Cultural Forms of Protest in Russia

Alongside the Arab Spring, the 'Occupy' anti-capitalist movements in the West, and the events on the Maidan in Kiev, Russia has had its own protest movements, notably the political protests of 2011–12. As elsewhere in the world, these protests had unlikely origins, in Russia's case spearheaded by the 'creative class'. This book examines the protest movements in Russia. It discusses the artistic traditions from which the movements arose; explores the media, including the internet, film, novels, and fashion, through which the protesters have expressed themselves; and considers the outcome of the movements, including the new forms of nationalism, intellectualism, and feminism put forward. Overall, the book shows how the Russian protest movements have suggested new directions for Russian – and global – politics.

Birgit Beumers is Professor of Film Studies at Aberystwyth University, Wales, UK.

Alexander Etkind is Professor of the History of Russia–Europe Relations at the European University Institute, Florence, Italy.

Olga Gurova is a Research Fellow in the Department of Social Research at the University of Helsinki, Finland.

Sanna Turoma is a Senior Research Fellow at the Aleksanteri Institute, University of Helsinki, Finland.

Routledge Contemporary Russia and Eastern Europe Series

Cultural Forms of Protest in Russia

Edited by Birgit Beumers,
Alexander Etkind, Olga Gurova,
and Sanna Turoma

LONDON AND NEW YORK

First published 2018
by Routledge
2 Park Square, Milton Park, Abingdon, Oxon OX14 4RN

and by Routledge
711 Third Avenue, New York, NY 10017

Routledge is an imprint of the Taylor & Francis Group, an informa business

British Library Cataloguing in Publication Data
A catalogue record for this book is available from the British Library

Library of Congress Cataloging in Publication Data
Names: Beumers, Birgit, editor.
Title: Cultural forms of protest in Russia / edited by Birgit Beumers, Alexander Etkind, Olga Gurova, and Sanna Turoma.
Description: Abingdon, Oxon; New York, NY: Routledge, 2018. |
Series: Routledge contemporary Russia and Eastern Europe series; 76 |
Includes bibliographical references and index.
Identifiers: LCCN 2017007691 | ISBN 9781138956650 (hardback) |
ISBN 9781315665610 (ebook)
Subjects: LCSH: Protest movements–Russia (Federation)–History. |
Political participation–Russia (Federation)–History. | Russia (Federation)–
Civilization. | Russia (Federation)–Politics and government–1991
Classification: LCC HN530.2.A8 C85 2018 | DDC 303.48/40947–dc23
LC record available at https://lccn.loc.gov/2017007691

ISBN: 978-1-138-95665-0 (hbk)
ISBN: 978-1-315-66561-0 (ebk)

Typeset in Times New Roman
by Out of House Publishing

Contents

Illustrations

Contributors

Birgit Beumers is Professor of Film Studies at the Aberystwyth University. She holds a DPhil from St Antony's College, Oxford, and has previously taught in the Russian Department at Bristol University. She specializes in contemporary Russian culture and has published on cinema and theatre. Her publications include *A History of Russian Cinema* (2009), *Performing Violence* (with Mark Lipovetsky, 2009), and *Aleksandr Sokurov: Russian Ark* (2016); she has edited *A Companion to Russian Cinema* (2016) and is editor-in-chief of the online quarterly *KinoKultura* and of the journal *Studies in Russian and Soviet Cinema*.

Marijeta Bozovic is Assistant Professor of Slavic Languages and Literatures, affiliated with Film and Media Studies and Women's, Gender, and Sexuality Studies at Yale University. A specialist in twentieth- and twenty-first-century Russian and Eastern European cultures with broad comparative interests, she is the author of *Nabokov's Canon: From Onegin to Ada* (2016) and the co-editor (with Matthew Miller) of *Watersheds: Poetics and Politics of the Danube River* (2016) and (with Brian Boyd) of *Nabokov Upside Down* (2017). She is currently working on her second monograph, *Avant-Garde Post– : Radical Poetics After the Soviet Union*. Bozovic is the co-editor of the journal *Russian Literature*, the co-curator of the 'Poetry after Language' colloquy for Stanford University's ARCADE digital salon, and a contemporary film and literature reviewer for *The Los Angeles Review of Books*.

Alexander Etkind is Professor at the Department of History and Civilizations of the European University Institute in Florence, Italy. Previously, he taught at the University of Cambridge and the European University at St Petersburg. He has been a visiting professor or researcher at Harvard, New York University, Georgetown, Wissenschaftskolleg in Berlin and others. From 2010 to 2013 he directed the European research project 'Memory at War: Cultural Dynamics in Poland, Russia, and Ukraine'. He is also an expert on Russian novel, film, and cultural forms of protest in the twenty-first century. He has published *Eros of the Impossible: The History of Psychoanalysis in Russia* (1997), *Internal Colonization: Russia's Imperial*

Experience (2011), and *Warped Mourning: Stories of the Undead in the Land of the Unburied* (2013). His new book, *The Right Side of History: An Intellectual Biography of William C. Bullitt*, is forthcoming.

Mischa Gabowitsch is a researcher at the Einstein Forum in Potsdam, Germany. He is a past editor-in-chief of the journal *Neprikosnovenny zapas* (Moscow) and was the founding editor-in-chief of *Laboratorium: Russian Review of Social Research* (St Petersburg). He is an alumnus of the Princeton University Society of Fellows. Spanning history and sociology, his research interests include protest and social movements, war memorials, and commemorative practices. He is the author of *Protest in Putin's Russia* (2016), a revised and updated translation of *Putin kaputt!? Russlands neue Protestkultur* (2013), the first book-length study of the 2011–13 Russian protests. He has also edited *Pamiat' o voine 60 let spustia: Rossiia, Germaniia, Evropa* (2005); *Kriegsgedenken als Event: Der 9. Mai im postsozialistischen Europa* (with C. Gdaniec and E. Makhotina, 2017); and *Pamiatnik i prazdnik: etnografiia Dnia Pobedy* (forthcoming). He is currently working on a history of Soviet war memorials.

Vladimir Gel'man is Professor of Political Science and Sociology at the European University at St Petersburg and Finland Distinguished Professor at the Aleksanteri Institute, University of Helsinki. His areas of expertise include Russian and post-Soviet politics in a theoretical and comparative perspective, regime changes, political institutions, electoral and party politics, federalism, and regionalism. He is the author and/or editor of more than twenty books, including *Making and Breaking Democratic Transitions: The Comparative Politics of Russia's Regions* (2003), *Authoritarian Russia: Analyzing Post-Soviet Regime Changes* (2015), *Authoritarian Modernization in Russia: Ideas, Institutions, and Policies* (2017), and numerous articles on politics and governance in post-Soviet Russia.

Olga Gurova holds a PhD in Cultural Studies and is the Academy of Finland Research Fellow at the Department of Social Research, University of Helsinki. Previously she has served as a docent at the National Research University – Higher School of Economics in St Petersburg and was a research fellow at the Helsinki Collegium for Advanced Studies, the University of Michigan at Ann Arbor, University of Illinois at Urbana-Champaign, and at the Central European University in Budapest. Her research interests include sociology of consumption, sociology of fashion, socialist and post-socialist cultures, and qualitative methods of social research. She is the author of *Fashion and Consumer Revolution in Contemporary Russia* (2016), *Soviet Underwear: Between Ideology and Everyday Life* (in Russian, 2008), and numerous articles on the culture of consumption in socialist and post-socialist Russia.

Ilya Kalinin is Associate Professor at the Department of Liberal Arts and Sciences, St Petersburg State University. His research focuses on early

Soviet Russia intellectual and cultural history, practices of self-fashioning of the Soviet subject, and the historical and cultural politics of contemporary Russia. He is editor-in-chief of the Moscow-based intellectual journal *Neprikosnovennyi zapas* and two book series published by Moscow Publishing House Novoe Literaturnoe Obozrenie (NLO). He has published in a wide range of journals, and his book *Istoriia kak iskusstvo chlenorazdel'nosti. Russkie formalisty i revoliutsiia* is forthcoming.

Jennifer G. Mathers is Reader in International Politics at Aberystwyth University. She received her undergraduate degree from Mount Holyoke College in the United States and her MPhil and DPhil from Oxford University. She joined the Department in 1992 while completing her DPhil thesis on Soviet ballistic missile defence policy from Stalin to Gorbachev. Her teaching and research spans two broad areas: Russian politics and security, and gender and war. She is the author of *The Russian Nuclear Shield from Stalin to Yeltsin* (2000) and co-editor, with Steve Webber, of *Military and Society in Post-Soviet Russia* (2005).

Kristina Norman is an Estonian artist and documentary filmmaker based in Tallinn. In her work she often explores the issues of collective memory and monuments. She is the author of videos and mixed-media installations including *Monolith* (2007), *Community* (2008) and *After-War* (2009), which deal with issues of cultural memory, collective identity, and belonging that surround the Bronze Soldier monument in Tallinn. In her artworks *0.8 Square Metres* (2012) and *Common Ground* (2013) Norman touches upon the issues of political imprisonment, migration, and displacement. She holds an MA in Visual Arts from the Estonian Academy of Arts and is currently a PhD student and a lecturer at the same institution.

Valentina Parisi holds a PhD in Slavic Studies from the State University in Milan (2005). She received a postdoctoral grant from the Istituto Italiano di Scienze Umane in Florence (2009–11). She researched as EURIAS Fellow at the Hanse-Wissenschaftskolleg (2014–15) and at the Central European University, Budapest (2012–13), on topics related to unofficial Soviet culture and *samizdat*. She is the author of the volume *Il lettore eccedente. Edizioni periodiche del samizdat sovietico, 1956–1990* (2013). She is currently at the Civica Scuola Interpreti e Traduttori, Milan.

Jonathan Brooks Platt specializes in Russian and Soviet literature, art and culture. He is the author of article publications on Zoya Kosmodemianskaya, Andrei Platonov, and Russian and American Art. His monograph *Greetings, Pushkin! Stalin's Cultural Politics and the Russian National* (2016) examines the idiosyncratic temporality of Soviet discourses of modernity and aesthetics in the Stalin era. He is currently at work on two new projects, one concerning Zoya Kosmodemyanskaya, and the other related to post-Soviet art.

Sanna Turoma is an Academy of Finland Fellow at the Aleksanteri Institute, University of Helsinki, Finland. She specializes in literary and cultural studies. Among her publications are *Brodsky Abroad: Empire, Tourism, Nostalgia* (2010) and *Empire Decentered: New Spatial Histories of Russia and The Soviet Union* (2013), which she co-edited with Maxim Waldstein. As a fellow of the Finnish Center of Excellence in Russian Studies she has co-edited special issues in Russian Studies for various journals, among them *Eurasian Economy and Geography* and *Transcultural Studies*. She is also the co-author and co-editor of a popular Finnish-language textbook on the history of Russian literature, *Venäläisen kirjallisuuden historia* (2011).

Alexandra Yatsyk is Visiting Researcher at the Uppsala Centre for Russian and Eurasian Studies, Sweden. She is also Director of the Centre for Cultural Studies of Post-Socialism at Kazan Federal University, Russia. She is a co-author of *Lotman's Cultural Semiotics and the Political* (2017) and *Celebrating Borderlands in a Wider Europe: Nations and Identities in Ukraine, Georgia and Estonia* (2016). Among her works are co-edited volumes and special issues, including *Borders in the Baltic Sea Region: Suturing the Ruptures* (2016), *Mega Events in Post-Soviet Eurasia: Shifting Borderlines of Inclusion and Exclusion* (2016), and *Vocabularies of International Relations after the Crisis in Ukraine* (2016). Her research interests include representations of post-Soviet national identities, sports and cultural mega events, art, and biopolitics.

Acknowledgements

The editors wish to thank above all Peter Sowden at Routledge for his support for this project. The idea and inspiration for this volume goes back to a seminar held at the Aleksanteri Institute in May 2014 and sponsored by the Academy of Finland Centre of Excellence, 'Choices of Russian Modernization'. Separately, Valentina Parisi, Olga Gurova and Birgit Beumers also wish to thank the Institute for Advanced Studies at Central European University, Budapest, and especially Eva Fodor, for encouraging early explorations of the protest movement during our fellowships there in 2013.

Note on transliteration

The Library of Congress system has been used throughout, with the following exceptions: when a Russian name has an accepted English spelling (e.g. Tchaikovsky instead of Chaikovskii, Yeltsin instead of El'tsin, Yakovlev instead of Iakovlev, Joseph Brodsky instead of Iosif Brodskii), or when Russian names are of Germanic origin (e.g. Eisenstein instead of Eizenshtein). We have also used the accepted spelling for towns and places (e.g. Bolotnaya Square instead of Bolotnaia, Nizhny instead of Nizhnii Novgorod). Where a source is quoted, the original spelling has been preserved. At the author's request, chapter 1 departs from the transliteration system (see chapter note).

Introduction

Genres and genders of protest in Russia's petrostate

Alexander Etkind

Many thousands of women and men marched through the Russian capital in the winter of 2011–12, protesting against election fraud, fearing the police, and surviving the frost. Nobody knew what would happen to their country during the next five years: the wars launched in Ukraine and Syria, massive recession, corruption scandals, and more election fraud. The participants in the Moscow rallies failed to prevent these historic events, though they warned about the coming catastrophe. But did they? Competing in witty slogans, they disguised their political protest under the classical forms of satire, parody, and utopia. For a social scientist, this carnival was not a prediction; it was not even a prophecy.

Precisely because the future is not accessible to our enlightened reason, it has always been a domain of religion, imaginative literature, and culture. From apocalyptic musings to political utopias to party programmes, people have produced a variety of cultural genres that struggle with the events to come. A major event of post-Soviet history, the Russian protest movement lacked many of these programmatic features. Emerging in a deeply troubled post-Soviet society, immersed in the convoluted East European politics, and combining the adverse influences of new nationalism, post-socialism, and neoliberalism, this movement did not formulate a social doctrine and failed to create a national consensus. Still, its impact on national and international politics was immense and remains underestimated. A link in the chain of the early twenty-first century protest movements that arguably started in Kiev, leapt to Cairo and Istanbul, touched New York and London, and shook Moscow and Athens, we need to explore Russia's political protest not in terms of its success or failure in transforming the political present, as either a continuation or a rebuttal of this country's historical past, but as a series of events that tested, provoked, prevented, or failed to prevent the future.

Looking back in time, this volume explores the cultural aspects of the Russian protest movement. In contrast to its participants, we do know a fragment of their future. Among its multiple functions, culture performs the role of fortune-teller, protesting against the foretold, representing the unknown, warning about the unknowable. This is why, in contrast to history that focuses largely on the past and political science that looks at the present, cultural studies of social movements zoom in on the future. Scrutinizing actions and texts of the participants as well as their gender, generation, historical experience, and political aspirations, this volume focuses on cultural forms, genres, and symbols of the movement. Unlike recent attempts at political, sociological, and philosophical interpretations of the protest movement, this volume predominantly, though not exclusively, employs the methods of cultural studies.[1] But we are also interested in the social, political, and economic underpinnings of the events. Distant, specialized, and fragmented in the modern world, culture becomes comprehensive and ubiquitous in moments of national crisis. Reflecting on all spheres of civil life – revising the past, depicting the present, and foretelling the future – the culture of the crisis deserves a comprehensive, respectful approach on the part of scholars.

Russia's decline had started well before the electoral crisis of 2011, but it was masked by exorbitant oil prices that were believed to be an organic, endless feature of the modern economy. Having accumulated much wealth that did not reflect the labour and knowledge of its people, the Russian state used this wealth for its own purposes, which were vastly different from those of the people. A petrostate, post-Soviet Russia experienced its richest and most powerful moment in 2011–12. It was fully dependent on oil and gas exports, and energy prices peaked in 2011–12, precisely when the Muscovites – geographically, the largest group of beneficiaries of Russia's oil trade – rallied on the streets and squares of Moscow.

The rallies started in December 2011 from the protest against widely perceived, though officially denied, fraud in the recent campaign in the run-up to legislative elections to the State Duma. No less intense was the disappointment with the political cheating at the executive level: Vladimir Putin, who was prime minister after having served as the Russian president for two terms, announced his intention to run again for presidency in 2012. Starting from technical issues connected to the parliamentary elections, the protest rallies increasingly focused on Putin's personality, his grasp on power, and the costs of his corrupted regime. Rarely did the slogans, caricatures, and political speeches of the protesters offer political alternatives; instead, they mocked the existing authorities, which the participants knew all too well, and protested against their continuation in the future. In Moscow, the protest was massive (some of the rallies were estimated to involve 60,000–100,000 participants). St Petersburg and major cities of Siberia and the Urals also saw some action, but the protest did not involve many other cities and provinces of Russia. It also failed to select a consensual leader who could confront those in power.

The protests were marred by the increasing violence on the part of the police, and by counter-rallies organized by the authorities. In response, some protesting groups both on the left and on the right of the political spectrum underwent rapid radicalization, but the majority of protesters tacitly acknowledged their capitulation. Still, the protests continued. In May 2012, when Putin was inaugurated for his third term, 400 people were arrested on the streets and squares of Moscow. In June, new laws seriously limited political freedoms and imposed heavy penalties on unauthorized actions; in the eyes of the Russian legislator, political protest became increasingly similar to 'terrorism', a concept that the authorities indiscriminately used to justify violent police actions. In fact, no senior Russian official fell victim to a terrorist attack during this period. But one of the most vocal leaders of the protest movement, Boris Nemtsov, was murdered in February 2015 in central Moscow very close to the epicentre of the bygone rallies, in circumstances that suggested foul play. He was mourned by a huge memorial rally, which marked the symbolic end of the Moscow protests.

Sociologists have depicted the protesters as young educated urbanites – the Moscow middle class, 'the advanced minority', the 'creative class'. The participants in the rallies were younger than an average Russian: 80 per cent had higher (university or equivalent) education (in Russia, only one-third of the population has college degrees); 65 per cent of the participants were men (a slight majority of Russians are women). According to sociological surveys, the participants were relatively prosperous; one measure indicated that, while 'materially satisfied' people constituted about one-third of the population of Russia and about half of the Muscovites, they made about 70 per cent of the participants in the rallies (Volkov 2012). This protest movement was not a manifestation of the economically deprived, but quite the opposite: the protesters came from the professional and, at the time, well-adjusted segment of the Russian population.

Paradoxically, the Moscow protests epitomized a whole decade of the steady growth of the Russian economy, which was fed by rising oil prices. Apart from the economic crisis of 2008, salaries in Moscow were growing at least by 15 per cent annually, and real-estate prices showed an even steadier growth. Many of the participants in the rallies owned apartments in Moscow, a treasure trove and often a source of income that the vast majority of Russians could not dream about (Anon. 2010). Most of the participants told sociologists that they learned the news from the internet rather than from television, while the overall Russian population prefers television as the source of news. Social media, especially Facebook, played a leading part in spreading information about the rallies. Talking about the reasons for their protest, participants mentioned their 'general dissatisfaction with the situation in the country' as frequently as their disappointment with the 'dishonest elections'. As their potential leaders, the participants named cultural celebrities – prominent journalists, writers, and public intellectuals – rather than professional politicians. Based on their interviews, sociologists also observed the lack of political experience, the individualist inclinations of many participants, and their aversion to organized, long-term political action (Volkov 2012).

However, Russian sociologists and philosophers refute the idea that 'the middle class' dominated the protests (Levinson 2012; Magun 2014a and 2014b). Preferring to believe that the protesters were representatives of a whole range of socio-economic layers, liberal experts are compliant with the idea that the Moscow protesters were part and parcel of the Russian 'creative class'. Introduced by the social scientist Richard Florida, this concept embraces an assortment of professional groups who create value by applying their knowledge-based skills in a post-industrial environment – programmers, designers, journalists, entertainers, and teachers. According to Florida, the decayed industrial cities could get a second breath by investing in cultural industries and cultivating the 'creative class' (Florida 2002). Whether those well-educated people who constituted the core of the Moscow protests match Florida's definitions or not, some of those people clearly preferred the trendy term of the post-industrial era, 'creative class', to the old-fashioned concept of 'intelligentsia', with its nineteenth-century origins and high-school connotations. However, the relations between these two concepts have never been clarified; though they belong to different eras and diverge in many important ways, their meanings in popular use might be identical.

In fact, the rallying professionals on Moscow's streets and squares were quite distant from Florida's entrepreneurial post-industrial craftsmen, the labour force of twenty-first century 'project capitalism' endowed with the ability to create knowledge, value, and businesses.[2] In Moscow, the vast majority of these journalists, professors, designers, cameramen, system administrators, and public relations specialists were financially dependent on the Russian state, directly or indirectly. Some of them worked for state-owned newspapers, universities, and corporations. Others worked for private companies that were largely dependent on governmental investments, orders, and tenders. One way or another, they were recycling oil and gas profits, the primary input of the Russian economy, into knowledge-based goods and services that were essential but increasingly marginalized by the Russian administration.

As a petrostate, Russia differs from its peers such as Nigeria, Venezuela, or Iran in several important respects.[3] One unusual feature is Russia's Soviet past; the great socialist experiment left a strong and peculiar legacy in many areas of life. The second particularity of Russia's petrostate is its relatively large and well-educated population. Thirdly, there is Russia's immense geography: the centres of population, such as Moscow, are separated from their main sources of income, the Siberian oil and gas fields, by thousands of kilometres. But, as happens in other petrostates, the government organizes the extraction of oil and gas, secures their transportation, and redistributes the profits for the benefit of 'the people', satisfying in the process the growing appetites of the state and security apparatus that oversees all these functions.[4] Only 1 per cent of the population of the Russian Federation takes part in the extraction and transportation of oil and gas, but in 2011–12 this trade secured about two-thirds of the state budget.

Russia's booming petrostate gives the clearest answer to the major question of contemporary history: why the protest movement failed in Moscow and succeeded in Kiev. A major post-socialist state that does not possess abundant resources, Ukraine has inherited the same Soviet institutions, value systems, and corruption as Russia. The diverging developments of Russia and Ukraine provide a critical experiment on the role of natural resources in the development of modern statehood. A petrostate gets its wealth directly from nature, with a little participation by the people. Since this state does not depend on taxes, but relies mostly on direct profits from exporting its resources, democratic representation in such a state is either underdeveloped or bogus. Since trade requires little labour, the workers lack the power to strike. In such a state, the wealth of the nation does not depend on the labour and the knowledge of its people. Healthcare, education, and the sociability of the population all become irrelevant to the national economy. Rather than being the source of the nation's wealth, people depend upon the charity of the state. In this environment, human capital decays in a vicious circle: the more the state relies on its natural resources, the less it invests in human capital, and the lower its development, the more resource-bound the state becomes.

Petrostates, with their 'oil curse', have become a popular subject of political science. Cross-country comparisons show that, from Norway to Nigeria and from Canada to Russia, oil-drilling countries are vastly different. In some cases, the detrimental consequences of the oil curse have been purposefully and successfully avoided; in other cases, they have led to a far-reaching deterioration of economy, culture, and society. Given this variety, it is proper to treat the oil curse as a self-imposed condition, a contingent political process that depends on the unique choices of the authorities and the population. The abundance of natural resources does not determine the social and cultural development of the country, but provides its ruling group with unique opportunities for using and abusing the income from the resource trade. These opportunities do not exist in countries that rely on their population instead. The oil curse did not determine Russia's arrested development; it only provided conditions that were eagerly used by the group in power.[5]

The oil curse is also a gender curse. Comparing Arab countries that have or do not have oil, Michael Ross has shown that though oil-trading states in the Middle East are richer than those that do not have oil, women in the latter have higher education, better employment, and more rights (Ross 2012). Another result from the Near East shows that the production of energy has a serious impact on real-estate prices, amplifying social differences and making houses and apartments less available for the majority of the population, members of which, in many of these countries, do not count as citizens. In Moscow, according to a recently published estimate, it takes 50 years for a medical nurse – some of them men but most women – to save money for a small studio apartment. For those men who are involved in the oil and gas sector it takes, on average, eight years to save money for a similar apartment (Anon. 2013).

The oil and gas industry needs equipment, knowledge, and qualified labour, but all that can easily be exchanged for a fraction of the oil and gas profits. Awash with cash, the Russian petrostate has been saving on hospitals, schools, roads, cities, and much more – in fact, on everything but its own security. During the time of the Moscow protests, more than 90 per cent of the software and information technologies that Russian corporations and manufacturers used for their work were of foreign origin. Relying on foreign technologies, the petrostate did not need a creative class; moreover, it was actively suppressing these people as a nuisance, an internal enemy and a source of potential rebellion. This was the true reason for the degradation of Russian science, technology, and the university system – in fact, of all the sectors that provided jobs and prosperity to the Soviet intelligentsia, with the exception of the propaganda machine that was booming. The dreams of modernization were abandoned for the sake of religious revivalism. State officials produced forged dissertations that were full of plagiarism; intellectuals were surprised by the speedy decay of the public sphere. The borders were still open, and the regime was effectively pushing astute and ambitious individuals out of the country. Many scientists, scholars, artists, and journalists emigrated (1.5 million people over the decade, though this is a rough estimate).

Several decades ago, Hannah Arendt identified the superfluity of the population as the common denominator of colonialism, Nazism, and Stalinism (Arendt 1966, 311). In the modern world, resource-dependent states also make their population economically and politically irrelevant for the purposes of the 'elites' that run these states. Deprived of its role in the economy of the country, the population responds with feelings of alienation, protest, and resentment. The concentration of wealth in the hands of the oil-and-security elite, the deterioration of human capital, and the gender disparity are all aspects of one and the same phenomenon.

Many commentators have revealed poor career prospects, lack of legal protection for women, and a new cult of masculinity in contemporary Russia (Iarskaia and Iarskaia-Smirnova 2002; Zdravomyslova et al. 2010; Goscilo and Lanoux 2006; Riabov and Riabova 2014; Sperling 2015). Significant disparities between men and women follow from the basic structure of Russia's political economy. Justified and amplified by the increasingly patriarchal propaganda machine, gender inequalities in wages and education are large and growing. In 2005, a United Nations study discovered that even though women's education level was increasing in Russia, women with higher education had lower chances of finding a job (men did not show this negative correlation) (Vasilev 2005). On the highest levels of professional qualification, employment chances for women decrease as status and salary increase: women constituted about 40 per cent of the staff of the institutes of the Academy of Sciences, but only 2 per cent of the directors of these institutes were women.

Two essential functions of the resource-bound state, extraction and protection, require labour that is performed in Russia almost exclusively by men. Worldwide, the mining industry is the economic sector with the highest gender disparity; in Russia, this source of inequality combines with the huge and, traditionally all-male, control-and-security apparatus. The leading employers, such as the oil and gas industry, the military-industrial complex, and the police and other security services, are almost exclusively all-male. In a word, the closer we come to the core of the petrostate and its resource-and-security trading elite, the more uneven is the gender balance, with men realizing all the key roles in extraction and protection, and therefore holding all the power and capital that results from it. With 1 per cent of the population working in the extraction of oil and gas, and probably about 5 per cent working for security services – almost all of them men – more than every tenth man is working in these privileged positions. Women are exiled to the secondary sector of this political economy, which recycles the profits from the resource trade through the redistribution and then retail of imported goods. They are entrusted with tasks that are connected to the production of human capital, such as education, healthcare, and social work, i.e. precisely those tasks that the petrostate undervalues and undermines. The synergy between the oil and gas trade and security services has created a hyper-masculine and misogynistic culture: *petromachismo*, as I prefer to call it.

Promoting archaic values of aggressive masculinity and unconditional loyalty to the sovereign, the country's overreliance on natural resources and security services denies the role of women as critical drivers of human capital. This situation explains, I think, the fascinating fact that, even though the majority of the protesters were men, the most successful symbols of these movements are feminine. At the turning points of these processes, rebellious, exaggerated femininity confronts the masculine state, with the manifestations of femininity and female sexuality acting as political symbols. Still, the female participation in Putin's 'vertical of power' was also significant; to give one example: many of those high-school teachers and municipal officials who organized the forged elections on the local level were women. Binary dichotomies work only on the symbolical level, and this is precisely the level that I wish to emphasize now. I am less concerned about the actual statistics of gender participation in the political protest or in the actions of the authorities than in those cultural forms of symbolization and political reification that were improvised on the Moscow (and, earlier, Kiev) squares. Groups such as Pussy Riot and Femen are characteristic here not only because they were all-women, but because they demonstrated their femininity as the ultimate argument against those in power.

Revealing the abuses of power, creative professionals on the streets and squares of Moscow protested against the pecking order of the petrostate, which discriminates against intellectuals and women. The protesters confronted the anxious and arrogant authorities, whom they perceived as cheating, confused, and corrupted. The protesters did not have a positive programme of social change, and they failed to shape a capable, popular leadership. But as the nearest future has demonstrated, these people had a historical feeling, a kind of collective intuition, of the forthcoming events: the decline of oil and gas prices that led to the rapid exhaustion of the state coffers and the erosion of social protection; the seemingly unexpected invasions in Ukraine and Syria that led to worldwide economic sanctions and Russia's increasing isolation and humiliation; and finally, the impoverishment of the people on the edge of the collapse of the state.

This volume explores the cultural dynamics of the Moscow protests, contextualizing them against the political development of Putinism and the cultural tradition of Russian dissent. Bridging the gap between political science and cultural history, Vladimir Gel'man contrasts two protest cycles, of 1989–91 and of 2011–12. One of them seemed triumphal, another failed, and their diverse experiences, argues Gel'man, were formative for entire generations. In his chapter, Gel'man defines three politically active generations and explains their political behaviour with reference to their formative experiences. Unusual for a political scientist, Gel'man finds that this long-term perspective provides a source of optimism: the protest mobilization in 2011–12 might be just the first stage in a political awakening of post-Soviet generations.

In contrast to this three-stage scheme that emphasizes continuity and change, Valentina Parisi compares the Moscow protests with the Soviet dissident movement, whose leaders had been active well before many participants in the Moscow protests were born. The differences are numerous, and Parisi focuses on a truly unprecedented political action, the performance of the punk group Pussy Riot in the Cathedral of Christ the Saviour in central Moscow, which launched a series of police investigations, court trials, and new acts of protest. Precisely because this performance was an entirely female event, it was entirely new: nothing similar had ever happened in the rich Russian and Soviet history of political dissent. These women prayed to the Madonna that she would kick Putin out of the way, and they structured the political space in a gendered way that was traditionally neglected by Soviet dissidents.

Ilya Kalinin also looks at the protesters of 2012 as if they were avid readers and followers of the twentieth-century Soviet dissidents. Andrei Siniavskii's dictum 'My differences with the Soviet State are stylistic ones' was definitely close to the hearts and minds of many protesters from the 'creative class'. However, this emphasis on style and form was not that common, even among Siniavskii's contemporaries. Polemically, the famous sculptor Ernst Neizvestnyi, whom Nikita Khrushchev severely criticized for 'formalism' and who later erected the memorial on Khrushchev's grave, said that his differences with the Soviet state were 'rather metaphysical'. In any case, we know that some leaders of the Moscow protests, such as the poet Dmitrii Bykov, knew the Soviet dissident tradition very well and referred to it frequently, while other leaders, such as the lawyer Aleksei Navalnyi, denied any relevance of the historical tradition to current political concerns (Stähle and Wijermars 2014). Emphasizing the election fraud and economic corruption, this legalist position sounds less relevant to a cultural scholar than the witty slogans, sophisticated critique, and juicy poetry of the aesthetic wing of the movement, but Navalnyi's growing political success demonstrates the viability of his position.

Mischa Gabowitsch illuminates the internal work of three minor social networks that created, in their horizontal interactions with myriads of others, the body of the protest movements. Transferring the reader from Moscow's squares to the on- and offline networks that span the Russian provinces from the Ukrainian border to Siberia, Gabowitsch both expands and subverts the narrow understanding of politics as a zero-sum power game with the state that has become traditional for Russian activists and scholars. This careful research disavows many accepted myths about Russian politics, e.g. the idea of its vertical structure and necessarily charismatic leadership. Having discovered these improvised, clandestine associations that perform the diverse functions of non-governmental organizations (NGOs), intellectual clubs, and edutainment, Gabowitsch demonstrates that these amorphous but ubiquitous cultural collectives survived the collapse of the Moscow protests very well. They have nothing to lose but their networks, and only the full shutdown of the Internet in the Russian territory – an apocalyptic project that has been often discussed in semi-official circles since the start of the Moscow protests – could tame them.

In the petrostate, citizens consume its profits according to the pecking order defined by the state. Many of these people work and create value in the myriads of industries and services, but their compensation for this work recycles the profits made far way from them, in the trade between Siberian oil fields and their European consumers. Thus the petrostate exacerbates the disproportions of capitalism to a degree not known to labour-bound societies, in which consumption depends on production. In her chapter, Olga Gurova surveys the practices of political consumption that the Muscovites reinvented during their protest actions. Everyone who has been to Moscow has seen its booming and bizarre consumerism – luxury cars parked under shabby Soviet-style projects, the well-heeled public in a McDonald's-style café, golden watches on the wrists of civil servants. In this environment, a self-conscious restraint in consumption is a political gesture – most frequently, an act of political protest. It is also true that Russia's extraordinary politics of recent years – its hybrid wars, declared or undeclared states of emergency, sanctions and counter-sanctions – address consumption more than production. While the petrostate depoliticizes the processes of production, aspiring to be selling oil and gas despite the political odds, it endows the processes of consumption with new magic powers.

The Moscow protesters were involved in subtle and complex games with the Kremlin authorities. Neither side in these games was homogeneous; the adversaries were multiple and changing. The Kremlin has 20 towers, which house different personalities, policies, and even ideologies; the same was true of the leaders of the rallies, though they did not have towers to protect them. The organizers of the protests had to ask for legal permissions for each rally; they would not get these permissions if they had not engaged one level of Russian power against another. These conflicts among different authorities were almost as important for the success of the protest movement as solidarity among its leaders. For some leaders, such as Nemtsov, these games with the authorities were lethal; many others received their initiation into political life, charged with risk, energy, and humour. Well depicted by Jennifer Mathers, this dramatic interaction between the citizenry and power was satiated with reciprocal, though not always satisfying, mimesis and historical reminiscences. Civil protest was typical in many historical moments in Russian history – the imperial, revolutionary, Soviet, and post-Soviet periods are no exception. Different agents led these protests with different results that varied from ignobility to revolution; but during the Moscow winter of 2011 and 2012, the initiative in these multi-step games firmly belonged to the protesters. In her chapter in this volume, Mathers explores this multilateral exchange between the protesters and the authorities. The protesters adopted white as their symbolic colour and wore white ribbons, which for them symbolized the winter frosts and also political innocence. In an aggressive response to these white ribbons, President Putin interpreted them as condoms. Mocking this demeaning language of power, at the next rally many protesters actually wore condoms on their coats, sometimes drawing Putin's portrait on the ends. As Mathers notes, the banners carried by pro-regime rallies proclaimed in Russian 'If not Putin, then who [*kto*]?' – a slogan that the anti-regime protesters easily subverted into 'If not Putin, then a cat [*kot*]?' But some of the more sophisticated protesters also carried the slogan, 'If not Putin, then who?' in English, translating it immediately as 'If not Putin, then a dick [*khui*]'. Does laughter represent the best hope for civil society? Yes, it does, if there is no other hope.

'The joyful science of occupying squares', sang the Pussy Riot group, analysed in this volume by Alexandra Yatsyk. Her biopolitical approach to the unprecedented success of this group contrasts with the legalistic stance of the Moscow court that refused to discuss its political message and ended up convicting the women for blasphemy. Begging the Madonna to eliminate Putin, these women in balaclavas exercised their joyful science better than others. Well-researched, the case of Pussy Riot poses important questions about the gender of the protest. The political success of specifically female protest groups – Pussy Riot in Russia, Femen in Ukraine, and some of their less-known followers – presents a much-discussed but still underappreciated phenomenon of the twenty-first century, possibly central for late post-socialism. These women made political statements by manifesting their femininity (the Femen group took this body technique to the extreme), and the specifically female performance shocked all-male, patriarchal, violent power to such an extent that it obediently arrested and tried these women, producing celebrated cases that amplified the political effect of the protests. Sociologically, we know that women were very active in the protest events of 2011 in Moscow and 2014 in Kiev, but men were in a majority there. Trained men had an advantage when the protests turned into physical confrontation. However, popular images from the rallies in Moscow and Kiev were full of women of all ages, peacefully confronting a line of all-male police officers. Is it a sort of cultural archetype that inspired the representation of the French revolution as 'La Marseillaise'? Disagreeing with this interpretation, Yatsyk takes this imagery literally, as a sociological fact. The Pussy Riot challenge to male power presented the most sincere message of Russian protest movement, and also a profound truth about the post-Soviet political economy. The petrostate is an all-male endeavour, with its central functions – extraction of oil and gas, their transportation, and securing the flow of energy and money – performed by men. It is the duty of women to take care of the reproduction of human capital and to perform all those jobs in education, healthcare, and social services that the petrostate deems secondary or even redundant. Interestingly, in the melancholic post-2012 period, Russian popular arts, which traditionally have been male-centred and male-voiced, have been switching to the feminine side. Rock star Sergei Shnurov, the heir to the brutal tradition of Soviet bards, sings songs and makes clips that are singularly concerned with the ordeal and revenge of young Russian women. Full of obscenities – now prohibited by Russian law, which is analysed in Birgit Beumers' chapter, these quasi-feminist elegies and parodies have made Shnurov extraordinarily popular.

In a time of deep national crisis – 'the state of emergency in the soul', as Walter Benjamin put it – many genres of representation betray the citizenry, including politics itself (Benjamin 2003, 73). Precisely because the future is unknown and the present unloved, radical art becomes a privileged arena, where the political subject tries to discern her politics, a preoccupation that does not soothe her despair but at least creates a language for conversation with peers. This turn to radical art, argues Jon Platt, 'forces the enemy to show its true face and the people to remember they have one'. Platt explores in detail one of the most scandalous performances of such art, in which a young woman inserts a frozen chicken into her vagina and leaves the supermarket with her hidden booty. Platt sees here a protest against private property; as an alternative reading, I suggest that the scene provides another visual parable of the horror of a woman's life. Going beyond the biopolitical stance of Yatsyk, which is now increasingly common in European scholarship, Platt applies the elusive idiom of American art criticism – partly psychoanalytic, partly Marxist, and usually deconstructionist – to the actionism of the Voina group and the most successful of Russian protest artists, Petr Pavlenskii. The results of this operation are striking, precisely because of the incompatibility of its subject, the Russian radical art with its tense and focused face that we know from Pavlenskii's performances, and Platt's playful and ambiguous method.

Zooming in on the post-2012 situation, Birgit Beumers draws an analogy between political protests and Russian obscenities, also banned by the post-Soviet state. She suggests that under Putin's hybrid regime, politics function through staged acts of dissent and despair, as 'an articulation of the people's speechlessness and voicelessness'. Sometimes banned and often ignored, such politics aims not to define a friend or foe, but to create a record, an audience, a public. Beumers depicts the panoply of cultural spectacles, all focused on the recent past that failed. A melancholic after-party, this condition is increasingly typical of our world. Temporary, this state of despair feels like eternity; contingent, it is recognized as destiny; local, it seems to be universal; and it is contagious. The twenty-first century has already presented us with many such moments, and post-protest Moscow is just an elaborated stage on which the worldwide despair flexes its muscles.

A successful artist and cultural activist turned cultural scholar, Kristina Norman offers a fascinating insight into post-socialist memory wars that are intrinsically connected to political protests. Her sophisticated study of her own artistic adventure is a wonderful example of the growing confluence of art, politics, and scholarship – a synergy which organically develops when a radical artist such as Norman turns into an agent provocateur, never missing a chance to document the show. An important feature of her case study is an uncompromisingly female gaze, which Norman throws onto the hyper-masculine protagonists of her narrative – the Iron Soldier, his gilded emulation, the embarrassed Estonian police, Russian patriots, etc. Having energized Norman's artistic performance, the same ironic and unorthodox gaze feeds her scholarship. In a macho-culture of petrostate, the female gaze is counter-cultural. The increasing popularity of this disrespectful gaze is arguably the most enduring legacy of Russia's protest movement.

While protest movements in the US and Western Europe are frequently connected with the political traditions of the democratic Left, the situation is more complex in Russia. Many decades of Soviet rule have materialized socialist teachings, and then several post-Soviet decades have materialized neoliberal teachings. Scarce ideological equipment remains uncompromised for a protest activist and thinker who rejects these legacies and looks for an alternative future. Marijeta Bozovic explores the unorthodox poetry of the young Russian Left, for whom the suppressed protests of 2011–12 remain the highest and noblest experience of their political life. Bozovic argues that for many of these poets, imitating the twentieth-century avant-garde with its revolutionary tradition is the way to subvert the discredited Left of state socialism. Working for their digital audiences, who appreciate the newly reinvented combinations of the visual and the textual, Russian radical poets (many of them female) engage in techniques of recorded performance that bring them close to silent actionists such as Pavlenskii, or the 'dancing maidens' of Pussy Riot.

Focusing on Dmitrii Bykov's poetic show *Citizen Poet* (*Grazhdanin poet*), Sanna Turoma asks a research question which is similar to Valentina Parisi's at the beginning of this volume: how new is this protest culture, and what has it inherited, critically or not, from the older culture of Soviet dissidence? Bykov is a seasoned intertextualist, the author of many volumes of sophisticated poetry, critical essays, and literary biographies that testify to his masterful, though sometimes unbridled, textual hermeneutics. But his incredibly popular *Citizen Poet* show was a politicized and, at the same time, commercial production. Its very success demonstrated the popular appeal of Bykov's political versification among millions of viewers – an appeal beside which the irreparably elitist, though historically triumphal, texts of the Soviet dissidents pale in comparison. Appreciating rhymes, deciphering allusions, and criticizing cyclicities, our profession often detects repetition where radical novelty rules the day. Though the Moscow protests failed as a political movement, they created a powerful culture that is not dead – in fact, not even dormant. In literature and theatre, in urban planning and literary criticism, in digital culture and everyday life, the long-lasting effects of those protests are strong and enduring. We do not know the future, but we are positive that it is coming. Whenever a new wave of Russia transformation arrives, the new generations of participants, observers, and historians talk about the revived tradition of the protest movement, as the authors of this volume discuss the tradition of Soviet dissidence.

Notes

1 See Volkov 2012; Ianitskii 2013; Zhuravlev, Savel'eva, and Erpyleva 2014; Erpyleva and Magun 2015; Ross 2015; Gabowitsch 2016. The most sensitive to cultural aspects of the protest movement are Arkhipova and Alekseevskii 2014; Jonson 2015; and 'Protestkulturen in Osteuropa' 2015.
2 On 'project capitalism', see Boltanski and Chiapello 2007.
3 For a comprehensive study of Russian energy politics which emphasizes Russia's differences from other petrostates, see Gustafson 2012. On the local manifestations of oil curse in one Russian province, see Rogers 2015. On the "resource" metaphors in the Russian authorities' political language, see Kalinin 2014.
4 International literature on petrostates is immense. The exemplary study remains Coronil 1997. Launched by Timothy Mitchell, a recent strain of books throws entirely new light on the subject (Mitchell 2011; Huber 2013; Di Muzio 2015). For a helpful perspective on the future of petrostates, see Wenar 2016.
5 See Gel'man and Marganiya 2012; Gaddy and Ickes 2013; Etkind 2015. For a discussion in Russian, see the special forum in *Neprikosnovennyi zapas* 2 (2013), http://magazines.russ.ru/nz/2013/2 (accessed 27 October 2016).

References

Anon. 2010. "Chem otlichaiutsia moskvichi ot rossiian." *Tol'kovatel'* 15 November. http://ttolk.ru/2010/11/15/москвичи-не-похожи-на-россиян/ (accessed 30 October 2016).
Anon. 2013. "Skol'ko let kopit' na kvartiru liudiam raznykh professii." *MirKvartir* 23 November. http://journal.mirkvartir.ru/analytics/2013/11/26/kopit-na-kvartiry-raznih-professii/ (accessed 30 October 2016).
Arendt, Hannah. 1966. *Origins of Totalitarianism*. New York: Harcourt.
Arkhipova, Aleksandra and Mikhail Alekseevskii. 2014. *My ne nemy! Antropologiia protesta v Rossii 2011–12 godov*. Tartu: Nauchnoe izdatel'stvo ELM.
Benjamin, Walter. 2003. *The Origin of German Tragic Drama*. London: Verso.
Boltanski, Luc and Eve Chiapello. 2007. *The New Spirit of Capitalism*. London: Verso.

Coronil, Fernando. 1997. *The Magical State: Nature, Money, and Modernity in Venezuela*. Chicago: Chicago University Press.

Di Muzio, Tim. 2015. *Carbon Capitalism. Energy, Social Reproduction and World Order*. London: Rowman.

Erpyleva, Svetlana and Artemii Magun, ed. 2015. *Politika apolitichnykh. Grazhdanskie dvizheniia v Rossii 2011–2013*. Moscow: Novoe Literaturnoe Obozrenie.

Etkind, Alexander. 2015. "Putin's Russia: An Exemplary Case of Super-Extractive State." *World Financial Review* 25 January. www.worldfinancialreview.com/?p=3472 (accessed 27 October 2016).

Florida, Richard. 2002. *The Rise of the Creative Class: And How it's Transforming Work, Leisure, Community and Everyday Life*. New York: Perseus.

Gabowitsch, Mischa. 2016. *Protest in Putin's Russia*. Cambridge: Polity Press.

Gaddy, Clifford D. and Barry W. Ickes. 2013. "Russia's Dependence on Resources." In *The Oxford Handbook of the Russian Economy*, edited by Michael Alexeev and Shlomo Weber, 309–339. Oxford: Oxford University Press.

Gel'man, Vladimir and Otar Marganiya, eds. 2012. *Resource Curse and Post-Soviet Eurasia: Oil, Gas, and Modernization*. Lanham, MD: Lexington Books.

Goscilo, Helena and Andrea Lanoux, eds. 2006. *Gender and National Identity in Twentieth-Century Russian Culture*. DeKalb: Northern Illinois University Press.

Gustafson, Thane. 2012. *Wheel of Fortune. The Battle for Oil and Power in Russia*. Cambridge, MA: Harvard University Press.

Huber, Matthew. 2013. *Lifeblood: Oil, Freedom, and the Forces of Capital*. Minneapolis: University of Minnesota Press.

Ianitskii, Oleg. 2013. "Protestnoe dvizhenie 2011–2012: Nekotorye itogi." *Vlast'* 2: 14–19.

Iarskaia, Valentina and Elena Iarskaia-Smirnova. 2002. "Ne muzhskoe eto delo: gendernyi analiz zaniatosti v sotsial'noi sfere." *Sotsiologichekie issledovaniia* 6: 74–82.

Jonson, Lena. 2015. *Protest and Art in Putin's Russia*. London and New York: Routledge.

Kalinin, Ilya. 2014. "Carbon and Cultural Heritage: The Politics of History and Economy of Rent." (Special Issue on "Studies on Russian Culture and Modernization", edited by Sanna Turoma). *Baltic Worlds* 2–3: 65–75.

Levinson, Aleksei. 2012. "Eto ne srednii klass – eto vse." *Vedomosti* 21 February. www. Vedomosti.ru/opinion/news/1509376/eto_ne_srednij_klass_eto_vse#ixzz 2fNoRd-MCr (accessed 27 October 2016).

Magun, Artemii. 2014a. "Protestnoe dvizhenie 2011–2013 v Rossii: Novyi populizm srednego klassa." *Stasis* 2 (1): 192–226. http://eupress.ru/uploads/files/PH-141_pages.pdf (accessed 27 October 2016).

Magun, Artemy. 2014b. "The Russian Protest Movement: A New Middle-Class Populism." *Stasis* 2 (1): 160–191. www.stasisjournal.net/all-issues/24-1-2014-revolutions-and-protest-movements/59-the-russian-protest-movement-of-2011-2012-a-new-middle-class-populism (accessed 27 October 2016).

Mitchell, Timothy. 2011. *Carbon Democracy: Political Power in the Age of Oil*. London: Verso.

"Protestkulturen in Osteuropa." 2015. *Religion und Gesellschaft in Ost und West* (Special Issue) 4–5.

Riabov, Oleg and Tatiana Riabova. 2014. "The Remasculinization of Russia? Gender, Nationalism, and the Legitimation of Power Under Vladimir Putin." *Problems of Post-Communism* 61 (2): 23–35.

Rogers, Douglas. 2015. *The Depths òf Russia. Oil, Power, and Culture after Socialism.* Ithaca, NY: Cornell University Press.

Ross, Cameron, ed. 2015. *Systemic and Non-Systemic Opposition in the Russian Federation. Civil Society Awakens?* London: Palgrave.

Ross, Michael L. 2012. *The Oil Curse. How Petroleum Wealth Shapes the Development of Nations.* Princeton, NJ: Princeton University Press.

Sperling, Valerie. 2015. *Sex, Politics, and Putin: Political Legitimacy in Russia.* Oxford: Oxford University Press.

Stähle, Hanna and Mariëlle Wijermars. 2014. "Forget Memory: Aleksei Naval'nyi's LiveJournal and the Memory Discourse of the Protest Movement (2011–2012)." *Digital Icons: Studies in Russian, Eurasian and Central European New Media* 12: 105–128. www.digitalicons.org/wp-content/uploads/issue12/files/2014/11/DI12_5_Staehle.pdf (accessed 27 October 2016).

Vasilev, Stephan [UN Resident Coordinator in the RF]. 2005. "Gender Equality and Extension of Women's Rights in Russia in the Context of the UN Millennium Development Goals." www.undp.ru/Gender_MDG_eng.pdf (accessed 27 October 2016).

Volkov, Denis. 2012. "Protestnoe dvizhenie v Rossii v kontse 2011–nachala 2012." *Vestnik obshchestvennogo mneniia* 112 (2): 73–86.

Wenar, Leif. 2016. *Blood Oil. Tyrants, Violence, and the Rules That Run the World.* Oxford: Oxford University Press.

Zdravomyslova, Elena, V. Pasynkova, A. Temkina and O. Tkach, eds. 2010. *Praktiki i identichnosti: Gendernoe ustroistvo.* St Petersburg: European University.

Zhuravlev, Oleg, Natal'ia Savel'eva and Svetlana Erpyleva. 2014. "Individualizm i solidarnost' v novykh rossiiskikh sotsial'nykh dvizheniiakh." *Zhurnal issledovanii sotsial'noi politiki* 2 (12): 185–200. http://cyberleninka.ru/article/n/individualizm-i-solidarnost-v-novyh-rossiyskih-grazhdanskih-dvizheniyah (accessed 27 October 2016).

Part I
Origins and traditions of protest

1 Fathers, sons, and grandsons

Generational changes and political trajectory of Russia, 1989–2012

Vladimir Gel'man

The wave of post-election protests which swept across Russia from December 2011 until the summer of 2013, and culminated in a number of mass rallies and manifestations in Moscow, St Petersburg, and some other cities, received broad coverage among observers of Russian politics and society (see Gel'man 2013; Robertson 2013; Greene 2014). No wonder that in analyses of the causes and effects of these protests some parallels were drawn with regard to several comparative referents, ranging from the experience of neighbouring post-Soviet 'Colour Revolutions' and the Ukrainian Euro-Maidan of 2013–14 to the geographically and politically more distant Arab Spring and the Occupy movement. While the scholarly potential of cross-national comparisons of anti-regime mobilization in authoritarian systems is certainly high and worthy of further elaboration, the cross-temporal within-nation comparison of the Russian protests of 2011–12 remains a relatively neglected item on the research agenda. Meanwhile, many striking similarities are noteworthy between mass protests on Bolotnaya Square and Sakharov Avenue in 2011–12 and the preceding 'protest cycle' (Tarrow 1994) of rallies and manifestations on Manezh Square and Luzhniki in 1989–91 (Urban 1997). Indeed, the participants in both protest cycles carried similar slogans of democratization, which were focused on fair elections, political and civil rights, media freedom, and the rule of law. Even though the targets of anti-regime protests, the mechanisms of mobilization, and the very repertoire of collective actions (Tilly 1978) were rather different in the two cases, both protest cycles can be seen as various stages of a continuing struggle for political democracy against (different) non-democratic regimes. Yet the protest cycle of 1989–91 greatly contributed to the overthrow of Communist rule and to the end of the Soviet system (Fish 1995; Urban 1997; Hough 1997), although ultimately it did not establish democracy, while the protests of 2011–12 suffered heavy blows (Gel'man 2013; Smyth and Soboleva 2014a), even if they can be perceived as a mere episode in a continuing battle against an authoritarian regime in Russia (Gel'man 2015) the outcome of which has not been determined as yet.

However, if we switch the focus from the macro level of anti-authoritarian mobilization under the slogans of regime change to the micro level of protest participation in terms of activism and leadership, which certainly affected the whole protest industry (Tilly 1978; Tarrow 1994), then the major differences between the two protest cycles will be more striking than the similarities. The protests of 1989–91, as part of a pro-democratic movement during perestroika, were led, organized, and populated to a major degree by representatives of the generation of the 1960s, the 'sixties' or *shestidesiatniki*, who were mature at the time of their political ascendance and who left the political scene soon after achieving their goal of destroying the Soviet system (see Fish 1995; Lukin 2000). The protests of 2011–12 brought to the streets mostly representatives of the young, post-Soviet generation, who had grown up after the Soviet collapse (see Volkov 2012; Smyth and Soboleva 2014a), and whose political future is still unclear. By contrast, most representatives of generation of the 1970s (the 'seventiers', or *semidesiatniki*), who were relatively young during perestroika, played a rather negligible role in the pro-democratic movement at that time and (with some exceptions) were not in the vanguard of the protest cycle of 1989–91. But representatives of this generation began to dominate Russia's political scene in the early twenty-first century and seem set to rule the country at least for the foreseeable future. Therefore the dynamics of the two protest cycles in Russia can be analysed not only through the lens of regime changes over a quarter-century, but also through the lens of generational change within the same period.

Perhaps ever since the time of Ivan Turgenev's famous novel *Fathers and Sons* (*Ottsy i deti*), first published at the height of Emperor Alexander II's reforms in 1862, tensions and contradictions between different generations in Russia have been at the centre of attention of various observers. An analysis of the problems of political change through the prism of generational change is important not only in rethinking both distant history and the recent past of Russian politics and society, but also for an understanding of the logic of the processes which determine current tendencies and Russia's political future. This chapter aims to contribute to the discussion of the role that different generations have played in late-Soviet and post-Soviet political change, followed by a reassessment of the impact of 'fathers' (or 'sixties') (Alexeyeva and Goldberg 1993; Vail' and Genis 1998; Zubok 2009), of 'sons' (or 'seventiers') (Yurchak 2006; Travin 2011), and of 'grandsons' (or the post-Soviet generation) (Mickiewicz 2014). I extend earlier arguments (Gel'man, Travin, and Marganiya 2014) and offer some conclusions about and tentative implications for the connection between political change and generational change in Russia and beyond.

From generation to generation: wine, vinegar, and cocktail

For the purpose of further analysis, I will depart from the standard functionalist sociological perspective, which links the phenomenon of generations to specific age cohorts (Eisenstadt 1956) and associates their formation with the process of socialization and adolescence. In this regard, the boundaries of age cohorts are not as important as the shared political context and collective experience of the generations, which significantly shape the formation and evolution of their 'mental models' (Denzau and North 1994), or the world-views of representatives from various generations and their subsequent effects on participation (or non-participation) in political action. This approach (Mannheim 1952) recently became more conventional for an analysis of late-Soviet society (Yurchak 2006; Zubok 2009) and applicable to the post-Soviet period as well (Gel'man, Travin, and Marganiya 2014). Also, my analysis is not concerned with generations as a whole, but rather focuses on the repre-sentatives of a political class – not only of elites, who affect meaningful polit-ical and policy decisions, but also of auxiliary actors: activists, professionals, experts, journalists, and the like. Since the major changes in late-Soviet and post-Soviet society were mainly initiated and implemented 'top-down' – as the product of the actions of the elite rather than the masses, with all the advan-tages and shortcomings of this, the focus on this tiny, but very important segment of generations appears relevant for the purposes of this discussion.

Based upon this angle, I consider three major generations which played decisive roles in political changes of 1989–2012. First, the 'sixties', whose political views were formed, and professional and public careers launched, in the period between the Twentieth Congress of the Communist Party in 1956 and the Prague Spring in 1968: these landmarks served as crucial points in their trajectories. Second, the 'seventiers', who had grown up and begun their active professional careers in the period between the Prague Spring and the beginning of perestroika (i.e. during the Stagnation), and who experienced the Soviet collapse and subsequent developments as a major turning point in their professional careers and public roles. Third, the representatives of the post-Soviet generation (no name given to it as yet), whose adolescence falls into the post-Soviet period, both the turbulent 1990s and the time of unpre-cedented economic growth in the 2000s, and for whom the public discontent of 2011–12 most probably was the first (but maybe not the last) major experi-ence of large-scale participation in contentious politics. I would argue that the collective experience of each of these generations affected their worldviews in various ways and, to a major degree, contributed to the modes of their pol-itical actions before, during, and after the critical junctures of 1989–91 and 2011–12.

In the historical novel *The Death of the Vazir-Mukhtar* (*Smert' Vazir-Mukhtara*, 1928), which focused on Russia in the late 1820s, Yuri Tynyanov made a major distinction between different generations: the 'people of wine fermentation' (*vinnogo brozheniia*), who flourished in the atmosphere of great expectations after the Patriotic War of 1812; and the 'people of vinegar fer-mentation' (*uksusnogo brozheniia*), who made their careers shortly after the suppression of the Decembrist uprising in 1825 (Tynianov 1985, 7–8). According to Tynyanov, the change in political climate in Russia after 1825 not only dealt an irrecoverable blow to the 'people of wine' generation, but also set back the country's progress by three decades, until the time of the 'people of vinegar' came to an end. The dichotomy proposed by Tynyanov to some extent is also relevant for the sixtiers and seventiers, each of whom ultimately got a chance to put their own ideas into reality. In a similar way, the critical junctures of the dividing lines between the late-Soviet and post-Soviet generations in the second half of the twentieth century were the suppression of the Prague Spring, which put an end to positive changes in the country's political climate, and the collapse of the Communist regime and of the Soviet Union in 1991. The first of these critical junctures put an end to the Thaw, that period of liberalization of the Soviet political system launched under Khrushchev. It interrupted the ascendance of the best and brightest sixtiers – the 'people of wine' – who intended to reform the system, and contributed to its 'long decline' (Zubok 2009, Chapter 9), which continued until pere-stroika. The second critical juncture not only marked the end of the previous political and economic system, but also terminated the hopes (or illusions) of the sixtiers, who soon lost the top positions in the country. At the same time, the Soviet collapse gave the seventiers – the 'people of vinegar', who had very limited aspirations before perestroika – the chance to build a new Russia on the Soviet ruins and to dominate the public scene for the next two decades and beyond.

Although it would be exaggerated to consider the 2011–12 protests as a new critical juncture in Russian politics, there is no doubt that these events brought to the centre stage of the public arena a whole group of representatives of the new post-Soviet generation, ranging from the anti-corruption activist and blogger Alexei Navalny to TV celebrity Kseniia Sobchak. It would be pre-mature to discuss their worldviews and modes of political action, although some studies have underlined certain differences between this generation and their predecessors (Tsimmerman et al. 2013; Mickiewicz 2014). However, one might argue that the political profile of the post-Soviet generation is far from monotonic: its representatives have received mixed signals from simultaneous changes both within and outside the country, experienced rapid globaliza-tion and technological changes, undergone a series of learning processes, and been faced with numerous new opportunities and new (and old) constraints. Therefore, extending Tynyanov's liquidity metaphor, the cocktail might be an appropriate image for this generation. But while the top positions in politics, governance, and business are still held by the seventiers (including Vladimir Putin and his inner circle), there is no doubt that intergenerational tensions are likely to increase over time. These tensions are related not only to the bitter struggle for the top positions but also to the different frames of refer-ence: for the seventiers, the Soviet Union, as a part of their personal experi-ence, is considered a role model in a positive and/or negative sense, while for their 'sons' (or the 'grandsons' of the sixtiers) this is more or less a matter of either a glorious or inglorious past. Thus, the expectations of the ageing sev-entiers have become more and more retrospect and backward-looking, chal-lenged by the rising post-Soviet generation, which is more forward-looking. Whether or not intergenerational tensions can be resolved in a peaceful way in the foreseeable future remains to be seen, but we will certainly observe a new wave of generational changes in Russia, which will again – for better or worse – change the country's political landscape.

The sixtiers: the last true believers

Khrushchev's Thaw, which coincided with the rise of the generation of the sixtiers, was a time of great expectations, in at least three important respects. First, the political liberalization against a backdrop of economic growth brought major hopes of reforming the Soviet political and economic system. Second, the ideas of building a 'socialism with a human face', which resonated not only in the slogans of the Prague Spring but also in the revival of the global Left in the 1960s, strengthened their belief in 'true Leninism' as a positive alternative to Stalinism. Third, the rapid technological progress of this period contributed to the illusion of a bright future within not-too-distant reach. These great expectations fuelled the rise of social activism and innovations on numerous fronts with the intention of improving the system rather than ruining it (Alexeyeva and Goldberg 1993; Vail' and Genis 1998; Grushin 2001–2003; Barkabadze 2007; Zubok 2009). The abrupt end of the Thaw and the following conservative turn in Soviet politics, which soon degenerated into almost two decades of decay and stagnation, had a devastating effect on the generation of the sixtiers. The Soviet reformers were faced with an increasing need to conform and adjust to the preservation of the status quo; their proposed solutions for an improvement of Soviet economy and society remained unclaimed, and the time-horizon for a new round of change became seemingly endless. Yet among the sixtiers there were many courageous people who opposed the Soviet system, either by openly criticizing the regime or by looking for possibilities to improve the country without breaking with Communism. But due to many constraints, only a limited number of brave dissidents chose to 'voice' (Hirschman 1970) their opinions against the regime, while most intellectuals and professionals took a forced 'exit' in various forms (ranging from emigration to alcoholism).

The long 1970s were an almost lost time for the sixtiers, not only in terms of inactivity but also in terms of the freezing of their ideas: the Soviet life experience did not broaden their knowledge and transform the worldviews that had emerged during the Thaw, but rather preserved them. Against the background of the Stagnation, intellectuals did not receive new incentives for analysis and had almost no opportunities for open discussion with real potential. Not only were all polemics aimed at the past, but any open debate, with the exception of 'kitchen talks', conformed to ideological censorship and was conducted in an 'Aesopian language' to avoid punishment for disloyalty to the authorities or for deviation from the true dogma. The intellectual environment in such conditions could not be very fruitful. Moreover, the evolution of the sixtiers was hindered by a lack of opportunities to turn words into deeds. Intellectual discussions held before perestroika had practically no relation to policy changes. Accordingly, the formulation of ideas, the elaboration of views, and finally the publication of a text, often written in Aesopian language, turned into a goal in itself. The dissemination of ideas was more important than putting them into action: the sixtiers probably did not think seriously about becoming true reformers, as the time for change seemed incredibly distant to them. Thus, the sixtiers were not concerned with the way in which their ideas would work in practice: they probably did not give much thought to how to achieve their goals. This was true for both regime loyalists and dissidents: with some notable exceptions (see Amalrik 1970), alternative visions for tackling the problems and improving the prospects of Soviet society were in short supply.

In the light of this ideational legacy, with the beginning of perestroika the Soviet Union seemed to return suddenly to the era of Khrushchev's Thaw for a while. Under Gorbachev, a number of reform-minded sixtiers occupied certain key positions in the power apparatus (e.g., Alexander Yakovlev or Anatoly Chernyaev); they dominated journalism (such as Yegor Yakovlev) and discussed key concepts for the development of Soviet society (for example, Yuri Afanasyev or Tatyana Zaslavskaya). They became major public figures: most popular pundits and media observers belonged to this generation – writers, scholars, and essayists who regularly expressed themselves on issues of the past, present, and future of the country. In a sense, perestroika was a last 'Hurrah!' of the ageing sixtiers, many of whom by that time were 50 years old or older, and they rightly considered this opportunity as the last chance for the Soviet Union and also for themselves. It wasn't the fault of the sixtiers, but rather their ill fortune that in terms of their knowledge and worldviews they proved to be insufficiently prepared to make use of the new opportunities for change that opened up with perestroika. At that time it was quite clear that many representatives of this generation almost entirely lacked a positive agenda. This was true in the case of Gorbachev and his intellectual advisors, but also for leading intellectual figures of the emerging pro-democratic groups, irrespective of their views. The title of a documentary film made in 1989 by the popular director Stanislav Govorukhin summarizes the argument of many sixtiers: *We Can't Live Like That* (*Tak zhit' nel'zia*). In other words, many sixtiers justly criticized the Soviet system, but it was completely unclear how to move out of this state of crisis and reach the ideals they envisaged. The numerous proposals made by leading sixtiers during perestroika often proved rather naïve, or somewhat wishful thinking, with little chance of practical implementation.

The lack of a positive agenda contributed to the inconsistency of the major changes launched during perestroika. In terms of economic reforms, the sixtiers began by experimenting with workers' self-government (which was employed in Yugoslavia in the 1960s and failed later on) and the legalization of private business (cooperatives), while they did not liberalize consumer prices or initiate large-scale privatization. Instead, partial and ill-considered reforms contributed to the rise of inflation, an increasing shortage of goods, and, in the end, a major recession which started in 1990 (Gel'man, Travin, and Marganiya 2014, Chapter 3). In terms of state- and nation-building, the sixtiers reacted sluggishly to the rise of nationalism and ethnic conflicts, or adopted one-sided partisan views but failed to propose viable solutions to the multiple troubles in the fading Soviet empire. Although these faults mostly resulted from poorly prepared and spontaneous moves by Gorbachev and his allies, the pro-reformist opposition intellectuals were no better prepared to change: they often spent their time in endless discussions aimed at blaming the Communist past rather than offer reasonable solutions for the future (Fish 1995; Lukin 2000).

While the sixtiers played a crucial role in the destruction of the Soviet system, they did not benefit from the outcome: rather, the almost simultaneous end of the Communist regime and the Soviet state resulted in a mutual annihilation of the two competing political camps during perestroika: the reformers and the conservatives. In fact, after 1991 the sixtiers soon lost their battle for leadership in politics, in government, and especially in business to the seventiers, and gradually left the public arena in the wake of the 'roaring' 1990s. This shift was only partly related to the natural ageing of the sixtiers. More importantly, the change of the country's agenda required new leaders from a new generation: those who primarily focused on deeds rather words.

The seventiers: politics without illusions

To some extent, the rise of the seventiers in the wake of the Soviet collapse marked by the appearance of Yegor Gaidar and his team in the vanguard of economic reforms (Aven and Kokh 2015) was the result of a political struggle and personal rivalry between Gorbachev and Yeltsin: Yeltsin did not trust the former members of Gorbachev's team, including his critics, and was not inclined to rely on the experience and ideas of the sixtiers unless there was some urgency. But to a large degree, the shift in policy leadership in Russia after 1991 was a side-effect of the inevitable process of generational change. In many ways the seventiers looked at things differently to the sixtiers. They were much more capable of not just arguing about big ideas but achieving at least small practical results. The approaches and values of the 'sons' proved to be very distant from the worldviews of their 'fathers' (see Travin 2011).

The seventiers grew up in rather different conditions than did the sixtiers. If in the Thaw era it seemed to young people that positive changes towards a bright future were possible in the short term, in the 1970s such hopes no longer existed, and so the rising generation of this time had to learn to live 'here and now' and to adapt to the existing political, social, and economic environment without any of those earlier dreams (Grushin 2001–2003). Instead of thinking about a collective bright future, each person had to formulate their own individual dream, i.e. a personal goal, and then try to achieve it within the framework of the Soviet system. These living conditions helped to develop pragmatism, and in many cases also cynicism, among the seventiers. It was only possible to achieve one's goal if one silently agreed to the Soviet 'rules of the game'. Yet there were also marginal non-conformist figures among the seventiers who tried to retain individual freedom and avoid following Communist rituals; they formed an alternative sub-culture (see Yurchak 2006). However, these exceptions do not reflect the nature of the major changes in the 1970s. The mainstream of young people adapted to the conditions set by the political regime, not wishing to eke out an impoverished living without the means to feed their families.

The pragmatism of the seventiers could take different forms: from a cynical acceptance of the political status quo for the sake of a successful career and a high salary, to the aspiration to become a well-qualified specialist in a certain field. Their indifference to Communist ideology did not mean their complete insensitivity to ideas. They simply perceived these ideas through the prism of pragmatic interests, i.e. not as goals for society, but as a means of realising individual desires. The seventiers supported ideas of market reform as a way of overcoming the inefficiency of the Soviet economy and of raising living standards. But they saw the ideas of democracy, which came to the fore in the late 1980s, in a rather ambivalent way. While they unequivocally approved of political liberalization as a way of eliminating the most awkward Soviet restrictions (limited access to information, bans on foreign travel, etc.), democracy as a model of elite competition and political representation met with a mixed reaction at best. They perceived long and often fruitless discussions on political issues as useless 'chatter', particularly against the background of the worsening crisis of the old system.

If reforms had not begun in the Soviet Union when Gorbachev came to power, the best and brightest seventiers would perhaps have remained in obscurity. But perestroika created better conditions in which to make use of their pragmatism and professionalism. No wonder that most of the seventiers (with a few exceptions) were not visible in the political movements of perestroika (Fish 1995; Urban 1997). Instead, many representatives of this generation chose the path of launching their private businesses in the turbulent environment of economic and political change. Despite failures and misfortunes, the most successful representatives of this generation reached the top of their entrepreneurial careers and formed the core of Russia's business elites by the end of the century (for some vivid descriptions, see Freeland 2000; Hoffman 2002). Others, who took up a career in government, were directly involved in reforming the Soviet political and economic system.

Unlike their predecessors, the seventiers had no illusions about socialism, equating it with the shortage of goods and hopeless egalitarianism. Rather, they focused from the beginning on ideas of a liberal market economy with private property, yet considered democracy as just one of several possible means to achieve this goal. They had their own views on how these changes should be implemented, and what sort of economy should be built as a result of the transformation of the Soviet system. However – and this also distinguished them from the sixtiers – they were prepared to adapt easily to changing circumstances, and if necessary make compromises to achieve results, while focusing on short-term goals rather than a vague 'bright future'. In other words, the seventiers preferred to have a bird in the hand rather than two in the bush.

Without entering into endless polemics about whether other scenarios for economic and political reform in Russia in the 1990s were possible, and whether these alternatives could have been carried out more success-fully than the actual reforms conducted by the seventiers, it is worth not-ing that the features of that generation had a considerable effect on the trajectory of transformation. They resulted in the choice of priorities and methods of achieving goals based on a pragmatic agenda: thinking about what was possible rather than what was desirable, a short-term planning horizon, flexibility, and a tendency towards compromise were combined with the willingness and ability to achieve goals. In addition, the unsuccess-ful experience of their predecessors, the sixtiers, who had lost their chance to transform the previous system during perestroika, gave the seventiers a clear signal about what not to do. In this situation, the approaches of the 'fathers' and the 'sons' almost inevitably were diametrically opposed, including in the choice of the sequence of the transformations of the eco-nomic and political system. The seventiers drew their lessons from previous experience, and they were able to achieve their goals at considerable cost, although their success proved to be incomplete and partial.

At the beginning of the twenty-first century, the seventiers seemingly got what they wanted. After a long and protracted recession, the rapid growth of the Russian economy brought a feeling of relative prosperity against the background of a major consumption boom and the abundance of goods and services. The increasingly authoritarian trends in Russian politics under Putin were perceived as trouble only for a tiny minority of ideationally driven seek-ers of freedom or for those who, for various reasons, did not find a suitable place in the new political and economic system. But even some successful seventiers faced bitter disillusionment about their achievements: the country lagged behind the developed world in many respects; dreams about Russia's partnership with the West did not materialize (Aven and Kokh 2015) and the crucial development issues ranging from law and order to public infrastruc-ture remained unresolved. While a number of successful seventiers opted for an 'exit' and took up residence outside Russia, for a large part of the gener-ation the growing resentment and nostalgic views towards the Soviet past, as well as anti-Western attitudes, became more and more widespread over time (for elite survey data, see Tsimmerman et al. 2013). The country is still run by the seventiers, who, now they are older, tend to perceive current develop-ments more or less retrospectively. Thus, the slogan of 'stability' as an idea of preserving the political, economic, and social status quo in the country – at least as the second-best solution – was proposed by the Kremlin, but largely resonated with the wishes of many seventiers who dreamed about a safe haven after the prolonged turbulence of the late-Soviet and early post-Soviet period. In a sense, this claim for 'stability' also resembled that during the Stagnation.

However, challenges to the status quo lay ahead, and a new wave of changes in the 2010s again coincided with a generation change.

The post-Soviet generation: a new turn?

The post-Soviet generation, which grew up in the turbulent 1990s, reached adolescence in the 2000s, when the Russian regime was enjoying a high degree of public support thanks to steady economic growth (Treisman 2011). However, despite these positive trends, the most ambitious representatives of the new generation found limited opportunities for upward mobility, given the rise of crony capitalism and electoral authoritarianism in Russia. Unlike the romantic-ideological sixtiers and the pragmatic-cynical seventiers, the post-Soviet generation perceived its role rather sceptically with regard to both the status quo in Russia and Western political and economic models (Mickiewicz 2014). While political careers required conspicuous and unconditional loyalty to the Kremlin within the framework of regime-sponsored activism (Lassila 2012), many young people dreamed of improving their lives through prestigious jobs in large state-owned energy companies or in the government: according to a Public Opinion Foundation 2009 survey, Gazprom and presidential administration were considered top employers among the Russian youth (see Petrov and Iadukha 2009). For non-conformist youngsters, who slowly began to be affected by the contagion of post-materialist values – pretty much like the Western European post-WWII generation (Tsimmerman et al. 2013) – the list of available alternatives was not rich. However, a visible number of young educated residents of big cities found themselves in milieus of social activism, which spread across Russian cities well before the protests of 2011–12 (Greene 2014). Emerging groups of environmental activists, cultural protection movements, and human rights defenders were often led by those for whom the Soviet period was a matter of the past. The relatively soft political climate of the 2000s and especially the interregnum of Dmitrii Medvedev's presidency from 2008–12 (Gel'man 2013; 2015) provided fertile ground for the advancement and politicization of new leaders, and for the emergence of new communities. In other words, social activism paved the way for generational change among the opposition, while the leadership in the ruling group remained in the hands of the same, ageing seventiers.

In many ways, the generational shift in political participation, which became visible in 2011–12 (Volkov 2012), had been prepared over the course of the previous years. During the new protest cycle, the opposition leaders from the generation of the seventiers were overshadowed by their younger counterparts, irrespective of their ideological position (liberals, democrats, socialists, or nationalists). This process was symbolically completed in July 2013, when the opposition party RPR-PARNAS (Republican Party of Russia – People's Freedom Party), co-chaired by 54-year-old Boris Nemtsov and 56-year-old Mikhail Kasyanov, nominated the 37-year-old Alexei Navalny as its candidate for the elections to the office of Moscow's mayor.

The generation change among the opposition greatly contributed to a 'negative consensus' against the political status quo. First, unlike their predecessors, post-Soviet leaders and activists were not so bitterly divided by old conflicts and by perceptions of the past (such as assessments of the Soviet collapse and of the reforms of the 1990s), but were ready to build a new political identity beyond conventional ideological barriers. Second, the populist discursive juxtaposition of the ruling class as 'crooks and thieves' as against 'the people', proposed by the representatives of the new generation, serves as a strong tool of anti-regime mobilization. Navalny, who identified himself through a combination of elements of both liberalism and nationalism, and who organized an excellent innovative campaign for Moscow's mayoral elections, receiving over 600,000 votes, became a prime example of this trend (Smyth and Soboleva 2014b; Gel'man 2015). Yet the protest cycle of 2011–12 was short-lived and did not bring any immediate success to the emerging opposition. Moreover, the harsh reaction of the Kremlin, which used repression and intimidation against its new (and old) rivals, prevented the spread of anti-regime mobilization, while Russia's annexation of Crimea and the aggravating conflict with the West over Ukraine undermined the foundations of the 'negative consensus' to a certain degree.

Despite all of these troubles, the natural advantage of the post-Soviet generation is their time horizon, which is certainly longer than those of the seventiers, whose capacity to offer attractive life chances to their successors will inevitably diminish over time. Therefore the 2011–12 protest cycle can be seen as the first (necessary, yet insufficient) step towards a new round of the country's democratization. This round is likely to take different forms and employ different mechanisms than the protest cycle of 1989–91 used, and not only because it may be driven from below, while the democratic movement during perestroika was by and large initiated from above (Hough 1997). The other important difference concerns the core of leaders and activists: a quarter-century ago, the anti-regime protests were the last battle of the sixtiers, while the most recent wave of protest mobilization in 2011–12 might be the first sign of a political awakening of the post-Soviet generation.

Conclusion

The conventional wisdom of scholars states that the public demand for democratization arises as a side-effect of economic growth, which encourages aspirations for greater political rights among the rising urban middle class and drives it into the political arena (Przeworski et al. 2000). The post-Soviet Russian experience provides rather mixed evidence (Treisman 2011) and also leaves open the question about the mechanism of conversion of public demands for political change from a latent to an explicit form. Judging by the experience of protest cycles in Russia, one might argue that the effect of generational changes has played an important role in this conversion. The differences between the sixtiers and the seventiers may explain the winding trajectory of the Russian reforms of the 1980s and 1990s, when the emerging public demand for free-doms shifted to a steady demand for wealth at the expense of freedom: the difference in the collective experience of these generations greatly affected their 'mental models' and played an important role in these changes. The intergen-erational differences were also crucial for the 2010s, when representatives of the post-Soviet generations, who had grown up in the 1990s and in the 2000s, came to the centre stage of Russian politics with their own 'mental models' formed against the background of a crucial reassessment of the experience of their predecessors. The evidence of intergenerational differences is very tenta-tive and far from conclusive, but it may well be the case that in the eyes of the new generation, public demands for freedom and wealth will be not juxtaposed as incompatible alternatives. If and when this happens, there will be some hope that Russia will not repeat the same flight from freedom that happened in the 1990s and 2000s. Therefore, the main slogan of opposition rallies – 'Russia Will Be Free!' – can be perceived not just as a call for action, but also as a key item on Russia's political agenda. Russia will indeed become a free country. The question for the new generation is exactly when and how this will happen, as well as what the cost will be of Russia's path to freedom.

Acknowledgement

This chapter is a part of the project 'Choices of Russian Modernization', a collective research project funded by the Academy of Finland.

Note on Transliteration

At the express wish of the author, this chapter departs from LoC transliter-ation for Russian first names with an accepted English spelling; and for the names of Tynyanov (Tynianov); Navalny (Navalnyi); Chernyaev (Cherniaev); Afanasyev (Afanas'ev); Zaslavskaya (Zaslavskaia); and Kasyanov (Kasianov).

References

Alexeyeva, Ludmilla and Paul Goldberg. 1993. *The Thaw Generation: Coming of Age in the Post-Stalin Era*. Pittsburgh: University of Pittsburgh Press.
Amalrik, Andrei. 1970. *Will the Soviet Union Survive Until 1984?* New York: Harper and Row.
Aven, Petr and Alfred Kokh. 2015. *Gaidar's Revolution: The Inside Account of the Economic Transformation in Russia*. London: I.B. Tauris.
Barkabadze, Mark, ed. 2007. *Shestidesiatniki*. Moscow: Fond Liberal'naia missiia. www.liberal.ru/upload/files/60-desyatniki.pdf (accessed 2 December 2014).
Denzau, Arthur and Douglass North. 1994. "Sharing Mental Models: Ideologies and Institutions." *Kyklos* 47 (1): 3–31.
Eisenstadt, Shmuel. 1956. *From Generation to Generation: Age Groups and Social Structure*. New Brunswick, NJ: Transaction Publishers.
Fish, Stephen M. 1995. *Democracy from Scratch: Opposition and Regime in the New Russian Revolution*. Princeton, NJ: Princeton University Press.

Freeland, Chrystia. 2000. *Sale of the Century: The Inside Story of the Second Russian Revolution*. Boston, MA: Little, Brown.

Gel'man, Vladimir. 2013. "Cracks in the Wall: Challenges to Electoral Authoritarianism in Russia." *Problems of Post-Communism* 60 (2): 3–10.

Gel'man, Vladimir. 2015. "Political Opposition in Russia: A Troubled Transformation." *Europe-Asia Studies* 67 (2): 177–191.

Gel'man, Vladimir, Dmitry Travin, and Otar Marganiya. 2014. *Reexamining Economic and Political Reforms in Russia, 1985–2000: Generations, Ideas, and Changes*. Lanham, MD: Lexington Books.

Greene, Samuel. 2014. *Moscow in Movement: Power and Opposition in Putin's Russia*. Stanford, CA: Stanford University Press.

Grushin, Boris. 2001–2003. *Chetyre zhizni Rossiii v zerkale oprosov obshchestvennogo mneniia. Ocherki massovogo soznaniia rossiian vremen Khrushcheva, Brezhneva, Gorbacheva i El'tsina*, 4 vols. Moscow: Progress-Traditsiia.

Hirschman, Albert O. 1970. *Exit, Voice, and Loyalty: Response to Decline in Firms, Organizations, and States*. Cambridge, MA: Harvard University Press.

Hoffman, David. 2002. *Oligarchs: Wealth and Power in the New Russia*. New York: Public Affairs.

Hough, Jerry F. 1997. *Democratization and Revolution in the USSR, 1985–1991*. Washington, DC: Brookings Institution Press.

Lassila, Jussi. 2012. *The Quest of Ideal Youth in Putin's Russia: The Search of Distinctive Conformism in the Political Communication of Nashi, 2005–2009*. Stuttgart: Ibidem-Verlag.

Lukin, Alexander. 2000. *Political Culture of the Russian "Democrats"*. Oxford: Oxford University Press.

Mannheim, Karl. 1952. "The Problem of Generations." In *Essays on the Sociology of Knowledge*, 276–320. London: Routledge & Kegan Paul.

Mickiewicz, Ellen. 2014. *No Illusions: The Voices of Russia's Future Leaders*. Oxford: Oxford University Press.

Petrov, Ivan and Viktor Iadukha. 2009. "Molodezh' mechtaet o trube." *Rbc.ru* 27 May. http://rbcdaily.ru/politics/562949979000840 (accessed 14 August 2015).

Przeworski, Adam, Michael E. Alvarez, José Antonio Cheibub, and Fernando Limongi. 2000. *Democracy and Development: Political Institutions and Well-being in the World, 1950–1990*. Cambridge: Cambridge University Press.

Robertson, Graeme. 2013. "Protesting Putinism: The Election Protests of 2011–2012 in Broader Perspective." *Problems of Post-Communism* 60 (2): 11–23.

Smyth, Regina and Irina Soboleva. 2014a. "Early Risers, Stalwarts and Protest Tourists: Differential Participation in the 'For Fair Elections' Movement." Paper for the 14th Annual Aleksanteri Conference, Helsinki, 22–24 October.

Smyth, Regina and Irina Soboleva. 2014b. "Gamesters: Electoral Innovation and the 2013 Moscow Mayoral Campaign." Paper presented at the ASEEES Annual Convention, San Antonio, 20–23 November.

Tarrow, Sideny. 1994. *Power in Movement: Collective Action, Social Movements, and Politics*. Cambridge: Cambridge University Press.

Tilly, Charles. 1978. *From Mobilization to Revolution*. Reading, MA: Addison-Wesley.

Travin, Dmitrii. 2011. "Semidesiatnutye – analiz pokoleniia." Working Paper 25. St Petersburg: Izdatel'stvo Evropeiskogo Universiteta v Sankt-Peterburge. www.eu.spb. ru/images/centres/M-center/Travin_25_09_11.pdf (accessed 2 December 2014).

Treisman, Daniel. 2011. "Presidential Popularity in a Hybrid Regime: Russia under Yeltsin and Putin." *American Journal of Political Science* 55 (3): 590–609.

Tsimmerman, Uil'iam [Zimmerman, William], Ronal'd Inglkhart [Ronald Inglehart], Eduard Ponarin, Egor Lazarev, Boris Sokolov, Irina Vartanova, and Ekaterina Turanova. 2013. *Rossiiskaia elita – 2020*. Moscow: RIA-Novosti. http://vid-1.rian. ru/ig/valdai/Russian_elite_2020_rus.pdf (accessed 22 July 2015).

Tynianov, Iurii [Tynyanov, Yuri]. 1985. "Smert' Vazir-Mukhtara." In *Sochineniia*, vol. 2. Moscow: Khudozhestvennaia Literatura.

Urban, Michael. 1997. *The Rebirth of Politics in Russia*. Cambridge: Cambridge University Press.

Vail', Petr and Aleksandr Genis. 1998. *60-e: Mir sovetskogo cheloveka*. Moscow: Novoe literaturnoe obozrenie.

Volkov, Denis. 2012. "Protestnye mitingi v Rossii kontsa 2011 – nachala 2012 gg.: zapros na demokratizatsiiu politicheskikh institutov." *Vestnik obshchestvennogo mneniia* 2: 73–85. www.levada.ru/books/vestnik-obshchestvennogo-mneniya-2112-za-2012-god (accessed 22 July 2015).

Yurchak, Alexei. 2006. *Everything Was Forever, Until It Was No More: The Last Soviet Generation*. Princeton, NJ: Princeton University Press.

Zubok, Vladislav. 2009. *Zhivago's Children: The Last Russian Intelligentsia*. Cambridge, MA: Harvard University Press.

2 Dissidents reloaded?
Anti-Putin activists and the Soviet legacy

Valentina Parisi

'I am not Sakharov, nevertheless I demand freedom for all political prisoners'. This slogan, which appeared on a self-made poster in April 2011 (Fig. 2.1) – that is, well before the escalation of anti-government protests in Russia – clearly reflects the ambiguity of the feelings nurtured by anti-Putin activists towards Soviet dissidents of the 1960s and 1970s. People who contested the results of the Duma elections in December 2011 and challenged the largely accepted model of a 'managed' (or 'sovereign') democracy (Petrov 2005) were generally aware of the fact that the nature of authoritarianism in Russia had radically changed after the collapse of the Soviet system. Some of the sharpest opponents of Vladimir Putin's regime even contested the cliché of an indisputable continuity among old and new dissidents by drawing on both historical and political reasons (Polukhina 2013). Thus, the historian and artist Il'ia Budraitskis complained about the fact that international media gave much more coverage to the Pussy Riot case than to the clashes between protesters and the police on Bolotnaya Square on 6 May 2012. As a consequence, he affirmed, the clashes re-enforced the 'well-established scheme of free, brave individuals struggling against Russia's oppressive power' that they inherited from the Brezhnev era (Budraitskis 2012).

Still, Soviet dissent seems to represent an unavoidable reference point for identifying and interpreting any sign of political activism, any demand for effective democratization on the territory of the former USSR. This proves to be true not only if we turn our attention to Western media as Budraitskis did, but also – more interestingly – if we look at the attempts at self-depiction by the protesters. Even if apparently denied or rejected, as in the case of the above-mentioned slogan, dissent still maintains a strong symbolic power over the imagination of those standing up against those in authority in Russia. Especially when issues related to human rights and the repression of freedom of opinion are at stake, anti-Putin activists experience the urge to confront this legacy and articulate their own position in respect to it. In my chapter I will try to illuminate some of the ways in which the category of dissent, and the symbolic potential it is invested with, have been appropriated or criticized by some government opponents, in particular by the Pussy Riot group. More specifically, I argue that Soviet dissent as a historical precedent provided both

Figure 2.1 The Voina activist Leonid Nikolaev before a poster demanding freedom for
all political prisoners, April 2011
Source: http://sakharov-today.ru/sf.

Putin's enemies and his allies with a tested rhetorical tool which, at a precise stage, became suitable for both of them. On the one hand, the reference
to Soviet dissident legacy allowed post-socialist protesters to place their own
strategy in a broader context and thus convey it towards a responsive Western
audience. On the other hand, the authorities looked back at the Brezhnev
era, too, and resurrected not only rhetorical imagery, but also the typically
Soviet penal allegation of hooliganism (*khuliganstvo*) in order to prosecute
anti-government activists and slander them in the eyes of the passive majority.

'Old' and 'new' dissenters

After the results of Duma elections were made public on 4 December 2011,
protests in the streets re-emerged in Russia as a significant political issue,
increasingly framed around a regime/opposition divide. After culminating
between December 2011 and February 2012, rallies diminished in size after
May 2012, when many activists were arrested on Bolotnaya Square. Although
protesters consistently reduced their presence in the public sphere because

of the laws enacted in June 2012, which imposed heavy penalties for unsanctioned gatherings, Western observers went on questioning the real significance and possible consequences of those demonstrations of civic unrest. For instance, in the summer of 2012 a study commissioned by the American Enterprise Institute (AEI) for Public Policy Research, the most prominent think-tank associated with American neo-conservatism, while welcoming the emergence of 'a new generation of politically active Russians', expressed the quite optimistic hope that 'a confluence of [...] "traditional" and "new" protesters could bring about a perfect political storm, which the regime will not be able to easily quell – or perhaps even survive' (Aron 2012, 5). These expectations of a perhaps imminent regime change relied on the assumption that '*just like past civil rights movements*, Russia's is led by a middle class that is seeking to effect vast political and social change through a personal and deeply moral effort' (Aron 2012, 6; my emphasis). A number of similarities between 'old' and 'new' Russian dissent – namely the absence of formal and permanent leadership and the participation of many exponents of the non-political sphere in the protest movement (Volkov 2012, 12–14), such as journalists, writers, and artists – encouraged the author of the survey to evaluate positively the situation and to define it as 'immensely favorable to America's geostrategy' (Aron 2012, 9) and to AEI's commitment 'to expanding liberty'.

The alleged return to a past that had never really gone away should not obscure the fact that – as Liudmila Alekseeva, a trained historian and founding member of the Moscow Helsinki Watch Group, remarked – Vladislav Surkov's 'sovereign democracy' is something definitely different from Soviet 'late socialism' (Kulagin 2012). 'I lived in a real totalitarian state and that was scary', she explained in December 2012 to Tat'iana Lokshina, deputy director of the Moscow office of Human Rights Watch. 'But now the country is different, people are different – you just cannot compare. Back in 1976, MHG (Moscow Helsinki Group) was the only independent group in the USSR. Now things just aren't the same' (Lokshina 2012). As a matter of fact, today's Russia seems rather to fit into the frame of what scholars call 'hybrid regimes', i.e. authoritarian regimes 'which speak the language of liberal democracy without fully adopting its practices' (Robertson 2011, 4). As Graeme B. Robertson has stated in his book devoted to street protests, Putin's strategy provides an excellent example for understanding the politics of repression in contemporary hybrid regimes, i.e. how contention of dissent works. Since leaders of such regimes do have at their disposal the full-blown repressive apparatus of closed authoritarian regimes and are forced to allow at least some public displays of opposition, politicians and protesters start to interact in ways which are completely unprecedented. This is the case, for instance, in contemporary Russia, where 'legitimate and public political competition coexists with an organizational and institutional playing field that renders this competition unfair' (Robertson 2011, 6), as Duma elections in December 2011 and Putin's re-election in March 2012 clearly showed.

Changes which occurred in the nature of authoritarian states after the end of Cold War and the rise of what Steven Levitsky and Lucan Way defined as 'competitive authoritarianism' (Levitsky and Way 2002; Levitsky 2010) caused significant transformations in oppositional tactics as well. In particular, the overt expression of anti-government positions ceased to be an elitist phenomenon, exclusively confined to the so-called 'creative class' (as it certainly was in the Soviet era) and was appropriated by an unprecedented number of people. Participants in oppositional rallies were bound together by some common features, being wealthier and better educated, and sharing a more critical attitude towards power holders, when compared to the majority of Russian citizens (Volkov 2012, 26); still, many observers have pointed out the heterogeneity of their individual positions. In this respect, they resemble the Soviet dissident movement, 'a sometimes odd, often unworkable amalgam of human rights activists, disappointed insiders, bloody-minded outsiders, fervent religious believers and nationalists of a wide range of Soviet nationalities' (Applebaum 2007).

Nonetheless, the emergence of such diverse, often conflicting, protesting identities, as well as the unexpected flourishing of various oppositional practices, can also explain why former Soviet dissidents at first did not particularly mix with new protesters. After the first rallies on Bolotnaya Square on 10 and 17 December 2011, elderly human rights activists were struck by the diversity of such a disjointed bunch of dissenters, including young hipsters and pensioners, right-wing nationalists and radical leftists. Natal'ia Gorbanevskaia, as well as Sergei Kovalev, remarked that the new protesters looked even more different from one another than Soviet dissidents were, and that their ideas often contradicted each other so much that it was hard to even see a common link between them. Kovalev recalled with nostalgia the sense of solidarity which brought together all opponents to the Soviet system, in spite of their often incompatible political views:

I hated the Russian nationalistic positions, but we accounted for Vladimir Osipov's articles in the *Chronicle of Current Events [Khronika tekushchikh sobytii]*. We thought we had no right not to acquaint the readers with ideas we did not share [...] We knew that our common enemy was Soviet ideology [...] And, in my opinion, our solidarity worked well.

(Pasternak 2012)

In spite of these critical remarks about fellow protesters, former dissidents started to express their solidarity with anti-government activists and especially those who had been arrested after the clamp-down following the 'March of Millions'. Among others, Alekseeva repeatedly praised the braveness of the Bolotnaya Square prisoners:

They are real heroes. They are all wonderful, beautiful, strong people. I deeply respect them and everyone who came to the Bolotnaya Square rally. Judging from this 'non-representative sampling', in other words random snatching, held by the Investigative Committee, I can say that the majority of those on the square […] must have been of the same strong sort.

(Polukhina 2013)

Some other dissidents began to feel a kind of proximity to jailed activists only after being explicitly addressed by them. This is the case for Gorbanevskaia, who declared in an interview that, despite 'all Pussy Riot's vulgarisms and primitiveness', she had a moral duty to support them, since they had decided to stage their performance 'Putin Pissed Himself' ('Putin zassal', 20 January 2012) on the Place of Skulls (Lobnoe mesto), i.e. the same place where on 25 August 1968 Gorbanevskaia and her comrades Vadim Delone, Pavel Litvinov, Viktor Fainberg, Vladimir Dremliuga, Konstantin Babitskii, Larisa Bogorazova, and Tat'iana Baeva demonstrated against the invasion of Soviet troops into the territory of the 'fraternal' Czechoslovak Socialist Republic. Namely, the explicit quotation of the slogan 'For your and our freedom' in Pussy Riot's songs provided the elderly dissident with a peculiar mirroring effect: 'Since they feel bonded to us, I have to feel bonded to them too. And it is not unlikely that we inspired them in some way with our example' (Gorbanevskii and Stroganova 2012).

Displaying protests

The establishment of individual relationships across generations and the participation of several former dissidents in the anti-Putin rallies has elicited – both in Russia and abroad – many comparisons with Brezhnev's Stagnation. Especially in Russia the question of similarities and differences between new and old protesters became the object of passionate debates among intellectuals (Lagunina 2007; Gutkin 2012). In this respect, Aleksandr Daniel' – whose father Iulii had been tried together with Andrei Siniavskii in Moscow in February 1966 and sentenced to five years of hard labour for anti-Soviet slander after having published his literary works abroad – made a very interesting point, by stating that Putinism is far more aggressive and appealing than communist ideology was in the 1960s and 1970s. Consequently, anti-government activists are much more isolated than Soviet dissidents were, and cannot rely on real support among Russia's silent majority.

While Russian observers generally tended to underline discrepancies rather than continuity between Brezhnev's Stagnation and Putin's sovereign democracy, Western journalists adopted the notion of dissent as a commonplace label to present Russian protesters to Western audiences. Irrespective of T-shirts with Stalin's portrait wore by Sergei Udal'tsov and regardless of Eduard Limonov's life-long mocking of émigré dissidents, the Western media started to speculate about a straight line of succession soon after the first anti-government rallies following the Duma elections in December 2011. The book by the British, Moscow-based journalist Marc Bennetts (2014) on what he calls the 'new generation of Russian dissidents' may serve as an example of such an attitude, as well as the article written by the American opinion-maker David Remnick for *The New Yorker* in August 2012 in reaction to the closing statements delivered by Nadezhda Tolokonnikova and Mariia Alekhina before the Khamovniki court in Moscow (Remnick 2012). The symbolic identification between old and new dissidents peaked a few weeks later in September 2012, when the members of Pussy Riot were nominated for the European Parliament's prestigious Andrei Sakharov Prize. The motivation, formulated by the Green Party member of the European Parliament Werner Schulz (who, in his turn, was a key figure of the opposition in the German Democratic Republic) stated: 'These young women have shone a light on and protested against an autocratic system with courage, creativity and inner force. They have embarrassed a patriarchal power and they have exposed judicial arbitrariness' (Anon. 2012; Garfield 2012).

Another discordant voice is the Russian-born journalist Vadim Nikitin, who replied to Remnick on 11 August 2012 in *The New York Times* – that is, on the eve of the Pussy Riot sentencing. He not only showed the flimsiness of the identification between old and new dissenters, but also warned American readers against the virtual danger of enthusiastically supporting the punk singers by mistaking them for Sakharov's granddaughters. In his opinion, at the core of much of the media fever over Pussy Riot lay a fundamental misunderstanding of what their controversial performances were about:

> Some outlets have portrayed the case as a quest for freedom of expression and other ground rules of liberal democracy. Yet the very phrase 'freedom of expression', with its connotations of genteel protest [...] is alien to Russian radical thought. The members of Pussy Riot are not liberals looking for self-expression. They are self-confessed descendants of the surrealists and the Russian futurists, determined to radically, even violently, change society.
>
> (Nikitin 2012)

In particular, referring to the orgy-performance staged by some Pussy Riot members and the group Voina (War) at the Moscow State Biological Museum (February 2008), Nikitin reminded readers that their actors 'come as a full package: you can't have the fun, pro-democracy, anti-Putin feminism without the incendiary anarchism, extreme sexual provocations, deliberate obscenity and hard-left politics'. Therefore, using them to score political points against the Russian regime would be, in his opinion, 'as dangerous as adopting a pet tiger: no matter how domesticated they may seem, in the end they are free spirits, liable to maul the hand that feeds them' (Nikitin 2012).

Nikitin makes a fundamental point here: while the Soviet dissidents of the 1960s and 1970s argued that the public actions of their movement were entirely legal and justified by the existing Soviet law, post-socialist art activists such as Pussy Riot or Voina deliberately situate their actions on the fringe between legal and illegal, questioning the moral right of a corrupted and corrupting power to prosecute them. While Vladimir Bukovskii identified his fellow dissidents with the norm and Soviet politicians with the norm breakers (Nivat 1998, 238), Pussy Riot members defined themselves as the norm breakers, who strive to challenge the validity of the norm and push the limits of what is deemed acceptable. No wonder that the Slovenian neo-Marxist philosopher Slavoj Žižek adopts the same reverse logic, while expressing his solidarity with Nadezhda Tolokonnikova and Mariia Alekhina: 'The true blasphemy is the state accusation itself, formulating as a crime of religious hatred something which was clearly a political act of protest against the ruling clique' (Tolokonnikova and Žižek 2014, 18).

This attitude resembles the radical agenda programmatically pursued by Voina, the art group to which Tolokonnikova belonged until 2009. As many other actionist artists, both Voina and Pussy Riot rejected commodifiable art practices, refusing the idea that art should produce a valuable object. Instead they staged unauthorized provocative guerrilla performances in highly symbolic urban locations (such as the Place of Skulls on Red Square, the Cathedral of Christ the Saviour, or the Liteinyi Bridge in St Petersburg, just opposite the headquarters of the Federal Security Service (FSB)), edited the original footage into videos, and posted them on the Internet. In this way, they were able to bypass both art-world institutions and the commercial gallery system and to incorporate public space in their practice in order to address socio-political issues. Their strategy included – especially in the Voina case – vandalism, destruction, or misuse of public property. By staging performances which deliberately displayed acts of hooliganism – such as overturning police cars in the street – Voina not only urged both authorities and conservative *maîtres à penser* to deny their practice any artistic value, but also intentionally strove to be prosecuted by the law. In the eyes of both Voina and Pussy Riot, being arrested by the police, charged with criminal offences, and prosecuted by penal courts, and serving a sentence, are not collateral effects, but consciously calculated consequences of their artistic strategies. Only the re-actions or contra-actions performed by the authorities enable them to shape themselves as defenders of freedom of thought and speech, political prisoners, victims, martyrs.

This radical approach accounts also for why Pussy Riot, from the very beginning, criticized opposition leaders for negotiating with the authorities the possibility of denouncing elections fraud within the 'acceptable' framework of sanctioned anti-government rallies. While stressing their dissatisfaction with what was happening in the sphere of civic protests ('The authorities will not get scared and make concessions because they are rallies that they sanctioned themselves'; Chernov 2012), Tolokonnikova and Alekhina repeatedly expressed their full admiration for the Arab Spring revolutionaries and referred to them as the right example to follow in the text of one of their songs: 'Egyptian air is good for our lungs, / let's do Tahrir on Red Square' ('Egipetskii vozdukh polezen dlia legkikh / Sdelai Takhrir na Krasnoi Ploshchadi'; Epshtein 2012, 25). In their opinion, only unauthorized, permanent gatherings in the style of Tahrir Square could help 'antigovern-ment forces to come to effective, collective actions despite political repression' (Pussy Riot 2011; Chernov 2012).

Therefore, Pussy Riot's provocative questioning of the right of the state to declare their actions illegal and prosecute them has really little or nothing to do with the stress on 'law, legality, and legitimized behavior', which, according to Serguei Oushakine, 'constituted the core of dissent in the Soviet Union and radically distinguished the Soviet dissident move-ment from previous oppositional political movements in the Soviet Union or Russia' (Oushakine 2001, 189). Art activists' incendiary radicalism is by no means reminiscent of the dissidents' strategy, which aimed rather at a gradual democratization of the system, i.e. an internal liberalization of the Soviet system, by exercising pressure from below in order to achieve conces-sions from above. What we see here instead – in Pussy Riot's case, but also in the visual arrangements of street protests – is rather a citational use of dissident discourse in order to create an image in which hinted references to Soviet dissidents can happily coexist with many other references, or overlap in a somehow unexpected or shocking way. An excellent example of this adaptation of the oppositional discourse to postmodernist aesthetics is the documentation of the Pussy Riot trial carried out by the Moscow-based artist Viktoria Lomasko in form of comics. From the very beginning a sup-porter of the punk group, she decided to eye-witness every single stage of the trial in the spirit of Frida Vigdorova, the Leningrad journalist who in 1962 documented Joseph Brodsky's trial by transcribing the contents of the interrogations, or in that of Aleksandr Ginzburg, who gathered materials on the Siniavskii-Daniel' trial in his self-published collection of documents (*dokumentalnyi sbornik*), titled *The White Book* (*Belaia kniga*, 1966). Still, the graphic "chronicle of resistance" kept by Lomasko from 4 December 2011 and until November 2012 (and including on-the-spot sketches not only of the Pussy Riot trial, but also of many other important protest-related events) is a very peculiar adaptation of this "dissident" genre to the lan-guage of popular culture, and includes both denunciation, pathos, and ele-ments of explicit mockery (Fig. 2.2).

Of course, identifying the whole protest movement with Putin oppo-nents from the radical artistic milieu such as Pussy Riot, Voina, or Lomasko would be misleading. Nonetheless, their contribution to the formulation of an oppositional discourse demonstrates that Soviet-era dissidents and post-socialist protesters are quite unlikely to fit into the model suggested by Marshall S. Shatz in his pioneering study of 1980, according to which Soviet dissidents formed a 'neo-intelligentsia' which basically repeated the strategy of the old radical intelligentsia of the previous two centuries by questioning and challenging the existing order (Shatz 1980).

Figure 2.2 'The Orthodox community demands harsh punishment'
Source: From Viktoriia Lomasko's graphic reportage from the hearing of the Pussy
Riot case, Taganskii District Court, Moscow, 19 April 2012. Courtesy of Viktoria
Lomasko.

Dissent of the dominant, dissent of the dominated

Still, the self-identification with Soviet dissidents undoubtedly played a major
role in the closing statements of the Pussy Riot trial. Here Tolokonnikova
and Alekhina tried to articulate their own position by appealing to civil
society and to the collective memory of the nation. Such a reference was the
logical reaction to the rhetorical argumentations post-Soviet officials had
resorted to. As a matter of fact, the similarities between the Pussy Riot case
and trials of the 1960s and 1970s are quite striking even from the legal viewpoint. The allegation itself, i.e. 'hooliganism motivated by religious hatred'
(under Article 282 of the Criminal Code of the Russian Federation), openly
references the notorious Soviet-era crime of 'hooliganism', which in the
Stagnation period was used 'as a catch-all clause for any type of opposition
to the regime' (van Galle 2013, 2). While the post-Soviet Criminal Code
of 1996 expressly raises the requirements for convictions of hooliganism
due to the problematic history of that article, in 2007 the elements of this
crime were expanded again as part of the legislative programme to combat
extremism.

Therefore, it is not surprising that the charge under which Pussy Riot were convicted echoed the allegations of sacrilege made against Daniel' and Siniavskii, who, by publishing their works abroad, allegedly wished 'to slander and curse everything that is dear to Soviet man' and expressed 'hatred for our system, vile mockery of everything dear to our Motherland' (Hayward 1966, 23). Not differently, the prosecution defined Pussy Riot's 'Punk Prayer' (Pussy Riot 2012), staged in the Cathedral of Christ the Saviour, as a 'vilification of the spiritual foundations of the state' (van Galle 2013, 3) and evidence of undisguised contempt for society. As a legal expert on the case had demonstrated, the arguments of the prosecution were based 'quite sweepingly on moral considerations, with express disregard for any legal discourse' (van Galle 2013, 3); on the other hand, the lack of clear-cut definitions of the two formal elements of the crime, i.e., hooliganism and religious hatred, led the court in the first instance to leave 'the finding of justice to the witnesses for the prosecution and the expert witnesses' (van Galle 2013, 4). In other words, the court did not explore whether the defendants' actions were protected by free speech laws; instead, they relied heavily on the subjective perception of religious believers (who declared themselves insulted by the violation of the general rules of the church) and on the opinion of selected expert witnesses. Similarly, to prove that the work of Siniavskii and Daniel' was 'sacrilegious in content and seditious in intent' (Hayward 1966, 23), the Soviet prosecution used in evidence the expressions of outrage received from an assorted collection of 'average citizens', as well as the expertise provided by state-loyal literary critics, who denied the relevance of Siniavskii and Daniel''s texts and testified to their intention of slander.

The comparison between the two trials is a subject which would probably deserve a separate analysis; nonetheless, for the purpose of this chapter, it is more relevant to focus on dissent as a historical precedent with the potential to trigger –among both oppositionists and officials – reactions which in part follow prearranged patterns. What has remained unmodified since Siniavskii and Daniel''s trial is not dissent as such, but the self-preserving policies of the contested political elite, i.e. the way authorities construct the official image of dissidents around the threat that they allegedly represent for the state. This turned out to be certainly true in the Pussy Riot case.

From time to time Pussy Riot's attitude towards the historical legacy of Soviet dissent has even shown signs of a competition. Let us consider, for example, Tolokonnikova's reference made from behind bars to the notorious case of Petr Iakir and Viktor Krasin, the two dissidents who broke down after their arrest, agreed to cooperate with the KGB and gave incriminating evidence against their fellow dissidents. Making an explicit comparison, Tolokonnikova declared:

> During the preliminary inquiry I could have withdrawn my opinion, shown contrition and therefore could have been released like Petr Iakir and Viktor Krasin in 1973. Anyway, nobody forced me to do that and I chose a strategy of honesty and coherence.
>
> (Tolokonnikova 2013)

But even before that, in their closing statements, both Tolokonnikova and Alekhina tried to legitimize their artistic endeavours by harking back to several recognizable dissident forerunners, above all Aleksandr Solzhenitsyn and Vladimir Bukovskii. In so doing, they strove to establish a possible intellectual genealogy for Pussy Riot's dissident actions. This genealogical principle is especially evident in Tolokonnikova's speech, insofar as she mentioned in (backward) chronological order Solzhenitsyn, the OBERIU poet Aleksandr Vvedenskii, Fedor Dostoevskii (a political prisoner for his involvement in the Petrashevskii Circle), St Stephen, and Jesus Christ. These names are only apparently chosen at random, eclectic as they sound. While the quotation of the last three names serves to demonstrate that Pussy Riot protest the regime's co-opted Christianity (that is, the alliance between Putin and Patriarch Kirill), and *not* the religion itself, the reference to Solzhenitsyn could be a response to Eduard Limonov, who had accused Pussy Riot of creating a rift between the secularized bourgeoisie and the Orthodox popular masses. Tolokonnikova here takes on a prophet-like role to explain that only Putin's repressive machine prevented her from finding a common language with the people:

> Let us enter into dialogue and contact with the country, which is ours too, not just Putin's and the Patriarch's. Like Solzhenitsyn, I believe that in the end, words will crush concrete. Solzhenitsyn wrote, 'the word is more sincere than concrete, so words are not trifles. Once noble people mobilize, their words will crush concrete.'
>
> (Tolokonnikova 2012)

At the same time, Tolokonnikova significantly chose not to refer to the charismatic, liberal Russian intellectuals of the eighteenth and nineteenth centuries, such as Aleksandr Radishchev, Petr Chaadaev, or Alexander Herzen, but rather hinted at the repressed poet Vvedenskii as one source of inspiration for Pussy Riot's own alogism and subversive strategy:

> The OBERIU poets remained artists to the very end, something impossible to explain or understand since they were purged in 1937. Vvedenskii wrote: 'We like what can't be understood, What can't be explained is our friend.' [...] Pussy Riot are Vvedenskii's disciples and heirs. His principle of 'bad rhythm' is our own. He wrote: 'It happens that two rhythms will come into your head, a good one and a bad one and I choose the bad one. It will be the right one.' What can't be explained is our friend.
>
> (Tolokonnikova 2012)

The reference to Stalin's Great Terror echoes an observation made by Alekhina and introduces another major problem related to political dissent: the problem of memory. In her own closing statement, Alekhina explicitly referred to the trial against Joseph Brodsky in 1963 as another farcical demonstration of the state's hostility to uncensored artistic expression. While attempting to demonstrate how little has changed in Russia, Alekhina glossed over the self-evident fact that Pussy Riot differ from their perceived predecessors in that they are an overtly political group that engages in a variety of art forms. Conversely, Brodsky was adamantly apolitical – but, by virtue of refusing to conform to Soviet state-sanctioned demands on art, his writing became a political act in and of itself. Still, the most significant moment is probably when Alekhina over-emphasizes the alleged inability of the government to learn from the past:

> It is very strange that in their reaction to our actions, the authorities completely disregard the historical experience of dissent. '[H]ow unfortunate is the country where simple honesty is understood, in the best case, as heroism. And in the worst case as a mental disorder,' the dissident Bukovsky wrote in the 1970s. And even though it hasn't been very long, now people are acting like Great Terror never occurred nor any attempts to resist it. I believe that we are being accused by people without memory.
>
> (Morgan 2012, 40)

Of course, Alekhina is not so naïve as to be truly surprised by Putin's (alleged) amnesia; what is more important to her is to emphasize the historical continuity that underpins every manifestation of political dissent in Russia. While on trial, Pussy Riot members repeatedly tried to obliterate the difference between the past and the present, because they perceived it as potentially disruptive for their own self-representation. It was more relevant at that point for them to 'create an image', to locate their own protest within the tradition of the never-ending opposition of the Russian intelligentsia to the power holders – that is, to situate this image within an eternal present. As Tolokonnikova put it:

> Katya, Masha and I are in jail but I don't consider that we've been defeated. Just as the dissidents weren't defeated. When they disappeared into psychiatric hospitals and prisons, they passed judgement on the country. The art of creating an image knows no winners or losers.
>
> (Tolokonnikova 2012)

From a different perspective, the self-identification with Soviet dissidents could also be interpreted as a peculiar manifestation of Soviet nostalgia, as a kind of bottom-up, subversive nostalgia opposed to the top-down nostalgia which is articulated and controlled by the power holders. But to conclude, I would like to mention another aspect, which is only apparently paradoxical. In his polemical essay 'The Terrifying Mimicry of Samizdat', and drawing on Pierre Bourdieu's theory of social fields, Serguei Oushakine has challenged the tradition of locating political resistance in Russia outside the field of power and within 'hidden areas in the underground, background or foreground of the dominant [discourse]' (Oushakine 2001, 192). Contrary to this interpretation, he argues that Soviet dissidents, by insisting that their public actions were fully legal and justified by already-existing Soviet laws, radically distanced themselves from previous oppositional movements in Russia and inevitably echoed and amplified the rhetoric of the regime rather than positioning themselves outside of or beneath it. In other words, according to Oushakine, Soviet dissidents failed to juxtapose a narrative of their own to the official one. Whereas Oushakine's conclusions about political *samizdat* are partially questionable, his essay succeeds in pointing out the relational character of political opposition and its 'dependence' on dominant discourses. It remains an open question whether anti-Putin activists, by referring to Soviet dissidents in search of self-legitimization, did not weaken the effectiveness of their actions – ultimately, they allowed government-controlled media to turn to the same rhetorical tools that the Soviet press used to defame dissenters as parasites, internal enemies, the fifth column of Western imperialism, agents paid by the CIA, or warmongers (that is, in the updated version of this discourse, mongers of Colour Revolutions). I think that recent political activism can provide an inspiration as well for a broader discussion of the ambiguous and open-ended relationship between the dominant and the dominated.

References

Anon. 2012. "Pussy Riot Nominated for Sakharov Prize." *Euronews* 25 September. www.euronews.com/2012/09/25/pussy-riot-nominated-for-sakharov-prize/ (accessed 1 March 2015).

Applebaum, Anne. 2007. "Russia's New Old Dissidents." *Washington Post* 27 November. www.aei.org/publication/russias-new-old-dissidents/ (accessed 1 March 2015).

Aron, Leon. 2012. "Russia's Protesters: The People, Ideals, and Prospects." *American Enterprise Institute* 9 August. www.aei.org/publication/russias-protesters-the-people-ideals-and-prospects/ (accessed 17 February 2015).

Bennetts, Marc. 2014. *Kicking the Kremlin. Russia's New Dissidents and the Battle to Topple Putin.* London: Oneworld Publications.

Budraitskis, Il'ia. 2012. "Pussy Riot: etika, politika i novye dissidenty?" *Polit.ru* 27 August. http://polit.ru/article/2012/08/27/ilbdr270812/ (accessed 1 March 2015).

Chernov, Sergei. 2012. "Female Fury. The Latest Sensation on the Russian Underground Music Scene Talks about Its Songs." *The St. Petersburg Times* 1 February. http://sptimes.ru/story/35092?page=1#top (accessed 1 March 2015); also as "Feminist Punk Band Become Unlikely Putin Foil." *The Moscow Times* 2 February. www.themoscowtimes.com/news/article/feminist-punk-band-become-unlikely-putin-foil/452197.html (accessed 25 July 2015).

Epshtein, Alek D. 2012. *Iskusstvo na barrikadakh. "Pussy Riot", "Avtobusnaia vystavka" i protestnyi art-aktivism.* Moscow: Izdatel' Viktor Bondarenko.

Garfield, Bob. 2012. "Russia's Expanding Definition of Treason. Transcript." *OnTheMedia* 28 September. www.onthemedia.org/story/240583-russias-expanding-definition-treason/transcript/ (accessed 1 March 2015).

Gorbanevskii, Iaroslav and Anna Stroganova. 2012. "Natal'ia Gorbanevskaia: 'Liuboi prigovor po delu Pussy Riot byl by nepravosudnym'." *RFI* 17 August. http://ru.rfi.fr/rossiya/20120817-natalya-gorbanevskaya-lyuboi-prigovor-po-delu-pussy-riot-byl-nepravosudnym/ (accessed 1 March 2015).

Gutkin, Mikhail. 2012. "Chem otlichaiutsia rossiiane, protestuiushchie segodnia, ot sovetskikh dissidentov?" *VOA – Golos Ameriki* 22 March. www.golos-ameriki.ru/content/russia-protests-discussion-2012-03-22-143912516/666161.html (accessed 25 July 2015).

Hayward, Max. 1966. *On Trial. The Soviet State versus "Abram Tertz" and "Nikolai Arzhak"*. New York, Evanston, IL, and London: Harper & Row Publishers.

Kulagin, Igor'. 2012. "Istoriia protesta: ot dissidentov do 'belych lentochek'." *Pravda* 26 March, www.pravda.ru/politics/parties/other/26-03-2012/1112370-disspro-1/ (accessed 1 March 2015).

Lagunina, Irina. 2007. "Vozvrashchenie poniatii 'dissidentstvo' i 'zastoi' v sovremennoi Rossii." *Radio Svoboda* 19 October. www.svoboda.org/content/transcript/417417.html (accessed 1 March 2015).

Levitsky, Steven. 2010. *Competitive Authoritarianism: Hybrid Regimes after the Cold War*. Cambridge: Cambridge University Press.

Levitsky, Steven and Lucan Way. 2002. "Assessing the Quality of Democracy." *Journal of Democracy* 13 (2): 51–65.

Lokshina, Tanya. 2012. "Back to the (Soviet) Future." *Foreign Policy* 6 December. http://foreignpolicy.com/2012/12/06/back-to-the-soviet-future/ (accessed 1 March 2015).

Morgan, Stephen. 2012. *Pussy Riot vs Putin. Revolutionary Russia*. CreateSpace Independent Publishing Platform.

Nikitin, Vadim. 2012. "The Wrong Reasons to Back Pussy Riot." *The New York Times* 20 August. www.nytimes.com/2012/08/21/opinion/the-wrong-reasons-to-back-pussy-riot.html?_r=0 (accessed 1 March 2015).

Nivat, Georges. 1998. "Nuzhno li plakat' po dissidentstvu?" *Kontinent* 8: 234–238.

Oushakine, Serguei Alex. 2001. "The Terrifying Mimicry of Samizdat." *Public Culture* 13 (2): 191–214.

Pasternak, Boris. 2012. "'Prilichnye zeki vsegda solidarny drug s drugom.' Pravozashchitnik Sergei Kovalev rasskazal, chem otlichaiutsia dissidenty 1970-kh ot oppozitsionerov 2010-kh." *Moskovskie novosti* 10 February. www.mn.ru/friday/20120210/311228736.html (accessed 25 July 2015).

Petrov, Nikolai. 2005. "From Managed Democracy to Sovereign Democracy. Putin's Regime Evolution in 2005." PONARS Policy Memo 396, Centre for Strategic and International Studies: 181–186. http://csis.org/publication/ponars-policy-memo-396-managed-democracy-sovereign-democracy-putins-regime-evolution-200 (accessed 25 July 2015).

Polukhina, Iuliia. 2013. "Lyudmila Alekseeva: 'Maybe by now they understand that there's no need to violate the public...'." *Novaia gazeta* 14 November. http://en.novayagazeta.ru/politics/60943.html (accessed 1 March 2015).

Pussy Riot. 2011. "Ot Khimkinskogo lesa k Takhriru. Iz bloga *Svobodnoe mesto*." *Grani.ru* 6 December, http://grani.ru/blogs/free/entries/193731.html (accessed 1 March 2015).

Pussy Riot. 2012. *Pussy Riot! A Punk Prayer for Freedom*. New York: The Feminist Press at the City University of New York.

Remnick, David. 2012. "The Pussy Riot Scandal." *The New Yorker* 11 August. www. newyorker.com/news/news-desk/the-pussy-riot-scandal (accessed 1 March 2015).

Robertson, Graeme B. 2011. *The Politics of Protest in Hybrid Regimes. Managing Dissent in Post-Communist Russia*. Cambridge: Cambridge University Press.

Shatz, Marshall S. 1980. *Soviet Dissent in Historical Perspective*. Cambridge: Cambridge University Press.

Tolokonnikova, Nadezhda. 2012. "The Closing Statements from Nadezhda Tolokonnikova in Trial 8 August 2012." *LiveJournal* 8 August. http://eng-pussy-riot. livejournal.com/4602.html (accessed 1 March 2015).

Tolokonnikova, Nadia. 2013. "Pis'mo Nadezhdy Tolokonnikovoi ot 11 oktiabria 2013 goda." *Lenta.ru* 12 October. http://lenta.ru/news/2013/10/12/letter/ (accessed 1 March 2015).

Tolokonnikova, Nadezhda and Slavoj Žižek. 2014. *Comradely Greetings: The Prison Letters of Nadya and Slavoj*. London: Verso.

Volkov, Denis. 2012. *Protestnoe dvizhenie v Rossii v kontse 2011–2012 gg.: istoki, dinamika, rezul'aty*. Moscow: Analiticheskii tsentr Iuriia Levady. www.levada. ru/books/protestnoe-dvizhenie-v-rossii-v-kontse-2011-2012-gg (accessed 25 July 2015).

van Galle, Caroline. 2013. "Failed for Now: Pussy Riot and the Rule of Law in Russia." *Russian Analytical Digest* 122: 2–5. www.css.ethz.ch/publications/Detail ansichtPubDB_EN?rec_id=2416 (accessed 25 July 2015).

3 Why 'two Russias' are less than 'United Russia'

Cultural distinctions and political similarities: dialectics of defeat

Ilya Kalinin

The intelligentsia and the state: a tradition of 'stylistic divergences'

'My divergences with the Soviet State are stylistic ones.' These are the words of one of the most subtle critics of the Soviet regime, Andrei Siniavskii, written some years after his emigration (Siniavskii 2002, 336). This sentence, which has become a widely known aphorism, appeared in the essay 'Dissidentstvo kak lichnyi opyt' ('Dissidence as a Personal Experience'), the striking title of which emphasizes the personal, existential dimension of non-conformism, presented as a path to individual rather than political or collective identity. Siniavskii's explanation of the phenomenon of Soviet dissidence directs attention to practices aimed at the formation of self rather than to any possible horizon for the formation of community. This position, which shifts opposition to the regime to the realm of cultural criticism and individual stylistic alternatives, has both advantages and disadvantages. Its positive potential has often been a topic of well-meaning and approving critical attention (see, for instance, Ar'ev 2012). Yet its inherent limitations as a basis for effective political criticism, and – what is more – for political action, have not often been closely examined. In this regard, one may offer several initial observations. Firstly, Siniavskii's thesis did not reduce the entire field of resistance to distinctions of taste; broadly apparent matters of style are in fact only the superficial and most evident material, or the objective markers of a rupture in worldviews and a non-correspondence of horizons of value. Secondly, it is precisely the articulation of an alternative language that should be considered one of the most productive forms of resistance, making possible an escape from the authoritative grammar of the hegemonic language. Paradoxically, however, for the majority of members of the dissident movement in the USSR, stylistic, aesthetic, and cultural positions that acted as central markers for a shared communal identity did not extend in a significant manner to the articulation of dissident discourse and to its rhetorical organization as such. Hence, dissident non-conformism in 'figures of thought' was expressed only weakly on the level of 'figures of speech'. In this regard, one may refer to Serguei Oushakine's essay 'The Terrifying Mimicry of Samizdat', in which – relying on the work of Michel Foucault and René Girard – the author discerns in the language of *samizdat* an example of 'mimetic resistance' – a reproduction, although in negated form, of the fundamental linguistic structures of a political opponent (Oushakine 2001). Possibly, the central element that may be recovered from Siniavskii's formula is its axiomatic opposition of power and style, power and culture, state authoritarianism and artistic autonomy, which – without explicit formulation – stands in need of no proof or explanation for the given community. It was in fact this axiomatic quality that served as a fundamental ideological position, establishing the boundaries of the dissident community as such.

This opposition has a deep historical tradition, which may be traced with confidence in one form or another as far back as the era of Alexander I in the first quarter of the nineteenth century, and quite possibly all the way to that of Catherine the Great in the second half of the eighteenth century (see, for instance, Lotman 1975). In retrospect, the tradition of intellectual, culturally oriented, and stylistically orchestrated rebellion was shaped by a series of recognizable conceptual *topoi*, emphasizing primarily the cultural dimension of civic opposition to the state, which was understood as a repressive apparatus for the limitation of individuality and for bureaucratic unification. 'Russian literature as a school for freedom of social thought and a space for social conflict'. 'Russian literature as the chief agent of Enlightenment in Russia'. 'The Poet as substitute for the saint in a secular era'. 'The intelligentsia as the salt of the earth'. One might easily continue the list of commonplaces, all of which boil down to the following: in circumstances of autocratic or authoritarian power, it was literature (and culture in general) that was constituted in Russia as the single locus of relative autonomy of the individual from the state, as a realm of free self-realization and self-representation, in terms of both individual creativity and social identity. For this reason, culture came to be recognized as a parallel and alternative sphere to that of the state – even at moments when the state was ostensibly in complete control of cultural life (and in fact, the state's elevated concern for the sphere of culture arose in response to the artistic and evaluative autonomy of culture as a site of alternative, non-state, practical and political socialization).

In this manner, culture was transformed into a central channel for the actualization of civil society and became responsible for the production of social, aesthetic, and even political values not mediated by the interests of the state. One might say that culture became civil society's sole justification – or even that culture, the field of cultural communication, became a displaced representation of an absent civil society, its discursive surrogate, transforming the absence of various socio-political practices into the basis of the socio-cultural imagination. Within this dispositif, cultural achievement, stylistic complexity, and aesthetic differentiation gained a political dimension, in opposition to the unifying, monolithic, and triumphalist style of the state. Agents of cultural production came to view themselves as the main emancipatory force in Russian society (ranging in significance from reform to revolution). These positions became the foundation for both the revolutionary-democratic legitimization of the intelligentsia and its critique (from *Vekhi* [*Landmarks*], the 1909 collection of essays about the Russian intelligentsia, to Aleksandr Solzhenitsyn's 1974 essay 'Obrazovanshchina' ['The pseudoeducated']; Solzhenitsyn 1991). The Soviet era constructed yet another level of this tradition in the form of theoretical characterizations of culture as a zone of autonomy in opposition to the state. Mikhail Bakhtin located this space of autonomy in the popular culture of the Renaissance (Bakhtin 1968); Leonid Batkin found it in the high humanistic culture of the same era (Batkin 1978; 1991); Georgii Pomerants saw it in the spiritual life of the individual (Pomerants 1995); Vladimir Bibler looked to the dialogue of cultures (Bibler 1975; 1991); and Mikhail Lotman imagined a special form of cultural semiosis that could introduce an element of unpredictability in the fabric of recurrent social reproduction (Lotman 2009). Typically for the late-Soviet period, these and other theoretical explanations of the emancipatory role of culture set it in opposition to the repressive and de-individualizing force of the state. The unofficial art from the 1950s and 1970s (from the Lianozovo group to Moscow Conceptualism) was founded on the same axiomatic base. Furthermore, this tradition of escape from the official political regime into the sphere of cultural production and consumption was not limited to theoretical constructions, specialized study of the humanities, and aesthetic experiments. Alexei Yurchak has discerned, in the very daily life of the late-Soviet era, related zones of cultural autonomy, which he, drawing on Bakhtin's analysis of the novel, describes as spaces of exteriority, or 'being *vnye*'. As Yurchak demonstrates, these spaces arose not without but within the hegemonic authoritative language, the vocabulary and grammar of which were subjected to performative shifts that made it possible to endow familiar signifiers and chains of signification with new meanings and to articulate novel, unusual structures out of familiar signs (Yurchak 2006, 36–77).

The question facing contemporary researchers is whether the tactics of independent cultural production, stylistic escape into alternative fields of individual freedom, and mobile autonomies of cultural protest continue to function in today's novel circumstances, in which culture has become not only a fundamental sector of production, but also a basic instrument for state administration of the social order and reproduction of symbolic hegemony. Does the system of distinctions described above – distinctions that undergirded the cultural community's ideology of resistance, articulating by means of culture itself its superiority over the political elite, the state apparatus, and those parts of the population loyal to it – still function in the same manner? In other words, does this system still function when the regime balances dynamically between the conservative assimilation of culture as a national historical legacy and the postmodern mediation of all historical contexts, restructuring the national tradition as a mosaic of elements that possess well-nigh absolute symbolic valency?[1] What is the emancipatory potential of positions based in the sphere of cultural production in opposition to a hybrid political regime that combines authoritarian governance with neoliberal economics?

The mechanisms for the systemic assimilation of the economic and political potential of culture in the late capitalist era, as well as the neoliberal practices of the creative industries, have been well described in works of the Frankfurt School (Adorno and Horkheimer 2002), Jameson (1991; 1998) and a range of contemporary critical theorists (Scott 2001; Cook 1996; Lash and Urry 1987; Throsby 2001). Widespread indifference to this critical context in the analysis of the Russian situation relates to certain fundamental miscomprehensions – a failure to recognize the contemporary, global, and neoliberal dimensions of Russian cultural and political processes. In consequence, strategies of protest founded on a simplistic conception of the regime as an authoritarian, trad- itionalist, paternalist, and conservative attempt to restore a Soviet model of power are ineffective and doomed to failure. The inadequacy of such views was among the central reasons that the strategies of resistance to the state deployed by the discursively dominant segment of the protest movement – strategies based in cultural distinctions – ultimately granted the state add- itional resources for the delegitimization of its challengers.

The protest of the 'successful and well-fed'

The topic of the present chapter is not the protest movement *per se*, nor even its forms of discursive and artistic activity (slogans, banners, photoshop mash-ups, memes, carnival costumes, etc.), but rather its emphasis on styl- istic creativity, which became not only a means for the articulation of pol- itical protest, but its very content – a central dimension of individual and collective self-identification for the movement's participants. I will focus on the hallowed Russian tradition of imagining creative, cultural activity that becomes a symbol of ethical and civic superiority as a worthy opponent to politics as embodied by state power. My discussion will therefore focus not on the multitude of actual meanings and motivations of participation in the protest movement (in this regard, see Berland and Stupakova 2012; Erpyleva 2015; Zhelina 2015; Zavadskaia and Savel'eva 2015), but rather on the dom- inant discourse for the representation of protest, which aspires to project a fundamental frame, embracing the total horizon of such motivations and self- descriptions. This discourse of protest, as articulated by representatives of the liberal intelligentsia and authoritative members of the artistic community, was concerned primarily with matters of self-expression, likely as a result of the primary professional habitus and the inherited traditions of opposition of these groups. For this reason, both political views and the civil right to cast one's vote figured as elements of the more general matter of the con- scious individual gesture, articulated in the language of cultural capital. The problem of expression of electoral will was conceived as the right to individ- ual self-expression: 'honest elections', the demand that the regime must take responsibility for its actions, the rejection of corruption, etc. were all rendered elements of personal choice, emanations of the rarified 'taste' of the contem- porary, culturally developed, stylistically advanced urbanite. Contemporary democratic politics was transformed into an element of contemporary urban bourgeois style, a necessary component of life in the modern city (and especially the modern megalopolis).

In what follows I will be concerned with the inherent limitations of this discourse of cultural autonomy, which derive from its inherent incapability – or from the lack of desire of its proponents – to step beyond the matrix of opposition between, on the one hand, culture (the sphere of autonomy and resistance, creative activity, broadly understood, and the field of individual freedom and self-respect) and, on the other, power (the unifying force that seeks to eliminate or, at the least, to instrumentalize in demagogic fashion all of the positive qualities just enumerated). It seems to me that the time has come to problematize this time-worn opposition in terms, which must necessarily be reimagined and reformulated in circumstances where the hegemonic language of power in its previous authoritarian and monolithic form – which is to say, the language in opposition to which it was possible to articulate the sphere of cultural autonomy, based on its special characteristics – no longer exists. At present, this hegemonic language is in fact a heterogeneous space of eclecticism, displacements of meaning, and semantic lacunae filled with contextual significance, all of which modally distances the subject from his or her speech. The language of contemporary power (both within Russia and beyond) long ago assimilated the situationist tactic of *detournement* and transformed it into an instrument of professionalized political trolling and populist play with clichés, repressed desires, and collective fears.[2] How is it possible to construct an effective field of cultural autonomy in a situation where the language of power operates in a continuous regime of falsification, imitation, cynical reason, and ironic rupture between signifier and signified, and in which the master subject of this language itself occupies the zone of 'being *vnye*', slipping away before it may be grasped? In opposing such a language of power, the appeal to symbolic values, rather than socio-economic realities, is frankly useless, for the language hegemon is quite capable of a limited appropriation of practically any category of symbolic value: liberal or conservative, national or imperial, democratic or statist. As such, it simply absorbs all alternative programmes, leaving the opposition with only one distinguishing characteristic – its pretensions to autonomy, to which the discourse of power, enriched at the expense of its opponent, graciously accords the status of social marginality, marking it as alien for the majority of the population.

In such a situation, any cultural alternative to the regime that seeks to articulate a zone of autonomy risks marking out instead just one more zone of 'being *vnye*' – an alternative space that, rather than subverting the hegemonic discourse of the state and its media apparatus, to the contrary reaffirms the pretensions of this discourse to govern a regime of heterogeneity, openness, demonstrative tolerance for all that is not forbidden by law, etc. Hence the self-representation of activists and participants in the protest movement, proclaiming autonomy in style and worldview, was quickly seized

upon and redirected by the regime in its own representations of the protesters, which reinterpreted the emphasis on autonomy as a figure of exclusion,
as an expression of arrogance and alienation from the majority, and finally as
a mark of marginality. In other words, the regime is quite content, as long as
the sphere of cultural production (as well as the protest movement, the social
basis and horizon of values of which were in many ways linked to this sphere)
aspires only to autonomy, for this makes it possible for the state to neutralize the energies of social activism, channelling them into spaces of cultural
autonomy. Thanks to a discursive opposition structured in this manner, other,
frequently more threatening, instances and forms of protest become far less
visible – forms of protest based not in the cultural but in the social and economic conditions of existence. These latter occasions for protest, as it turns
out, are impossible to articulate in terms of cultural distinction, which has
become at present the dominant language for description of the opposition
between the powers that be and 'normal, intelligent, educated, creative, and
contemporary people'. How, for instance, could it be possible to describe in
these terms the protest movement that delivered a quite actual shock to the
regime in 2015, that of the long-haul truck drivers opposed to the introduction of a new system of fees for the use of federal highways?[3] The majority
of these protesters were 'normal guys' in quilted jackets, sporting St George's
ribbons – that is to say, precisely the category of people who served as a negative example in the self-descriptions of protesters in 2011–12.

In the words of the sociologist Aleksandr Bibkov,

> in the initial stages of protest the aesthetic dimension was decisive: aes-
> thetic discontinuity with the activities of political figures became a special
> system of identification [...] 'beautiful faces' became as important an ele-
> ment of a successful formulation of protest as 'jolly' slogans.
>
> (Bibkov 2013, 66–67)[4]

To my mind, the aestheticized form and self-sufficiency of the protests were
themselves less significant than the fact that an orientation on the aesthetic,
on matters of culture and taste, constituted the internal content of the protest
movement (or at least, of its liberal-democratic wing), its *raison d'être* and
motive force, definitive of the limits of the community that appeared on the
streets of Russia's larger cities. A strongly articulated aesthetic dimension was
merely a symptom of conceptions of cultural identity as a necessary and sufficient principle of political distinction that precisely defined a space for the
expression of dissatisfaction with the actions of the regime. This space might
be described as the space of style in the sense of Karl Mannheim (1986). In
that thinker's terms, 'style' or 'thought style' is a means of mediating and giving shape to the position of a particular social group. Style is a reflection of
the views of the group with regard to its own position and development, while
'basic intention' is the dominant associated with each thought style, with each
given approach to the world (Mannheim 1986, 7–15). Turning to definition of

the thought style of the typical subject of the protest movement (aggregated from a variety of intersecting social groups, differentiated in various ways: the urban middle class, the liberal intelligentsia, the creative class), we may propose that its basic intention, its dominant, was style itself – a collection of cultural coordinates, the polyvalent semantic structure of which made it possible to express meanings in any register: aesthetic, existential, social, or political.

In this sense, it is essential to discuss not only a specific style, embodied by the intelligentsia and its worldview (as does Il'ia Budraitskis, drawing on Mannheim; Budraitskis 2013), but also the fact that style itself (formal-aesthetic features, encompassing everything from forms of thought to forms of everyday life) constituted the *content of the thought style* of those who made up the protest movement's base (if perhaps not in demographic or social terms, then at the least in discursive ones). The *political* figured here as one more attribute of *style*, and political protest became a sign demonstrating the rupture between 'we the cultured' and 'those uncultured others'. As noted above, the tradition of this means of articulation of difference reaches back in the history of relations between the intelligentsia and the Russian state, to eras when it was precisely culture that acted as a field for the displacement of social-political problems to the nominal plane of symbolic production. In the case of the protest movement of 2011–12 this old intelligentsia tradition was charged with the new ideology of creativity (creative cities, creative labour, the creative class) that constructed yet another barrier between those who had made the 'correct' choice of alignment with the post-industrial present and future and those who were hopelessly stuck in the industrial past (Florida 2002). And so the liberal-democratic tradition of cultural opposition to the state (that had always been reflected on the level of an unavoidable, although frequently bewailed, cultural alienation from the people) received a neoliberal-creative 'upgrade', and in consequence quite openly, without a trace of traditional intelligentsia hand-wringing, articulated a sharp cultural border between the 'smart and sexy, mobile and active' agents of the new non-material economy and the 'passive' majority that ostensibly 'preferred' smaller cities to the post-Fordist metropolis with its new industries and new styles of life; that 'preferred' work in a machine shop to work in a hair salon (see the chapter 'The Machine Shops and the Hair Salon' in Florida 2002, 85–102); that 'preferred' watching television in the evenings to prosumption on the World Wide Web 2.0.

In this manner, transparent politics and fair elections turned out to be in large part (and possibly in the main) elements of good taste, the base ingredients of which were 'European character', 'civilization', and 'normality'. In a discussion of the make-up of the protest community of 2011, the poet Ol'ga Sedakova characterized it as composed of 'calm, independently thinking, freely speaking [...] normal people [...] Russian Europeans [...] possessed of the absolute right to speak for the country as a whole' (Sedakova 2012). I will set aside theories of political representation and the postcolonial dilemma of legitimate cultural leadership, although we may easily discern in Sedakova's words familiar conceptual *topoi*, deeply intertwined with the traditions of the Russian intelligentsia, accustomed to addressing power in the name of the 'Russian people' and in the language of 'high culture'. More significant for the present discussion is the logic distinguishing participants in the protests from the passive majority of 'simple people' (Sedakova 2012) who, in Sedakova's view, constitute the social product of ideological indoctrination and commercial mass culture. Separating the 'normal people', who participated in the protest movement from these 'simple people', who did not, is none other than the space of cultural distinctions, which is imagined according to this thought style as more fundamental than the social and economic conditions that dictate distinct life possibilities and even access to cultural consumption, let alone production. Civic-mindedness, it seems, is an expression of one's level of cultural achievement, and the latter, in turn, is an emanation of a fundamental, anthropological 'normality' that is not dependent on socio-cultural factors.

The even more frankly elitist system of oppositions developed in protest discourse – people vs. herd, citizens vs. mob (*bydlo*), agitated urbanites vs. moronic patriotic majority – was markedly indifferent to social, economic, and political determinants (as well as to any actual agenda dependent upon them), and instead constituted a structural objectification of cultural, stylistic differences. 'It's impossible to stop being people, but one may stop being part of the mob. One may become a citizen, but you must not become a vulgar, primitive, dull-witted slave' (Bykov 2011). This thesis of the well-known writer, literary critic, and liberal publicist Dmitrii Bykov and the words of the poet, translator, and orthodox thinker Sedakova (who otherwise have very little in common) reproduce the formula of 'stylistic divergences' generated several decades earlier by Andrei Siniavskii. Civil protest stands in opposition not to any political or economic programme fostering increased social inequality, and not to the continuing retreat of the state from social programmes, but rather to 'vulgarity', 'the primitive', and 'dull-wittedness' (Platt 2013). Furthermore, these qualities are ascribed not to the regime – which, according to this construction, is viewed not as dull-witted, but as cynical – but rather to those who support it. Or, to be completely accurate, it is ascribed to those who do not support the protest movement. One may add that, perhaps unsurprisingly for this discourse of protest which mediates political and cultural preferences, the language of cynicism turns out to be far more palatable for many of the leaders of and participants in the protest movement than the so-called 'idiotic mumbling of the mob', which falters before the sophisticated language games of cynical reason. Consider, too, the impressively active and 'inventive' interaction that arose between the Kremlin's creative geniuses and the protesting 'creative class' with regard to mutual trolling, the definition and redefinition of a bevy of new terms such as 'office plankton', 'internet hamsters', the 'Bandar-log', and so forth (see the glossary of novel terms composed by the journal *Bol'shoi gorod*, Kashin et al. 2011). This dialogue offers a great deal of evidence of a common language uniting the protesters with the regime, problematizing to a great degree the stylistic divide affirmed in protest discourse itself.[5]

In this connection we may observe a characteristic confusion of cultural-stylistic and socio-economic characteristics: the protest comes to be described as an expression of the dissatisfaction of the multitude of 'successful and well-fed people', as the 'successful' journalist and producer Leonid Parfenov expressed in an interview on TVTs:

> This is a protest of the well-fed. It arises not because people are living poorly, but rather because they are generally living well, but have woken up to the fact that they are living in unfreedom [...] They are people living successful lives, but they want to make them even better.
>
> (Parfenov 2011)[6]

The motivating logic of the protest that is presented here – those who came out into the streets are 'living well, but want to live even better' – set the protesters in opposition not to the regime, which consists of people who are no less (and are possibly more) 'successful and well-fed', but rather implicitly to the 'mob', to those who are 'living poorly'. The absence inscribed in this utterance is that of those who cannot be inserted into the neoliberal logic of the new creative life – those who were unable to realize themselves in the 'roaring aughts'. In this manner, all of these people (who were subsequently claimed by the regime as the 'Putin majority') were from the start excluded from the realm of the protest movement. Their interests could not be reflected there, for they belonged to another, more 'primitive and dull-witted' dimension of unresolved material needs, which rendered them *a priori* distinct from the culturally sophisticated problem of civil freedoms. *Quod severis metes*, it was this very 'mob' that, with its silent acquiescence, allowed the regime to defeat the 'successful and well-fed' protesters who came out onto the streets of Moscow and St Petersburg with their aspirations to 'live better, and in freedom to boot'.

As a consequence, a linkage was established between the 'successful and well-fed' characteristics of one group and the 'vulgarity and dim-wittedness' of the other – that is, between dispositions that reference completely distinct evaluative terms (relating to matters of economics, profession, and income on the one hand, and to cultural and intellectual inadequacy on the other). This discursive linkage had a decisive negative effect on the development and eventual fate of the protest movement – an effect not consciously planned by those who, thanks to their professional positions and accumulated cultural capital, were central agents of the rhetorical articulation of the goals and significance of the protest movement (naturally, the positions of the many individual participants in the protests, as expressed in social networks and various polls, were considerably more variegated). Yet it was in consequence of this linkage, it seems to me, that the protest movement experienced such a quick decline following the completely fair and honest presidential elections of early 2012, towards which the regime was able to mobilize the very same 'vulgar, primitive, and dim-witted slaves' that the 'successful and well-fed' representatives of the protest movement had so passionately denounced. As a result, the army of observers launched into action by the protesting minority during the presidential elections was compelled to register the *de facto* existence of the loyal majority orchestrated by the regime. Yet the causes of this successful mobilization are to be found not only in the state's control of its potent propagandistic machine, administrative resources, and media infrastructure. For, ultimately, this pro-regime mobilization was also supported by the fundamental discursive strategies deployed by the opposition, which were structured by the matrix of cultural distinctions.

'Sha Pu Na Na' vs. 'Bo Ro Di No'

The cultural strategies of the regime and the opposition may be schematically described by means of two characteristic examples. These examples illustrate the cultural gulf that came to be recognized as well-nigh the fundamental indicator of difference between the regime and the opposition. The discussion of political alternatives in terms of cultural distinctions, as it was initiated by the opposition, allowed the regime to easily outmanoeuvre its challengers by deploying the organic national tradition in response to the new, Western, 'foreign' category of creativity. The 'creativity' of the protests was expressed in various aesthetic experiments, from the articulation of '"jolly" slogans' (Bibkov 2013, 66–67) and images, the ironic inversion of official slogans, and the composition of photoshop mash-ups, to the rock-parody of Artemii Troitskii, written and performed during the Bolotnaya Square demonstration of 4 February 2012 – his 'hit of the season' song 'Sha Pu Na Na' (an acronym for 'Send Putin's Gang to the Prison Bench) [Shaiku Putina na nary]), to which it was 'good to cavort, since it's rock-n-roll' (Troitskii 2012). In distinction from Boris Yeltsin, who himself danced to rock-n-roll during his presidential election campaign of 1996, Putin selected a different strategy of cultural opposition to his political opponents. In his speech to a gathering of supporters at the Luzhniki Stadium on 23 February 2012, Putin cited lines from Mikhail Lermontov's poem 'Borodino', calling on listeners to swear to 'die in defence of Moscow', and identifying the Patriotic War of 1812 with the political contest of 2012. In conclusion, Putin proclaimed: 'The battle for Russia continues! But victory will be ours!' (Putin 2012). His response to the contemporary creativity of the protest movement was formulated on the basis of the school programme in Russian literature. Yet this response was founded not only on a justified expectation that these lines, with the support of state educational standards, would have broad resonance with listeners; it was also founded on the complete range of discursive strategies characteristic of the protest movement itself: *detournement* (the reappropriation and remediation of original utterances), the reformation of primary significances in order to achieve new instrumental uses (the defence of the country from an external foe became a frame for conflict with the internal opposition), and eclectic, cynical pastiche, combining Lermontov's well-known lines with the no less well-known words of Viacheslav Molotov, chairman of the Council of People's Commissars, in his radio address following the attack of Nazi Germany on 22 June 1941.

The discursive trap that allowed the regime to describe its risky situation in terms of a culture war – a trap into which the liberal wing of the anti-systemic opposition fell from the very start – was predetermined by a perhaps unintentional internal split in the critical address of the speeches, interviews, and publicistic writings of the most well-known leaders of the protest movement (Bykov, Boris Akunin, Parfenov, Troitskii, Kseniia Sobchak, and others). Its immediate addressee was the regime that had falsified the results of the parliamentary elections of 2011, the 'Party of Crooks and Thieves', yet its concealed addressee, the internal horizon that in fact constituted the dominant and profound basis for the axiological structure of the publicly dominant protest discourse, was the 'mob' – the same category that was soon to be redescribed by the regime as the 'majority that chooses stability and the traditional values of our national culture', that 'does not wish to rock the boat', and that has no need for political convulsions. Bibkov has noted the peculiar 'cultural racism' characteristic of the protest movement, based on the opposition between 'we the cultured' and the 'uncultured regime' (Bibkov 2013). However, the accusation of 'unculturedness' addressed to the regime was in reality directed at those who, in the imagination of protest participants, represented the regime's social basis. Further, behind this emphatic strategy of cultural differentiation from the vulgar tastes and undeveloped civic consciousness of the mass stood the postcolonial anti-populism that has long been characteristic of post-Soviet cultural elites.[7] The discourse of protest simply projected this postcolonial anti-populist rhetoric against the state, the hegemonic discourse of which had been, in contrast, more and more focused during the 2000s around the populist rhetoric of cultural autarky and imperial patriotism.

The regime responded with enthusiasm to this challenge, setting the voice of representatives of mass industrial production in opposition to the discourse of creativity, of contemporary urban style, and of the post-Fordist economy. In contrast to the pop divas, music critics and authors, entrepreneurs and poets, to which it proved quite easy to reduce the public face of the protest movement, the state offered the figure of the factory worker, the representative of the masses, whose effectiveness was based not on wit, inventiveness, stylistic sophistication, and advanced consumer taste, but rather on the time-tested image of heavy industry, that guarantor of defensive capabilities, political stability, and the labour market – an image that was familiar to those who possessed neither the initial opportunity nor the acquired skills needed to navigate the creative knowledge economy. As the sociologists Aleksandrina Van'ke and Maksim Kunaev note with some justification: 'Whereas in classic Marxist discourse the workers are linked to revolution and the transformation of the social order, in the present hegemonic discourse of the Kremlin the term "worker" is linked to "stability", "order", and "staying the course"' (Van'ke and Kulaev 2015a, 12).

And so the social lioness Sobchak faced off with Igor Kholmanshikh, foreman of the assembly line from the Ural Railroad Car Factory, who during Vladimir Putin's annual televised meeting with the people offered to help the president remove protesters from the streets of capital cities: 'the boys and I are ready to come ourselves and defend our stability' ('Razgovor s Vladimirom Putinym' 2011). The structure of Russian society left little room for doubt as to who would emerge the victor in this discursive 'battle' for symbolic hegemony – as to who was the more obvious figure for mass identification. As paradoxical as it might seem, it was precisely the opposition that structured the field of communication in such a manner that its actors were defined as a minority proclaiming its cultural superiority (and let us note that the orientation on cultural superiority nearly inevitably implies a minority status, since superiority is buttressed by rarity) in opposition to a subordinate (by the logic of this matrix) disaffected majority, which was therefore prepared in advance for assimilation by the opposed, official camp.

The discourse of protest described itself through the figure of exclusivity. Employing what would appear to be the maximally universal terms 'people' and 'normal people', it implied instead only a small part of the people: the cultured, educated people, capable of forming their own life strategies and distinguished from those who do not satisfy these 'norms' ('the simple people', 'slaves', and 'mob'). In this connection it is of little importance who made the first move, organizing the social field by means of a set of cultural distinctions (from forms of consumption and lifestyle to forms of historical memory) and articulating the division of society into a modernizing minority and a unmodernizable majority. What is, however, of importance is that neither side expressed any doubt concerning the objectivity and propriety of this division of society. In her interview, Sedakova completely correctly identifies the 'simple person' as a construct employed by the regime as 'an instrument of politics and ideology' (Sedakova 2012), yet the problem remains that, as is eloquently demonstrated by the protest movement of 2011–12, this construct was called into being simultaneously by the discourse of the Kremlin and by that of the protesters. In the resulting mirror-like optical system, both sides could apprehend the reality of the *majority* that was composed of these 'simple people'.

Thanks to a lack of concern for social-economic problems (medicine, education, systems of pre-school preparation and continuing education, labour reform, communal infrastructure, etc.) that are in fact important for the masses who have been dumped at the roadside by the neoliberal mainstream, the Putin elite was able to present itself as the defender of these same masses' interests. The emphasis on cultural and stylistic divergences allowed the regime to restructure and reformat the matrix of real socio-economic distinctions and tensions, further reinforcing the cultural component of protest and turning it against itself. Cultural capital, the possession of which inclined influential members of the opposition to turn to the matrix of cultural distinctions as their central and most advantageous field of battle, rendered them hostages of this matrix, hindering the access of the protest movement to the social groups against which these distinctions discriminate.[8] Hence it was an easy task for the regime to take hold of this very matrix and to present, in opposition to the values of contemporary cultural production and its defining ethos (individualism, human rights, freedom of expression, personal dignity, etc.), other cultural values, reflective of the national tradition, the state, national history, and collectivism. In sum, *social and economic dispositions*, which mark out the more and more firm actual distinction between, on the one hand, the political elite, bureaucracy, symbiotic business elites, and, on the other, the majority of the population of Russia, were cast into the shadow of *cultural dispositions*, that distinguish between, on the one hand, the traditionalist part of the Russian population, firmly attached to the outmoded, standardized, industrial base, along with the regime that aligns itself with it, and, on the other, that part of the population of the large cities that has successfully assimilated to the post-industrial creative economy.[9] The result of these discursive substitutions was the appearance of the 'pro-Putin majority' that so thoroughly frightened and disheartened liberal social elites and that became a powerful source of social legitimacy for the regime and its policies.

Later, this discursively constructed majority gained social objectivity as a result of the presidential elections, as well as sociological objectification as a result of the work of the polls. Still later, it poured into the *topos* of the president's '86 per cent approval rating', that serves both the legitimization of the regime and the internal self-justification of the liberal intelligentsia, which can refer to it as the insurmountable and objective cause of the failure of the protest movement. In fact, the social reality of the '86 per cent' that took shape in 2014 had discursive roots in the political stand-off of 2011–12. Before it took shape in support for the national leader and his foreign policy actions it had already been articulated in the discourse of the liberal opposition, thanks to the figure of the 'herd' of politically passive, socially de-privileged, and culturally backward 'slaves', who were incapable of making the emancipatory ethical and aesthetic gesture that their more modern compatriots made in going out into the streets to demonstrate. All the discourse of power had to do was to make use of the structural possibilities created by the rhetoric of the liberal opposition, reflecting its dispositif and projecting back a mirror-image reversal of that very opposition as an egoistic minority, indifferent to the fates of both the 'simple people' and 'the Russian state'. And so, by the efforts of both sides of the conflict, the construction of the 'two Russias' was shaped, comprising a pro-Western minority and a patriotic majority – a construction that ensures the continuing reproduction of current political elites and of the present status quo, yet which nevertheless is supported in parallel by the regime and the liberal opposition, by nationalists (such as Maksim Sokolov and Egor Kholmogorov) and left-leaning adepts of the imperial idea (such as Aleksandr Prokhanov and Zakhar Prilepin). The motivating logic in this for the regime and for the 'nationalists' and 'empire-ists', who support it in one way or another, is clear. One may wonder, however, what the liberal intelligentsia gets out of the reproduction of this construction, which dooms it to a marginal position in the system of distinctions. Possibly, social marginality allows the liberal intelligentsia to generate cultural capital derived from its broadly comprehended stylistic autonomy, which in the given situation is supported and even amplified by socio-political marginality.

The logic of cultural distinctions constructed by the representatives of the liberal intelligentsia and the creative class in the context of the protest movement, which was perhaps even more actively promulgated following its decline, automatically triggered a specific hierarchical organization of relations between various forms of capital and fields of production. Pierre Bourdieu, in describing the field of cultural production, distinguished between two forms of hierarchical organization: heteronomous (when the field of culture depends on the field of power and on the political and economic positions that penetrate it) and autonomous (when this dependence is negated: political or financial success is interpreted as a sign of stylistic compromise and betrayal, while failure is taken as a sign of high distinction) (Bourdieu 1993, 29–74). In our case, the burst of cultural production in the moment of the protests, followed by the ever more strident affirmation of cultural distinctions after they had passed, was both a marker and an effect of this sought-after cultural-stylistic autonomy. In the course of the protest demonstrations themselves the emphasis on cultural autonomy was among the main reasons that the movement could not achieve a truly mass level of participation (and also, in complementary fashion, one of the main factors that allowed the regime to neutralize the protest movement by describing it as egoistic, indifferent to the 'fate of Russia', and oriented exclusively on the individualist values of 'Western culture'). Yet after the movement's defeat this emphasis made it possible for its participants to justify this outcome and their own role in it, while also, paradoxically, further raising their own sense of cultural status by reaffirming once more the exclusiveness of the minority in the face of the passive majority that had been 'rendered idiots by the television and by Putin's propaganda'. This evaluation of developments is supported as well by the fact that in the course of their participation in the movement, its leaders, the representatives of the liberal wing of the cultural elite, rather than converting their cultural capital into political capital, instead simply grew their own cultural capital by means of political activism, becoming ever more recognizable as journalists and authors, poets and artists, media-producers and music critics.

Conclusions

As we have seen, the strategies of stylistic resistance and cultural differentiation ostensibly made it possible for the opposition to create an alternate discursive space, escaping the mimetic mirror-image reproduction of the hegemonic language. However, this same cultural logic of protest, that placed its fundamental hopes for emancipation on the creation of new forms of representation and artistic creativity, very quickly encountered its own internal limits of development. The absence of any articulated political programme (which, in the case of the Russian protest movement of 2011–12, was limited to critique of one particular figure, along with an appeal for honest elections and the fight against corruption) ultimately rendered the protest movement relatively harmless for the regime, which could co-opt or moot (following the conclusion of the election cycle) the majority of the protest agenda. Even more importantly, the stylistic and cultural element of the protest movement, interpreted by the 'creative class' as its main achievement on the road to new forms of self-representation, possessed a completely idiosyncratic character (both in stylistic and in social terms). It was this artistic-stylistic specificity that in the main prevented the movement from development into a truly mass social protest. And this led ultimately to a reinforcement of the logic of cultural distinctions. Oppositional liberal discourse turned to an explanation of the decline of the movement as a reflection of the 'backwardness' of the electorate, supposedly hypnotized by official mass media, while official discourse simply proclaimed that the programme of the protest movement was from the start 'extraordinarily distant from the people'. Nevertheless, it must be recognized that the description of the protest movement in the language of cultural distinctions was conceived not by the regime, but by the liberal, westernized, culturally enlightened community, which preferred enunciation of the cultural division into 'two Russias' to the attempt to deprive the regime of a 'United Russia' – to seizing hold of the truly economically and socially downtrodden majority, which is in reality in no way represented by the regime.

Concerning the concept of 'two Russias', much ink has already been spilled. Its organizing system of oppositions is variable and has been worked out with a high degree of creativity: advanced/backwards; television viewers/internet users; older generation/younger generation; 'Soviet'/creative class; individual consumption/mass and standard consumption; enlighteners/objects of enlightenment. The journalist Valerii Paniushkin has offered one of the most frank expressions of cultural distinction: 'I think that oysters and truffles are delicacies (whether this is snobbery or my developed taste is unknown). For the people, a delicacy is a Siberian dumpling' (Paniushkin 2012).

The turn of the regime, in response, to the language of culture, which reached its climax in the years following the disappearance of the protest movement, possessed a more inclusive character and was far more successful (Kalinin 2014; 2015). In place of the liberal opposition's discussion of 'two Russias', emerging out of cultural matrices that are increasingly distant from one another, the regime speaks of a 'United Russia', bound together by a common national cultural tradition. In the discourse of the Kremlin, the language of culture aspires to address matters of importance for all (for instance, national identity). In a situation of social stratification, growing economic inequality, ever-increasing differentiation in lifestyles and evaluative orientations, it is precisely culture that begins to act as bastion of mass democratic participation and as the horizon of the values and legacies that belong to each and every member of society and that must be the focus of concern and care. In this discourse, it is precisely national culture that unites the bureaucrats with the shuttle traders, the IT-managers with the combine operators, the businessmen with the doctors, the show-business stars with the rural schoolteachers, the Duma members with the voters who don't know their names.

The symbolic riches of culture are offered as a compensation for the absence of material goods, relieving in this manner tension between various positions in the social pyramid. In other words, although you have nothing and you are excluded from participation in political life and from collection of rents from the resource economy and income from business, you can participate all the same in the active defence of the 'common' cultural legacy. It is precisely as a reflection of this pragmatic logic of simulation that I comprehend the newly awakened interest of state elites in intensive cultural politics, which began with the 2013 discussion of the 'Bases of State Cultural Politics', adopted in 2014. Whereas for the participants in the protest movement culture was a marker of social activism, an impetus for the transformation of the political situation in the country, in the state discourse of cultural construction that arose in response to this challenge culture figures as a sphere for the active participation of those whose opinion is absolutely irrelevant in every other way.

The concept of a culture which arises in the discourse of the state is founded on values that are imagined to be inalienable and common to all: perhaps you do not have a large apartment, but you do have traditional family values; you may not have a car, but you have the wonderful Russian language (which, as the Russian proverb says, will 'take you all the way to Kiev'); you cannot choose not to re-elect Putin, but you have your Pushkin; you have a small salary, but you are an heir to the grandeur of Russian culture; and, even if you do not have a job, you have your national pride and heteronormative sexuality. In sum, the same category of 'culture' that in the course of the modern era has been defined as a zone of freedom, autonomy, and alternative thought begins to function in support of the existing regime, in opposition to the protest movement, which chose to emphasize the new, post-industrial, individualized creativity, presenting instead the idea of a national culture that ostensibly unites all, with no demand to reject any part of one's own past, rooted in the standardized school programmes that arose to meet the demands of the industrial era.

Acknowledgement

I am grateful to my friend and colleague Kevin M. F. Platt for his invaluable help in work on this paper.

Notes

1 In fact, these two strategies of work with culture, nominally 'conservative' and 'postmodern', constitute the thesis and antithesis of a dialectical development. Such strategies for the reproduction of cultural hegemony may be termed either 'postmodern in form and conservative in content', or 'conservative in form and postmodern in content'.

2 In this regard, as well, the current Russian regime has made no new discoveries and merely imitates its Western Other, once more demonstrating its own (post-) contemporary character, which is very far from both the monolithic authoritarian discourse of high Stalinism and the rigid, ever more formalized discourse of late socialism.

3 The company entrusted by the state with the task of developing the new payment system and collecting fees for highway use belongs to the son of a close friend of Vladimir Putin, Arkadii Rotenberg, who has himself for many years topped the rating 'State Contract King'. On the protests, see Anon 2015a; Anon 2015b; on a more recent surge in this situation, see Ismailov 2016.

4 'Beautiful faces' was a frequent element in descriptions of the protest community during sociological interviews with participants.

5 Applying the terms of linguistics, this divide may be discerned on the level of the utterance, but not on the level of the speech act itself, the supposedly opposed subjects of which possess similar rhetorical resources, cultural competencies, and even literary coordinates.

6 The coincidence of the representation of the protest movement in coverage on state television channels with the self-representations of its participants is also quite telling. On state-controlled television, interviews focused (both in the case of celebrities and in that of rank-and-file participants) on members of the business community or the creative class. Self-representations of participants, too, consciously or unconsciously focused on personal success, commonly featuring explanations of how, following a demonstration on Saturday, participants planned to drive back to their suburban houses, to head home and drink a bottle of fine wine, or to visit a restaurant or café. In consequence of this complete harmony between biased television coverage and perhaps ironic self-presentations of the characters it covered, a standard image of participants in the protest movement arose. Ultimately, the social frame generated in this coincidence of what were ostensibly opposed discursive strategies (those of the state-controlled media and those of the protesters) rendered impossible any identification of Russian society as a whole with those who sought to represent it and who proclaimed, to quote Sedakova once again, 'their right to speak for the country as a whole' (Sedakova 2012).

7 On post-Soviet anti-populism, see Dzhagalov 2011; Platt 2013; Matveev 2015. On anti-populism in Eastern Europe as an expression of the postcolonial relation of elites to the ostensibly insufficiently westernized people, see Gagyi 2012.

8 See, for instance, the project of the fashionable Moscow journal *Afisha*, which in spring 2012 invited 43 musicians, poets, artists, journalists, critics, and representatives of various creative industries to write their own manifestoes, articulating their views of 'what is to be done' and 'how to live from now on' ('43 Manifesta' 2012).

9 Compare, for instance, Putin's characteristic discursive move that, although it appeared during his press conference on 18 December 2014, referred to the cultural battles of the protest era: 'the elites of Russia are in fact its workers and peasants [...] I consider all other categorizations of elites to be absolutely unfounded' (Putin 2014; see also Van'ke and Kulaev 2015b).

References

"43 Manifesta." 2012. "Muzykanty, khudozhniki, poety i drugie zhilteli strany o tom, chto delat'." *Afisha* 18 May. www.afisha.ru/article/manifesto/ (accessed 11 August 2016).

Adorno, Theodor and Max Horkheimer. 2002. *Dialectic of Enlightenment*. Edited by Gunzelin Schmid Noerr. Stanford, CA: Stanford University Press.

Anon. 2015a. "Dal'noboishchiki obeshchaiut 'polnuiu blokadu' Moskvy, esli Rotenbergov i Medvedeva ne nakazhut za 'Platon'." *Newsru.com* 27 November. www.newsru.com/russia/27nov2015/blokadamsk.html (accessed 17 August 2016).

Anon. 2015b. "Dorozhnaia karta. Protest dal'nobopishchikov." *Mediazona* 19 November. https://zona.media/online/2015/19/11/antiplaton (accessed 17 August 2016).

Ar'ev, Andrei. 2012. "Esteticheskie predpochteniia samizdata." *Zvezda* 2. http://magazines.russ.ru/zvezda/2012/2/aa14.html (accessed 17 August 2016).

Bakhtin, Mikhail. 1968. *Rabelais and His World*. Translated by Hélène Iswolsky. Cambridge, MA: MIT Press.

Batkin, Leonid. 1978. *Ital'ianskie gumanisty: stil' zhizni i stil' myshleniia*. Moscow: Nauka.

Batkin, Leonid. 1991. *Vozobnovleniia istorii: Razmyshleniia o politike i kul'ture*. Moscow: Moskovskii rabochii.

Berland, Irina and Marina Stupakova, eds. 2012. *Razgnevannye nabliudateli. Falsifikatsii parlamentskikh vyborov glazami ochevidtsev*. Moscow: Novoe literaturnoe obozrenie.

Bibkov, Aleksandr. 2013. "Samoispytanie protestom." *Khudozhestvennyi zhurnal* 91: 59–69. http://moscowartmagazine.com/issue/5/article/30 (accessed 11 August 2016).

Bibler, Vladimir. 1975. *Myshleniia kak tvorchestvo*. Moscow: Politizdat.

Bibler, Vladimir. 1991. *Ot naukoucheniia – k logike kul'tury. Dva filosofskikh vvedeniia v dvadtsat' pervyi vek*. Moscow: Izdatel'stvo politicheskoi literatury.

Bourdieu, Pierre. 1993. *The Field of Cultural Production*. New York: Columbia University Press.

Budraitskis, Il'ia. 2013. "Intelligentsiia kak stil'." *Khudozhestvennyi zhurnal* 91: 71–78. http://moscowartmagazine.com/issue/5/article/31 (accessed 17 August 2016).

Bykov, Dmitrii. 2011. "Vystuplenie Dmitriia Bykova na Bolotnoi ploshchadi." 9 December. www.youtube.com/watch?v=v6IOhyMzKHk (accessed 11 August 2016).

Cook, Deborah. 1996. *The Culture Industry Revisited*. Lanham, MD: Rowman & Littlefield.

Dzhagalov, Rosen [Djagalov, Rossen]. 2011. "Antipopulizm postsotsialisticheskoi intelligentsii." *Neprikosnovennyi zapas* 1: 134–153.

Erpyleva, Svetlana. 2015. "'Na mitingi ia ne khodil, menia roditeli ne otpuskali': Vzroslenie, zavisimost' i samostoiatel'nost' v depolitizirovannom kontekste." In *Politika apolitichnykh: grazhdanskie dvizheniia v Rossii 2011–2013 godov*, edited by Svetlana Erpyleva and Artemii Magun. 106–143. Moscow: Novoe literaturnoe obozrenie.

Florida, Richard. 2002. *The Rise of the Creative Class: And How It's Transforming Work, Leisure, Community and Everyday Life*. New York: Perseus.

Gagyi, Agnes. 2012. "Anti-Populism as an Element of Postsocialism." Paper presented at the 44th Annual Convention of the Association for Slavic, East European and Eurasian Studies, New Orleans, LA, 19 November.

Ismailov, Ruslan. 2016. "Esli nas ne uslyshat i v etot raz, to vyidem na ulitsy." *Znak. com* 21 June. www.znak.com/2016-06-21/protest_dalnoboychikov_protiv_platona_ poluchil_vtoroe_dyhanie (accessed 17 August 2016).

Jameson, Fredric. 1991. *Postmodernism, or, the Cultural Logic of Late Capitalism.* Durham, NC: Duke University Press.

Jameson, Fredric. 1998. *The Cultural Turn: Selected Writings on the Postmodern, 1983–1998.* London and New York: Verso.

Kalinin, Il'ia. 2014. "'Nash parovoz...': Kul'tura kak instrument demodernizatsii." *Neprikosnovennyi zapas* 6: 85–94.

Kalinin, Il'ia. 2015. "Prazdnik identichnosti." *Neprikosnovennyi zapas. Debaty o politike i kul'ture* 3: 250–261.

Kashin, Oleg, Aleksei Minupov, Iurii Saprykin, Aleksei Zimin, Iuliia Tarnavskaia, Linor Goralik, Anastasiia Krasil'shchik, Irina Kaliteevskaia, Inna German, Marusia Gorina, and Lena Kraevskaia, eds. 2011. "Slovar'-2011." *Bol'shoi gorod.* http://bg.ru/city/slovar_2011-9875/ (accessed 11 August 2016).

Lash, Scott and John Urry. 1987. *The End of Organised Capitalism.* Cambridge: Polity Press.

Lotman, Iurii. 1975. "Dekabrist v povsednevnoi zhizni (Bytovoe povedenie kak istoriko-psikhologicheskaia kategoriia)." In *Literaturnoe nasledie dekabristov,* edited by V. G. Bazanova and V. E. Vatsuro, 25–74. Leningrad: Nauka.

Lotman, Juri [Iurii]. 2009. *Culture and Explosion (Semiotics, Communication and Cognition).* Translated by Wilma Clark, edited by Marina Grishakova. Berlin and New York: Mouton de Gruyter.

Mannheim, Karl. 1986. *Conservatism: A Contribution to the Sociology of Knowledge.* London: Routledge and Kegan Paul.

Matveev, Il'ia. 2015. "'Dve Rossii': kul'turnaia voina i konstruirovanie 'naroda' v khode protestov 2011–12 gg." In *Politika apolitichnykh. Grazhdanskie dvizheniia v Rossii 2011–2013 godov,* edited by Svetlana Erpyleva and Artemii Magun, 292–311. Moscow: Novoe literaturnoe obozrenie.

Oushakine, Serguei Alex. 2001. "The Terrifying Mimicry of Samizdat." *Public Culture* 13 (2): 191–214.

Paniushkin, Valerii. 2012. "Chto obshchego u menia s narodom." *Snob.ru* 3 April. www.snob.ru/selected/entry/47631 (accessed 11 August 2016).

Parfenov, Leonid. 2011. "Reportazh pro miting na Bolotnoi ploshchadi." *TVTs* 9 December. http://leonidparfenov.ru/reportazh-pro-miting-dlya-programmy-moskva247/; www.youtube.com/watch?v=5Dbikl8UyRM (accessed 11 August 2016).

Platt, Kevin M. F. 2013. "Moia tvoia ne ponimai: Intelligentsiia v poiskakh obshchego iazyka s narodom." Paper presented at the conference "Malye bannye chteniia. Slovo i delo: Intellektualy, khudozhniki, poety i obshchestvenno-politicheskie protsessy v Rossii," St Petersburg, 1–2 March.

Pomerants, Georgii. 1995. *Vykhod iz transa.* Moscow: Iurist.

Putin, Vladimir. 2012. "Putin dal kliatvu vernosti Rossii v 'Luzhnikakh'." 23 February. www.youtube.com/watch?v=Ta1GePGqu0g (accessed 11 August 2016).

Putin, Vladimir. 2014. "Bol'shaia press-konferentsiia Vladimira Putina 18 dekabria 2014 goda." *Kremlin.ru* 18 December. http://kremlin.ru/transcripts/47250 (accessed 11 August 2016).

"Razgovor s Vladimirom Putinym." 2011. Stenogramma programmy. *Premier.gov.ru* 19 December. https://archive.is/NRkG (accessed 11 August 2016).

Scott, Allen J. 2001. *The Cultural Economy of Cities.* London: Sage.

Sedakova, Ol'ga. 2012. "Byt' khristianinom po pravde." Interview with Olga Sedakova by Dmitrii Uslaner. *Russkii zhurnal* 2 April. www.russ.ru/Mirovaya-povestka/Byt-hristianinom-po-pravde (accessed 11 August 2016).

Siniavskii, Andrei. 2002. "Dissidentstvo kak lichnyi opyt." In *Puteshestvie na Chernuiu rechku*, 315–456. Moscow: Izografus, Eksmo Press.

Solzhenitsyn, Aleksandr. 1991. "Obrazovanshchina". *Novyi mir* 5: 28–46.

Throsby, David. 2001. *Economics and Culture.* Cambridge: Cambridge University Press.

Troitskii, Artemii. 2012. "Miting za chestnye vybory. Moskva, Bolotnaia ploshchad'." 4 February. www.youtube.com/watch?v=JWzly1euDrI (accessed 11 August 2016).

Van'ke, Aleksandrina and Maksim Kulaev. 2015a. "Rabochie v rossiiskom novostnom televizionnom diskurse: kontekst politicheskikh protestov." *Neprikosnovennyi zapas. Debaty o politike i kul'ture* 5: 11–23.

Van'ke, Aleksandrina and Maksim Kulaev. 2015b. "Representatsiia rabochikh v rossiiskoi pechatnoi presse." *Zhurnal issledovanii sotsial'noi politiki* 14 (1): 23–38.

Yurchak, Alexei. 2006. *Everything Was Forever Until It Was No More. The Last Soviet Generation.* Princeton, NJ, and Oxford: Princeton University Press.

Zavadskaia, Margarita and Natal'ia Savel'eva. 2015. "'A mozhno ia kak-nibud' sam vybery': vybory kak 'lichnoe delo,' protsedurnaia legitimnost' i mobilizatsiia 2011–12 gg." In *Politika apolitichnykh. Grazhdanskie dvizheniia v Rossii 2011–2013 godov*, edited by Svetlana Erpyleva and Artemii Magun, 219–270. Moscow: Novoe literaturnoe obozrenie.

Zhelina, Anna. 2015. "'Ia v eto ne lezu': vospriiatie 'lichnogo' i 'obshchestvennogo' sredi rossiiskoi molodezhi nakanune vyborov." In *Politika apolitichnykh: grazhdanskie dvizheniia v Rossii 2011–2013 godov*, edited by Svetlana Erpyleva and Artemii Magun, 143–180. Moscow: Novoe literaturnoe obozrenie.

4 Are copycats subversive?

Strategy-31, the Russian Runs,
the Immortal Regiment, and
the transformative potential of
non-hierarchical movements

Mischa Gabowitsch

Some of the most visible, original, and geographically extensive recent movements and initiatives in Russia, across the political spectrum, cannot be accurately described as either bottom-up or top-down. They are copycat movements, in that the initial idea for a new type of public activity spreads quickly across numerous locales with minimal organizational efforts on the part of those who originated it. In this chapter I analyse three such movements, chosen because they exhibit structural similarities even though their ideological background, objectives, and popularity differ widely: the Strategy-31 protests for the freedom of assembly; the ultranationalist temperance movement known as Russian Runs; and the commemorative processions titled Immortal Regiment. My overarching question is whether the very nature of such movements as flat, horizontal networks endows them with subversive or transformative potential. I conclude that the features that make copycat movements distinctive also make them especially vulnerable in the Russian context; still, I argue that they have already had tangible effects despite the ostensible failures of all three initiatives considered here, and that we will probably see many more such movements in the future.

Bottom-up and top-down movements in Russia

Recent years have seen increased scholarly interest in social and political movements in Russia and increasing sophistication in their analysis. Several detailed studies describe the emergence of *bottom-up* movements and initiatives, including those focusing on the environment, urban construction and preservation, car ownership, or electoral fraud (e.g. Gabowitsch 2013, 147–166; Greene 2014, 145–201; Erpyleva and Magun 2015; Kleman 2013; Kleman, Miriasova, and Demidov 2010). There has also been interest in Astroturf-style movements built from the *top down*, though not so much NGOs, as in the United States (Eliasoph 2011), but rather state-orchestrated organizations such as the youth movements Idushchie Vmeste and Nashi (Hemment 2015; Lassila 2012; Mijnssen 2012). What all of these movements have in common are relatively close links between the different parts and multiple hierarchical levels.

While grassroots local movements are often analysed as weak and vulnerable, in successful cases their path of development seems to be to go through organic growth, joining up with other movements to form a 'movement of movements' spanning a city or region (Kleman 2013, 502–540; Kleman, Miriasova, and Demidov 2010, 661–664; Turovets 2015), or to grow, however briefly, into countrywide single-issue movements, as in the case of the anti-monetization protests of 2005 or the fair-election protests of 2011–13. Whenever that happens, it raises questions of representation: who is allowed to speak for the whole movement? How are tactical and strategic conflicts going to be resolved (Gabowitsch 2013, 170–184)? These questions have been analysed in the US context under headings such as 'democracy in social movements' (Polletta 2002) or 'the dividends of dissent' (Ghaziani 2008). When they fail to be answered satisfactorily (as they almost invariably have been in Russia), the movement is torn apart by the push of state repression and the pull of co-optation. The upshot seems to be that these are movements that require both large numbers and internal consolidation in order to succeed on their own terms.

In the case of more centralized movements or organizations, the problem is the opposite: how can their headquarters ensure that local members toe the line? This has been a problem in particular for legal Russian political parties integrated into the system of managed democracy. Because of the paramount importance of personal networks rather than similarities in ideology or social background for local party formation, there has been considerable diversity among local party representatives concerning, for example, acceptance of state policies or participation in protests (Brenez 2011; Lobanova and Semenov 2015).

The movements I analyse in this chapter differ from both of these. For want of a better term, I call them 'copycat movements', a term that is not meant to be pejorative. Another option would be 'snowball movements', but that would suggest that what matters is the larger whole rather than its parts, whereas I want to argue that such movements can have a local impact even when their connections with others are weak, and even if they fail to develop a momentum that would make them unstoppable. They could also be called 'viral', but that term has acquired overly commercial overtones; it also potentially diminishes the agency of the local organizers and overstates the centrality of the Internet, which – though important – only partly accounts for the spread of such movements. Finally, the three movements discussed here are clearly indebted to flash mobs, which became increasingly popular in post-Soviet countries in the new millennium, in that they represent *ad hoc* aggregations of individuals rather than displays of pre-existing ties. They differ from flash mobs, however, in that they are not one-off events that strive to appear spontaneous, but regular occurrences whose timing is known in advance.

Copycat movements

Built as relatively decentralized, non-hierarchical networks, copycat movements eschew the traditional question of how to ensure democracy or just representation in social movements. Earlier, the assumption was that a movement is engaged in concerted action towards a common goal. This requires mass events and other types of mass action, and such events need to be organized jointly. Thus the main questions are ones of collective decision-making, democratic procedure, and delegation. Network movements are different: they are 'flat' and built around weak, non-hierarchical ties with a low level of commitment and centralized control; they can be geographically very spread out. Crucially, the lack of such control means that commitment is graduated: activists decide on their own degree of involvement, and there are no bodies such as party tribunals or local labour union cells to discipline them if they fail to live up to their commitments. This can make such movements less effective, but it also makes them more flexible and creates a low threshold for involvement. Globally, the demise of traditional organizations such as trade unions encourages the individualism that contributes to the proliferation of such movements. So does technological change, well beyond the rise of the Internet (Gabowitsch 2012).

In addition to these general tendencies, there are particular reasons why copycat movements have become especially prominent in Russia. Denied access to state institutions, political oppositionists of various hues have increasingly resorted to street protest. Lacking a committed base that could be mobilized in hierarchical fashion, they have attempted to build loose networks and coalitions. At least as importantly, grassroots 'social' protesters have traditionally been wary of institutionalization, which is often seen as distancing them from genuine local concerns, increasing the risk of being captured by politicians and making them more vulnerable to state repression. A similar logic goes for many non-governmental organizations, primarily in the human rights segment. Thus, Memorial, for example, had long constituted itself as a confederation of local groups rather than a centralized organization, in part because of its grassroots origins, but also to increase its resilience in the face of potential repression.

However, in some ways the networks constituted by grassroots protesters or non-governmental organizations remain traditional: the frequent requirement to organize mass events (e.g. protest) or the need to have someone speak on behalf of the entire movement puts the problem of representation back on the agenda and gives individual activists in the network an incentive to try to influence the direction of the collective activity as a whole by voicing their opinion. In another sense, this is true of crowdsourcing-style activism, such as in the massive wave of volunteer election monitoring between 2011 and 2013, which was effective to the extent that there was a central organizing body engaged in collecting, collating, and systematizing the information gathered.

Yet there is a particular type of movement where the importance of central coordination has receded even more: these I call copycat movements. These are movements which start with an idea for an activity that is first implemented locally, but is then taken up by others who may not have any links with the originator, and which require only local, but no central, coordination. They differ from purely local grassroots movements in that they do not respond to an intrusion into the local life-world. And yet local *spaces* are usually crucial to their message: they often express their message by temporarily occupying or 'liberating' symbolic or central urban spaces.

During the 2011–13 protest wave, activities of this type played a prominent role, even though they were often underreported by Western and Muscovite media overly focused on events in Moscow and ignorant or dismissive of the numerous protest events taking place elsewhere in Russia. These demonstrations were, in a sense, an example of copycat-style organization: there is ample evidence that the role of parties and other organized groups was limited in most cases, and there was little to no coordination between protests in different cities beyond their synchronicity. The horizontal, non-hierarchical aspects of the demonstrations influenced post-2012 engagement: many of those disillusioned with the fair-election rallies went on into local activism (Zhuravlev 2015).

Case selection and sources

The three case studies examined here are of Strategy-31, the Russians Runs, and the Immortal Regiment. I have chosen these movements for several reasons. Firstly, they started in different places, though each has a precise date of origin: Strategy-31 began in Moscow on 31 July 2009; the first Russian Run took place in St Petersburg on 1 January 2011; and the first procession of an Immortal Regiment took place in Tomsk on 9 May 2012. While they all had precursors, it was after those dates that each one of them very quickly spread to other parts of Russia, and eventually to other countries with sizeable populations of Russian-speakers. Nevertheless, Strategy-31 and the Russian Runs in particular have so far not been studied outside their respective places of origin, and thus the replication that makes them both special and unexpectedly similar to each other has not been reflected in the social science literature.

Secondly, the three cases cover a broad political spectrum while at the same time escaping easy identification with existing political traditions: Strategy-31 is often associated with the radical nationalist writer Eduard Limonov, leader of the National Bolshevik Party and its successor, Other Russia, but it was launched during a period when Limonov was allied with a broad coalition of other (mostly liberal) opposition parties and supported by several civil rights groups. Outside Moscow it was taken up by a diverse range of activists, usually small groups that exhibit considerable internal diversity in terms of declared ideology. The Russian Runs fall much more clearly within the nationalist spectrum, but unlike traditional nationalist gatherings that were usually structured by negative discourse and communitarian affect (against Jews, Muslims, immigrants, etc.), they were built around a positive message of physical fitness and health and used a discourse of individual, therapeutic self-improvement that had been imported in recent years from the United States through popular culture and fused with traditional Russian collective critiques of the individual. The Immortal Regiment is especially interesting, as it concerns an area – war commemoration – that is often (simplistically) associated with state-directed patriotism. It was launched, however, by a group of liberal Tomsk journalists, whose TV station was eventually shut down for being too independent and critical of the regional authorities, and whose stated intention was to democratize state commemoration and strip it of political, commercial, and militaristic overtones.

In addition to secondary online sources and the work of colleagues who have studied the movements under consideration, my discussion of the three cases draws on my own research, including fieldwork in Cheliabinsk in 2012 as well as electronic communication with some of the organizers and, finally, data collected as part of two large-scale collective projects on Victory Day celebrations that I co-directed in 2013 and 2015. For the Immortal Regiment, I draw in particular on interviews with organizers in Tomsk, Vologda, and Berlin conducted between 2013 and 2015 by Azat Bilalutdinov, Cordula Gdaniec, and myself.

A subversive defence of the Constitution? Strategy-31

The Strategy-31 demonstrations have attracted considerable media attention and, more recently, have been the subject of detailed historical analysis (Horvath 2015b). However, both journalists and scholars have focused almost exclusively on the Moscow demonstrations. A coalition that initially included liberal youth groups and Drugaia Rossiia (a reincarnation of the banned National Bolshevik Party) began holding political protests in favour of the freedom of assembly in 2009. By July, the campaign had been given a title and logo that referred to Article 31 of the Constitution, which guaranteed that freedom, and a regular date: the last day of each 31-day month. Eduard Limonov, Drugaia Rossiia's flamboyant leader, managed to rally several well-known human rights defenders to his cause. The regular Strategy-31 demonstrations became the latest and most prominent in a series of supra-partisan protests of the extra-parliamentary opposition, attracting liberal, nationalist, and left-wing participants – perhaps about 1,500 people at their peak in mid-2010. However, the organizers soon split over their strategy. Upstaged by the fair-election protests and other mass rallies and marches starting in December 2011, the Strategy-31 demonstrations in Moscow were eventually reduced to partisan events, losing their freedom-of-assembly orientation and – following the occupation of Crimea – reflecting most National Bolsheviks' new pro-regime orientation.

This story, masterfully summarized and explored in Robert Horvath's recent account (2015b), is limited to Moscow. Despite much smaller numbers, however, Strategy-31's impact outside the capital was no less significant.

By mid-2011, the organizing committee's website listed 70 cities in Russia (mostly but not exclusively regional capitals) with locations (typically central squares) and times (usually 6pm) of regular Strategy-31 demonstrations, in addition to solidarity demonstrations that were taking place abroad, often in front of Russian embassies ('Regiony' 2012). The organizers, let alone the participants, were by no means limited to Drugaia Rossiia activists, or to members or sympathizers of other Moscow-based groups, such as the liberal Solidarnost'. The composition of the demonstrations reflected local configurations. Thus, in most cases the Communist Party of the Russian Federation (CPRF) ignored the demonstrations, yet in others it joined them. In Vladivostok, for example, where the massive regional protests against restrictions on car imports were still in full swing, the CPRF sided with Solidarnost', the left-wing Union of Communist Youth and the TIGR party, which had emerged out of the protests, to hold several joint Strategy-31 demonstrations (Fomchenkov 2010). In other regions, participants ranged from neo-pagan Russian nationalist groups to members of the social-liberal Yabloko party (both of these were present at protests in Barnaul; see Fomchenkov 2010).

In some cases there were initially no organizers at all, and indeed some demonstrations started out as mere entries in the online list before anyone felt responsible for organizing them. In Cheliabinsk in September 2012, I interviewed the three men in their twenties who had become the local organizing committee after meeting at the first Strategy-31 event on 31 July 2010. That demonstration had consisted of five people. One of my interviewees told me that he had travelled to Cheliabinsk from his home town, 120 kilometres west of the regional capital, after reading about the event on the Moscow website.

> I came and saw that the local chapter of the Communist Party was holding a rally on the square. I walked around and looked, but couldn't find anyone. Then I saw some young lads. I thought: interesting, perhaps they are not with the Communists, but are the ones I need. I approached [one of them] and asked: are you Strategy-31? Did you come for the rally? He was a clever lad, he said: we have come to defend the foundations of the Constitution of the Russian Federation.
>
> (Strategy-31 interview 2012)

The participants were unable to determine who had posted the original announcement. Yet by the time of the next demonstration on 31 August, they had themselves become the organizing committee, submitting a notification of the event to the authorities (just before the deadline, to prevent a veto) and answering questions from potential participants online.

Thus Strategy-31 sometimes demonstrated the distinctive features of copycat movements in pure form: giving text-message-sized information about a

time and place, no central organization is necessary, nor is the prior existence of a network. What organizing efforts went into preparing the protests
were related to the notoriously fraught procedure of notifying the authorities
of an assembly. Central coordination from Moscow was limited to publishing online information about the local events on Strategy-31's website and
reposting short news items or other reports in a LiveJournal blog (31svo-
boda.livejournal.com). As with other copycat movements, this did mean that
even single-person events (in this case, pickets, as in Sochi on 31 May 2011;
Kravchenko 2011) could be presented as instances of the larger campaign,
creating an imagined movement even in the face of very limited attention
from traditional media.

In many ways the provincial demonstrations, just like the ones in Moscow
and St Petersburg, prefigured the much larger fair-election protests that began
in December 2011. Freedom of assembly was generic enough as a topic to
be able to attract protesters of varying stripes, who often became aware of
their commonalities and forged new solidarities precisely through participating in the same events and experiencing the same repression as their nominal
rivals or foes across the ideological aisle. Once the protests became regular events, groups in the VKontakte network, a Russian Facebook clone,
emerged to prepare and discuss future iterations – similarly, in the 2011–
13 protests, VKontakte was the principal organizing tool for most protest
events. Activists who had first met during the Strategy-31 demonstrations
sometimes went on to play an important role in the 2011–13 protests, not
least because – unlike most new protesters and even some participants in
local grassroots movements – they had had experience in dealing with the
authorities. In Cheliabinsk, the tiny group of Strategy-31 activists came to
act as consultants for and defenders of protest newcomers who were only
learning to organize demonstrations, but also as one of the links between
different groups of grassroots protesters – those demonstrating against urban
infill construction, environmental damage, or attacks on the city's architectural heritage (Gabowitsch 2013, 155–162). Although differences in political
opinion between the three persisted, they essentially came to act as professional defenders of the freedom of assembly not entirely unlike dissidents in
the 1960s and 1970s. Similarly, in many other places Strategy-31 gradually
merged with local or regional protest movements or with the fair-election
protests. Despite smaller numbers, Strategy-31's effect of keeping a protest
movement in abeyance (Taylor 1989) may have been more significant in many
provincial towns than it was in Moscow, precisely because – unlike in the
capital, with its larger political scene – a tiny group of activists willing to risk
arrest and persecution and amassing valuable experience in dealing with the
authorities could make a real difference.

In many places (again, Cheliabinsk can serve as an example) there were no
Limonov sympathizers among the core group of Strategy-31. Indeed, some
of those outside Moscow who knew about their local Strategy-31 demonstrations were unaware of the original connection with Limonov and Drugaia

Rossiia (this has been confirmed in some of my interviews, e.g. with Perm activists who came to Moscow for the 6 May 2012 'March of Millions'); others were overtly hostile. Natal'ia Novozhilova, a journalist and liberal political activist in Vladimir, recalls:

> There was never a single *natsbol* [...] Note that the title of my protest differed from Limonov's. His was 'Strategy 31', mine was 'Article 31 of the Constitution'. That way I deliberately dissociated myself and my fellow participants from the *natsboly* [...] I was greatly scandalised by the illegality, injustice and brutality towards people who were demanding that the Constitution be observed, and especially towards the very elderly Liudmila Alekseeva. (I would have protested on the 31st earlier, but I strongly disliked Limonov, and that held me back.)
>
> (Novozhilova interview 2016)

The protests in Vladimir continued regularly throughout the year 2010. Thus the splits among the organizers in Moscow were not directly mirrored elsewhere, although of course the basic tension between radical and conciliatory positions has dogged local protest in similar ways. And yet the Strategy-31 protests barely survived the demise of the 2011–13 protest wave. As with the larger protests, I would argue, the reasons for this were both internal to the movement and due to the state's response.

In terms of internal protest dynamics, the 2011–13 protests, with their mass rallies, marches, Occupy-style camps, and car/sledge/bicycle parades, provided a far larger arena than the Strategy-31 demonstrations ever had for protesters of different backgrounds and political persuasions to get to know each other and test out their common ground and differences. As I have argued elsewhere (Gabowitsch 2013; 2016a), this resulted in initial euphoria about not being alone, followed by disappointment as it became clear that mere repetitions of rallies with a rote choreography would not bring about change. Generic political protest became distinctly unpopular, and those (including thousands of people newly politicized by the 2011–13 protests) who continued their activism often stressed that they wanted to effect real change from below, by focusing on 'real' local issues (Zhuravlev 2015). Moreover, the violent response to some of the post-election protests had made Strategy-31 seem naïve and dated. Finally, the 2011–13 protest cycle itself provided protesters with new symbolic dates to commemorate with new demonstrations: 5 December, 10 December, and 6 May all became more significant than the 31st.

Much more important, however, was the direct effect of the state's response to the 2011–13 protests. Increased penalties and new limitations on the freedom of assembly passed after Putin's return to the presidency had a much more tangible effect in provincial Russia than in Moscow. Thus the cost of public protest has become prohibitive for all but the most committed activists. In addition, Russia's occupation of Crimea split oppositional scenes (and each individual ideological segment of those scenes) more radically than disa-greements over protest strategy ever had (see e.g. Horvath 2015a).

The rapid spread of the Strategy-31 demonstrations and their large-scale acceptance as common platforms for political oppositionists and grassroots protesters across the political spectrum proved their effectiveness in showing the hollowness of liberalization during the nominal Medvedev interregnum. What proved effective was not just the legalistic basic premise, which Limonov astutely adapted from the dissident heritage to create a supra-partisan plat-form, but also the copycat format of the idea. A place and time (and, as an added bonus, a website and brief charter) sufficed as a starting point. By adopting the basic format locally, activists could make a point about an issue of countrywide relevance while forging local links that were adapted to their city's specific configuration. Instead of merely following events in Moscow, as many had, for example during the upheaval of 1991 and 1993, they could identify local places with symbolic meaning, trying – however fleetingly – to challenge the authorities' control of their significance.

Yet the demise of Strategy-31 – and of the larger 2011–13 protests – clearly demonstrated the vulnerability of copycat movements. The format had allowed individuals or small groups to appear as an extensive movement even when they spoke for no one but themselves. But the stepped-up reprisals that followed Putin's return to the presidency left such protesters defenceless in the absence of strong local support groups or milieus. Horizontal ties proved of little use when those so connected turned out to be too few for effective mutual support. Taken at face value, Strategy-31 has been a failure: Article 31 of the Russian Constitution is less respected now than it has ever been. The real importance of the protests, however, may well lie in their unintended effect of providing protesters across Russia with a limited but real experience of organization and supra-ideological solidarity. They have also been some-what of a template for other copycat movements, as my next example shows.

Subversive temperance? The Russian Runs

Because of the roots of social movements studies in progressive, often left-wing movements, ultranationalism has rarely been studied as a social move-ment, just as self-organized ultranationalist (or Salafi) activity is usually excluded from consideration of civil society, relegated to an 'uncivil' society at best. However, abandoning such normative blinkers can yield cognitive ben-efits (see e.g. Caiani, Della Porta, and Wagemann 2012).

Similar to liberal opposition groups, ultranationalist activists found their scope of action increasingly circumscribed under Putin, despite a selective inclusion of nationalist ideas and political figures into the system of managed democracy. As the state apparatus became more and more adept at identify-ing ultranationalist symbols and began to keep a tight rein on organized pol-itical groups, the relevant scenes increasingly engaged in activities other than pure violence or political activism. In particular, various forms of physical education came to acquire even greater significance than they had before. This was also indicative of a larger cultural transformation in Russian ultranationalism. Soviet-era culture wars that focused on anti-Semitism were eclipsed by sub-cultural (such as skinhead) youth scenes in mid-sized towns, a dramatic increase in xenophobic violence, and a new role for 'Southerners' (from the Caucasus and Central Asia) as the main enemy. This reflected a shift of rivalries and anxieties to areas that require physical rather than intellectual efforts, such as blue-collar labour and the state's security apparatus.

The Russian Runs were a result of this new situation. Focusing on the individual body as well as the collective body of the nation, they advocate an abstinent and athletic lifestyle expressed in the slogan '"Russian" means "sober"'. The first of these runs took place on New Year's Day 2011 in St Petersburg (the only place where they have been studied so far: Omel'chenko 2015), as a counterpoint to a holiday often associated with binge-drinking; soon the idea was taken up in many other Russian cities and by Russian minority activists in other post-Soviet countries. In some places, they soon took place almost every weekend, attracting up to several hundred young participants who go for a run regardless of weather, sporting black, yellow, and white imperial flags and other nationalist symbols, though they are usually careful to avoid symbols of political parties. The initiative has survived various splits and reprisals. Preparing for the fifth anniversary of the Russian Runs, the ruszabeg_ru group in the VKontakte (VK) network listed 30 cities where runs were going to take place on 1 January 2016, and discussions in that community and various local groups indicated that the list was really much longer ('Russkaia probezhka' 2015). In an informal poll in the same group that has been running since 2012, 520 of 7,764 participants (6.7 per cent) claimed that they had not just participated in but also organized Russian Runs in their towns (Malovichko 2012). While at first these runs mostly took place in parks, they were quickly moved to central streets and in sight of stunned passers-by. A manifesto of the movement refers to the 'brilliant format which does not fall under Federal Law no. 54' – the law on the freedom of assembly. The manifesto rejects 'patronage from any political parties or religious confessions'. 'The movement does not have a single centre', it goes on; 'in every city there is an autonomous Russian Run with its own leaders [...] All important decisions are taken collectively by means of debates online or in assemblies.' It defines 'creating a cell of civil society as an institution of unmediated popular sovereignty [*narodovlastie*]' as one of the movement's aims. Finally, similarly to Strategy-31, the manifesto refers to the Constitution: 'We are not fighting for power, it is our birthright. We are guaranteed its unmediated exercise by the Constitution' (Sinyakov 2011).

Several things are striking about the Russian Runs. Firstly, they represent a novel form of activity, yet one that is rooted in long-standing nationalist traditions. Physically training the nation's youth has been an important aspect of European nationalist ideology and practice since they first developed in the nineteenth century. In Russia, for almost as long, the idea that Jews and other enemies have been turning the Russian people into drunkards has been a staple of nationalist ideology. The fact that alcoholism and other forms of substance addiction are widespread in male-dominated small-town milieus where ultranationalist ideas have gained a particular foothold gives the topic special urgency (Gabowitsch 2013, 291–329).

Secondly, despite constant references to a larger collective that is usually circumscribed as the Russian (*russkii* or *rossiiskii*) people or, Russian doll-style, as 'You – Family – People – Motherland', the Russian Runs are clearly a product of a post-Soviet culture influenced by discourses and practices of individual self-improvement. Imported from the United States and mediated by countless self-help books, seminars, and TV shows, this ideal has seeped into areas as diverse as corporate culture, patriotic youth camps, and lifestyle magazines (Lerner 2015). It merged with earlier Soviet projects of individual improvement, which implied ritual confessions and denunciations within the working collective (Kharkhordin 1999). The local discussion boards for the Russian Runs are full of posts such as this one from the Stary Oskol group, accompanied by photos of scantily clad male and female athletes in gyms: 'If you are waiting for someone to accept you "the way you are", then you are simply lazy. Because usually "the way you are" is a sad thing to behold. Change, work on yourself!!!' ('Russkie probezhki' 2013).

Thirdly, leaving aside its nationalist ideology, the network-based organization of the Russian Runs is astonishingly similar to that of Strategy-31 as well as a range of other initiatives to reclaim public space. Unlike the stationary protests of Strategy-31, the Russian Runs resemble Critical Mass events, in which cyclists, skaters, and others try to wrest city streets from motorized traffic. More than the two other cases discussed here, they are also reminiscent of flash mobs, which became increasingly popular in Russia after 2003 thanks to the spread of the Internet.

However, the similarities with Strategy-31 go further. In both cases, legislation played an important role in structuring the initiative, although Strategy-31 was launched *in defence* of a legal norm (Article 31), whereas the Russian Runs explicitly exploit a legal loophole – the lack of provisions for athletic events in Law no. 54, which regulates 'assemblies, rallies, demonstrations, marches and pickets' but does not mention sports. In both cases, nationalists were demonstrating that they now subscribed to a rhetoric of collective self-organization and civil society – a discourse that has been even more prevalent than that of individual self-improvement. One forum user in Novocherkassk ('Adminer' 2013) cited the local Russian Runs as proof that civil society there was not limited to ethnic minority associations. 'The Russian Runs', one central site for the initiative proclaimed in 2011,

> are a means of civic self-organization on the part of conscientious Russian youth, aiming to protest against the authorities' failure to act on the problems of alcoholism, drug addiction and the moral decline and cultural degradation of Russian (*rossiiskoe*) society.
>
> ('Russkie za ZOZh' 2011)

In both cases, the initiators took pains to present their campaign as 'non-political'. In both cases, events attended only by small groups or individuals were inscribed in the larger collective by virtue of taking place under the same heading: 'If your group is no longer active', one of the moderators of the ruszabeg_ru group wrote in the local Cheliabinsk forum for the Runs, 'we ask those interested to conduct a Run themselves! Remember that even if there is only 1 of you, you are not alone! Companions-in-arms in other cities are running with you!' ('Russkie probezhki' 2016).

The initiative spread via networks of Russian ultranationalist activists. Although invitations to Runs usually feature prominent calls not to bring party flags or symbols, the events are often organized by members of local ultranationalist associations. Asmik Novikova, who studied local nationalist scenes in the Voronezh, Komi, and Kirov oblasts in 2014–15, has observed that local activists are very eager to try out new, low-risk types of public activity that do not put them in direct conflict with the authorities, unlike open protest or violence (Novikova interview 2015). They are also interested in using neutral formats to attract young newcomers to their groups while at the same time regularly demonstrating their existence in physically intimidating ways.[1]

Yet the Runs were even less tied than Strategy-31 to the originators in St Petersburg. In fact, predictably, disagreement soon developed about who had come up with the original idea. As with Strategy-31, the initiative's 'date of birth' marked the emergence of an activity packaged for imitation and given a catchy name and set of rules, rather than the birth of an idea: after all, it would be hard to claim the invention of going for a run instead of consuming alcohol. Some authors would later claim that the initiative had first been discussed online, and that as early as 1 January 2011 Russian Runs took place simultaneously in 'approximately 11 cities' (Anon. 2015).

The St Petersburg Runs soon split over the issue of ideological ostentatiousness and involvement with the larger 2011–13 protests. However, as with Strategy-31, these disagreements did not necessarily register with local organizers of Russian Runs elsewhere in Russia, where responses by the authorities, as usual, have run the full gamut from repressive to permissive. Taken up by a range of groups whose ties to organized ultranationalism varied in intensity, the idea merged with similar initiatives, incorporating disciplines such as 'Russian bench pressing' and patriotic rap songs about healthy living ('Russkii Patriot REP' 2016).

Have the Russian Runs had a subversive effect? Their contribution to spreading the idea of a healthy lifestyle is a moot point, yet that laudable goal can hardly count as subversive unless one subscribes to the idea that the Russian state or some ominous enemy is purposely keeping Russians drunk. Nor do the Runs seem to have contributed to creating or fostering an ultranationalist scene capable of posing any real challenge to the state – the very publicity of the events has made it easy for Extremism Centres and other parts of the security apparatus to keep track of organizers and participants. Nevertheless, the structural effect of the Runs has been similar to that of Strategy-31, and perhaps even more lasting, given that the latter have involved more young people and, unlike the former, are continuing to this day: by allowing participants to come together on a comparatively neutral platform (in this case, one that tries to overcome the usual divisions between rival groups of nationalists) and by giving a large number of people an experience of self-organization and collective agency in public space, they have done more to spread potentially subversive skills than any centrally coordinated nationalist campaign ever has. (One must, of course, be careful not to equate subversiveness with inclusion or democratization: participants in Russian Runs have been involved in violent homophobic and xenophobic attacks.)

Subversive war commemoration? The Immortal Regiment

War commemoration is one of the main areas of collective action and civic activity in the post-Soviet world. It includes tens of thousands of volunteers (*poiskoviki*), who search for the remains of fallen soldiers from the Second (and, more rarely, the First) World War, and also associations that go on secular pilgrimages to Soviet war memorials and cemeteries abroad, local veterans' councils, and much else. These activities are usually ignored by observers interested in civil society and social movements, perhaps because most such initiatives espouse a patriotic discourse and are therefore suspected of being orchestrated or at least co-opted by the state. Yet the relations between commemorative associations and state bodies cover a much broader spectrum than this suggests, and have done so since at least the 1950s, when veterans' associations wrought significant concessions from the Soviet authorities (Edele 2008). While most commemorative initiatives receive some form of support from the state or are even created by state actors, many are keen to stress their autonomy from state institutions (Gabowitsch, Gdaniec, and Makhotina 2007).

The Immortal Regiment has quickly become one of the best-known such initiatives. It has two components. On the one hand, it involves processions during the Victory Day celebrations on 9 May, where each participant holds up a portrait of a relative who participated in the war effort against Nazi Germany, usually including the person's name and dates of birth and – if deceased – death. On the other hand, the initiative's website (moypolk.ru) collects the life stories of such people in a centralized register. Launched in Tomsk in 2012 with a claimed 6,000 participants in its first event, the Immortal Regiment spread to more than 100 cities and towns across Russia and some neighbouring countries; by 2015 local organizers had staged processions in at least 15 countries, including Israel, Germany, and Norway (Bilalutdinov 2017). Yet by then many observers saw the Immortal Regiment as a state initiative. That year half a million people took part in the Moscow procession, which was broadcast live on several TV stations, later earning a prize as 'the main TV event of the year'. Vladimir Putin joined its ranks with a portrait of his father, and media photos of the event showed numerous Russian flags and banners of various organizations.

The initial impulse behind the Immortal Regiment was critical of established state practices. It was launched as a local project in Tomsk by three journalists – all of them grandchildren of war participants – affiliated with the liberal Tomsk Media Group (Tomskaia mediagruppa), best known for TV2, a station that was shut down in February 2015, despite a wave of popular protest, for being overly independent and critical of the regional authorities. They have stated that they were frustrated with the political, commercial, and militaristic overtones of the standard commemorative events such as military parades, and wished to create an alternative (Bilalutdinov 2017). Given the extent to which war commemoration has come to frame and permeate Russian political discourse, education, and everyday life, this intention has no less potential significance than the struggle for democratic institutions and rights, and is in fact intertwined with them.

Like Strategy-31 and the Russian Runs, the Immortal Regiment started out as a local event. As a safeguard against politicization and state co-optation attempts, the initiators – journalists Sergei Lapenkov, Sergei Kolotovkin, and Igor' Dmitriev – wrote a brief charter that defined the Regiment as a 'non-commercial, non-political, non-state civic initiative' that could not be 'personalised in one, even highly respected, individual, be it a politician, a public figure or an official. The Regiment consists of the millions of deceased and their descendants.' They also stressed the idea of unity across differences: 'Every citizen, regardless of creed, ethnicity, political or other views can join the ranks of the regiment. The Immortal Regiment unites people. Anything that serves other purposes is unacceptable to us. One country – one Regiment' (Lapenkov 2012).

Comparative historical studies have shown that war commemoration all over the world follows a similar dynamic, one that has been described as a 'democratisation of death' (Koselleck 1979) or 'individualisation of memory' (Hettling 2013) – from glorifying monarchs and military leaders to commemorating each individual soldier or war victim. However, such individualization has often meant bureaucratization: the fallen are mentioned individually, but in the form of standardized lists of variables that matter to the state: surname, date of birth, and death (Gabowitsch 2014; Madigan 2014). More recently we have been witnessing a new tendency of *personalized* commemoration, where life stories, narratives of personality, and intimate attachments, as well as personal objects, come to play a central role (King 2010).

Personalization has been an important part of the Immortal Regiment's appeal. In recent years, the massive commemorative database OBD Memorial, assembled under the auspices of the Russian Ministry of Defence, has made the kinds of formalized data on soldiers' wartime fate that can be found in state-produced sources available to a large public for the first time. The Immortal Regiment's website went beyond that, offering space for more detailed personal stories, even if many of them are largely reconstructed on the basis of sources such as OBD Memorial. Many participants produce their own portraits or signs, often in non-standard formats and with ample additional information.

Lapenkov, Kolotovkin, and Dmitriev undertook more concerted efforts than the organizers of either Strategy-31 or the Russian Runs to spread their idea and oversee the growth of their network, using their journalistic contacts to identify potential local organizers. Nevertheless, the initiative still spread in copycat style (as Lapenkov phrases it in an interview, 'we had to decide whether we are some sort of vertical structure or a confederation'; Lapenkov interview 2015): since 2013, organizers in numerous regions have staged processions having had no or only minimal contact with the initiators in Tomsk, who have been happy to acknowledge those events as long as they use the suggested format and observe the Charter. As with the Russian Runs, the flipside of this loose structure means that the initiators have very few resources to sanction violations of their rules. This problem quickly came to a head. By 2014, the Russian state, acting through the United Popular Front, started making attempts to appropriate the initiative by issuing centralized instructions on its organization to its local representatives. The erstwhile Moscow coordinator, Nikolai Zemtsov, decided to accept help from United Russia and the Moscow city authorities, and eventually created his own parallel organization. In 2015 he let United Russia distribute leaflets about the Immortal Regiment that were branded with its own symbols; he also encouraged organizers of the Regiment in war-torn Donetsk to add portraits of those who had died as separatist fighters in the ongoing conflict in south-eastern Ukraine. The Tomsk team rejected the move but could not sanction such behaviour: 'In the end the council voted to exclude Zemtsov from among the coordinators of the Immortal Regiment, which had absolutely no consequences, as we do not issue or confiscate party cards' (Lapenkov interview 2015).

It soon became apparent that the state's take-over of the initiative was going beyond occasional co-optation of local organizers. In May 2015 online and offline media started discussing accusations that the Tomsk organizers had stolen the idea from a retired policeman in Tyumen and were using it for publicity and personal gain (Rykovtseva 2015). The attacks followed the time-honoured tradition of anonymously leaking *kompromat* (compromising information) to damage political opponents (Ledeneva 2013) and seemed designed to cut the authors of the Immortal Regiment out of its history.

That a copycat movement should have had precursors was not in itself surprising. Ivanov had indeed launched an idea very similar to the later Immortal Regiment; he had first proposed it under the heading 'Take a portrait to the parade' in 2007, and it had been implemented in Tyumen since the 2008 Victory Day parade.[2] However, writing mostly to regional governors in Russia and neighbouring countries and occasionally to regional newspapers, he had largely failed to spread the idea outside his home region (Rykovtseva 2015), although it was taken up in some places by United Russia or its affiliated organizations under the new heading of 'Victors' parade'.

The Immortal Regiment has had a transformative effect that is by no means obliterated by its partial domestication. The initiative has already expanded Russia's commemorative repertoire. It has provided a framework through which to express a need that is obviously felt near-universally by the generation of war participants' grandchildren – the need for individualized, personalized commemoration. It has done so through a horizontal initiative that has given local organizers and participants a sense of agency. It forced the state to adapt official events to this new format, giving more airtime to the Immortal Regiment than the traditional military parade. Even though Russian state and para-state agencies such as the United Popular Front have undertaken efforts to fuse the new format with loyalty to the political regime, the very idea of personalization and the early history of the Immortal Regiment will continue to act as a potential source of critique – similarly to the 1980s, when newly emerging *poiskoviki* groups challenged the state for not living up to its own mantra of 'No-one is forgotten, nothing is forgotten' (Tumarkin 1994). Even if the initiators of the Immortal Regiment are sidelined, the manipulability of commemoration clearly has its limits: state-ordained practices such as forced participation or centralized distribution of portraits could easily backfire, turning the processions into yet another empty ritual that does not attract the kind of emotional involvement inherent in the initial idea.

This suggests two things about the evolution of copycat movements in Russia. Firstly, movements that do not rely on the state apparatus paradoxically seem to have greater chances of spreading widely and quickly, not least because non-state actors are more flexible in the face of bureaucratic obstacles and hierarchies, but also because such initiatives tend to spread beyond Russia's borders and thus beyond the immediate reach of its authorities. Secondly, an initiative of this kind needs to be formatted as a media product in order to be quickly taken up and to be recognized as a single movement despite its diversity. The Immortal Regiment's distinctive title, Charter, and website turned it into an easy-to-copy kit, and while the internet-savvy originators often offered little more than encouragement to local organizers, their quick response seems to have contributed to the rapid growth of numerous offshoots (N. N. interview 2015).

Conclusion

The differences between the three movements examined here are so obvious they hardly need to be stated. Their similarities are all the more striking.

1. All three are parasitical on, or a response to, a repertoire deployed by the state. The earliest Strategy-31 protests were in response to loyalist demonstrations taking place at the same time. The Russian Runs respond to increased state control over the ultranationalist scene by exploiting a loophole in the law on assemblies. The Immortal Regiment starts with a

date – Victory Day – whose significance and set of most visible practices has been shaped by the state, and tries to introduce a new practice into it.

2.   While the originators, and some central organizers, have played a role in all three movements, they can in no way be seen as 'movement leaders' in any traditional sense of the term. Following a recent suggestion in social movement studies (Quednau 2013), it would be more accurate to call them 'instigators' – a type that belongs to the broader family of 'key figures' in movements without assuming a leadership role.

3.   In all three cases, the instigators' contribution was strikingly similar: they took an idea that was not in itself novel and packaged it for effortless imitation by giving it a short, memorable title, a logo or other visual symbol, and a website with a brief charter and list of places, thus providing local organizers with an easy kit that could be used to reproduce events.

4.   All three movements experienced rifts among the organizers or instigators, but in no case were these fatal to the initiative, the way they often have been in both top-down and bottom-up movements. In the case of Strategy-31 and the Russian Runs, local events persisted long after the team behind the original events in the two capitals had split; for the Immortal Regiment, the rift between Tomsk and Moscow gave the state an opportunity to step in, but for the time being this has not sapped the initiative's energy.

5.   The same goes for reprisals against individual organizers: for Strategy-31, arrests of prominent figures were a calculated part of the dilemma that the movement wanted to create for the state, and the highly publicized detention of Liudmila Alekseeva actually gave the campaign a strong impetus. For the Russian Runs, the arrest of Maksim Kalininchenko did not prevent their spread across Russia and beyond.[3] In the case of the Immortal Regiment, the blow dealt to TV2, which had been the instigators' institutional base, hardly registered with most participants.

6.   All three movements were based on the idea of temporarily occupying a centrally located public space, providing a framework for individuals to congregate and engage in a communal activity. Unlike earlier attempts at analysing masses, recent work in social psychology (Hopkins et al. 2016) suggests that being part of a crowd is very often an empowering experience that provides participants with a sense of agency rather than suppressing it. That insight applies to all three cases considered here. Participants have often experienced the very sense of agency that is a prerequisite to social engagement.

7.   The crowds involved in Strategy-31 and the Russian Runs in particular have often been small. To a degree, however, the internet-driven structure of the movements has allowed even individuals to experience the enhanced agency effect. This has been a factor in the movements' quick spread, and a template for the 2011–13 protests. Yet it has also been a major weakness: a thin, horizontal network cannot replace a locally rooted, tightly knit community, especially when it comes to protecting

individual members against reprisals. The only protest movements that have been partially successful in defending themselves against such reprisals have been regional ones based on interests explicitly shared by a large part of the population, such as the Save Khopyor movement on the borders of the Voronezh, Volgograd, and Tambov regions (Turovets 2015).[4] Copycat movements have not become networks of solidarity.

8. Most importantly, perhaps, all three initiatives have been at pains to present themselves as being non-political. The rhetorical rejection of politics also follows a general pattern among Russian protesters; one research collective has even identified the 'politics of the apolitical' as the central theme in Russian social movements (Erpyleva and Magun 2015). While the repudiation of politics has been a tactical advantage for the initiatives examined here, it has also left them strategically vulnerable, as it meant acknowledging the state's right to define and delineate the realm of the political, as it has, for example, in selecting 'foreign agents' engaged in 'political activity'.

The experience of Strategy-31, the Russian Runs and the Immortal Regiment suggests that we should be cautious of the idea that an original format can, in itself, help a movement succeed – in the absence of broad social base that shares the movements' ideals, administrative resources will always trump horizontal networks.

The copycat will remain a common type of activist. The format's subversive potential seems to lie in its ability to attract relatively large numbers of previously uninvolved participants to a novel type of activity. Instead of pursuing the goal (both limited and elusive) of transforming the Russian political system, copycat movements may well have the more profound effect of changing social practices. Whether any of these movements has actually had such an effect, however, remains to be seen.

Note and acknowledgements

I wish to think Azat Bilalutdinov, Johannes Due Enstad, Cordula Gdaniec, and Asmik Novikova for their valuable advice. Both the theoretical and the empirical parts of this chapter had to be shortened for reasons of space; the complete version has been published in Gabowitsch (2016b).

Notes

1 Several of my Cheliabinsk informants mentioned that they felt threatened by the Runs, which have been particularly large there, taking place along a stretch of the central Lenin Prospect.

2 Ivanov has been systematically trying to draw attention to his authorship of the idea in various online forums, though his efforts were hardly noticed until mid-2015. He has also been critical of the Immortal Regiment's charter, writing that a ban on Soviet symbols is ahistorical since many Soviet soldiers went to war with

those symbols (see Ivanov 2016). I wish to thank Gennadii Ivanov for providing me, in December 2015 and January 2016, with ample documentation of his commemorative activities since 2007.

3 Maksim Kalinichenko, an ultranationalist activist and Russian Runs organizer, had also been an election observer and published a 'Manifesto of Russian Youth' after the first mass protests on 5 December. He was arrested on his way to a joint protest rally on 10 December and charged with having called for violence against the police. One of the earliest victims of the state's response to the mass protests, he was placed under arrest for a year and, in February 2013, sentenced to a two-and-a-half-year suspended prison sentence on flimsy evidence (Politzeky.ru 2013).

4 A broad-based popular protest movement against nickel mining in the rural Khopyor river basin on the border of Voronezh and Volgograd regions. Remarkably resilient in the face of repression, though with little tangible success so far, the movement has been active since 2012. See also Gabowitsch 2016a, 138–140.

References

"Adminer". 2013. "Grazhdanskoe obshchestvo Novocherkasska." *Novocherkassk. net* 16 May. http://новочеркасск.net/viewtopic.php?t=90146&p=1469404 (accessed 7 January 2016).

Anon. 2015. "Russkaia probezhka." *Traditsiia. Russkaia entsiklopediia.* https://traditio.wiki/Русская_пробежка (accessed 11 December 2015).

Bilalutdinov, Azat. 2017. "Das Unsterbliche Regiment." In *Kriegsgedenken als Event. Der 9. Mai im postsozialistischen Europa*, edited by M. Gabowitsch, C. Gdaniec, and E. Makhotina, 126–140. Paderborn: Ferdinand Schöningh.

Brenez, Lou. 2011. "Les partis 'partenaires du Kremlin' à l'épreuve des dynamiques locales. Formes et pratiques de 'l'opposition constructive'." *Revue d'études comparatives Est-Ouest* 42 (1): 65–89.

Caiani, Manuela, Donatella Della Porta, and Claudius Wagemann. 2012. *Mobilizing on the Extreme Right: Germany, Italy, and the United States.* Oxford: Oxford University Press.

Edele, Mark. 2008. *Soviet Veterans of the Second World War: A Popular Movement in an Authoritarian Society 1941–1991.* Oxford: Oxford University Press.

Eliasoph, Nina. 2011. *Making Volunteers: Civic Life after Welfare's End.* Princeton, NJ: Princeton University Press.

Erpyleva, Svetlana and Artemii Magun, eds. 2015. *Politika apolitichnykh: grazhdanskie dvizheniia v Rossii 2011–2013 godov.* Moscow: Novoe literaturnoe obozrenie.

Fomchenkov, Sergei. 2010. "'Strategiia-31' v regionakh RF. Itogi." *WaybackMachine Internet Archive* 2 June. https://web.archive.org/web/20101225101218/http://strategy-31.ru/?p=1460 (accessed 7 January 2016).

Gabowitsch, Mischa. 2012. "Social Media, Mobilisation and Protest Slogans in Moscow and Beyond." *Digital Icons* 7: 213–225. www.digitalicons.org/issue07/social-media-mobilisation-and-protest-slogans-in-moscow-and-beyond/ (accessed 8 August 2016).

Gabowitsch, Mischa. 2013. *Putin kaputt!? Russlands neue Protestkultur.* Berlin: Suhrkamp.

Gabowitsch, Mischa. 2014. "Umkämpfte Tote. Gefallene Soldaten, Angehörige und der Staat." *Mittelweg 36*: 47–53.

Gabowitsch, Mischa. 2016a. *Protest in Putin's Russia.* Cambridge: Polity Press.

Gabowitsch, Mischa. 2016b. "Are Copycats Subversive? Strategy-31, the Russian Runs, the Immortal Regiment, and the Transformative Potential of Non-Hierarchical Movements." *Problems of Post-Communism* doi:10.1080/10758216.2016.1250604.

Gabowitsch, Mischa, Cordula Gdaniec, and Ekaterina Makhotina, eds. 2017. *Kriegsgedenken als Event. Der 9. Mai im postsozialistischen Europa.* Paderborn: Ferdinand Schöningh.

Ghaziani, Amin. 2008. *The Dividends of Dissent: How Conflict and Culture Work in Lesbian and Gay Marches on Washington.* Chicago: University of Chicago Press.

Greene, Samuel A. 2014. *Moscow in Movement: Power and Opposition in Putin's Russia.* Stanford, CA: Stanford University Press.

Hemment, Julie. 2015. *Youth Politics in Putin's Russia: Producing Patriots and Entrepreneurs.* Bloomington: Indiana University Press.

Hettling, Manfred. 2013. "Nationale Weichenstellungen und Individualisierung der Erinnerung. Politischer Totenkult im Vergleich." In *Gefallenengedenken im globalen Vergleich. Nationale Tradition, politische Legitimation und Individualisierung der Erinnerung,* edited by M. Hettling and J. Echternkamp, 11–42. Munich: Oldenbourg Verlag.

Hopkins, Nick et al. 2016. "Explaining Effervescence: Investigating the Relationship between Shared Social Identity and Positive Experience in Crowds." *Cognition and Emotion* 30 (1): 20–32.

Horvath, Robert. 2015a. "The Euromaidan and the Crisis of Russian Nationalism." *Nationalities Papers* 43 (6): 819–839.

Horvath, Robert. 2015b. "'Sakharov Would Be with Us': Limonov, Strategy-31, and the Dissident Legacy." *The Russian Review* 74 (4): 581–598.

Ivanov, Gennadii. 2016. "Gennady Ivanov." *VK Public Profile.* https://vk.com/id204923774 (accessed 7 January 2016).

Kharkhordin, Oleg. 1999. *The Collective and the Individual in Russia: A Study of Practices.* Berkeley: University of California Press.

King, Anthony. 2010. "The Afghan War and 'Postmodern' Memory: Commemoration and the Dead of Helmand." *The British Journal of Sociology* 61 (1): 1–25.

Kleman, Karin, ed. 2013. *Gorodskie dvizheniia Rossii v 2009–2012 godakh: na puti k politicheskomu.* Moscow: Novoe literaturnoe obozrenie.

Kleman, Karin, Ol'ga Miriasova, and Andrei Demidov. 2010. *Ot obyvatelei k aktivistam: zarozhdaiushchiesia sotsial'nye dvizheniia v sovremennoi Rossii.* Moscow: Tri kvadrata.

Koselleck, Reinhart. 1979. "Kriegerdenkmale als Identitätsstiftung der Überlebenden." In *Identität* (Poetik und Hermeneutik Band VIII), edited by O. Marquard and K. Stierle, 255–276. Munich: W. Fink.

Kravchenko, Svetlana. 2011. "V Sochi pravozashchitnik Basmanov provel piket v ramkakh aktsii 'Strategiia-31'." *Kavkazskii Uzel* 1 June. www.kavkaz-uzel.ru/articles/186441/ (accessed 7 January 2016).

Lapenkov, Sergei. 2012. "Ustav Polka." *Bessmertnyi polk.* http://moypolk.ru/ustav-polka (accessed 7 January 2016).

Lassila, Jussi. 2012. *The Quest for an Ideal Youth in Putin's Russia II: The Search for Distinctive Conformism in the Political Communication of Nashi, 2005–2009.* Stuttgart: ibidem.

Ledeneva, Alena. 2013. *How Russia Really Works: The Informal Practices That Shaped Post-Soviet Politics and Business.* Ithaca, NY: Cornell University Press.

Lerner, Julia. 2015. "The Changing Meanings of Russian Love: Emotional Socialism and Therapeutic Culture on the Post-Soviet Screen." *Sexuality & Culture* 19 (2): 349–368.

Lobanova, Olesya and Andrey Semenov. 2015. "Civic Protests in Tyumen Region: December 2011–September 2012." In *Systemic and Non-Systemic Opposition in the Russian Federation: Civil Society Awakens?*, edited by C. Ross, 179–198. Farnham: Ashgate.

Madigan, Edward. 2014. "'The Burden of Our Sorrow'. Zum Umgang mit den britischen Kriegstoten des Ersten Weltkriegs." *Mittelweg* 36: 62–71.

Malovichko, Nikolai. 2012. "Russkie probezhki. Russkie za ZOZh. Rus'! '[Opros] A ty privel druga(podrugu) na russkuiu probezhku za ZOZh?'." *VK Blog* 9 June. https://vk.com/topic-22668555_26657394 (accessed 7 January 2016).

Mijnssen, Ivo. 2012. *The Quest for an Ideal Youth in Putin's Russia I: Back to Our Future! History, Modernity and Patriotism According to Nashi, 2005–2012.* Stuttgart: ibidem.

Omel'chenko, Elena. 2015. "Riski i udovol'stviia na stsenakh molodezhnogo aktivizma sovremennoi Rossii." In *Puti Rossii. Al'ternativy obshchestvennogo razvitiia. 2.0*, edited by M. Pugacheva and A. Filippov, 25–47. Moscow: Novoe literaturnoe obozrenie.

Politzeky.ru. 2013. "Kalinichenko Maksim Sergeevich." www.politzeky.ru/politzeki/uslovnye-sroki/40844.html (accessed 7 January 2016).

Polletta, Francesca. 2002. *Freedom Is an Endless Meeting: Democracy in American Social Movements.* Chicago: University of Chicago Press.

Quednau, Tobias, ed. 2013. "Anstifter, Strippenzieher, Urgesteine. Schlüsselfiguren in sozialen Bewegungen." Thematic issue of *Forschungsjournal Soziale Bewegungen* 4.

"Regiony." 2012. Blog. *WaybackMachine Internet Archive* https://web.archive.org/web/20120310205135/http://strategy-31.ru/?page_id=25 (accessed 7 January 2016).

"Russkaia probezhka". 2015. "Russkaia probezhka 1 ianvaria 2016 goda (Siuda skidyvaite spisok gorodov)." *VK Blog.* https://vk.com/topic-22668555_32982868 (accessed 7 January 2016).

"Russkie probezhki". 2013. "Russkie Probezhki! Russkie za ZOZh! g.Staryi Oskol." *VK Blog* [Cached]. http://webcache.googleusercontent.com/search?q=cache:KbO1PShczzIJ:vk.com/ruszabeg_oskol_2+&cd=1&hl=de&ct=clnk&gl=de&lr=lang_de%7Clang_en%7Clang_es%7Clang_fr%7Clang_it%7Clang_ru%7Clang_uk (accessed 7 January 2016).

"Russkie probezhki". 2016. "Russkie probezhki! Russkie za ZOZh! Cheliabinsk!" *VK Blog.* https://vk.com/ruszabeg1 (accessed 7 January 2016).

"Russkie za ZOZh". 2011. "O nas." *Russkie za ZOZh* official website. www.ruszabeg.ru/ (accessed 7 January 2016).

"Russkii Patriot REP". 2016. *VK Discussion Board.* https://vk.com/rus_patriot_rap (accessed 7 January 2016).

Rykovtseva, Elena. 2015. "Son Gennadiia Ivanova." *Radio Svoboda* 13 May. www.svoboda.org/content/article/27014615.html (accessed 8 August 2016).

Sinyakov, Alexander. 2011. "Manifest 'Russkoi probezhki'." *VK Blog* 25 September. https://vk.com/topic-23240913_25455632 (accessed 7 January 2016).

Taylor, Verta. 1989. "Social Movement Continuity: The Women's Movement in Abeyance." *American Sociological Review* 54 (5):761–775.

Tumarkin, Nina. 1994. *The Living and the Dead: The Rise and Fall of the Cult of World War II in Russia*. New York: Basic Books.

Turovets, Mariia. 2015. "Protivostoianie depolitizatsii: dvizhenie protiv dobychi nike-lia v Voronezhskoi oblasti." In *Politika apolitichnykh: grazhdanskie dvizheniia v Rossii 2011–2013 godov*, edited by Svetlana Erpyleva and Artemii Magun, 408–444. Moscow: Novoe literaturnoe obozrenie.

Zhuravlev, Oleg. 2015. "Chto ostalos' ot 'Bolotnoi': novyi start lokal'nogo aktivizma v Rossii." Unpublished manuscript.

Interviews

Lapenkov, Sergei. 2015. One of the initiators of the Immortal Regiment. Interviewed by Azat Bilalutdinov in Tomsk, 14 May.

N. N. 2015. Forty-year-old owner of a small cosmetics business, originally from the Cheliabinsk region in Russia, in Germany since 2000. Interviewed by Mischa Gabowitsch in Berlin, 30 March.

Novikova, Asmik. 2015. Sociologist, Moscow. Skype interview, 11 December.

Novozhilova, Natalia. 2016. Journalist and liberal activist from Vladimir, now residing in Bulgaria. Electronic interview, 4 January.

Strategy-31. 2012. Three organizers of the Strategy-31 demonstration in Cheliabinsk. Interviewed by Mischa Gabowitsch in Cheliabinsk, 14 September.

5 Political consumerism in Russia after 2011

Olga Gurova

Introduction

In 2012–13, when the company Yves Rocher sued the political opposition leader Aleksei Navalnyi for what is believed to be a fabricated allegation (Navalnyi and his brother Oleg provided courier services to Yves Rocher), a group of bloggers and activists started a campaign to boycott Yves Rocher products. Vsevolod Chernozub, one of the activists in this campaign, stated on its web page that in Russia,

> consumption is still Soviet in nature. We take what is given to us and think all these boycotts are absurd. As if you punish yourself. However, a boycott is our deliberate political choice, our conscious way to spend money – is the only way to influence business […] is one of the most interesting instruments of civil society.[1]

In this chapter I argue that consumption has recently become a tool for expressing citizenship and civic concerns in Russian society. It has also become a resource for collective identification and for creating consumption communities based on political views. The protests of 2011–12 have made visible and prompted this process. The topics of consumption and politics became even more acute in 2014–15 and spread to the wider population after sanctions against Russia were introduced by the European Union, the US, and other countries in response to the annexation of Crimea, provoking another huge wave of bans and embargos from the Russian authorities on the one hand, and a wave of citizens' engagement on the other. These processes have highlighted the fact that consumption in Russia had become an arena for the construction of a national belonging, in which the state, businesses, and citizens participate. Consumption has furnished the state with yet another area in which and resource with which to consolidate the nation. It has also provided citizens with an opportunity to express their own belonging and concerns. In order to make a profit, producers of consumer goods play on the nationalist and patriotic feelings of loyal citizens as well as the oppositional mood. How and why does consumption become a means for expressing citizenship?

How has consumption been used as a tool for political consumerism by the state, by businesses and citizens in Russia recently? I will here discuss these questions in the framework of an increase of political consumerism in Russia.

What is political consumerism?

One of the key categories describing the connection between consumption and citizenship is political consumerism. 'Political consumerism' comprises the ways of using consumer choices in the market with the purpose of influencing society and politics in a broad sense, as a decision-making process (see Strømsnes 2009). The concept of political consumerism has gained importance in Western democracies during the past two decades. Scholars have explained its popularity as an addition to conventional political participation. Citizens' participation in politics has turned towards more direct engagement in relation to particular political, social, or cultural issues. Researchers characterize this as a shift from conventional ('old') to post-conventional ('new') methods of political participation. Political consumerism is often described as a form of participation that appeals to citizens who tend to find themselves marginalized and alienated from formal political settings (Strømsnes 2009; Micheletti 2003).

Different categories are used to label consumer behaviour for the purpose of influencing politics and society (see Carrigan, Szmigin, and Wright 2004). For instance, Michel Micheletti utilizes the above-mentioned term 'political consumerism' (Micheletti 2003). Juliet Schor favours the category of 'conscious consumption' to emphasize the contemporary purchasing practice of consumers who are 'mindful' of the larger political and social context (see Littler 2009, 6). 'Ethical consumption' is perhaps currently the most commonly used term; it refers to conscious and deliberate choices of consumption on the basis of personal and moral beliefs (Carrigan, Szmigin, and Wright 2004). Other terms include 'green consumption', i.e. avoiding certain types of products that cause pollution, or that are associated with cruelty to animals, and purchasing instead environmentally friendly products, as well as recycling (Carrigan, Szmigin, and Wright 2004). Further categories with similar meanings are 'sustainable consumption' and 'responsible consumption'. In this chapter I use the category of 'political consumerism', first because it goes beyond environmental concerns to a broader set of issues; and second, because it allows me to embrace the actions of agents other than individuals.

Political consumerism supposes an interaction between various agents: the state, businesses, and citizens. Each has its own strategies and forms of participation. In Western democracies scholarly attention is given to the actions of consumers. Citizens practise political consumerism in different forms: through 'positive buying' ('buycott'), when products are bought for certain reasons; or 'moral boycott' ('boycott'), i.e. negative purchasing and company-based purchasing. These two forms – boycotting and buycotting – are often considered as major forms of political consumption (Neilson 2010, 214). An individual consumer as a sovereign agent is capable of significantly influencing the structures and practices of consumer culture (Autio, Heiskanen, and Heinonen 2009, 40). One can boycott or buycott in order to resist or support state politics, corporations, and groups of interest. As sociologists have argued, political consumers recognize that despite the dominant power of the state and corporations, consumers still have the power to meaningfully interact with and influence them. Therefore, political consumerism gives power and agency to the consumer. Political consumerism can be observed in various movements, including anti-globalist, anti-corporate, and ecological movements, as well as in practices of eco-consumption, collaborative consumption, street art, and others.

The category of political consumerism can potentially explain consumer patterns in today's Russia, where the state plays a significant role in the regulation of consumption and consumer practices, while the forms of citizens' political participation are limited. The actions of the state and the way in which the state practises political consumerism can be explained through the concepts of 'biopower' or 'biopolitics', a technology of power which implies the state's exercising of political power over its citizens' bodies (Foucault 2009; 2010). Biopolitics as a technology of disciplining citizens' bodies targets such areas as health, sexuality, hygiene, and others. It can also extend into the domain of consumption as a sphere of private life and the bodily practices of the citizen. Andrei Makarychev and Sergei Medvedev argue that Russia is currently going through a 'biopolitical turn' – with the extension of state power into private lives with the purpose of legitimizing and strengthening the regime (Makarychev and Medvedev 2015). Biopolitics is usually approached as a set of political regulations and actions of state-affiliated institutions, i.e. attention is focused on biopolitics 'from above'. At the same time, various agents can be involved in political consumerism. In this chapter I show how ordinary consumers communicate with the state while exercising political consumerism and, thus, try to reclaim their power 'from below'.

State, political consumerism, and nation-building in Russia

In Russia, political consumerism means that the state takes an active part in shaping national belonging through consumption. This situation is not new or specific to contemporary Russia. The 'top-down' approach to consumption was a feature of the socialist era. Also, there are many examples of how the state shapes consumption in different contexts, including in Western democracies; for instance, in the US the state has launched campaigns based on the patriotic motive of purchasing American consumer goods to support the economy in times of crisis (Cohen 2001). One of the differences here is that in Russia the approach of the state is built on rejection of others – for instance, Western European and American products – and enforced by anti-Western propaganda and economic measures, as we will see below. In the USA, this campaign is enforced by consumption of American goods rather than rejection of non-American products. The role of the state in shaping consumption and national belonging has been discussed in relation to other historical, cultural, and political contexts, such as, for example, fashion in the totalitarian regimes of fascist Italy (Paulicelli 2004), Nazi Germany (Guenther 2004), and Maoist China (Chen 2001); other examples include contemporary Turkey (Özkan and Foster 2005) and post-socialist Lithuania (Klumbyte 2010).

In Russia, the state regulation of consumption, or state-led political consumerism, is implemented through different measures both outside and inside the country. Outside the country, state-led political consumerism can be seen through economic actions, such as embargos, or partial or complete trade prohibitions with a particular country. During the last two decades Russia has had rich experience of bans on different consumer products from a range of countries. Since 2006, the Russian government has banned wines and mineral water from Georgia, Polish meat, Moldovan wine, Latvian fish, Belarusian dairy products, and Ukrainian sweets, among other goods. Interestingly, the major reasons for such embargos are biopolitical and include Russian citizens' health: namely, that these products fall short of proper certification, or that they do not meet hygienic requirements and, therefore, are 'hazardous' and pose a health risk (Smolchenko 2006). Yet experts suggest that this reasoning 'is suspicious' (T. J. 2013). Rather, Russia uses the bans 'as a weapon against countries that align themselves against Moscow' (Anon. 2014c). In other words, experts suppose that the major reason for such embargos, rather than healthcare, is to target political non-allies through economic mechanisms. The banned goods are often export products which contribute significantly to the other country's national economy. Among the banned import countries were also those that had created or planned to create better relations with the US and the EU.

Consumption in the country is shaped similarly by economic sanctions backed by the argument of taking care of citizens' health. For instance, recent measures of state-led political consumerism include inspections of the fast-food chain McDonald's. In August 2014 12 branches of McDonald's across the country were temporary closed over 'allegations of sanitary violations' (Anon. 2014b). An interesting set of interpretations has been offered to explain this fact. The state officially accused McDonald's of inadequate hygiene conditions. Experts and journalists emphasized the political explanation, stating that the closure 'coincided with the heightened tensions over the Ukrainian crisis of 2014' (Anon. 2014b). The American urban sociologist Saskia Sassen, who visited St Petersburg at the time, commented on this situation and emphasized that,

> if McDonald's leaves Russia, the market will stay anyway, because the chain will leave the market not because consumers abandoned it. Therefore, a place for local business will open up [...] So if McDonald's is leaving, the positive side has to be seen – an opportunity for a local business.
>
> (Galkina 2014)

Sassen's opinion falls into an anti-globalist and anti-capitalist discursive framework typical of the criticism of McDonald's in Western democracies. On the one hand, indeed, McDonald's is a multinational corporation, an 'evil servant' of capitalism that – if it appears in the neighbourhood – takes over both clientele and cash from small, local businesses. Yet this kind of criticism eliminates the role of the state as an agent of political consumerism in Russia. Through economic sanctions the state intervenes the market, tries to control various agents from transnational corporations to small local firms, promotes the East/West confrontation, and takes control over its citizens' lifestyle choices and bodies.

Another strategy of the state to exercise power through political consumerism is through the production of a patriotic subject. In Russia consumption has recently served as a sphere in which debates around national identity have taken place. From this point of view, the nation is considered as an 'imagined consumer community'. Consumption serves as a resource for political identification and a unifying force across the nation (see Trentmann 2007; Foster 1999). In 2014 the official, state-led discourse combined national identity and consumption through such categories as 'patriotism' and 'self-respect'. Several examples highlight how the state shapes the bodies, appearance, and consumer behaviour of its citizens. On 1 July 2014 Russia (along with Belarus and Kazakhstan, the other members of the Customs Union) banned the production and export of lacy underwear manufactured from synthetic fibre. This regulation aims to protect consumers 'against synthetic garments which do not absorb enough moisture. That could cause skin problems' (Kottasova 2014). In turn, experts have argued that lacy underwear does not cause harm; yet this measure will make the prices go up and open yet another door for bribery and for restructuring the market (the share of imported underwear in Russia is about 80 per cent), allowing the state to control yet another part of citizens' lives and bodies. Finally, this regulation removes agency from the consumers, restricting their ability to decide what kind of underwear to buy and wear (Abrosimova 2014).

Various regulations concerning the body and appearance can be traced in the speech of fashion historian Alexander Vasiliev at the State Duma. Vasiliev talked about a 'Russian style in fashion', associating it with pre-revolutionary traditional dress. He suggested that it was time to give up 'plastic flowers from Hong Kong' and instead wear the Russian national head-dress (*kokoshnik*). Thus Vasiliev offered a way of constructing a national identity through the utilization of historical dress and dress codes.[2] In general, addressing past fashion trends is a well-known strategy of nation-building (Kalinina 2014). But why, then, should such a progressive sphere as fashion turn to pre-revolutionary traditional dress rather than, for instance, to post-revolutionary trends known for their experimentation and modernity? The answer is that the proposed changes have to fit the neo-conservative agenda that has been pushed forward by the Russian authorities in various spheres of cultural and social life, and to which traditional clothing corresponds better than modern, experimental designs.

In addition, Vasiliev criticized the way women dress in the State Duma, advising them not to wear high heels, above-the-knee skirts, and loose hair, suggesting that these features are an expression of sexuality (Anon. 2014d). Besides, one of the members of the State Duma introduced a proposal to prohibit high heels, sneakers, and ballerinas, as they supposedly posed a danger to the health of Russians, causing 'flat-foot, varicose veins and chronic venous insufficiency' (Anon. 2014e). In fact, such bans, although neither of them were in the end implemented, targeted the lifestyle of the middle class, among whom sneakers and ballerina shoes were popular at that time. The middle class was coincidentally also the group that protested loudest against election fraud and thus against the authorities during the Snow Revolution of 2011–12. Two arguments are used to support the actions of the state: one of 'returning to the roots', meaning conservative ideals from the past, and one about citizens' health.

These ways of shaping a patriotic subject through fashion and clothing exemplify the principle of biopolitics 'from above', or the technologies of discipline and control of institutions affiliated with the state over its citizens' bodies. Besides the state, other agents also take part in political consumerism: business companies and corporations, as well as citizens, are involved in the sphere of the cultural production of fashion.

Consumer nationalism and cultural producers in Russia

Producers and sellers seek popular support on the market: they want to make a profit by offering consumer goods that are in demand. This market-driven political consumerism has been called 'neoliberal nationalism' (Foster 1999, 264; Özkan and Foster 2005). Neoliberal nationalism is expressed through the market activities of producers and resellers in the promotion and sale of consumer goods which express national belonging.

Russian producers and resellers actively develop the patriotic agenda offered by the state and deploy it in their production and marketing strategies. Many examples can be seen in stores, which offer patriotic T-shirts and other products with a large range of printed inscriptions. Some are quite neutral, such as 'Made in Russia', while others are rather aggressive, such as 'My grandfather did not need a visa for his trip to Berlin in 1945'.[3] This aggressive form of negative nationalism turns its back to the world, isolating the country and seeing others as enemies (see Özkan and Foster 2005).

A new discursive frame, combining consumption and nationalism, is currently in the process of formation in Russia: this frame may be called 'patriotic fashion'. Clothing designers – as cultural intermediaries – participate in creating this trope. The well-known Russian designer Leonid Alekseev, who had a boutique in St Petersburg, participated in fashion weeks, and was quite successful in the fashion business, at some point closed down his label and started to work as designer for the Russian Ministry of Defence. In an interview he summarizes this patriotic fashion trope:

Patriotism is an inner feeling; that's why it can't pass: you either rejoice in the success of your native country or you don't. I may love other countries, people who live in other cities and their creative work, but that doesn't prevent me from being a patriot. We are eventually ridding ourselves from that complex of embarrassment when you meet your compatriots abroad. We begin to realize that we can be educated, cultured and interesting. We are slowly accepting ourselves as Russians.

(Karpova 2014)

The collection of patriotic clothes includes military balaclavas, sweatshirts, shorts, trousers, and parkas with patriotic inscriptions; it illustrates how patriotic feeling is marketed and monetized in fashion.

Another example of patriotic fashion is the products manufactured by the designer duo ANYAVANYA (Anna Trifonova and Ivan Ershov). The duo has produced T-shirts with 15 different prints, including Vladimir Putin's portrait. The designers explained their choice as follows: 'All these developments speak of the strengthening of our country in the world. This is ultimately thanks to Vladimir Putin; he is a strong president and we are proud of him' (Redaktsiia 2014). A delivery of 5,000 T-shirts caused a queue in the State Department Store (GUM) in Moscow and was sold out within a day. Another designer duo, Anastasiia Zadorina and Kseniia Mel'nikova, also produced T-shirts for people who identified themselves as 'patriots' and wanted to express their (fashionable) patriotism through clothing choices. The designers launched the campaign 'Fashionable Sanctions' in response to the US and EU sanctions against Russia, with the purpose of 'showing the world that Russia is not afraid of sanctions' and proving that 'it is possible to be fashionable and patriotic simultaneously'.[4] During this campaign people could exchange any piece of old clothing (T-shirt, sweatshirt) for a patriotic T-shirt with inscriptions. Interestingly, this campaign was supported by the Committee of Public Relations in Moscow, i.e. a state body. Therefore, neoliberal nationalism in this case is also state-driven.

Alternatively, the designer Katia Dobriakova, known for her projects and collaboration with the political opposition in Russia, offered her version of Putin's look on a T-shirt with a line from a Russian fairy-tale, 'If I were a tsarina…', right after the protests in 2011. Dobriakova noted that the T-shirt allowed self-expression and communicated social standing or preferences (Vorkova 2014). She is known for her other projects with the political opposition, such as creating T-shirts for the TV personality and media celebrity Kseniia Sobchak, who was involved in the Russian opposition movement in 2011–12.

Good buy, glamour: welcome, patriotic fashion

One of the most interesting examples of patriotic fashion as a biopolitical strategy is the recent discussion on glamour, which reflects the production of patriotic subjects in a state-led discourse. In the article 'The Misery of

Glamour', written in Soviet propaganda style in the leading state-sponsored newspaper *Rossiiskaia gazeta*, the cult of consumption and glamour that has developed in Russia during past 20 years is questioned and severely criticized (Orlov 2014). The basis for this criticism is the Western origin of glamour as an ideology of a consumer society and of the glossy journals which promote it. At first sight, the content of glossy journals, the glamour ideology, and the 'cult of consumption' are not dangerous. But the author of the article concludes that glossy magazines are 'not without danger', because they have a significant influence over people, especially the younger generation: they produce new heroes and promote types that are approved by the Western businesses which pay for advertisements. 'What will happen if it becomes unfashionable to respect your own country'?, the newspaper asks.

Glamour has been the ideology of the elite and the middle class in Russia during the first decade of the 2000s. The state has used various methods to get control over the middle class since the protests of 2011–12; yet it is not the middle class which is the immediate focus of criticism in this particular article. Rather, the article targets the opinion makers and leaders, such as It-girls, fashion models, bloggers, and designers, most of whom belong to the elite as they are wives and/or daughters of tycoons and politicians. These It-girls, blogger Miroslava Duma, fashion model Elena Perminova, designers Ul'iana Sergeenko and Vika Gazinskaia, are known outside of Russia thanks to social media and their reputation in the fashion world. In Orlov's article they are called 'glamour dissidents': while participating in global fashion to represent Russia, they also criticize and 'belittle their home country' (Orlov 2014). For example, Miroslava Duma, according to the newspaper, refused to support young fashion designers from Russia who were sponsored by the state at the Milan Fashion Week. Vika Gazinskaia (rightfully) condemned the domestic fashion industry for problems with the infrastructure, low levels of education, and lack of state support (Orlov 2014). Ul'iana Sergeenko complained that 'people in Russia do not like her nor her brand [...] They do not want to develop, be successful and have a job. Instead they prefer to be aggressive towards everything around. It is hard to call our country very successful' (Orlov 2014).

The core of the criticism lies in the differences in the newspaper journalist and the designers' understandings of patriotism. While they are involved in the global fashion scene, these It-girls present their Russian identity and, at the same time, they have to be cosmopolitan in order to communicate this identity and be understood elsewhere, acting thus as 'cosmopolitan patriots' (cf. Nussbaum 1994). It is largely thanks to them that Russian fashion has appeared on the global map (Belaia 2014). The designers use national culture as an inspiration for their collections, as is the case for Sergeenko's feminine retro-style. They also allocate the production of clothing to Russia. Kseniia Sobchak has supported the It-girls in her column, stating that 'even in a not so simple political situation they continue to be proud of their nationality and, whenever possible, avoid complicated issues of geopolitics'

(Sobchak 2014). These designers are 'real' patriots, who build their brands on Russian heritage and create jobs for Russian citizens, claims Sobchak. Indeed, Ekaterina Kalinina, who conducted research on Russian clothing designers, proves in her article that designers in Russia have a 'very strong national identity' (Kalinina 2013). This cosmopolitan way of communicating Russian identity is not accepted by *Rossiiskaia gazeta*. For the Russian state, patriotism and patriotic fashion should be a new glamour. In the context of ideological competition with the West, one has to be clearly on one or the other side, and criticism of the country is perceived as sabotage; therefore the designers are labelled 'dissidents' in the newspaper.

Lifestyles and consumer citizenship

It is not only state and cultural intermediaries who are involved in political consumerism; ordinary citizens also take an active part in it. The key term that reflects the combination of consumption, nationalism, and agency is 'citizen-consumer', which refers to a person who makes consumer choices from the point of view of a larger public interest rather than from an egoistic interest of self-indulgence and pleasure-seeking, as do 'customer-consumers' (see Cohen 2001).

Consumer citizenship has seen a tremendous increase during and after the protests of 2011–12. Fashion has always played a significant role in expressing one's identity, but at this time it became a sign of political concern. A quick glance at newspapers headings – 'Dress to impress before you protest', 'Russian protests as a fashionable affair', 'White protest ribbons all the rage for chic Russians' – supports this argument. Also, the blog 'Fashion on the Barricades' (*Moda na barrikadakh*), created by fashion designer Aleksandr Arutiunov, reflects the connection between fashion and protests.[5] According to these sources, the identities of the protesters were to a large extent defined by their looks and, more generally, their lifestyles. As a result, certain looks were politicized. Several categories were applied to identify the protesters: they were labelled as belonging to the 'creative class', following Richard Florida, defining people as belonging to the academy, the sciences, and various creative professions (architecture, design, education, and arts, among others), whose economic function is to create new ideas, technologies, and products of original content (Florida 2011, 23). As Florida notes, the creative class has a particular style, which is exemplified by their liberal attitude to clothes: they do not appreciate uniforms and, in general, heavily rely on clothes as a means of self-realization. The style of the protesters in Russia was creative: hip and with self-irony. The protests were also called 'mink coats protests' to emphasize the wealth of the people involved. The most common fashion item, however, was the white ribbon as a symbol of fairness and honesty: 'students sympathetic to the cause sport them on backpacks while socialites tie them to their Prada purses' (Brinkworth 2012). On the opposite side to the protesters stood the working class; one of the noticeable figures among them was the young pro-Kremlin activist Sveta from Ivanovo, with her infamous line in broken Russian: 'We started to dress more better' (Gurova 2015, 1). Later, such working-class patriots and supporters of the Kremlin were labelled with reference to their clothes as '*vatniki*' (a pejorative term for 'quilted jacket', commonly worn by blue-collar workers and soldiers). This term, however, does not reflect their clothing choices directly and is a metaphor that refers to the class background of the Kremlin supporters and the lack of reflexivity towards the ruling regime.

Therefore, consumption and clothing have given Russian citizens possibilities for expressing their views, whether complying with the biopolitics of the state institutions or not. Citizens have used consumption not only to communicate their belonging, but also to support people and activities with similar views. For example, protesters have initiated boycotts of the television channel NTV, Procter & Gamble, and Yves Rocher for political reasons, as mentioned at the beginning of this chapter. They use lifestyle choices to express their belonging: for instance, the subscription to the anti-government television channel Dozhd' is in this sense a form of buycotting. Such actions are also known as 'alternative political actions' that allow 'inclusion for groups excluded from the formal body politics' (Trentmann 2007, 149).

Boycotts and buycotts are used not only by the opposition, but at both ends of the political spectrum: in 2012 supporters of the current government called for a boycott of 'made in Finland' goods because of the – they believe – biased policy of the Finnish social services which act against mothers with Russian citizenship (and, hence, against Russia) in the case of family issues involving children.

Political consumerism and popular support

In 2011–12 the actions of citizens that could be described as political consumerism were quite sporadic, whereas by 2014–15 the wider population had become more involved in issues of consumption and politics. In August 2014, when Russian sanctions were implemented in response to the European and American sanctions against Russia, which meant that Russia prohibited the import of grocery products from the EU, the US, and several other countries, more than 70 per cent of the Russian population approved of the sanctions, according to data from the Levada Centre (Gorbachev 2014). The majority of the population supported the sanctions towards groceries. For example, in response to the question of whether Russia had to respond to sanctions implemented against the country by Europe and the US, 39 per cent answered 'definitely', 33 per cent 'probably', 12 per cent 'probably not', 6 per cent 'definitely not', and 10 per cent gave no answer (Gorbachev 2014). In February 2015, 69 per cent of Russians said that Russia should continue its policy in response to the Western sanctions. They considered the sanctions a sign that the West fears Russia and, therefore, respects the country (Elkina 2015). Consumption for patriotic reasons also became more and more popular. For example, over 63 per cent of the inhabitants of Novosibirsk reported that they have positive emotions when they hear the words 'Made in Russia', because they feel proud and patriotic (Anon. 2014a). Yet the important feature of this kind of patriotism is that it is selective: citizens support the sanctions towards food, but do not support them in case of clothing, footwear, and other non-food items. Interestingly enough, the Russian government did not implement sanctions against non-food items at the time, probably taking into account these popular attitudes.

The question remains whether such actions can be classified as political consumerism and consumer citizenship. On the one hand, political consumerism and consumer citizenship both imply agency on the part of the consumer. In the case of support for sanctions, Russians act as political consumers and buy local products. At the same time, such actions might not be deliberate, since citizens are put in this position by the state and do not have much choice. Nevertheless, through the support for state policies in the area of consumption, i.e. sanctions, the wider population has become aware of how consumption can be used for political purposes. In this sense, people become involved in political consumerism, deliberately or not.

Why has consumer citizenship become widespread? One explanation comes from the point of view of increased well-being in Russia; during the first decade of the twenty-first century the country moved from a lower-income to a higher-income society. In the 1990s the level of subjective well-being was low: the majority of people were unhappy and dissatisfied with their lives (Inglehart 2000, 218). After a certain threshold (US$10 000 GNP per capita), people begin to emphasize quality of life, to show concern for such issues as environmental protection and, in general, post-materialistic values – among them environmental values, self-expression, a role in society, tolerance towards others and towards exotic things, and cultural diversity as interesting rather than threatening (Inglehart 2000, 218–219). Therefore, this concept can well explain the increase in political consumerism during 2011–12. Another explanation is that Russia has been maturing as a consumer society and its citizens have learnt to use consumption as a mechanism which has political implications.

In 2014–15 the economic conditions worsened due to economic crisis in Russia. The state started losing popular support and resorted to an intensified biopolitical discourse in order to discipline its citizens and take them under control (Makarychev and Medvedev 2015). The ideological competition with the West became a vital propaganda tool in the state's attempts to maintain popular support. Consumption continued to be one of the spheres in which this competition was constructed and implemented. Experts talk about 'the war between the fridge and the television' (Travin 2015), meaning that due to the recession, the lifestyle acquired over the past 10–15 years by Russian citizens – and not only by middle-class citizens – is currently falling; therefore propaganda is needed to strengthen the connection between consumption and patriotic feeling. To be patriotic means to support your own country and local producers, and to be prepared to limit consumption in times of austerity. In authoritarian regimes, such as Russia, the state uses televised propaganda to launch and maintain a campaign in support of this (Guriev and Treisman 2015). Whether this state strategy will work and help local producers and the domestic economy as well as citizens' well-being remains to be seen, because for such regimes political support is more important than economic success and the well-being of the citizens. Moreover, according to Inglehart (2000) – and judging by recent history, when well-being increases, citizens start protesting. Since the wider population has already gained the experience of political consumerism, we might hypothesize that they will use it in the future to express their own concerns vis-à-vis the state, if needed.

In lieu of a conclusion

The increase in political consumerism can be observed not only in Russia, but also across other former socialist states. Yet the perception and interpretation of political consumerism differs across nations. In Estonia, back in the 1990s, the consumption of Western (European, Scandinavian) consumer goods signified national independence and national belonging (Rausing 1998). At the beginning of the 2000s, in Lithuania the consumption of goods labelled 'Soviet' – for example, 'Soviet' sausages – was already seen not as a means of colonization and a threat to independence or democracy, but as a form of political engagement and a way of expressing the post-Soviet and European identities of the country (Klumbyte 2010). In Slovenia, scholars talk about 'commercial nationalism', which means 'taking responsibility for the nation's economic development' and, hence, 'maximizing individual prosperity' (Volcic and Andrejevic 2011). In Ukraine, the 'Don't buy Russian' campaign is an example of nation-building and consumer citizenship in the context of war. Hence, the question can be raised of what makes the Russian case different.

   The history of consumption contains many examples of political consumerism and expressions of national belonging through consumption. The differences lie in the agents who initiate such campaigns – the state or the citizens – and in the motives – whether economic, political, or socio-cultural. For example, in Russia the state acts as a strong agent of political consumerism with the political motive of seeking popular support. In comparison, in Estonia, Lithuania, and Ukraine political consumerism has grown 'from below' and was pushed by the citizens rather than the state (see Klumbyte 2010, 24). The meanings of such activities are also different, as mentioned above. In Russia, the meanings of political consumerism reflect to a certain extent Russia's postcolonial identity, i.e. the inferiority complex of the former empire that has lost its power and is trying to get it back. At the same time, many agents and groups utilize political consumerism differently and for different purposes, as is typical for democratic societies: to express their civic concerns, to communicate with the state and the market, and to express their political and national belonging as well as their class and other identities. In this sense, in recent years consumption has been embraced as an instrument of civil society in Russia and used in a way that it had not been before.

Notes

1 'Boycott Yves Rocher': www.boycottyvesrocher.com (accessed 22 July 2015).
2 The 'conservative turn' in Russia in various spheres is another phenomenon discussed (see Makarychev and Medvedev 2015). This and other examples illustrate that the conservative turn can also be observed in the sphere of consumption.
3 FuckAmerica.ru, internet store for patriotic goods: http://fuckamerica.ru/index. php?route=product/category&path=57 (accessed 3 April 2015).
4 Blog "Modnyi otvet – sanktsiiam net!": http://otvetim-net.ru/ (accessed 10 February 2015).
5 Currently the blog is non-existent; it used to be located at http://fashionprotest.ru/.

References

Abrosimova, Svetlana. 2014. "Komu 'zhmut' kruzhevnye trusy?" *Rosbalt* 21 February. www.rosbalt.ru/generation/2014/02/21/1236125.html (accessed 1 March 2015).
Anon. 2014a. "Bol'she poloviny zhitelei Novosibirska gordiatsia tovarami rossiiskogo proizvodstva – sotsiologi." *Sib.fm* 24 November. http://sib.fm/news/2014/11/24/bolshe-poloviny-zhitelej-novosibirska-gordjatsja-tovarami (accessed 11 February 2015).
Anon. 2014b. "McDonald's Says 12 Branches Closed over Food Safety Concerns." *The Moscow Times* 29 August. www.themoscowtimes.com/business/article/mcdonald-s-says-12-branches-closed-over-russian-safety-concerns/506135.html (accessed 1 March 2015).
Anon. 2014c. "Russia Tightens Screws on Ukraine with Candy Import Ban." *The Moscow Times* 5 September. www.themoscowtimes.com/news//business/article/russia-bans-sweets-imports-from-ukraine/506483.html (accessed 1 March 2015).
Anon. 2014d. "V Gosdume – anshlag. Istorik mody Aleksandr Vasil'ev posovetoval narodnym izbrannitsam 'zakazat' zhemchuzhnyi kokoshnik, chtoby vygliadet' prilichno khot' raz v zhizni'." *Znak.com* 1 October http://znak.com/urfo/news/2014-10-01/1029295.html (accessed 15 March 2015).
Anon. 2014e. "V Gosdume predlozhili zapretit' kedy i vysokie kabluki." *Lenta.ru* 19 June. http://lenta.ru/news/2014/06/19/shoes/ (accessed 3 April 2015).
Autio, Minna, Eva Heiskanen, and Visa Heinonen. 2009. "Narratives of 'Green' Consumers – the Antihero, the Environmental Hero and the Anarchist." *Journal of Consumer Behaviour* 8: 40–53.
Belaia, Alena. 2014. Pochemu mir rossiiskogo glamura obvinili v izmene rodine." *Wonder* 6 October. www.wonderzine.com/wonderzine/style/opinion/202057-russians-go-hard (accessed 1 February 2015).
Brinkworth, Dennis. 2012. "Trending: Russian Protests is a Fashionable Affair." *Haute Living* 29 February. www.hauteliving.com/2012/02/trending-russian-protests-is-a-fashionable-affair/258161/ (accessed 11 February 2015).
Carrigan, Marylyn, Isabelle Szmigin, and Joanne Wright. 2004. "Shopping for a Better World? An Interpretive Study of the Potential for Ethical Consumption within the Older Market." *Journal of Consumer Marketing* 21 (6): 401–417.

Chen, Tina Mai. 2001. "Dressing for the Party: Clothing, Citizenship, and Gender-formation in Maoist China." *Fashion Theory* 5 (2): 143–172.

Cohen, Lizabeth. 2001. "Citizens and Consumers in the United States in the Century of Mass Consumption." In *The Politics of Consumption: Material Culture and Citizenship in Europe and America*, edited by M. Daunton and M. Hilton, 203–221. New York: Berg.

Elkina, Mariia. 2015. "Rossiiane predlagaiut vvesti zhestkie otvetnye sanktsii protiv zapada." *Izvestiia* 3 February. http://izvestia.ru/news/582590 (accessed 12 February 2015).

Florida, Richard. 2011. *Kreativnyi klass: Liudi, kotorye meniaiut budushchee.* Moscow: Klassika-XXI.

Foster, Robert. 1999. "The Commercial Construction of 'New Nations'." *Journal of Material Culture* 4 (3): 263–282.

Foucault, Michel. 2009. *Security, Territory, Population. Lectures at the College de France, 1978–1979.* London: Picador.

Foucault, Michel. 2010. *The Birth of Biopolitics. Lectures at the College de France, 1978–1979.* London: Picador.

Galkina, Iulia. 2014. "Ekonomist Saskia Sassen o tom, pochemu bedneiut goroda". *The Village* 16 September. www.the-village.ru/village/city/city-interview/164629-saskiya-sassen-o-peterburge (accessed 18 September 2014).

Gorbachev, Aleksei. 2014. "Otvetnye sanktsii – eto pravil'no." *Nezavisimaia gazeta* 8 August. www.ng.ru/politics/2014-08-08/3_opros.html (accessed 11 February 2015).

Guenther, Irene. 2004. *Nazi Chic? Fashioning Women in the Third Reich.* Oxford: Berg.

Guriev, Sergei, and Daniel Treisman. 2015. "The New Authoritarianism," *Vox* 21 March. www.voxeu.org/article/new-authoritarianism (accessed 15 March 2015).

Gurova, Olga. 2015. *Fashion and the Consumer Revolution in Contemporary Russia.* London and New York: Routledge.

Inglehart, Ronald. 2000. "Globalization and Postmodern Values." *The Washington Quarterly* 23 (1): 215–228.

Kalinina, Ekaterina. 2013. "Venäjän luovan luokan kuoppainen tie." *Idantutkimu* 3: 19–36.

Kalinina, Ekaterina. 2014. *Mediated Post-Soviet Nostalgia.* Huddinge: Sodertorns Hogskola.

Karpova, Aleksandra. 2014. "V lichnom tvorchestve ia kodiroval svoi idei, a zdes' rasskazyvaiu o tom, chem ivliaetsia armiia." *Time Out St Petersburg* 1 December. www.timeout.ru/spb/feature/439194 (accessed 23 July 2015).

Klumbyte, Neringa. 2010. "The Soviet Sausage Renaissance." *American Anthropologist*, 112 (1): 22–37.

Kottasova, Ivana. 2014. "Protests over Russia, Belarus and Kazakhstan 'Ban' on Lacy Underwear." *CNN* 21 February. http://edition.cnn.com/2014/02/21/business/kazakhstan-lace-underwear-ban/ (accessed 1 March 2015).

Littler, Jo. 2009. *Radical Consumption. Shopping for Change in Contemporary Culture.* New York: Open University Press.

Makarychev, Andrei and Sergei Medvedev. 2015. "Biopolitics and Power in Putin's Russia." *Problems of Post-Communism* 62: 45–54.

Micheletti, Michele. 2003. *Political Virtue and Shopping: Individuals, Consumerism and Collective Action.* New York: Palgrave.

Neilsen, Lisa A. 2010. "Boycott or Buycott? Understanding Political Consumerism." *Journal of Consumer Behaviour* 9: 214–227.

Nussbaum, Martha. 1994. "Patriotism and Cosmopolitanism." *The Boston Review* 1 October. www.bostonreview.net/martha-nussbaum-patriotism-and-cosmopolitanism (accessed 11 August 2016).

Orlov, Petr. 2014. "Glamurnaia nishcheta." *Rossiiskaia gazeta* 3 October. www.rg.ru/2014/10/03/fashion.html (accessed 1 February 2015).

Özkan, Derya and Robert Foster. 2005. "Consumer Citizenship, Nationalism, and Neoliberal Globalization in Turkey: The Advertising Launch of Cola Turka." *Advertising and Society Review* 6 (3). www.volkskunde.uni-muenchen.de/vkee_download/derya/oezkan_colaturka.pdf (accessed 11 August 2016).

Paulicelli, Eugenia. 2004. *Fashion under Fascism: Beyond the Black Shirt.* Oxford: Berg Publishers.

Rausing, Sigrid. 1998. "Signs of New Nation: Gift Exchange, Consumption and Aid on a Former Collective Farm in North-West Estonia." In *Material Cultures: Why Some Things Matter*, edited by D. Miller, 189–213. Chicago: University of Chicago Press.

Redaktsiia. 2014. "'Samye vezhlivye futbolki' vyzvali kolossal'nyi azhiotazh." *Ridus* 12 June. www.ridus.ru/news/161887 (accessed 10 February 2015).

Smolchenko, Anna. 2006. "Russia Says Banned Wines Contain DDT." *The Moscow Times* 7 April. www.themoscowtimes.com/sitemap/free/2006/4/article/russia-says-banned-wines-contain-ddt/205745.html (accessed 1 March 2015).

Sobchak, Kseniia. 2014. "O svete russkikh zvezd. Otvet Petru Orlovu," *Snob* 7 October. http://snob.ru/profile/24691/blog/81990 (accessed 11 February 2015).

Strømsnes, Kristin. 2009. "Political Consumerism: A Substitute for or Supplement to Conventional Political Participation?" *Journal of Civil Society* 5 (3): 303–314.

T. J. 2013. "Why Has Russia Banned Moldovan Wine?" *The Economist* 25 November. www.economist.com/blogs/economist-explains/2013/11/economist-explains-18 (accessed 1 March 2015).

Travin, Dmitrii. 2015. "Voina televizora s kholodil'nikom." *Novaia gazeta* 9 February. http://novayagazeta.spb.ru/articles/9480/ (accessed 15 March 2015).

Trentmann, Frank. 2007. "Introduction: Citizenship and Consumption." *Journal of Consumer Culture* 7 (2): 147–158.

Volcic, Zara and Mark Andrejevic. 2011. "Nation Branding in the Era of Commercial Nationalism." *International Journal of Communication* 5: 598–618.

Vorkova, Vasilina. 2014. "Katia Dobriakova: 'Vse, chto my delaem, dolzhno byt' 'wow!'." *Look.tm* 22 December. http://look.tm/content/blog/katya-dobryakova (accessed 31 March 2015).

6 Even the toys are demanding free elections

Humour and the politics of creative protest in Russia

Jennifer G. Mathers

Introduction

In January 2012 the city of Barnaul in Siberia was the scene of one of the most unusual forms of political activism of Russia's protest winter of 2011–12: dozens of teddy bears, action figures, and Lego characters appeared overnight, grouped together in the snow, in a prominent place in the city. The toys were posed to mimic the stances that protesters had been taking in Moscow, St Petersburg, and other cities in Russia during December 2011 and January 2012, when they came together regularly to object to the manipulation of results in the December Duma elections, including the tiny banners that they held, which reproduced the slogans and demands of their human counterparts. The toy protest arose after local activists were repeatedly refused permission by the city's authorities to hold a more conventional meeting, and represented a form of double protest: against the city's officials and their ruling as well as against the way that the elections had been conducted in order to produce the predetermined results. This chapter sets Siberia's toy protest in the wider context of trends in Russia's protest movement before, during, and after the winter of 2011–12 and argues that humour, which was so apparent in the toy protest but also used extensively in other forms of protest, was a cleverly chosen tool that both expanded the appeal of the opposition's message and made it difficult for the regime to counter it effectively without risking looking (even more) foolish and inviting further laughter at its own expense.

Nano-meetings in the snow

One protester's banner reads, 'I support honest elections'. Another's simply displays '146%', a reference to the official voter turn-out in the Rostov oblast' in the December 2011 Duma elections, while a third holds a sign mimicking the insignia of the ruling United Russia party but with a monkey instead of a bear standing beneath the colours of the Russian flag. All of these messages and images regularly appeared on the signs carried by participants in the protests that took place in cities across Russia during the winter of 2011–12, when tens of thousands of people regularly came out onto the streets to express their anger at the conduct of Duma and presidential elections. What was different about this protest, however, was that the participants were only a few inches high and most were made of plastic. These were scenes from the toy protest in the Siberian city of Barnaul (Fig. 6.1).

Barnaul's citizens had been as outraged as their counterparts in Moscow when, in September 2011, Dmitrii Medvedev announced blandly that he would not be standing for a second term as Russia's president in March 2012 and would instead be stepping aside to allow Vladimir Putin to return to that office. Approximately 2,000 people came out onto the streets in Barnaul on 10 December, the first of a series of nationwide days of election protests in Russia following the announcement of the results of the disputed Duma vote (Elder 2012a). The size of the demonstration was large for a small city such as Barnaul, which has a population of around 700,000. While the proportion of protesters to city residents was less than 1 per cent, this was also the case for protests in the major cities, including Moscow. Encouraged by the obvious strength of local feeling about this issue, a group of activists sought permission from the city authorities for further demonstrations on other dates that had been announced as national days of protest. The city authorities in Barnaul refused these requests, unlike their counterparts in Moscow. One of the observed patterns of large-scale, explicitly political protest actions in Russia is that they tend to be focused in the major cities, particularly Moscow but also St Petersburg and, to a lesser extent, some other large urban areas. This has been explained by scholars of political science as reflecting cleavages in the political attitudes of Russian society between the metropolitan centres and the regions (Busygina and Filippov 2015). Another relevant explanatory factor, however, is that the officials in charge of considering requests for permits to stage protests – and policing those events – are well aware that events in the major cities will be under greater scrutiny from the world's media than those further from the public eye. This has, somewhat paradoxically, meant that it can be far easier to gain permission to hold a march or rally in Moscow, in the shadow of the Kremlin, than it is to hold a similar – or indeed much smaller – event in a location that is far from the centre of power and international attention. The experience of Barnaul bears this out.

After their requests for permits to hold more conventional gatherings were repeatedly denied, the leaders of the Barnaul protest group decided instead to organize an unconventional form of political participation: what Russian media reports described as a flash mob using toys, coordinating the action through the social networking website VKontakte. The first 'nano meeting' was held on 7 January 2012, outside the city's drama theatre, followed by a second, larger gathering in the same place a week later. For the 14 January event approximately 170 toys were collected to form what the organizers termed the 'all-Russia nano-action protest' (Nim 2012, 172). One of the organizers, a student named Liudmila Aleksandrova, described the refusal of the officials to grant a permit for protests as 'absurd' and explained that the local activists

Figure 6.1 Toy protest in Barnaul
Source: Sergey Teplyakov/VKontakte.

'wanted to hyperbolize this attempt and show the absurdity and farce of officials' struggle with their own people' (Elder 2012a).

The reaction of the police and other city officials to the January toy actions seemed to underline Aleksandrova's characterization. On the days of the toy protests the police solemnly photographed and took note of each figure and tiny placard, later releasing a statement that described the nano-meetings in rather sinister terms as an example of the use of 'new technologies' by the opposition and confirming that the action was nevertheless unsanctioned and therefore illegal. The protest organizers sought official permission again – but this time for a further toy protest on 4 February, to coincide with the next national day of action in advance of the presidential elections due one month later. The permit was requested for 100 Kinder Surprise toys, 100 Lego people, 20 model soldiers, 15 soft toys, and 10 toy cars, but it was refused on the grounds that the toys (particularly imported toys) were not citizens of Russia and indeed were not even people – a tongue-in-cheek response that suggests the humour of the situation was also appreciated by the city's officials (Nim 2012; O'Flynn 2012). The final act of the Barnaul toy protest took place on 19 February, when the organizers decided to hold an individual protest, in which only one toy was posed holding a placard, while another group of toys gathered nearby, waiting for their turn (Nim 2012).

The toy protest in Barnaul would appear to be an entertaining, whimsical but ultimately ephemeral episode in the 2011–12 winter of protests, with little importance beyond the fleeting amusement that it sparked as an overnight media and internet sensation, although it did inspire activists to organize their own nano-meetings in other Russian cities, including Irkutsk, Kazan, St Petersburg, Omsk, and Tomsk (Nim 2012, 179). To dismiss this unusual action on the part of activists in Barnaul as insignificant, however, would be to miss an opportunity to consider the light that it sheds on a distinctive feature of the 2011–12 protests in Russia: the important role played by the protesters' use of humour. The use of humour in protests is a feature that cuts across many of the geographical, generational, class, political, and cultural divisions of Russia and reveals something very interesting about the winter of election protests as well as the possibility for the further development of civil society in Russia in future.

Setting the toy protest into context: the use of humour in Russian protests

The use of humour in citizens' responses to the absurdities of both high and low politics is not a new phenomenon in Russia, of course. There is a long tradition of using humour to poke fun at everyday frustrations and the non-sense of political lies that must be ostensibly accepted at face value, even though bureaucrats and ordinary citizens alike are well aware of the yawn-ing chasm between official versions of reality and what happens in real life. Political satire was a feature of the Tsarist period and became highly devel-oped in the Soviet Union, particularly in the form of jokes, but also surfacing in novels, plays, films, and songs. Political jokes and anecdotes would spread quickly in Soviet society, and were so popular precisely because they revealed truths about the weaknesses, failures, and absurdities of the political and eco-nomic system that everyone understood but were too dangerous to express in other ways (Zlobin 1996; Davies 2007). In the early years of post-Soviet Russia, the political atmosphere was sufficiently open to allow the production and transmission of *Kukly* (*Puppets*), a popular television programme shown on NTV in the 1990s that used puppets to mock the speech and actions of prominent politicians.

The use of humour as a feature in protests against the arbitrariness, cor-ruption, or incompetence displayed by representatives of the state was rela-tively slow to emerge in post-Soviet Russia. Before December 2011, most of the protest actions that succeeded in attracting hundreds if not thousands onto the streets and in getting some kind of concessions from officials were serious affairs that focused on very specific problems that affected people's everyday lives (Evans 2012, 238). For example, in January and February 2005, pensioners gathered in major cities across Russia to protest against changes to state benefits that had recently come into effect. This so-called 'cotton revolution' (*sitsevaia revoliutsiia*, named for the cotton dresses worn by older women during the Soviet period) demonstrated the strength of feeling against the regime felt by a group – the elderly – that had previously contained its staunchest supporters (Robertson 2009, 532–534). Other protests between

2005 and 2011 were initiated, for example, by local people to try to prevent the destruction of their own homes, by motorists against a rise in the tariff on imported cars, by employees against the closure of factories, and by citizens against the withdrawal of local authority services (Evans 2012, 237). Threats to the environment joined threats to economic interests as a motivation for protest action, such as in the case of the Movement for the Defence of Khimki Forest, founded and led by Evgeniia Chirikova, in which citizens have come together since 2007 to oppose a major road-building scheme that combined illegality (at the time that it was launched) with the destruction of a swathe of protected woodland and a substantial reduction in the quality of life of local residents (Evans 2012, 234–236).

But while most of these protests reflecting the everyday concerns of ordinary people were not notable for their use of humour, there were some signs that more creative and whimsical forms of action were creeping into the repertoire. The 2005 pensioners' protests referred to above were remarkable for the cooperation of different opposition factions. This included youth groups, who began to develop creative and performative forms of protest, such as throwing food or flowers at prominent political figures, engaging in street theatre, and organizing flash mobs (Robertson 2009, 534–536). Perhaps the first protest group both to make extensive use of humour and to gain widespread popular attention and support for its cause was the Society of Blue Buckets (*Obshchestvo sinikh vederok*).

Since 2009 car owners in several cities (including, but not limited to, Moscow and St Petersburg) have staged protests against the abuse of *migalki*, the spinning blue lights that high-ranking officials are entitled to place on their cars in order to speed through traffic and get them to important appointments on time. The reckless driving of many of these cars on crowded city streets is responsible for traffic accidents on a regular basis. The spread of dashboard-mounted cameras in Russian cars has made it easy for outraged drivers to upload footage of this behaviour onto the Internet, raising awareness of the problem and generating anger at the contempt shown by officials towards the safety of ordinary citizens (Elder 2010). In addition to angry responses to the abuses of the *migalki* by those who were entitled to use them, it was common knowledge that the distribution of *migalki* was spread much more widely than to those who held certain official posts. The handing out of the blue lights and the privileges they bestowed as a way of granting favours or as payment for bribes was therefore an additional source of anger, further reinforcing the perception that many of those occupying public office in Russia saw no need to follow the rules that they were charged with upholding.

The response by motorists to the abuse of *migalki* was not to organize a more traditional protest, such as a rally outside government offices. Instead, they placed blue plastic buckets on their cars and drove in processions on major avenues of Russian cities (Evans 2012, 237). The choice to use such humble objects in their protests was an inspired move: it ensured that the means of expressing outrage were accessible to all (unlike the real *migalki*) and it provided a stark and humorous contrast to the trappings that self-important officials used to separate themselves from the ordinary citizens whose taxes paid their salaries. The mimicry by the blue bucket drivers poked gentle fun at a ridiculous situation while also drawing attention to popular outrage at an example of abuse of power that placed Russians in real danger and was costing lives. The responses of officials were generally muted and limited to minor fines, while promises were made to rein in the abuses of *migalki*. Opinion polls conducted in 2010 indicated that a clear majority (68 per cent) of Muscovites approved of the actions of the Society of Blue Buckets (Evans 2012, 237), suggesting that some combination of the cause, the universality of the experience (millions of road users in Russia would have had personal experience of sitting in traffic while watching a car with a spinning blue light speed past them), and the form that the protest took resonated with Russian society.

The Blue Buckets protest against the abuse of *migalki* is an intriguing example of an issue that affects ordinary people – and thus fits the pattern of successful protest identified above, in which the target of the protest is an issue that affects people in their everyday lives – but at the same time also crosses the line into criticism of the political failure of the state. Evidence of corrupt practices and personal gain on the part of elected officials are clearly political issues, and they are damning indictments of the state's failure to provide a basic level of equitable treatment of its citizens, especially concerning the even-handed enforcement of the state's own laws.

The state's refusal to enforce its own laws and to deliver on its own promises of free and fair elections, of course, was at the heart of the 2011–12 winter of protests, together with a strong sense of outrage that, with Putin and Medvedev swapping places, fundamental decisions about the political order in Russia were taken in ways that showed contempt for ordinary people (Vasilyeva 2012). What has fascinated scholars of political science and international relations, however, is the willingness of so many Russians to take to the streets in a series of explicitly political demonstrations in sharp contrast to the well-established practice described above, where more concrete and less-obviously political issues motivated Russians to take action (Robertson 2009; Evans 2012; Gel'man 2015). This sense of outrage at the Putin-Medvedev deal for deciding who should occupy the most powerful political position in the country, which many people regarded as a crime against them on a personal level – the removal of their opportunity to make a choice, the stealing of their votes – was undoubtedly a key factor. It is also possible that the tone and atmosphere of many of the protests themselves contributed to the unprecedented willingness of so many to come out repeatedly onto the streets in favour of the ability to exercise a political right. The accounts of many of the participants in the protests refer to the relaxed, sociable, and even light-hearted manner in which the vast majority of the actions were conducted (see, for example, Vasilyeva 2012 and Levinson 2012). Many of the protests had a festive atmosphere, in spite of the presence of large numbers of police and other security services in riot gear, and it was not unusual for participants to bring young children and pets with them to the demonstrations and marches (Jonson 2015, 206). The use of creative forms of protest, and especially the good-natured sense of humour that largely prevailed, was an important component of this atmosphere.

Creativity and humour were integral to the opposition discourse that developed even before the December 2011 Duma elections, for example through Aleksei Navalnyi's successful campaign to popularize the term 'Party of Crooks and Thieves' (*Partiia zhulikov i vorov*) as an alternative slogan for United Russia. In the weeks before the December 2011 Duma elections, Navalnyi and his supporters photographed and disseminated on social media examples of United Russia posters and stickers that had been replaced or defaced with the 'Party of Crooks and Thieves' slogan. These were signs, well before the actual examples of election fraud came to light, that the elections would be met not only with disbelief and anger, but also with mocking and satire. Protesters turned to humour at the very beginning of the actions: once the results were announced and the first, spontaneous demonstration against them on the evening of 5 December was forcibly broken up by the police, Navalnyi took a photo of his fellow protesters and tweeted it from inside the police van where they were being held (Kelly et al. 2012), setting a trend for protesters to take photos of themselves under arrest and post them to social media websites, sometimes accompanied by commentary on the poor quality of the signals they were able to pick up on their phones while inside police vehicles.

The incorporation of humorous, imaginative, and whimsical features permeated the winter and spring of protests, alongside more conventional and traditional forms of action such as marches and rallies addressed by leading activists. The protesters quickly adopted the colour white as a symbol of the winter of election protests, wearing white ribbons when they attended marches or rallies. This expanded to the wearing of white scarves and the carrying of white flowers or balloons and, in some cases, tying white balloons to cars as they were driven around on protest days. This was most notable on 29 January and 19 February, when motorists sympathetic to the protests were encouraged to tie white balloons and ribbons to their cars and drive them slowly around Moscow's Garden Ring. The weekend following the second, white-bedecked car action (which was also the final weekend before the presidential elections) was the occasion of 'The Big White Ring'. This was a pedestrian action, in which people were asked to wear or carry something white and stand side by side along the Garden Ring, with would-be protesters directed to a Facebook account to reserve their places (Levinson 2012).

The humorous dimension of the protests was clearly dynamic, and evolved in response to the state's – and especially Putin's – reactions to them. In the course of his 15 December 2011 annual live television phone-in programme, during which Putin speaks to journalists and takes telephone questions posed by citizens across Russia, Putin famously claimed to have mistaken the white ribbons worn by the protesters at the first large-scale demonstration on 10 December for condoms. Undaunted by this attempt to belittle the symbol of their protests, participants in subsequent actions did actually wear condoms on their coats as well as carrying signs and banners that referred to Putin's comment. The regime also responded to the white ribbon protests by staging their own, pro-regime and pro-Putin rallies, composed largely (although not entirely) of those who had been intimidated or paid into participating. In addition to the contrast between the prevailing motives for participating in the pro- and anti-regime actions, there was a visible disparity between the uniformity of the accessories (pins, scarves and jackets, signs) worn and carried by the pro-Putin marchers and the more homespun, individualistic opposition equivalents (Ioffe 2012). One of the messages on many of the banners and placards carried by pro-regime protesters was 'If not Putin, then who?' (*Esli ne Putin, to kto*), referring to the lack of alternative candidates commanding comparable levels of support from across the country. Some of the participants in the white ribbon protests responded with the rival slogan, 'If not Putin, then a cat' (*Esli ne Putin, to kot*) – both a clever play on words, reversing the last two letters of the Russian word 'who' (*kto*) to form the word 'cat' (*kot*), as well as a clear indication that the protesters refused to take seriously the notion that Putin was irreplaceable.

Even after the 6 May 2012 rally at Moscow's Bolotnaya Square that turned into violent clashes with the police and led to the arrest of more than 400 protesters, creativity and good humour continued to be a feature of the white ribbon protests. The action in Moscow that followed the 6 May arrests was a series of flash mobs, with participants assembling in public places and camping out overnight. One group settled in a plaza on Chistye Prudy boulevard near a statue of the nineteenth-century Kazakh poet Abay Kunabayev, which quickly turned into a camp that became known as 'Occupy Abay' (Englund 2012; Elder 2012b). The camp was maintained for more than a week by a shifting collection of protesters who sang songs and conducted more and less serious political discussions, and who represented different age groups and socio-economic classes as well as different political views, from leftists to nationalists (Vasilyeva 2012). Although by June the camp was dismantled by the police, before that happened there was another notable protest action in Moscow linked to 'Occupy Abay': a peaceful stroll through the city of approximately 15,000 protesters wearing white ribbons, led by a group of prominent writers including Boris Akunin and Liudmila Ulitskaia. Participants and journalists remarked on the friendly and good-humoured atmosphere. This included the attitude of the police lining the route, who seemed to go out of their way to aid rather than impede the strollers (Elder 2012b; Englund 2012). Similar 'Occupy' camps and strolls took place in other cities across Russia in May 2012, including St Petersburg, Novosibirsk, Nizhny Novgorod, Astrakhan, and Vladivostok (Garmazhapova et al. 2012).

Although the regular, frequent staging of mass protests effectively came to an end in the spring of 2012, the use of creative and humorous formats for registering dissatisfaction with the state continued. One such example is the 'Make Bureaucrats Work' campaign in Yekaterinburg that emerged later that year, which was focused on the failure of local officials to maintain the roads. Activists drew attention to this dereliction of duty by spray-painting the portraits of those responsible around the potholes (with the holes forming the enormous, open mouths of the officials), together with quotations from promises made by the same officials to fix the problem. The action initially met with attempts at concealment, as one supporter of the campaign pointed out:

> At first, municipal services either painted over the pictures or removed a layer of asphalt. At night [campaign] initiators left additional graffiti 'To paint over isn't the same as fixing!' By morning, municipality workers had fully patched all the holes.
>
> (Konnander 2012)

The cause of maintaining Russia's roads was also taken up by Aleksei Navalnyi, who launched the 'RosYama' (Russian Hole) campaign in 2012, which featured his characteristic focus on using his knowledge of the details of Russian laws to hold officials to account – and to ridicule. RosYama operates a website that informs citizens of officials' obligation under Russian law to repair or cordon off any holes in the road that are larger than a specified size and invites road users to photograph potholes (with an indication in the photo of the size and location of the offending hole) and upload them. This generates a letter to the traffic police, notifying them of the infringement of the law and requesting action, which the driver can print and send. According to the website, more than 15,000 potholes have been repaired across Russia following the receipt of these letters. Navalnyi later added to the RosYama campaign with RosZhKKh (*Zhilishchno-kommunal'noe khoziastvo*, or Russian Communal Services), a website that provides a similar service to tenants who are struggling to get the local authorities to make large or small repairs to their homes (Loginov 2013). The accessible, engaging style of these campaigns combined with the practical support for citizens in solving practical problems provides an easy way for ordinary people to gain some experience in successfully challenging the state – even at a very local and mundane level.

What does fun have to do with political protest?

The literature on the role of humour in political protest highlights the ways that humour can act as a unifying force, drawing together otherwise disparate elements of a community and helping to forge a common identity (see, for example, Helmy and Frerichs 2013), as well as changing the dynamic between a regime and its opponents (Sorensen 2008). There were some striking similarities between the style of the Russian protests in 2011–12 and the extent to which protesters used creative and humorous forms of action in the wave of demonstrations in the Middle East that began in 2011. The protests in Cairo's Tahrir Square in January 2011 and subsequent overthrow of Hosni Mubarak have been called 'the laughing revolution' (Helmy and Frerichs 2013), while the occupiers of Gezi Park in Istanbul in June 2013 made extensive use of satire, bilingual jokes, and visual humour, much of it shared through social media (Yigit 2015; Gurel 2015).

These examples, as well as comparisons with the use of humour, mocking, and satire during the Soviet period, suggest that finding ways of laughing at authority attracts popular participation and support for protest movements in states with tightly controlled regimes. The importance of folk humour, parody, and laughter in creating an opportunity for ordinary people to challenge the holders of power was recognized by Mikhail Bakhtin and identified as dating back to medieval times and the tradition of the carnival or world turned upside down (Bakhtin 1984, 4–8). But while humour is sometimes described as a weapon of the weak or powerless (Davies 2007, 291), this weapon has a power of its own, and this is a power that rulers and regimes fear (Zlobin 1996). As Michel de Certeau noted, 'laughter can kill power that plays the role of Jupiter and that thus cannot tolerate it' (in Ward 2000, 65). When society finds the rules, structures, and leaders governing them comical, it suggests that the people have ceased to believe in the political realities created by the regime, and even calls into question the very legitimacy of that system of authority (Davies 2010). As Nikolai Zlobin has pointed out, 'ridicule is absolutely deadly, politically speaking' (Zlobin 1996, 223).

Perhaps this is why the pro-regime demonstrations and leading political figures for the most part did not themselves make use of humour in their actions. On the rare occasions when Putin mocked the protesters (such as his pretended confusion between white ribbons and condoms referred to above), it simply provided the opposition with more material for their mockery of him. The differences in social class and education levels between those attending white ribbon protests and those at pro-regime rallies may also be an important part of the explanation for the presence of creative and humorous forms of protest in the former and their absence in the latter. A survey of the participants in the 24 December 2011 protest in Moscow revealed that 62 per cent of them had experience of higher education, while those present at the 23 February 2012 pro-regime gathering at Luzhniki stadium were described as more traditionally defined working class (Wood 2012, 17).

Some of the leading figures in the Russian opposition movement have confirmed that the use of humour in the 2011–12 protests was a self-conscious choice: 'We considered that serious things are better presented through the prism of irony. What is said with pathos, people usually receive badly' (Jonson 2015, 134). Efforts were made by the organizers to make the forms that many of the protest actions took not only fun and engaging, but open to everyone. They were literally accessible to all, because the only props that they required were inexpensive, common objects that are not necessarily regarded as the tools of protest: children's toys, blue plastic buckets, cans of spray paint, balloons, ribbons. Such forms of protest are also accessible in the ways that they deliver their messages. The mechanisms are not difficult to understand in the way that they are conveyed – motorists mocking the driving behaviour of arrogant officials; caricatures of the holders of local offices with large, gaping mouths formed by the potholes in the roads they are responsible for maintaining; toys placed in the formations adopted by human protesters, carrying signs with the same slogans. Such protests also deliver their messages using forms of humour and mockery that can be widely understood. It is not necessary to have an advanced knowledge of or sympathy with difficult or controversial philosophies in order to understand that the wielders of bureaucratic power are being mocked when their caricatures are composed in part of enormous potholes.

These humorous forms of protest are also accessible in the sense that they are unlikely to cause offence to large sections of the population. There is a clear contrast here between the gentle mockery of placing blue plastic buckets on cars or protest placards in the hands of toys and the more bitingly sarcastic, confrontational – and obscure – forms of protest adopted by Pussy Riot. Even many of those who shared Pussy Riot's objections to the close ties between Putin's regime and the Russian Orthodox Church were offended and upset by their decision to use a cathedral – and one of the holiest of places within the cathedral, the space in front of the altar – as the venue for staging a protest against that relationship.

The contrast between creative and humorous forms of protest and the more traditional forms can be seen by considering the example of Strategy-31, a group whose mission is to raise popular awareness of Article 31 of the Russian Constitution, which guarantees Russian citizens the right to freedom of assembly, and to shame the Russian state for its failure to permit citizens to exercise that right. Since 2009 the group has conducted a campaign of civil disobedience by staging public gatherings on the 31st day of those months with 31 days. The organizers of Strategy-31 see themselves as the modern-day heirs of the Soviet-era dissident movement, both in their aims and in their choice of action, which echoes the dissidents' practice of holding regular demonstrations at particular locations at predetermined times (Horvath 2015). Strategy-31 and its actions, however, are relatively unknown to most Russians. While the message of their protest is very important, the rather abstract cause (the right to freedom of assembly in general rather than as a means to advance a particular issue) does not attract widespread support (Jonson 2015, 200). Perhaps another reason for the lack of public enthusiasm for its actions are their far more serious character, which lack whimsy or particularly memorable, imaginative, and creative forms that might attract and retain attention.

In addition to its benefits in attracting ordinary people to the protest movement, humour also provides a screen that can help to temper the responses of officials and security services. While security services know how to react to conventional protests and to violence, they find less conventional formats, and particularly those that involve absurdity, much more difficult to address. Responding in a heavy-handed way and using force in such situations risks making them look ridiculous and giving the movement further new material (Sorensen 2008, 183). This dynamic was borne out in the 2011–12 protests in Russia. For the most part, the police treated gently those protesters whose actions took good-humoured and less conventional forms, while those who engaged in more conventional forms of protest, such as the rallying, anti-regime speech for example, attracted more focused attention and more usual responses from the regime, namely the curtailment of events and arrests.

Conclusions

The examples discussed in this chapter suggest that the use of creative and humorous forms of protest – particularly the more gently mocking variety on display in the toy protests in Barnaul – both reflected and helped to perpetuate the character of the election protests in Russia during the winter of 2011–12. Ordinary people found the quirky, whimsical, and funny aspects of the actions accessible, appealing, and enjoyable. As one participant remarked, 'It's like [being] with friends' (Englund 2012). But although the use of humour helped to sustain the protests, it has also been criticized by some as a sign that the protesters did not take their actions seriously enough, paying too much attention to socializing and having fun and not enough to the business of politics. Indeed, the mass street protests ended without the regime agreeing to any of the demands of the protesters, most notably fair elections.

But while the 2011–12 protests did not achieve their political ambitions, there are signs that the use of unconventional forms of protest, including humour, mockery, and the absurd, are still seen as useful mechanisms for expressing ordinary citizens' dissatisfaction with the regime. More than three years after the original toy protest in Barnaul, the city was the source of another unexpected and humorous overnight media and internet sensation when, in December 2015, a group of citizens nominated a cat for election as mayor. Launched in the wake of multiple corruption scandals involving local elected officials, the campaign to make Barsik the cat the city's new mayor gathered considerable momentum. With the slogan 'Only mice don't vote for Barsik' (Fig. 6.2), the campaign managed to attract support from over 90 per cent of those participating in an unofficial online poll. As one local pensioner explained, 'People don't know who to trust anymore. They have come to the conclusion that they can't trust the authorities' (AFP 2015).

A distrust of the authorities in itself is not a sufficient condition for political activism, but the experience of recent years would suggest that this sentiment, together with the periodic use of creative, unexpected, and humorous

Figure 6.2 'Only mice don't vote for Barsik'; poster, Barnaul
Source: vk.com/altaionline.

forms of action, helps to engage ordinary Russians in the search for solutions to political problems, both large and small. Laughter may, therefore, represent the best hope for the development of civil society in Russia in both the short and the longer term.

References

AFP (Agence France-Presse). 2015. "Disgruntled Siberian City Wants Cat for Mayor." *The Guardian* 16 December. www.theguardian.com/world/2015/dec/16/disgruntled-siberian-city-wants-cat-for-mayor (accessed 8 February 2016).

Bakhtin, Mikhail. 1984. *Rabelais and His World*. Bloomington: Indiana University Press.

Busygina, Irina and Mikhail Filippov. 2015. "The Calculus of Non-Protest in Russia: Redistributive Expectations from Political Reforms." *Europe-Asia Studies* 67 (2): 209–223.

Davies, Christie. 2007. "Humour and Protest: Jokes under Communism." *International Review of Social History* 52: 291–305.

Davies, Christie. 2010. "Jokes as the Truth about Soviet Socialism." *Folklore* 46: 9–32.

Elder, Miriam. 2010. "Moscow's Limos Halted by Blue Buckets." *The Guardian* 28 May. www.theguardian.com/world/2010/may/28/russia-moscow-blue-buckets-cars (accessed 8 February 2016).

Elder, Miriam. 2012a. "Doll 'Protesters' Present Small Problem for Russian Police." *The Guardian* 26 January. www.theguardian.com/world/2012/jan/26/doll-protesters-problem-russian-police (accessed 8 February 2016).

Elder, Miriam. 2012b. "Russian Protests: Thousands March in Support of Occupy Abay Camp." *The Guardian* 13 May. www.theguardian.com/world/2012/may/13/russian-protests-march-occupy-abay (accessed 8 February 2016).

Englund, Will. 2012. "Russian Protesters, Led by Prominent Writers, Take a Peaceful Stroll in Moscow." *The Washington Post* 23 May. www.washingtonpost.com/world/europe/russian-protesters-led-by-prominent-writers-take-a-peaceful-stroll-in-moscow/2012/05/13/gIQAFkTpMU_story.html (accessed 8 February 2016).

Evans Jr, Alfred B. 2012. "Protests and Civil Society in Russia: The Struggle for Khimki Forest." *Communist and Post-Communist Studies* 45: 233–242.

Garmazhapova, Aleksandra, Kristina Farberova, Iaroslav Gunin, Aleksei Dmitriev, Dmitrii Trunov, Sergei Tepliakov, Dmitrii Antonenkov, and Ivan Petrov. 2012. "Okkupai RF!" *Gazeta.ru* 22 May. www.gazeta.ru/politics/2012/05/21_a_4595469.shtml (accessed 22 October 2016).

Gel'man, Vladimir. 2015. "Political Opposition in Russia: A Troubled Transformation." *Europe-Asia Studies* 67 (2): 177–191.

Gurel, Perin. 2015. "Bilingual Humor, Authentic Aunties, and the Transnational Vernacular at Gezi Park." *Journal of Transnational American Studies* 6 (1). https://escholarship.org/uc/item/2md6f6fr#page-1 (accessed 8 February 2016).

Helmy, Mohamed M. and Sabine Frerichs. 2013. "Stripping the Boss: The Powerful Role of Humor in the Egyptian Revolution 2011." *Integrative Psychological and Behavioral Science* 47 (4): 450–481.

Horvath, Robert. 2015. "'Sakharov Would Be With Us': Limonov, Strategy-31, and the Dissident Legacy." *The Russian Review* 74: 581–598.

Ioffe, Julia. 2012. "Protest and Pretend in Moscow." *The New Yorker* 4 February. www.newyorker.com/news/news-desk/protest-and-pretend-in-moscow (accessed 8 February 2016).

Jonson, Lena. 2015. *Art and Protest in Putin's Russia*. London and New York: Routledge.

Kelly, John, Vladimir Barash, Karina Alexanyan, Bruce Etling, Robert Faris, Urs Gusser, and John Palfrey. 2012. "Mapping Russian Twitter." The Berkman Center for Research Publication No. 2012–3. http://papers.ssrn.com/sol3/papers.cfm?abstract_id=2028158 (accessed 8 February 2016).

Konnander, Vilhelm. 2012. "Russia: Paving Political Potholes." *Global Voices* 28 July. http://vilhelmkonnander.blogspot.co.uk/2012/07/paving-political-potholes.html (accessed 8 February 2016).

Levinson, Alexei. 2012. "The Free City of Moscow: Reflections on Russia's Protest Movement." *OpenDemocracy* 4 May. www.opendemocracy.net/od-russia/alexei-levinson/free-city-of-moscow-reflections-on-russia%e2%80%99s-protest-movement (accessed 8 February 2016).

Loginov, Mikhail. 2013. "Aleksei Navalny Takes On 'the Fools and the Roads'." *OpenDemocracy* 5 August. www.opendemocracy.net/od-russia/mikhail-loginov/aleksei-navalny-takes-on-%E2%80%98fools-and-roads%E2%80%99 (accessed 8 February 2016).

Nim, Evgeniia [Eugenia]. 2012. "Protest v miniatiure: 'Nanomitingi' kak mediaso-bitiia" [Miniature Protests: 'Nanodemonstrations' as Media Events]. *Digital Icons* 7: 171–180. www.digitalicons.org/wp-content/uploads/2015/10/7.5.7_Nim.pdf (accessed 22 October 2016).

O'Flynn, Kevin. 2012. "Toys Cannot Hold Protest Because They Are Not Citizens of Russia, Officials Rule." *The Guardian* 15 February. www.theguardian.com/world/2012/feb/15/toys-protest-not-citizens-russia (accessed 8 February 2016).

Robertson, Graeme B. 2009. "Managing Society: Protest, Civil Society, and Regime in Putin's Russia." *Slavic Review* 68 (3): 528–547.

Sorensen, Majken Jul. 2008. "Humor as a Serious Strategy of Nonviolent Resistance to Oppression." *Peace and Change* 33 (2): 167–190.

Vasilyeva, Nataliya. 2012. "Moscow's Quiet Protest a New Tactic for Frustrated Russian Opposition." *The Republic* 14 May.

Ward, Graham, ed. 2000. *The Certeau Reader*. Oxford: Blackwell Publishers.

Wood, Tony. 2012. "Collapse as Crucible: The Reforging of Russian Society." *New Left Review* 74 (March–April): 1–22.

Yigit, Ahu. 2015. "Those Who Laugh Together, Belong Together: Online Satire in Turkey." *Turkish Policy Quarterly* 13 (4): 61–69.

Zlobin, Nikolai. 1996. "Humor as Political Protest." *Demokratizatsiya* 4 (2): 223–231.

Part II

Artistic and performative forms of protest

7   Biopolitics, believers, bodily protests

The case of Pussy Riot

Alexandra Yatsyk

Introduction

The minute-long performance by five colourfully dressed girls in balaclavas on 21 February 2012 in Moscow's Cathedral of Christ the Saviour (Fig.
7.1) triggered one of the most notorious and politically accentuated debates
in post-Soviet Russia. Members of the Pussy Riot group, which was little-
known at that time, danced and 'prayed' at the most sacred site of the Russian
Orthodox Church (ROC), the soleas and ambon, thus ignoring the taboo
on access to those areas and evoking awe among other visitors.[1] A few days
later, a fully-fledged video of the event, with added sound, circulated on the
Internet. Millions of people watched the 'Punk Prayer' entitled 'Mother of
God, Chase Putin Away'. A few weeks later, three participants in the event
were arrested and accused of a criminal offence. Two of them, Nadezhda
Tolokonnikova and Mariia Alekhina, were convicted of 'disrespect to society
and disruption of public order with motives of religious hatred and enmity'
(Anon. 2012a), and sentenced to two years in a penal colony.

This short performance was not the only cultural statement of Pussy
Riot. By the time of the Punk Prayer, they already had a history of partak-
ing in the projects of the art group Voina (War) and had staged their own
actions as an independent feminist band. Like the Punk Prayer, most of these
actions had also denounced the Putin regime, yet without directly criticizing
the Russian Orthodox Church, and the chosen venues for their performances
had not been sufficiently 'sacral' to draw the ROC's attention. In fact, the
group's previous performances, whether on the roof of a pre-trial detention
centre ('Death to Prison, Freedom to Protest' [*Smert' tiurme, svobodu pro-
testu*], 14 December 2011), or in the Moscow metro and atop a trolleybus
('Release the Cobblestones' [*Osvobodi brushatku*], November 2011), or even
on Red Square ('Putin Pissed Himself' [*Putin zassal*], 20 January 2012), had
not triggered such fierce public resonance.

The effect achieved by Pussy Riot can be compared with that of the
two notorious exhibitions titled 'Beware, Religion!' (*Ostorozhno, religiia!*,
2003) and 'Forbidden Art 2006' (*Zapretnoe iskusstvo*, 2007), held in the
Sakharov Centre in Moscow. Both provoked a broad public reaction, followed

Figure 7.1 Pussy Riot in the Cathedral of Christ the Saviour, 21 February 2012

Source: Still from Garadzha Matveeva's video at www.youtube.com/watch?v= GCasuaAczKY (accessed 27 November 2016).

by criminal charges against their curators. Similarly to the Pussy Riot performance, these exhibitions were widely recognized as political actions rather than offences against the religious norm (Bernstein 2014a). The Pussy Riot *Punk Prayer*, however, became known worldwide. Since 2012 the group has been nominated for an unprecedented number of prestigious prizes, in fields ranging from human rights protection (such as the Sakharov Prize for Freedom of Thought, or the Lennon-Ono Grant for Peace in 2012) to music (nomination for NME 'Hero of the Year 2014' Award). The Pussy Riot performers were ranked fifty-seventh in the 2012 ArtReview 'Power 100' list of the most influential contemporary art figures,[2] and sixteenth in the US *Foreign Policy* list of 100 top global thinkers in 2012 (together with Barack Obama and Hillary and Bill Clinton).[3] Due to its human rights focus, as well as the fervent art practices, the Pussy Riot protest was not only noticed, but also well understood in the West, by observers ranging from top-rank celebrities (Paul McCartney, Björk, Elton John, Sting, John Malkovich, Madonna) to civil rights activists (Yoko Ono), politicians (Hillary Clinton), and NGOs (Amnesty International). In Russia, however, the band's case did not find the same level of understanding, which has been interpreted by many scholars as an indication of the deepening split between 'two worlds' – the 'Russian' and 'Western' ones (Engström 2014; Rutland 2014; Storch 2013).

The scope of works dedicated to the Pussy Riot case is extensive. Numerous scholars have studied this performance in its manifold aspects, focusing on feminist (Gapova 2014; Kizenko 2013; Sperling 2014; Yusupova 2014), artistic (Bruce 2014; Manderson 2013; Shaw 2013; Steinholt 2013), memory (Etkind 2014), political (Sharafutdinova 2014; Storch 2013; Yablokov 2014), religious (Bernstein 2013; 2014b; Džalto 2013; Tolstaya 2014; Uzlaner 2013; Voronina 2013), and mass media and marketing (Cangro 2013; Strukov 2013) issues. Despite these differences, analysts are mostly consensual in dubbing this affair a trigger for the consolidating of Putin's majority and the solidifying of the nexus between the state and the ROC (Bernstein 2013; Gapova 2014; Rutland 2014; Sharafutdinova 2014). Meanwhile, some of the authors point out that the ROC clergy has interpreted this 'Prayer' very differently, which testifies to heterogeneity of the Russian religious community, with multiple post-secular hybrids within it (Storch 2013; Uzlaner 2013).

Yet some questions still remain unaddressed: for example, how we can conceptualize differences between the strategies of Pussy Riot and those of the state and assess their coherence and consistency? In trying to address these questions I include in my analysis the ROC, which serves as references point for both Pussy Riot and the state.

My contribution to the ongoing unpacking of the Pussy Riot phenomenon consists in proposing a biopolitical perspective based on works of Michel Foucault. This analysis is juxtaposed to Carl Schmitt's idea of the implicitly theological basis of the (conservative) state, as well as Judith Butler's concept of precarious life, which appears helpful to understanding the nature of artistic protest in contemporary Russia. The ideas developed by Foucault and Schmitt, being drastically dissimilar on most theoretical counts, are nevertheless (at least partly) compatible with each other in one particular respect, namely the role of the church as a specific type and source of power. Despite the predominant liberal connotations of the idea of biopolitics in Foucault's works, Russia is among the countries that refocus and reconceptualize biopolitics as an instrument of authoritarian power, which leaves ample room for theorizing on the state–church relationship with the help of Schmitt's work.

The first section of this chapter portrays the pillars of the current Kremlin discourse that can be conceptualized as biopolitical conservatism. Then I analyse the specificity of post-Soviet cultural protests as represented by actions of the Voina group, Petr Pavlenskii's performances, and Pussy Riot's artistic statements. I argue that the shrinking public sphere in Russia and its hegemonization by the Kremlin's biopolitical discourse stipulate a corporeal character of counter-discourses which, in turn, represent attempts to (re)politicize protest by means of body language. The final part of the chapter is devoted to an analysis of the ROC's discourse on the Pussy Riot affair, which I describe as corporeal and largely depoliticized by the state. In this discussion I mainly draw on discourse analysis of Orthodox critics of Pussy Riot and the legal proceedings of the trial.[4]

Turning the optics of biopolitical conservatism

The concept of biopolitical conservatism grasps the core of the ideology of Russia's officialdom, often formulated in cultural terms (see Makarychev and Yatsyk 2015). The idea of biopolitics has been developed in the late works of Michel Foucault (Foucault 2003b), who treated it as the application of a number of regulatory mechanisms aimed at inciting, yet also disciplining and constraining, human bodies. Biopolitics is usually referred to as a relatively soft (but rather pervasive) technology of power and governance targeted at such areas as health, sanitation, birth rate, and sexuality (Finlayson 2010, 97). In biopolitical reasoning, human life is part of political calculations and mechanisms of power and security (Dillon and Lobo-Guerrero 2008, 266). This chapter follows Foucault's understanding of biopolitics as the product of a disciplinary society, related to a government's concern about regulating people's life through various disciplinary institutions (Foucault 2003a, 377–378).

An explicitly permissive attitude of the state to a plethora of issues of corporeality and body politics can be seen as an essential part of an informal social contract and a precondition for a relative balance between state and society during the first two decades after the fall of the Soviet Union. This balance was undermined by the new conservative turn in the Kremlin's policy as a reaction to growing demands for social and political change that emerged since autumn 2011 (Remizov 2013).

In Russia, biopolitics not only gives an additional set of tools of power to the authorities; more importantly, it is an intrinsic element of debates on the essence and borders of Russia's political community. Specifically, Russian biopolitics is a set of instruments that define the belonging to this 'imagined' community on the basis of loyalty to official policies, while simultaneously ostracizing those who either do not share the official ideology or do not fit into the biopolitical standards imposed from the top down. Biopolitical regulations, implemented through bans and restrictions, become a key tool for articulating the rules of how Russia is shaped as a political community and how its political borders are drawn, i.e. how biopolitical distinctions from other communities are established. With their restrictive effects, these bans unveil mechanisms of 'inclusive exclusion': 'if someone is banned from a political community, he or she continues to have a relation with that group: there is still a connection precisely because they are outlawed' (Vaughan-Williams 2009, 734). The practices of political incarceration, ostracizing LGBT people, and fuelling anti-migrant feelings among the population are cases in point.

The proliferation of biopolitical ideas and practices in Putin's Russia has to be understood as a specific instrument for the 'suture' of the hegemonic discourse that, since the fall of the Soviet Union, lacked coherence and was intrinsically fragmented. This discourse lacked effectively functioning and widely shared 'quilting', or nodal points, which led to its decomposition into culturally divergent and often competing narratives of Russia's 'collective self'. The idea of biopolitical normalization, an epitome of Putin's version of conservatism, is meant to stabilize and consolidate this discourse as the pivotal hegemonic strategy of power, and attests to the growing state authoritarianism.

The Russian conservative turn also absorbed the political ideologeme of *katechon*, developed by Russian right-wing thinkers during the last decades. Theologically, the concept of *katechon* (from the Greek 'withholding') originated in the Byzantine Empire and claimed to protect the world from the advent of the Antichrist. In Russia it was introduced through the idea of Moscow as the Third Rome, dating back to the sixteenth century. Its appearance in the Kremlin's discourse can be traced to the post-Soviet re-actualization of Carl Schmitt's political theology (Engström 2014), as exemplified by the works of Arkadii Maler or Aleksandr Dugin. As Maria Engström points out, the concept of *katechon* was injected into the early post-Soviet discourse by those intellectuals who promoted the ideology of empire for the sake of establishing a new social order (Engström 2014, 358). Interestingly, it was the liberal politician Anatolii Chubais who polemically characterized Russia's future as that of a 'liberal empire', thereby symbolically legitimizing this concept for further ideological implementation (Engström 2014, 361). On the opposite political flank, three godfathers of Russian conservatism – Aleksandr Prokhanov, Sergei Kurginian, and Aleksandr Dugin – have been developing their own imperial image of Russia since the 1990s. Furthermore, Dugin is known as an active commentator on Schmitt's works, which he discusses in his *Katechon and Revolution* (Dugin 1997) in the light of state-based Messianism. A former student of Dugin, Arkadii Maler has favourably popularized the concept of *katechon* in the Russian media.[5] In post-Soviet art this concept evoked ambivalent representations of Russia as 'the Restrainer and the Apollo-Dionysius ambivalence of the Russians as the keepers of the heart of the earth and in the same time "the door-keepers" of chaos' (Engström 2014, 368). The concept was touched upon by Pavel Krusanov in literature, Aleksei Balabanov in cinema, and Aleksei Beliaev-Gintovt in painting, where the latter developed the so-called neo-Eurasian style (Engström 2014, 368).[6]

The Pussy Riot affair has illuminated another argument by Carl Schmitt: that all concepts used by the state stem from secularized theological ideas; therefore the system of modern law has taken on the functions of religion (Schmitt 2000). This explains the ultimate merger of state and church discourses, exemplified by the fact that Pussy Riot were persecuted for 'hooliganism' (Anon. 2012a), which meant violation of social practices appropriate in a specific community and causing moral suffering to churchgoers. From the viewpoint of the state, believers are not simply one of the endless numbers of social groups, but are representatives of the state's core ideology, which in turn considers it essential to protect them. By so doing, the state also constructs a boundary that divides 'encroachers' and their 'victims', whose sacred and tabooed hard core was overtly contested.

By the beginning of 2012, when Pussy Riot performed their Punk Prayer, Russia's dominant discourse was becoming increasingly conservative and biopolitical, with a strong accent on the idea of state Messianism and Orthodox aesthetics. In these circumstances, one of few possible ways for artists to make political statements was through body language, which, as represented by the Pussy Riot case, paradoxically has been excluded from the sphere of politics through official attempts to reformulate the whole story in legal categories, based on the biopolitical ability of the state to regulate the appropriateness of the protest.

Corporeal protest

In this section I focus on those forms of cultural protest that, in one way or another, react to state authoritarianism, including biopolitical conservatism, which matured after the widely contested Duma election in December 2011. I argue that the shrinking space for public politics under Putin, along with the growing repressions against the 'radical opposition' – with the trials of Aleksei Navalnyi since 2013 and the assassination of Boris Nemtsov in February 2015 as the most eloquent examples – have had a major influence on the structure of counter-discourses. These have achieved greater visibility when expressed through the language and imagery of cultural and performative representation. Concomitantly, many artists in Russia have played political roles and are widely perceived as bearers of different political messages addressed to broad audiences.

In qualifying certain acts as political, I need to specify what I mean by politics. Politics eludes neat and precise definitions, since it can often be expressed through or justified by moral or ethical reasoning. In a narrow sense, one may define politics as 'a sphere of constant struggle among competing definitions of what the good and the right is' (Cozette 2008, 672), or reduce it to Schmitt's distinction between friend and enemy (Beckstein 2011, 35). Yet in a wider sense, politics can, and in my view should, be understood as a type of power relation where an inherently conflicting interplay of *equivalence* and *difference* is produced, transformed, and subverted. Politics always involves practices of contests between dominating discourses of policy principles. As R. B. J. Walker (2010, 81) has argued, modern politics is 'a system of separations' and discriminations (Walker 2010, 110), including those between insides and outsides. Therefore, politics presupposes a component of line-drawing (Walker 2010, 95), but a political experience also encompasses the deconstruction of boundaries between jurisdictions, identities, social or cultural groups.

I agree with Chris Thornhill that:

> society cannot be stripped of its eminent politicality [...] and it is always capable of momentarily configuring itself around its politicality and its

general demands for legitimacy [...] The attempt to eradicate political primacy from the society is therefore not plausible.

(Thornhill 2007, 513–514)

Yet, at the same time, 'there is no stable core of the political' (Ungureanu 2008, 310), and 'political order is never a definitive, once and for all, done deal' (Horton 2010, 440). Politics might have many facets and groundings that, even if repressed, can be reactivated on the basis of claims for the constitution of a new legitimacy and universality. In this sense, the political 'designates the moment of openness, of undecidability, when the very structuring principle of society, the fundamental form of the social pact is called into question, whereas politics describes the positively determined outcome of that process' (Paipais 2014, 360).

With hindsight, the most common instrument of Russian cultural protests in the 2000s has been the scandalized body. The performance 'Fuck for the Heir Puppy Bear' (*Ebis' za nadslednika Medvezhonka*, 28 February 2008), staged by the art group Voina in protest against the undemocratic mechanisms for delegating power in Russia under Medvedev (whose surname derives from *medved'*, for 'bear'); Voina's drawing of a phallus on the drawbridge in front of Russia's Federal Security Service headquarters in St Petersburg, 'Dick Captured by the FSB' (*Khui v plenu u FSB*, 14 June 2010); as well as Petr Pavlenskii's performances, such as the public nailing of his scrotum to the cobbles of Red Square as an illustration of the 'fixed' position of Russia's citizens under the yoke of the state ('Fixation', [*Fiksatsiia*], November 2013); or 'The Separation' (*Otdelenie*, October 2014), when he cut his earlobe to contest the practice of psychiatrically 'disciplining' dissenters (Anon. 2014). All these actions are closely related to the European traditions of actionist art, as exemplified by the Viennese Actionists of the 1960s, with bloody performances using animal corpses and shocking self-inflicted injury, or by radical feminist groups such as Fierce Pussy, Guerrilla Girls, or Riot Grrrl.

What is different in the Russian protest art of the 2000s is the circumstances of the artists' speech act, characterized by the almost abraded political sphere of Putin's third term as president. In their numerous interviews and their lyrics, the Pussy Riot artists have emphasized the primordial significance of feminist and LGBT rights issues for contesting the current political regime in Russia through artistic protest. 'The joyful science of occupying squares / The will to power, without these damn leaders / Direct action – the future of mankind! / LGBT, feminists, defend the nation! / Death to prison, freedom to protest', they sang in their 'Death to Prison, Freedom to Protest' piece (Alekhina, Tolokonnikova, and Samutsevich 2012, 15). Pussy Riot's actionism is an attempt to point to the dangers of a convergence between the state and the Orthodox Church as the key source for the dominant homophobic practices of ostracizing alternative lifestyles and detaching sexual minorities from the normalized body of the nation (see Bernstein 2013; Bremer 2013; Džalto 2013; Manderson 2013; Steinholt 2013; Uzlaner 2013).

Contestation of biopolitical regulations was particularly strong in Nadezhda Tolokonnikova's letters from prison, where she protested against the sexualized practices of beauty contests among female convicts and other sexist rituals (caseofpussyriot 2013).

With the cementing of the biopolitical language in the dominant Russian discourse, aimed at 'taking care of a flock' and its bodies through disciplinary institutions and practices (Bernstein 2013; 2014b; 2014c), political contestation of the hegemonic discourse included the role of individual bodies as generators of claims for the individual right to injure themselves, or even to dispose of their lives, thus rendering the body useless for the sovereign power. Writers and commentators on the Pussy Riot affair mentioned that the members of the group were fully aware of the potential consequences of their performance and expected to be convicted and imprisoned (Kichanova 2012; Obukhova 2012).

Seen from this angle, the Pussy Riot performance – with all its corporeality – was a political statement, to which the Kremlin (as locus of power) responded with a strategy of depoliticization by means of reducing the meaning of that performance to its bodily aspects. This strategy fully harmonized with the biopolitical core of Putin's regime, with a priority on bans and bodily discipline.

At the same time, the Pussy Riot Punk Prayer in the Cathedral of Christ the Saviour was not based exclusively on a speechless corporeal language of protest, since the song's lyrics were a substantial element of the performance. However, the key point of the prosecution boiled down to their physical conduct in the cathedral. As the chair of the ROC Synodic Department of Information, Vladimir Legoida, commented, 'the church is not the place for political actions' (Anon. 2012c), although the cathedral is undoubtedly a place where the political is represented through forging exceptional relations between the church and public authorities.

Meanwhile, most of the complaints against Pussy Riot in court dealt with their physical appearance in the cathedral, which challenged the corporeal regulations of the church. Specifically, the artists were charged with standing on the soleas and ambon, which are forbidden areas for women; wearing inappropriate attire for a religious place; and making unacceptable gestures, such as dancing in can-can style and imitating a prayer (Anon. 2012a). Yet the claimants also mentioned the absence of direct 'political outcries' in the Punk Prayer[7] – probably because the performance in the cathedral was too short and the band had not enough time to finish the song. The key point of the indictment was mostly grounded in a number of 'corporeal' claims that it allegedly caused emotional distress to believers.

This corporeal tilt in the prosecution appears to depoliticize an originally political artistic utterance: the state reduced Pussy Riot's performance to biopolitical categories – indecent clothing and gestures and the physical location of the artists in forbidden areas – leaving aside the political content of their message. Yet this depoliticization can be effectuated only on the basis of the deeply political sovereign right to enforce exceptionalization by means of legally prioritizing one social group (believers) over another. On the reverse side of this sovereign practice, Pussy Riot can be understood in terms of Agamben's *homo sacer*: as outcasts ('internal others') bracketed outside of the 'normalized' political community through imprisonment and multiple verbal animadversions (Bernstein 2013). Later the Pussy Riot artists made efforts to publicize their *homo sacer* status through accentuated victimization exposed in short videos with scenes of the public humiliation and harassment that they suffered in Nizhny Novgorod and at the Sochi Olympics (Walker 2014). In a more performative form, Tolokonnikova and Katrin Nenasheva (who is not a member of Pussy Riot) played a similar role in sewing a huge Russian flag on Red Square on Russia Day 2015, thus performatively imitating the tasks of female convicts, with whom they here expressed solidarity (Gordon 2015). The trajectories of Alekhina and Tolokonnikova following their release from prison also confirms their detachment from the hegemonic discourses in Russia: most of their public appearances took place in Europe and the US, which became better places in which to pursue their media-channelled human rights campaigns, though with much less political vigour.

Against this backdrop, the corporeal works of Petr Pavlenskii look even more radical. As a gesture of support for Pussy Riot, he sewed his mouth shut ('Stitch' [*Shov*]) in July 2012, and claimed that Jesus Christ would be on their side.

> Russia is transforming into a totalitarian state which demands all of us to shut up, and which deems that no one has right to express her/his opinion. The question is what kind of state is this – still a secular or already a religious one? [...] And does the Russian Orthodox Church support Christian or other types of culture? These two fundamental questions reveal contradictions inside the ideological apparatus.
>
> (Pavlenskii in Volchek 2013)

As he noted about his action entitled 'The Carcass' (*Tusha*), performed at the St Petersburg Legislative Assembly in May 2013 (Fig. 7.2):

> A series of legal acts aimed at suppressing civil activity and intimidating the population, the constantly growing number of political prisoners, restrictive laws regulating NGOs, the 18+ law, the activity of Roskomnadzor,[8] the anti-gay propaganda law – all these laws are not against criminal activity, but against the people. This also includes the recent law against offending religious feelings. This is why I staged my performance. The human body is naked, like an animal's carcass; it has nothing on and is surrounded by wire intended for cattle. These laws, like the wire, keep people in individual paddocks: the persecution of political activists, the prisoners of 6 May,[9] and the state-orchestrated repressions are metaphors for this herding in a wired camp. This is done to convert

people into securely protected, gutless cattle that can only consume, work and breed [...]

I understand the body in my own way. The human body as part of the mechanisms of power, authority and society is something that is accused, convicted, and damaged. As an artist I was eager to show that I do with my body pretty much the same as the state does with our society. I expose these processes on my body, since it is part of a bigger social body; this is how a metaphor of what is going on with the social body appears.

(Pavlenskii in Volchek 2013)

Interpreting his actions, Pavlenskii draws a parallel between Foucault's concept of 'power of nomination' and practices of the symbolical 'fixture' of Russia's population by the Kremlin. He claims that the state, which labels him mentally unstable, schizoid, or criminal, turns his protest into a banality by so doing.

The narrative of the state is 'listen, repeat, obey'. The voice of art calls to 'speak, contest, resist'. This is an eternal opposition, since the authorities are interested in people being subdued like animals [...] Struggling for

Figure 7.2 Petr Pavlenskii, 'Carcass'. May 2013
Source: Private archive, courtesy of Petr Pavlenskii.

their subjectivity, people cease to be an obedient subaltern and become a dissenter.

('Territoriia vzgliada' 2014)

These cases of flesh expose one of the key structural characteristics of the Putin regime: it devalues and disavows any form of communication with its opponents. In the case of Pussy Riot, the impossibility of communication sprang from a collision of the political hard core of provocative art protest with the largely depoliticized reaction of the state. In the case of Pavlenskii, it was the non-verbal language of his performances that predetermined the communicative border: his scandalous corporeal installations were staged in a semantic register inaccessible to his opponents in the Kremlin, which can be interpreted as his gesture of fixing the borderline between his corporeal revolt and officialdom.

Vulnerable orthodoxy

Following the Pussy Riot case, there were many voices accusing the ROC of monopolizing the spiritual sphere, declaring all dissenters enemies and advocating a militant approach. In this section I relate the roots of the militant position adopted by the ROC in this case to the re-actualization of the church's traumatic experience during Soviet times. It is through the prism of this historical trauma of submission to a dominant godless power that one can explicate the sensitivity of the Orthodox community to actions challenging its moral authority and questioning its close collaboration with the current regime.

The discourse of the key Orthodox opponents to Pussy Riot can be dubbed 'militant clericalism', since it presupposes a clear demarcation between religious people and the three female artists along with their multiple supporters. Most radical ROC speakers have defined the performance as an act of aggression, against which the Orthodox community should react accordingly (Rybko 2012). Valentin Lebedev, the head of the Union of Orthodox Citizens of Russia, claims that:

> only inveterate marginals and poky blind men fail to accept that the blasphemous Pussy Riot and their sympathizers are soldiers of a single anti-Church, anti-Russian front. Their task is clear: to de-sacralize the consciousness of the people. The question is whether the people, unable to defend the shrines, will be capable of standing up to defend the Motherland?

(Lebedev 2012)

Corporeal language can also be inscribed into this discourse. Hieromonk Macarius draws a direct parallel between the Pussy Riot performance and the LGBT-permissive policies of European governments (Markish 2012). Andrei

Kuraev, an Orthodox priest, proposed to substitute incarceration of the artists with flogging (Kuraev 2014), a method that contains strong biopolitical allusions.

The overall ROC strategy in the Pussy Riot affair can be qualified as discursive hegemony by means of equating one particular group (Orthodox believers) with the whole of Russia. The Orthodox critique of Pussy Riot is replete with references to the idea of a holy war as the basis for national unity (the war against Napoleon in 1812, the Great Patriotic War of 1941–45), which is meant to reiterate the katechonic thesis of Russia's mission in the world. In this context, Pussy Riot represents a threat tantamount to the revolutionary upheavals of the early twentieth century, while the combat against dissenters is equated with the salvation of the Russian nation. The usage of universalizing concepts signifying national unity (such as 'Stalingrad', referring to the discourse of the Great Patriotic War as a nodal point of Russian national identity) in the religious critique of Pussy Riot (despite all obvious communist connotations of this metaphor) testifies to the profoundly ambiguous nature of the ROC's discourse. The church has to resort to, and borrow from, concepts belonging to a drastically different political register in order to sustain its own vigour, vitality, and traction. In this respect the discursive strategy of the ROC can be dubbed trans-ideological, resembling the equally trans-ideological posture of the state that compensates the weakness of its ideational resources with promiscuous instrumentalization of arguments from different parts of the political spectrum.

Yet the hegemonic project of the ROC is inherently unstable, ambivalent, and vulnerable. This stems from the glaring inconsistency between the church's intention to develop its own religious discourse, not necessarily congruent with that of the state, on the one hand, and the intrinsic insufficiency and incompleteness of these attempts on the other. By exposing its hegemonic articulations through attempts to discursively identify the ROC with the entire nation (if not the whole 'Russian world'), the church in fact sustains the key argument of its opponents in Pussy Riot.

The Pussy Riot case unveiled not only the conflation of Putin's regime and the ROC, but also the precarious status of the latter. The negative reaction of the Kremlin to the actionist performance by Pussy Riot can be understood as the state's policy of sacralization of religious space based on tabooing it from public activity. This policy stems both from the long history of the state–Orthodox 'symphony', which reached its heyday with the motto 'Orthodoxy, Autocracy, Nationality', and the communist experience of the ostracizing and marginalizing of the religious sphere. As a cultural protest, Pussy Riot's Punk Prayer contested this twofold policy of sacralization and victimization of the ROC, thus laying their claims not only against the ROC as representative of Orthodox faith, but against Putin's regime as such. The Kremlin, eager to install the state ideology based on the conservative 'agenda of spiritual bonds', has refocused the political gist of the performance and interpreted it as an offence against the religious community that requires legal action.

The concept of taboo in this context has more than one meaning. As one commentator put it, the most tabooed element in the church discourse is 'the right to sacrilege' (Baranova 2007). Seen from this perspective, the ROC considered the Pussy Riot affair as a case of blasphemy (Anon. 2012d) aimed at contesting the church monopoly on drawing boundaries between the religious and the secular. The Pussy Riot performance, from the ROC viewpoint, was an unauthorized attempt to redraw those borders (Uzlaner 2013, 101).

By the same token, Pussy Riot also challenged both the monopoly of the ROC on the discursive production of borders and the Kremlin's monopoly on its ideological appropriation. In fact, the Putin regime hijacked and re-signified the religious discourses, which diminished the ROC's ability to generate alternative narratives and reduced its role to that of the Kremlin's mouthpiece.

The political motives behind the ROC's reaction to Pussy Riot were based on a precarious foundation for two reasons. First, the ROC oscillates between dependence on the state, which builds its current political philosophy on apparently religious aesthetics, on the one hand, and attempts to articulate its own 'religious diplomacy' and 'soft power' toolkit, with the idea of 'the Russian world' at its core, on the other. Traumatic memories of past submission to the state add greater fragility and controversy to this precarious balance. Second, the church discourse itself was far from consolidated, with many voices not only contesting the hegemonic insistence on harsh punishment for Pussy Riot, but also accepting the performance as part of Russian carnivalesque culture.

Conclusion

In the Pussy Riot case, the opponents – the group itself on the one hand, and the state and the ROC on the other – used different frames and languages, and produced two different strategies, of politicization and of depoliticization respectively. Both turned out to be intrinsically unstable and, at a certain point, prone to merging, blurring the distinction between them and making politicization and depoliticization contextual, contingent, and transformable.

On the surface, the qualification of the case as political seemingly stems from Pussy Riot. The artists claimed that their main target was not the ROC, but the undue and inappropriate liaisons between the church hierarchy and the Kremlin. Those in society who welcome these 'symphonic' liaisons read Pussy Riot's message as a sacrilege (Chaplin 2012), while their opponents had all the grounds necessary to interpret the performance as a parody (Kuraev 2012), thus challenging the characterization of this specific form of protest as having anything to do with either 'instigating religious hatred' or 'insulting feelings of believers'.

Apparently, against this backdrop the state tried to avoid political connotations and, in their stead, to portray the case as purely legal. By so doing, the Kremlin only not showed reluctance to engage in a political debate with its opponents, but also an eagerness to diminish the political importance of each protest. Yet under closer scrutiny, the state's putative depoliticization of the Pussy Riot case masked an indubitable political core hidden behind the attempts to wrap the case in legal categories. First, the legal qualification of artistic protest became possible only because the state made an exception for a specific social group – religious people – and warranted their protection against what might be vaguely dubbed insults to their feelings. This is a political gesture as such, since it is based on the logic of prioritizing one particular group over others.

Second, on a couple of occasions President Putin de facto confirmed the insufficiency and incompleteness of the legal qualification of the whole case by pointing to Pussy Riot's previous actions which, in his interpretation, contained homophobic (as well as anti-Semitic and anti-migrant) messages (Anon. 2012b). Besides, Putin – perhaps unintentionally – engaged in political polemics with Pussy Riot, making a case for the ethical inappropriateness of their performances involving group sex scenes, as well the very name of the band (Anon. 2012b). The fact that the President could not avoid the temptation of – albeit indirectly – debating with the Pussy Riot artists such issues as their explicitly political identity attests not only to Putin's politically motivated misreading of their public messages, but also to the structural impossibility of keeping the entire issue within a purely legal frame. The discussion on 'genuine Russianness' unleashed by the Pussy Riot affair (Gapova 2012), and then enhanced in the context of Russia's policy towards Ukraine, betrays the inherently political core of the state–church merger.

What adds further intricacy to this analysis is that the strategy of politicization pursued by Pussy Riot had its limitations and ultimately integrated into the globally hegemonic discursive structures of human rights protection. Of course, the legacy of Pussy Riot could have been reproduced in other political contexts, such as the Rahvere punk festival in Estonia in August 2015, where the famous anti-Putin song became one of the hits (Erlikh 2015). Yet the integration into the global industry of mass media and entertainment came at the cost of losing the authenticity of Pussy Riot's original appeal, which ultimately resulted, in 2015, in the group declaring the end of the project (Pussy Riot 2024 [sic]).

This analysis proves that the political is an ineradicable element of antagonism in human affairs, while politics is the articulation of the enactment of social identities (Wenman 2003, 63). The ability to exclude from and include in the community are the most visible 'signals of politics', which the Kremlin has clearly demonstrated. In the meantime, there is always an inherent uncertainty and ambiguity in the concept of politics, which was expressed by Foucault in his assertion that no one has a monopoly on dictating the terms of politics. This leaves 'the question of how politics is ultimately defined' to its subjects (Kiersey, Weidner, and Rosenow 2010, 150), and undermines the absolutization of notions such as essence and grounds as applicable to the domain of politics.

Notes

1 According to the rules of the Russian Orthodox Church, and the Cathedral of the Christ the Saviour in particular, it is strictly prohibited for women to access the ambon and soleas.
2 http://artreview.com/power_100/ (accessed 3 September 2015).
3 http://foreignpolicy.com/2012/11/26/the-fp-top-100-global-thinkers/ (accessed 3 September 2015).
4 I have analysed the publications of the official website of the Russian Orthodox Church (www.patriarchia.ru), the internet journal *Pravoslavie i mir* [Orthodoxy and the World] (www.pravmir.ru), and posts on the blog 'Pravoslavnaia politika' (Orthodox Politics) on *LiveJournal* (http://pravoslav-pol.livejournal.com) from 2012 to 2015.
5 See Maler's *LiveJournal* page http://arkadiy-maler.livejournal.com. He is the founder and leader of the club (2007) and almanac (2005) Katechon, and an internet portal (www.katehon.ru).
6 See Beliaev-Gintovt's projects on www.evrazia.tv/category/alieksiei-bieliaiev-gintovt.
7 Testimonies of S. V. Vinogradov, V. A. Anosov, V. I. Tsyganiuk, S. N. Beloglazov, S. A. Shilin, V. V. Potan'kin (Anon. 2012a).
8 Roskomnadzor: Federal Service for Supervision in the Sphere of Telecom, Information Technologies and Mass Communications.
9 Pavlenskii refers to a group of protesters against the Putin regime who were convicted for unauthorized public demonstrations on 6 May 2012.

References

Anon. 2012a. "Prigovor Pussy Riot." *Snob.ru* 22 August. http://snob.ru/selected/entry/51999 (accessed 3 September 2015).
Anon. 2012b. "Putin – Merkel': odna iz Pussy Riot 'veshala chuchelo evreia'." BBC Russian Service 16 November. www.bbc.co.uk/russian/russia/2012/11/121116_putin_merkel_pussy_riot.shtml (accessed 3 September 2015).
Anon. 2012c. "V. P. Legoida: Tserkov' ne mesto dlia politicheskikh aktsii." Russkaia pravoslavnaia tserkov', 30 April, www.patriarchia.ru/db/text/2192902.html (accessed 3 September 2015).
Anon. 2012d. "Zaiavlenie Vysshego Tserkovnogo Soveta v sviazi s prigovorom po delu ob oskvernenii Khrama Khrista Spasitelia." *Pravmir.ru* 17 August. www.pravmir.ru/zayavlenie-vysshego-cerkovnogo-soveta-russkoj-pravoslavnoj-cerkvi-v-svyazi-s-sudebnym-prigovorom-po-delu-lic-oskvernivshix-svyashhennoe-prostranstvo-xrama-xrista-spasitelya/#ixzz3VaDnOrEM (accessed 3 September 2015).
Anon. 2014. "Net mochki terpet'." *Grani.ru* 19 October. http://grani.ru/Politics/Russia/activism/m.234126.html (accessed 3 September 2015).
Alekhina, Mariia, Nadezhda Tolokonnikova, and Ekaterina Samutsevich. 2012. Application no. 38004/12. Mariya Vladimirovna Alekhina and others against Russia. Lodged 19 June 2012. European Court of Human Rights. http://hudoc.echr.coe.int/sites/eng/pages/search.aspx?i=001-139863 (accessed 3 September 2015).
Baranova, Ol'ga, ed. 2007. "Zapis' diskussii 'Tabu v sovremennom russkom iskusstve'." Sakharov Center 28 March. http://old.sakharov-center.ru/museum/exhibitionhall/forbidden-art/tabu-art/texts/ (accessed 3 September 2015).
Beckstein, Martin. 2011. "The Dissociative and Polemical Political: Chantal Mouffe and the Intellectual Heritage of Carl Schmitt." *Journal of Political Ideologies* 16 (1): 33–51.

Bernstein, Anya. 2013. "An Inadvertent Sacrifice: Body Politics and Sovereign Power in the Pussy Riot Affair." *Critical Inquiry*, 40 (1): 220–241.

Bernstein, Anya. 2014a. "Caution, Religion! Iconoclasm, Secularism, and Ways of Seeing in Post-Soviet Art Wars." *Public Culture* 26 (3): 419–448.

Bernstein, Anya. 2014b. "Forgiveness as a Sovereign Exception: Pussy Riot, Winter Olympics, and the New Russian Biopolitics." *In the Moment* 6 January, 13–15.

Bernstein, Anya. 2014c. "The Impossible Object: Relics, Property, and the Secular in Post-Soviet Russia." *Anthropology Today* 30 (2): 7–11.

Bremer, Thomas. 2013. "The Pussy Riot Trial and the Russian Orthodox Church." *Russian Analytical Digest* 122: 6–8.

Bruce, Caitlin. 2014. "The Balaclava as Affect Generator: Free Pussy Riot Protests and Transnational Iconicity." *Communication and Critical/Cultural Studies* 12 (1): 42–62.

Cangro, Stephanie L. 2013. "When 'Girl' Is A Four-Letter Word: A Case Study of Pussy Riot in Western and Social Media." MA project, American University. www.american.edu/soc/upload/Stephanie-Cangro-Capstone.pdf (accessed 3 September 2015).

caseofpussyriot. (2013). "Nadezhda Tolokonnikova obyavlyaet golodovku i rasskazyvaet ob IK-14." *LiveJournal.com* 23 September. http://caseofpussyriot.livejournal.com/33753.html (accessed 3 September 2015).

Chaplin, Vsevolod. 2012. "Tserkvi i vlasti suzhdeno trudit'sia vmeste radi blaga liudei. Vystuplenie Vsevoloda Chaplina." *Pravoslav.Pol LiveJournal* 10 October. http://pravoslav-pol.livejournal.com/22544.html (accessed 3 September 2015).

Cozette, Murielle. 2008. "What Lies Ahead: Classical Realism on the Future of International Relations." *International Studies Review* 10 (4): 667–679.

Dillon, Michael and Luis Lobo-Guerrero. 2008. "Biopolitics of Security in the 21st Century: An Introduction." *Review of International Studies* 34 (2): 265–292.

Dugin, Aleksandr. 1997. *Katekhon i revoliutsiia.* Moscow: Arktogeia. http://arctogaia.com/public/templars/kateh.htm (accessed 3 September 2015).

Džalto, Davor. 2013. "Religion, Politics, and beyond: The Pussy Riot Case." *Journal of Religion and Society* 15: 1–14.

Engström, Maria. 2014. "Contemporary Russian Messianism and New Russian Foreign Policy." *Contemporary Security Policy* 35 (3): 356–379.

Erlikh, Evgenii. 2015. "Pussy Riot – khorovoi pank-moleben v Estonii." *YouTube* 24 August. www.youtube.com/watch?t=69&v=DaYpHdH-Ams (accessed 3 September 2015).

Etkind, Alexander. 2014. "Post-Soviet Russia: The Land of the Oil Curse, Pussy Riot, and Magical Historicism." *Boundary 2* 41 (1): 153–170.

Finlayson, Gordon. 2010. "'Bare Life' and Politics in Agamben's Reading of Aristotle." *The Review of Politics* 72 (1): 97–126.

Foucault, Michel. 2003a. *Security, Territory, Population: Lectures at the Collège de France 1977–1978.* New York: Picador.

Foucault, Michel. 2003b. *Society Must Be Defended. Lectures at the Collège de France, 1975–1976.* New York: Picador.

Gapova, Elena. 2012. "Delo 'Pussy Riot': feministskii protest v kontekste klassovoi bor'by." *Neprikosnovennyi zapas* 85 (5). http://magazines.russ.ru/nz/2012/5/g2.html (accessed 3 September 2015).

Gapova, Elena. 2014. "Becoming Visible in The Digital Age." *Feminist Media Studies* 15 (1): 18–35.

Gordon, Jeremy. 2015. "Pussy Riot's Nadya Tolokonnikova Arrested in Moscow." *Pitchfork* 12 June. http://pitchfork.com/news/59930-pussy-riots-nadya-tolokonnikova-arrested-in-moscow/ (accessed 3 September 2015).

Horton, John. 2010. "Realism, Liberal Moralism and a Political Theory of Modus Vivendi." *European Journal of Political Theory* 9 (4): 431–448.

Kichanova Vera. 2012. *Pussi Raiot: Podlinnaia Istoriia.* Moscow: Hocus-Pocus.

Kiersey, Nicholas J., Jason R. Weidner, and Doerthe Rosenow. 2010. "Response to Chandler." *Global Society* 24 (2): 143–150.

Kizenko, Nadezhda. 2013. "Feminized Patriarchy? Orthodoxy and Gender in Post-Soviet Russia." *Signs* 38 (3): 595–621.

Kuraev, Andrei. 2012. "Maslenitsa v khrame Khrista Spasitelia," *LiveJournal* 21 February. http://diak-kuraev.livejournal.com/285875.html (accessed 3 September 2015).

Lebedev, Valentin. 2012. "Pochetnaia missiia babushki amerikanskoi popsy." *Pravoslav.Pol LiveJournal* 13 August. http://pravoslav-pol.livejournal.com/20179.html (accessed 3 September 2015).

Makarychev, Andrey and Alexandra Yatsyk. 2015. "Refracting Europe: Biopolitical Conservatism and Art Protest in Putin's Russia." In *Russia's Foreign Policy: Ideas, Domestic Politics and External Relations,* edited by David Cadier and Margot Light, 138–155. Basingstoke: Palgrave Macmillan.

Manderson, Desmond. 2013. "Making a Point and Making a Noise: A Punk Prayer." *Law, Culture and the Humanities* (online publication) June: 1–13.

Markish, Makarii [Ieromonakh]. 2012. "Nichego lichnogo, ili Stalingrad v Khamovnikakh."*Pravmir.ru* 14 August. www.pravmir.ru/ieromonax-makarij-markish-nichego-lichnogo-ili-stalingrad-v-xamovnikax/ (accessed 3 September 2015).

Obukhova, Aleksandra. 2012. "Avdei Ter-Ogan'ian: 'Pussy Riot – eto kachestvenno sdelannaia popsa'." *Colta.ru* 13 September. http://archives.colta.ru/docs/5567 (accessed 3 September 2015).

Paipais, Vassilios. 2014. "Between Politics and the Political: Reading Hans J. Morgenthau's Double Critique of Depoliticisation." *Millennium – Journal of International Studies* 42 (2): 354–375.

Pussy Riot. 2024 [sic]. "Ia UBILA PROTEST!!!!" *LiveJournal* 4 March 2015. http://pussy-riot.livejournal.com (accessed 3 September 2015).

Remizov, Maksim. 2013. "Konservatizm i sovremennost'." *Svobodnaia mysl'* 5. www.svom.info/entry/281-konservatizm-i-sovremennost (accessed 3 September 2015).

Rutland, Peter. 2014. "The Pussy Riot Affair: Gender and National Identity in Putin's Russia." *Nationalities Papers* 42 (4): 575–582.

Rybko, Sergii [Igumen]. 2012. "Pussy Riot neobkhodimo nakazat', inache zavtra u nikh budut posledovateli." *Pravmir.ru* 17 August. www.pravmir.ru/igumen-sergij-rybko-pussy-riot-neobxodimo-nakazat-inache-zavtra-u-nix-budut-posledovateli/#ixzz3VaAdFQsk (accessed 3 September 2015).

Schmitt, Carl. 2000. *Politicheskaia teologiia.* Moscow: KANON-press.

Sharafutdinova, Gulnaz. 2014. "The Pussy Riot Affair and Putin's Démarche from Sovereign Democracy to Sovereign Morality." *Nationalities Papers* 42 (4): 615–621.

Shaw, Claire. 2013. "'Fashion Attack': The Style of Pussy Riot." *Digital Icons* 9: 115–128. www.digitalicons.org/issue09/claire-shaw/ (accessed 3 September 2015).

Sperling, Valerie. 2014. "Russian Feminist Perspectives on Pussy Riot." *Nationalities Papers* 42 (4): 591–603.

Steinholt, Yngvar B. 2013. "Kitten Heresy: Lost Contexts of Pussy Riot's Punk Prayer." *Popular Music and Society* 36 (1): 120–124.

Storch, Leonid. 2013. "The Pussy Riot Case." *Russian Politics and Law* 51 (6): 8–44.

Strukov, Vlad. 2013. "From Local Appropriation to Global Documentation, or Contesting the Media System." *Digital Icons* 9: 87–97. www.digitalicons.org/issue09/vlad-strukov/ (accessed 3 September 2015).

"Territoriia vzgliada." 2014. "Petr Pavlenskii. Iskusstvo i politika: aktsionizm protiv dispozitiva." *OTB Kharkiv TV Channel* 7 October www.youtube.com/watch?v=mmyM0XhuHpk (accessed 3 September 2015).

Thornhill, Chris. 2007. "Niklas Luhmann, Carl Schmitt and the Modern Form of the Political." *European Journal of Social Theory* 10 (4): 499–522.

Tolstaya, Katerina. 2014. "Stained Glasses and Coloured Lenses: The Pussy Riot Case as a Critical Issue for Multidisciplinary Scholarly Investigations." *Religion and Gender* 4 (2): 100–120.

Ungureanu, Camil. 2008. "Derrida on Free Decision: Between Habermas' Discursivism and Schmitt's Decisionism." *Journal of Political Philosophy* 16 (3): 293–325.

Uzlaner, Dmitrii. 2013. "Delo 'Pussy Riot' i osobennosti rossiiskogo postsekuliarizma." *Gosudarstvo. Religiia. Tserkov'* 2: 93–133. http://religion.rane.ru/sites/default/files/%E2%80%9EThe%20Pussy%20Riot%20Case%E2%80%9C%20and%20the%20Peculiarities%20of%20Russian%20Postsecularism_%202%202013.pdf (accessed 3 September 2015).

Vaughan-Williams, Nick. 2009. "The Generalised Bio-Political Border? Re-Conceptualising the Limits of Sovereign Power." *Review of International Studies* 35 (4): 729–749.

Volchek, Dmitrii. 2013. "V strastnuiu piatnitsu." *Radio Svoboda* 8 May. www.svoboda.org/content/article/24978110.html (accessed 3 September 2015).

Voronina, Olga. 2013. "Pussy Riot Steal the Stage in the Moscow Cathedral of Christ the Saviour: Punk Prayer on Trial Online and in Court." *Digital Icons* 9: 65–85. www.digitalicons.org/issue09/olga-voronina/ (accessed 3 September 2015).

Walker, R. B. J. 2010. *After the Globe, Before the World*. Abingdon: Routledge

Walker, Shaun. 2014. "Pussy Riot Attacked with Whips by Cossack Militia at Sochi Olympics." *The Guardian* 19 February. www.theguardian.com/music/2014/feb/19/pussy-riot-attacked-whips-cossack-milita-sochi-winter-olympics (accessed 3 September 2015).

Wenman, Mark A. 2003. "What is Politics? The Approach of Radical Pluralism." *Politics* 23 (1): 57–65.

Yablokov, Ilya. 2014. "Pussy Riot as Agent Provocateur: Conspiracy Theories and the Media Construction of Nation in Putin's Russia." *Nationalities Papers* 42 (4): 622–636.

Yusupova, Marina. 2014. "Pussy Riot: A Feminist Band Lost in History and Translation." *Nationalities Papers* 42 (4): 604–610.

8   Hysteria or enjoyment?

Recent Russian actionism

Jonathan Brooks Platt

In recent years it has become quite common for Russian artists and activists to pronounce the death of actionism. In the late 2000s, the Voina (War) group and their splinter faction, Pussy Riot, achieved international recognition with a number of 'loud' (i.e., high-profile) actions that accompanied the build-up to the Moscow protests of 2011–12. This provocative form of performance art usually traces its origins to the bloody, scatological, and erotic displays of the Viennese Actionists in the 1960s. However, recent Russian actionism also derives from a rich native tradition. Late-Soviet non-official groups like Collective Actions and the Necrorealists often took their practices into public spaces (or at least into the forest), and the Moscow art scene in the 1990s was dominated, on the one hand, by the actionism of Oleg Kulik and Aleksandr Brener (both associated with the gallerist Marat Guelman) and, on the other hand, by the more overtly political actions of Anatolii Osmolovskii and the Radek group.[1] The 2000s also saw the emergence of a vibrant street activism that at times crossed over into performative actions.[2] Now, however, many of the same people who participated in this movement are lamenting its demise.

Still, despite the sombre mood, actions and would-be actionists remain quite prevalent in Russia today. In August 2014, for example, an activist swam the Fontanka River in St Petersburg with a sign reading 'Putin is Eternal/ Crippled' (*Putin vechen/uvechen*). The work evoked an eloquent, if somewhat overly literary, set of associations: the lonely river of time (the documentation's soundtrack is 'Que sera, sera') and the inevitable fate of any Ozymandias. The problem was the reaction, or lack thereof. In fact, the stormiest response came from the artist himself, who was deeply disappointed that the mainstream media failed to cover the story. As he reasoned on his Facebook page: the era of loud action ended when Vladimir Putin quashed the Russian protest movement and began his reactionary third term (following the more moderate interim presidency of Dmitrii Medvedev). The activist explained the problem in terms of a typology of political regimes. America has no need for such interventions because its free media make true transgression impossible (a somewhat dubious but commonplace argument). Meanwhile, hardcore authoritarian states like post-Bolotnaya Russia or North Korea (!) can simply ignore them. The only fertile soil for art actions is a 'soft' authoritarianism.[3]

Pussy Riot's Nadezhda Tolokonnikova expressed similar sentiments on her own Facebook page on 8 August 2014, blaming not the state-controlled media but the regime's turn from its original 'stability' paradigm to the aggressive popular mobilization that reached a frenzied pitch with the annexation of Crimea. According to Tolokonnikova, Putin resembles the total-artist Stalin from Boris Groys' seminal analysis, since he seems to have taken up the mantle of the actionist avant-garde himself, far surpassing his teachers when it comes to undermining the political (now geopolitical) order, pushing trigger points and provoking conflict.[4] This argument resonates with the enthusiasm many well-known actionists and performance artists expressed for the annexation of Crimea, including Oleg Vorotnikov of Voina. The suggestion seems to be that when Voina fled the country in 2012, they left the regime to launch its own actionist project, now taking the fight to the smug liberal West in the form of little green men and drunken Cossacks shooting down passenger jets. However one might feel about such claims, Pussy Riot certainly have not been keeping the fight alive, as Tolokonnikova and Mariia Alekhina appear increasingly enamoured with their status as international celebrities, producing MTV-style protest videos and abandoning their original riot-grrrl aesthetic.[5]

Nonetheless, there does remain one Russian actionist still capable of loud interventions: Petr Pavlenskii, who rose to prominence in 2012 with 'Stitch' (*Shov*), sewing his mouth shut to protest the Pussy Riot trial (Fig. 8.2), and went on to produce two more living-pain sculptures with 'Carcass' (*Tusha*) – crawling naked into a cocoon of barbed wire – and, the loudest of all, 'Fixation' (*Fiksatsiia*), nailing his scrotum to Red Square (Fig. 8.3). In February 2014, Pavlenskii and other activists created a burning barricade on St Petersburg's Malo-Koniushennii Bridge with 'Liberty' (*Svoboda*), mimicking the Maidan events in Kiev. With this action, a new turn seemed visible in Pavlenskii's work: 'speaking', as he put it, 'for the first time about freedom and not prison' (Pavlenskii 2014). However, he returned to his self-harming roots in October 2014, when he sliced off his earlobe while sitting atop the infamous Serbskii Institute for Forensic Psychiatry in Moscow (Fig. 8.1). The work was called 'Separation' (*Otdelenie*), a word that can also refer to a hospital ward. Here many a dissident was declared mentally ill for non-conformist beliefs during Soviet times, and Pavlenskii has himself been forced to undergo psychiatric evaluation after several of his actions.

My central question in this chapter is whether it is correct to see Pavlenskii as continuing the actionist project. On the surface, the connections seem self-evident. His work focuses on provoking the police with transgressions that revolve around the body and its limits. His actions are designed for mass media consumption and pay little or no attention to the institutional framework of the art world. Common negative appraisals of his work also link it to his immediate predecessors. For example, in September 2014 at the St Petersburg conference 'No Radical Art Actions are Going to Help Here…: Political Violence and Militant Aesthetics after Socialism' that I organized as part of

Figure 8.1 Petr Pavlenskii, 'Separation'. October 2014
Source: Private archive, courtesy of Petr Pavlenskii.

the Manifesta 10 Biennale of Contemporary Art, a number of scholars and artists expressed the opinion that recent Russian actionism takes the (ineffectual) posture of the hysteric with regard to power. The actions of Voina, Pussy Riot, or Pavlenskii are not really performed for the mass viewer; rather, their intended audience is state power itself, personified by the police. They challenge the organs of social control by laying bare the 'castration' of society, demonstrating the failure of power on their own bodies.[6] The problem is that such hysterical actionism is vulnerable to Jacques Lacan's famous critique of the student uprisings of 1968 (frequently cited by Slavoj Žižek): 'What you aspire to as revolutionaries is a master. You will get one' (Lacan 2007, 207).[7] From this perspective, the hysteric only performs castration as a demand for the assertion of phallic authority.

There is much to suggest that Pavlenskii is indeed cultivating a version of this hysterical position. However, I argue here that such a strategy in fact represents a significant divergence from the Russian actionist tradition. To demonstrate this thesis I will examine in detail one characteristic Voina action and then highlight its differences from Pavlenskii's practice. My claim is that Voina's strategy (more traditional in the Russian context) is not the hysterical challenge to power but, rather, a staged enjoyment of bare life, cultivating 'festive indistinction' from power by revelling in the abject condition to which modern sovereignty reduces its subjects.

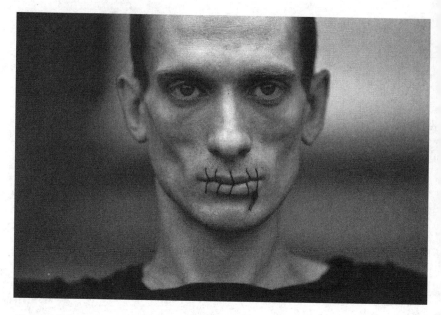

Figure 8.2 Petr Pavlenskii, 'Stitch'. July 2012
Source: Photo by Maksim Zmeev (Reuters), courtesy of Petr Pavlenskii.

In my view, this strategy reflects one of the most potent trajectories of Russian art – from the Mit'ki and the Necrorealists to the Moscow action-ists – a tradition marked by passion for ambiguity and 'zones of indistinc-tion' (a term, by the way, which was popularized by Andrei Monastyrskii's Collective Actions group in the 1970s long before Giorgio Agamben used it to define the juridico-political order of our times in *Homo Sacer*).[8] Occupying spaces between life and death, human and animal, the individual and the col-lective body, not to mention aesthetic autonomy and activist engagement, these performative practices flourished though emancipatory enjoyment of every category's slippage, every law's emptiness. Instead of Mikhail Bakhtin's public square, these artists worked in spaces at once open and closed, exposed and hidden – whether in a forest, a communal apartment, or the street in front of a gallery, or as a clandestine action displayed openly on the Internet.

Enjoyment leads to a certain deformation in these practices, reducing the subject to what Agamben calls 'bare life' – a life at once lacking and exces-sive, suspended between the biological and the political (Agamben 1998). As Eric Santner writes, the zone of indistinction is a site of metamorphosis, where we glimpse 'what remains once one's entitlements to enjoyment have been reduced to the minimal one to *enjoy bare life*' (Santner 1999, 47; emphasis in the original). In this formulation Santner uses the term 'enjoy-ment' (from the French *jouissance*) in the sense of enjoying rights. However, in the Russian tradition I am describing, particularly in Voina's actions, it is the ambivalent word's other semantic centre that comes to the fore: an erotic enjoyment that is obscene, even traumatic, and which troubles the desiring, disciplined subject.

In a discussion of Alenka Zupančič, Santner also links bare life (or, in his terms, 'creaturely flesh') to the site of castration. Here the two meanings of enjoyment are entwined. The antithetical Lacanian term *plus-de-jouir*, which means both 'more enjoyment' and 'no more enjoyment,' captures how symbolic castration introduces a twofold split in the speaking subject. On the one hand, the subject comes to enjoy symbolic rights and entitlements that do not naturally belong to it. These 'phallic' prostheses are 'castrating' because they introduce a gap between the subject's being and social role. On the other hand, erotic enjoyment emerges as the retroactive effect of our division into sexed beings. Here again castration doubles as lack and surplus – the mythic loss of some pre-Oedipal capacity for enjoyment is retroactively produced by the appearance of its remainder as something autonomous and separate from the subject – not an 'amputation' but an 'appendix', as Zupančič puts it (Santner 1999, 79–80; Zupančič 2008, 192).[9]

If Pavlenskii's works revolve around the neurotic, hysterical display of 'amputations', Voina and their predecessors in the Russian tradition more perversely seek out castration as a site of enjoyment. Traumatic reduction to bare life is recast as an explosion of bare enjoyment. This reversal often looks like a carnivalesque identification with power, laying bare the creaturely flesh that both the sovereign and *homo sacer* share. From this perspective, Voina practises a tactic of subversive affirmation, ironically over-identifying with power to expose its injustice. But subversive affirmation assumes a meta-position from which the artist or activist observes and performs his/her critique (see Zaitseva 2010). Voina may hint at the existence of such a position, but they never leave it uncompromised. Instead, they cultivate an elusive irony, protecting the site of festive indistinction from the dialectic of transgression, which always threatens to divert the action into something much more predictable. This irony can also be linked to the non-official Soviet practice of *stiob*, a widespread form of deadpan irony that Alexei Yurchak has associated with the Necrorealists and Mit'ki, as well as the poetry of Voina's mentor, Dmitrii Prigov. *Stiob* often takes the form of over-identification with ritualized official language, suspending performance between seriousness and irony, making it 'impossible to tell whether it [is] a form of sincere support, subtle ridicule, or a peculiar mixture of the two' (Yurchak 2006, 250). In its more everyday articulation, this uncertainty is usually either partial or temporary; subtle 'winks' or a final burst of laughter give the game away. However, the more radical *stiob* that Voina and their predecessors practise never fully surrenders uncertainty, never lays down its cards. Moreover, since over-identification is also directed at the contexts and characters the artists themselves create – the Mitek, the Necrorealist 'non-corpse' (*netrup*), Kulik's dog-man, Brener's coprophilic idiots, the great poet Dmitrii Aleksandrovich Prigov, Voina's heroic outlaws, and so on – this uncertainty means that the viewer can never catch the artist in a distinct subject position, especially not a political one. Pavlenskii, as I will show, is much more serious.

Snatching Chicken

Let us consider one of Voina's typical actions, first as the vast majority of its viewers experienced it, i.e., through online video documentation. The setting is St Petersburg, July 2010. A young woman with shoulder-length blonde hair is walking down Nevskii Prospekt. She seems relaxed, even a bit hunched, as she ambles along, dangling a white handbag. Off camera, someone gets upset about something, 'What do you mean, "sorry"?', and the woman's lips curl into a sardonic, almost devious smile. She turns into the supermarket of the high-end 'Passage' Shopping Centre, and we cut to her pushing a trolley towards the back of the shop. 'Voulez-vous coucher avec moi?' plays over the speakers. The woman asks a shop assistant if they have any chickens, and she is pointed in the right direction. She examines the cling film-wrapped birds with enthusiasm – 'Fucking amazing little chickens' (*Okhuennye tsypliata*) – and fills her basket. Next she is joined by several companions, and together they start asking some bemused security guards about the quality of the poultry and the different options on offer. 'Are they fresh?' 'Is this for making soup?' 'This is for cats, right?' They sniff at the chickens and compare sizes. When asked how they plan to cook the bird, a second woman in the group answers, 'We want to stuff it' (*Khotim zapikhivat'* – not the usual culinary term for stuffing, which is *farshirovat'*). A little boy with a shaved head pulls some chickens off a shelf and treads on one triumphantly.

Then things begin to get tense. The group splits up among the aisles, carrying large signs with letters painted on them in a clumpy, brown substance that looks like excrement. The shop assistants are getting upset, shouting at the group to stop filming and leave. Meanwhile, the woman with the handbag has removed her panties and is trying with great difficulty to stuff (*zapikhat'*) a raw chicken up her vagina. After some help from a male companion, she gets the bird part-way inside, puts her panties back on, and fixes her dress. The rest of the crew now has the signs in place, holding them up in different parts of the shop, one group of letters for each of the four security cameras: *bez, blia, d, no*. The letters come together on the guard's monitor to form the word *bezbliadno* (a play on *besplatno*, 'for free', that replaces the root *plat*, 'payment', with *bliad*, 'whore'). They hold the signs for 15 seconds and then fold them up. The woman with her secret galline cargo walks calmly past a security guard and out of the shop. Once outside, she lets the stolen carcass drop with an audible gasp: 'Opa'.

This action – usually titled 'Why Did They Snatch the Chicken?' (*Poshto pizdili kuru?*) – was not Voina's most scandalous (the orgy in the Moscow Biological Museum holds that honour), nor their most confrontational (the 'Palace Coup' action, in which they overturned a police car, earned them jail time), nor their most successful (they won the prestigious Innovation Prize for the giant phallus painted on Liteinyi Bridge, which stood through the night opposite the local headquarters of the Federal Security Service (FSB)). Indeed, the chicken action has only achieved the renown of these others because of a false rumour (which any viewing immediately disproves), namely that the young woman is Tolokonnikova. Although the idea of her having had intimate relations with a chicken suited the smear campaign against Pussy Riot very well, Tolokonnikova in fact had nothing to do with the action, having split to form her own Voina faction with Petr Verzilov in 2009.[10]

Still, despite its reputation, the chicken action is much more than a crude piece of shock-art. First, it illustrates Voina's core principle of rejecting the use of money in favour of stealing. The photographic documentation is even presented as part of an instruction manual titled (in English), 'Voina DIY Handbook. Section 1. How to Snatch Chicken'.[11] This mock didacticism is then repeated at a linguistic level, as the action realizes the metaphor behind the slang word, *pizdit'*, a verb form of 'cunt' (*pizda*) that means, 'to steal'.[12] Voina is thus not only teaching us how to steal; they are also explaining the logic behind this magic name for the thief's practice. And this is no cold pun like the titles of so many artworks from the 1990s (think of Damien Hirst's bisected cow and calf, titled 'Mother and Child Divided'). In the Voina action, the dead metaphor explodes into life, as the taboo word contributes its sacral power to the group's mythic self-presentation as an outlaw underground, at once joyously vulgar and nobly righteous.

Like nearly every Voina action, 'Why Did They Snatch the Chicken?' revolves around a confrontational encounter between the group – the militant band of heroes – and a disciplinary apparatus. While the usual target is the police, the chicken action focuses on Voina's second favourite enemy: the supermarket. As an institution, the supermarket dazzles and taunts us with its cornucopia of food, but then restricts consumption by charging money. At the simplest level, the chicken theft calls this disciplinary authority into question and thwarts it. Indeed, the surface intention of most Voina actions can be described in a similar way. As the DIY manual suggests, the group's triumphant defeat (disturbance, duping) of the apparatus is intended as a model for emulation, teaching us how to resist.

However, Voina actions also indulge in a level of irony that makes such a straightforward reading problematic, rendering the action's relation to any conceivable 'reality' of struggle decidedly ambivalent. The call to emulation feeds off the action's authenticity – the fact that the risk, the conflict, and the chickens are all exhilaratingly 'real'. It is this authenticity that grounds the imperative to resist: Voina steals chickens, why don't you? But, at the same time, the scenario of the action – the literalization of the word *pizdit'* – renders this very reality absurd, showing no concern for actual conditions or tactics. The would-be militant viewer is thus faced with two distinct versions of the imperative. The outrageously literal version urges us to 'follow instructions' and 'snatch' our own chickens. Behind this call (and dependent on its disavowal as mere allegory or metaphor) is something more abstract: 'Live for free! Don't die a whore!' (*Zhivi besplatno! Umri bezbliadno!*).[13] Taken together, the two imperatives suspend the viewer in a zone of indistinction between authenticity and utopia, absurdity and the call to action, far removed from the stark dialectic of law and its transgression.

The ultimate effect of this ambivalence in the action is to render the question of power – and thus any relation between hysteric and master – undecidable. Despite the call to conflict and resistance, it is in fact impossible here to settle the old Leninist question of *kto kogo?* (literally 'who, whom?', i.e., who is the active subject and who is the passive object).[14] The action may seem to be about antagonism. On one side, there are the supermarket employees, mere *obyvateli* (everyday people, much like the police in other Voina actions) who are dehumanized through their incarnation of the disciplinary apparatus. On the other side, there are the heroic activists, who invade the site to lay bare the disciplinary logic that marks its borders (both internal and external). But the encounter also involves a third party: the young woman, who mediates and brings together these two worlds.[15] Her attire marks her out from the group of activists, who are all in clothing appropriate for making mischief on a hot day: T-shirts, jeans or shorts, and backpacks (Vorotnikov is shirtless). By contrast, the woman is wearing an elegant brown dress and carrying a snakeskin bag. When she appears alone in the first scene, there is no reason to suspect she is any kind of activist at all. She seems like a normal consumer, perfectly equipped to pay for her chicken.

However, when she finds the chickens and exclaims that they are 'fucking amazing', a transformation begins: the Russian word she uses – *okhuennye* – is an adjectival form of *khui* (cock), and this sets the sexual charge that goes off when the word *pizdit'* is later brought to life. In between, the engagements with the shop assistants and security guards – which are quite amiable, if a bit wild and aggressive – serve to emphasize the chickens' corporeal presence. As the Voina activists poke at the birds, step on them, press their noses against them, and so on, the relationship between consumer and commodity increasingly comes to resemble something closer to predator and prey, or lover and beloved.

When the woman finally pulls the wrapper from the chicken she intends to 'snatch', this relationship becomes even more complex and over-determined. The mad effort to stuff the chicken up her vagina evokes, first of all, a carnivalesque fusion of eating and sexual reproduction. Both processes involve the openness of the body, and the woman revels in their grotesque hybridization. At the same time, this revelry merely lays bare the supermarket's own extravagant luxury. As the phallic moniker given to the chicken suggests, the supermarket aisles offer, as it were, 'a smorgasbord of cocks for orgiastic cunt stuffing' – so many signifiers of desire calling us to enjoy. But, as any seasoned consumer knows, the appropriate response to this call is a castrated one. I will only enjoy what I can afford, waiting patiently in line with my safely wrapped chicken, disavowing the abundance all around me. The alienating process of monetary exchange mediates my encounter with the supermarket, as I accept the meagre pleasure my purchases bring. The woman, by contrast, responds as if there are no obstacles to fulfilling the supermarket's call completely. 'Yes, thank you, I will enjoy! I will stuff it up my cunt right now!'

So, who is the victor in this encounter with disciplinary power? It is impossible to say. The supermarket has been forced to reveal its hidden obscenity, but the consumer, however captivated by Voina's outlaw spirit, still submits to the call to enjoy. As a result, one cannot say that the action articulates a hysterical demand for the law to come and put things right. The supermarket and the outlaws come together, mediated by the willing consumer, in a single scene of festive enjoyment.

A similar effect occurs with the signs the actionists hold up, spelling the word *bezbliadno*. The Western-style supermarket with all of its aisles, racks, displays, security cameras, and so on, has only existed in Russia for 15 years or so, slowly replacing the old Soviet system. In the old system – the dominance of which only began to fade in the late 1990s – one had to scurry back and forth from the counters of different departments, quizzing shop assistants, getting things weighed, taking tickets to the cashier's desk, and only then returning to collect one's goods. Shopping for food used to be much more about negotiation, argument, jostling for places in line, and so on. The alienated rationality of the Western system, founded on an economy of abundance rather than Soviet deficits, swaps (often unpleasant) intimacy with one's neighbour for a closer connection to the items on sale. Now you can hold them, squeeze them, read their labels, return them to the shelves or drop them in your basket, all silently, unmolested, making your way through the labyrinthine space towards the checkout. The only thing to worry about in a capitalist supermarket is either how much money you have in your pocket (if you are honest), or where the lens of the security camera is pointed (if you are not). When Voina brings the word *bezbliadno* together under this gaze to protest against its alienated 'whoring', it stages a reunification of the fragmented space. And yet, all the while, the process of reunification is intercut with the theft of the chicken, hidden from view in a way that is only possible with just such a capitalist floor plan. Which is it, then? Are we meant to enjoy the crevices of invisibility or claim the right to unify the space under our own gaze? If the goal of the action is to liberate 'cunt' (*pizda*) from 'whore' (*bliad'*) – replacing alienated buying and selling with theft, as a more 'organic' form of acquisition – why does this mythic unity remain so dependent on fragmentation and the interstices of the alienated space?

As the follow-up to their phallic masterpiece, 'Dick Captured by the FSB', described above, the chicken action arguably tests whether a vaginal approach to such confrontations can have a similar impact. In terms of desire, the effect is indeed the same. Just as the eroticized chicken theft both revolts against the supermarket and acquiesces to its most basic command, at once transforming the supermarket site and appropriating its logic, the cock-bridge simultaneously stands in opposition to the secret police and erotically responds to

their power, rising in admiration. The manifestation of this duality is arguably the fundamental effect of Voina's practice – surface antagonism delivers
the inner secret of festive collusion. When the site of antagonism gradually
opens as a zone of indistinction, and there is no clear answer to the question
of *kto kogo?*, the power of the outlaw ceases to be one of simple transgression.
Instead of breaking the law – an act that only reaffirms the law's authority,
thus fulfilling the hysteric's demand – Voina erodes and effaces it, revealing
the heterogeneous spaces in which the law also seeks to enjoy. And it does so
by enjoying along with it.

Pavlenskii's Law

As I have argued, Voina's strategy of enjoyment lends their actions a markedly festive quality, and, on the surface, this festiveness has much in common
with Bakhtin's well-known concept of carnival. The 'material-bodily lower
stratum' is paraded everywhere, while symbols of authority are overturned
and debased (Bakhtin 1984). However, the effect is different. If carnival turns
the world upside down in order to maximize the dialectical tension between
high and low, closed and open, the beautiful and the grotesque – harnessing
the energy of transgression – Voina's festive world revolves around an enjoyment that collapses distinctions and undermines the very logic that enables us
to tell up from down in the first place.

In the chicken action, for example, one can argue that the target of Voina's
over-identification is not just the supermarket's injunction to enjoy but also
the group's own militant rejection of money, framed as an injunction to steal.
They subversively exaggerate adherence to their own law. The logic of radical *stiob* also extends beyond the content of Voina's self-presentation and
into its form, contaminating the actions' authenticity with distortions in the
documentation. Aleksei Plutser-Sarno's decidedly carnivalesque LiveJournal
reports are always deeply discordant with the visual record of the action.
Sara Stefani, for example, has noted that in his reports of the chicken action
and the orgy in the Biological Museum, Plutser writes of wild, intoxicating
excesses of bodily enjoyment, while the visual documentation shows something much more awkward and nervous (Stefani 2013).[16] Although the young
woman in the chicken action clearly struggles to get the poultry stashed away,
Plutser describes her genitals as 'The Sixteen-Feet Wide Gates' (*Semiarshinye
vrata*) and the 'Bottomless Pit of Hell' (*Adskaia bezdonnaia propast'*)
(Plutser-Sarno 2010).

The video documentation of the action engages in inflation and narrativi-
zation in its own way as well. There are at least four different supermarkets
in the video, and at least two different scenes of chicken snatching (only one
of which is successful). The *bezbliadno* display appears to have occurred at
an entirely different time from the chicken theft. Even the chicken used in the
successful snatching seems suspiciously smaller than those handled in other
parts of the film; it is very limp, as if more skin than bones. But through the

magic of montage, the viewer is encouraged to ignore the subtle evidence that the action's authenticity is quite removed from the mythic narrative on display. In other words, the action is at once staged and authentic, theatrically overblown and utterly serious – the hallmark of *stiob*.

Turning now to Pavlenskii, let us first consider the argument that his actions resemble those of Voina as a hysterical form of protest. To paraphrase Keti Chukhrov's remarks at the above-mentioned 'No Radical Art Actions' conference, actionism's focus on transgressive, hysterical self-exposure forecloses any real engagement with society and the spaces it inhabits. The actionist may display extreme courage in his/her confrontation with power, offering a heroic example to others, but s/he also turns his/her back on these others, caught up in narcissistic self-display. In this sense, Voina's chicken snatching is little different from Pavlenskii's living-pain sculptures. Each hysterically lays the body bare to the violence and obscenity of power. And, in this way, each begs the master to come and put them in their place.

However, as I have shown, Voina does not limit its practice to transgression – the sovereign decision to transgress is too immersed in festive indistinction – and exposure is always combined with concealment. With Pavlenskii's actions the hysteria argument is a better fit, although it still requires modification. Pavlenskii made a number of strong statements in the press after his recent actions. Along with the dramatized transcripts of his interrogations after *Liberty – The Interrogation of Petr Pavlenskii: A Play in Three Acts*, from which I quoted earlier, Pavlenskii also gave three long interviews, first to *Ukrainian Pravda* after his visit to the Maidan in December 2013 (Lan'ko and German 2013), and then twice to Dmitrii Volchek (2014a and 2014b) of Radio Free Europe/Radio Liberty, once after the publication of the *Liberty* play and then again after 'Separation'. In these texts the artist calls for preserving at all costs a strict divide between art and the state, referring, for example, to Manifesta 10 as political prostitution (mere decoration for the regime) and broadly defining art as any and all emancipatory practice. Maidan is the true festival of revolt that artists should look to for inspiration.

This position has a distinguished ancestry in political theory. From Georges Sorel, who argued that the proletariat should answer all gestures of compromise from the bourgeoisie with 'black ingratitude', to Frantz Fanon's celebration of violent conflict with the colonizer as a means of political subjectivization, many have argued that a resistance movement must maintain the force and ferocity of its dialectical encounter with the oppressor to the bitter (or ecstatic) end (Sorel 1999, 77; Fanon 1963, 56–58). Otherwise, the dynamic of contradiction fails, leaving us stranded in yet another frozen conflict, 'fixated' by defeat. Still, it is not difficult to see how the proletariat and the colonized in these arguments might fail to emerge as revolutionary subjects and instead drift into the position of either the hysteric, forever exposing the impotence of power, or the *homo sacer*, persisting in bare life in anticipation of some messianic moment to come. Neither of these positions offers much in

Figure 8.3 Petr Pavlenskii, 'Fixation'. November 2013
Source: Private archive, courtesy of Petr Pavlenskii.

the way of hope. The first easily suggests the idea of resistance's futility (simply waiting for a real master), while the second often seems to encourage an infinite deferral of revolt.

Even without these dangers, the efficacy of such an antagonistic strategy requires taking account of objective conditions. Who is the oppressor in Russia today? A number of interesting diagnoses have recently been proposed to explain the psychology of the regime's aggressive turn. Alexander Etkind traces its roots to the hyper-extractive oil and gas economy, which leaves the state wholly independent of the population and promotes a 'petro-macho' posture, ignoring the needs and subject positions of artists, intellectuals, and women (Etkind 2013a). Artemii Magun, by contrast, offers a diametrically opposed argument, likening Russia to a neglected wife, smashing dishes in a hysterical outburst. The modus of Putin's new foreign policy agenda desperately exposes the global order as castrated (hypocritical, empty, based on double standards, etc.), all in the hope of getting a little attention from the West (Magun 2014). Pavlenskii himself interprets the situation in a more idiosyncratically Russian way, according to the old saying: 'the problem isn't that my cow died, but that my neighbour's cow is still alive'. In other words, no one thinks of lamenting the failure of the 2011–12 protests in Russia, but it is humiliating that the clashes with police in Kiev did not fail in the same way. And so Pavlenskii offers his actions as a call to resist. If the state is alternately macho towards the populace and hysterical towards the West, and the people themselves wish only for everyone to share in the 'happiness' of being subject to such maddening vacillation, perhaps radical art actions can be deployed to force the enemy to show its true face and the people to remember they have one.

What is peculiar about Pavlenskii's position, however, is his identification of such radical non-cooperation with the autonomy of art. In the dramatized transcripts of his *Liberty* interrogations, the character 'Pavlenskii' takes an exceedingly defensive posture, resisting all attempts by the 'investigator' to blur the lines between the actionist's practice and his own (at one point the investigator even calls himself an 'artist of justice'). At every turn Pavlenskii seeks to uphold and protect the authority of art's autonomous law from that of the state. If the cop wants to be an artist, he must enrich art's symbolic codes, conceptualize his work within the narratives of art history, and communicate his message to an audience, particularly the fact that he is engaged in producing art. He must overcome himself like any true artist by doing something others find impossible. Meanwhile, the investigator gradually moves in the opposite direction, admitting that the law he embodies is empty, that he is only an instrument, that his own moment of historical accountability is coming (he resigned from his job soon after the drama was published),[17] that he has no idea what forces are behind the investigation, and – the best bit of all – that 'everyone says: we have capitalism. But in America they have democracy [...] But it's actually a lot stricter there. Really, a lot stricter and more brutal' (Pavlenskii 2014).

Caught in the maw of power's unintelligibility, the sentimental cop still wants to believe in a soft authoritarianism that might protect him from the coming flood. Pavlenskii, by contrast, wants something harder. He decries the compromises of contemporary Russians – particularly oppositional artists who participated in Manifesta – repeatedly diagnosing such behaviour as 'schizophrenic' (Volchek 2014a). But is this not a call for the same kind of disciplinary clarity – the segregation of the insane from the sane – that he critiques in 'Separation'? Choose sides, no compromises – *enough madness*. Though cutting off his earlobe clearly involved an homage to Vincent Van Gogh, Pavlenskii's call for clear boundaries is quite antithetical to the painter's own use of the gesture. Van Gogh famously gave his ear to a prostitute, saying 'guard this object carefully', thus passing the artwork (the ear) from one place of segregation to another – from madness to illicit desire. But Pavlenskii passes his ear from art's place of power to that of the police: you have your law, and I have mine. And the object itself is lost: 'I didn't get my knife or my earlobe back', Pavlenskii wryly commented after the action (Nikulin 2014). Despite such moments of humour, Pavlenskii has clearly abandoned the tradition of festive indistinction. Even his *Liberty* – meant to imitate the great 'festival' of Maidan – seemed a rather gloomy affair, its flaming tyres and rhythmic pounding of sheet metal only momentarily disturbing the winter morning's quiet darkness before the fire brigade dutifully arrived.[18]

Nevertheless, Pavlenskii's insistence on autonomy may not be as rigorous as it seems. In fact, his statements on the relationship between art and politics often verge on their own kind of schizophrenia. Maidan is a total installation, he tells us. This could mean the distinction between art and politics no longer exists, but it is also a strangely contemplative act of aestheticization, lifting the revolt out of the immediacy of struggle. The signature of one of his investigators uncannily resembles the swirling form of his 'Carcass' (see Lan'ko and German 2013). Perhaps this is evidence, as Pavlenskii claims, that he is unmasking the hidden codes of power. But the gesture also falls into line with his virtuoso ability to pull the police into the frame of his artworks and 'recode' them in his own way. Volchek compares Pavlenskii's work to the end of Vladimir Nabokov's *Invitation to a Beheading* (and the artist approves), when Cincinnatus realizes his prison and jailers are only a poorly constructed illusion and the true 'reality' is a higher-level work of artistic imagination (the novel itself). But does such a radical retreat into art not contradict Pavlenskii's own references to Kazimir Malevich, who defined art's truth as a power and mastery (*gospodstvo*) possible only through the rejection of autonomy, creating the forms of nature directly? All of these contradictions seem to escape Pavlenskii's notice. Perhaps there is some slippage behind his iron law of art after all.

It is significant, however, that these signs of ambivalence have very little to do with the undecidability of radical *stiob*. Rather, the confusion seems largely to be a side-effect of a more fundamental vacillation in Pavlenskii's practice, which is quite similar to the diagnoses of the Russian state discussed above. After all, in Chukhrov's comments, it is not simply hysterical self-exposure that defines the political inefficacy of actionism; the artists' 'extreme courage' also serves to foreclose true engagement with the other, now in the form of a 'macho' display of strength and endurance.

In the 2009 action, 'Cock in the Ass: A Punk Concert in the Taganskii Courthouse', which provided the model for Pussy Riot, Voina invaded the trial of Andrei Erofeev over his 'Forbidden Art 2006' exhibition. Launching into an impromptu punk concert, they screamed over their guitars: 'All cops are bastards, remember this'. But when the cop-bastards rushed in to stop the show, they ended up joining it, forming a mosh pit with the artists (and if you look closely, they are clearly enjoying themselves) (Plutser-Sarno 2009). Following Voina's example, Pavlenskii's actions always hinge on the moment the police arrive – a moment of great festive potential. This is when we lose our bearings regarding the question of *kto kogo?* – asking who the real 'victim' is in the action, the self-mutilating artist or the baffled police who have to decide what to do with him.

However, Pavlenskii always remains deadly serious at these moments. No doubt he is too preoccupied with remembering who the bastards and the whores are to join them in the dance. But, at the end of the day, the dance is the site of emancipation, where revolutionary action confronts the bastard and whore in each of us, and where we all must question our lineage and the cost of our desire. Instead, both the artist and the state oppose one another, each vacillating between two equally phallocentric postures: the obscene enforcement of an empty law and hysterical declarations of its emptiness. Perhaps a new slogan is needed: 'All laws are castrated, remember this'. But, then again, the lesson of Voina is not so much about memory as enjoyment: 'Enjoy your place of indistinction before the empty law'.

Conclusion

As Yurchak has shown, the late socialist period was marked by a suspension of the political, as creative practices occupied the abandoned conceptual spaces of the necrotic Soviet state (Yurchak 2006). To thrive in such conditions typically required a *stiob* ethos, practising an irony that, in its most radical form, refrains from announcing itself as such – a carnival that forgets what is up and what is down. These cultural practices did not disappear after 1991, but continued to evolve in the new context of triumphant neoliberalism. Now that the post-Soviet order has been solidified under a newly invigorated authoritarianism, it is no accident that artists and activists are wondering if the traditions of the past have outlived their usefulness. Pavlenskii clearly understands his actions in different terms, articulating their meaning from a distinct meta-position and insisting on his autonomous law. Despite the links between his practice and the earlier actionist tradition, he is serious to the core, uninterested in the festive potential of the encounters he stages with power. Many find the clarity of his work inspiring and certainly not as politically problematic as that of Voina.

However, it is precisely Pavlenskii's seriousness that makes him susceptible to vacillation between hysterical displays of castration and macho-heroism, making his practice into a mirror image of the regime itself. Neither side is a pure hysteric. Each desires a master, but neither has any hope he will come, and so hysteria must double as heroism. By contrast, Voina's strategy – the *stiob* enjoyment of bare life – sought to liberate our castrated modernity from such quashed hopes, remaking it as a site of festive indistinction. Voina was never in the business of forming the militant subjects of a more traditional revolutionary movement à la Sorel and Fanon. Rather, it worked to erode the structures of ideological interpellation that prop up the repressive social order from within.

Nevertheless, when the state began to take notice of Voina's actions and pursue them in the courts, they also seemed to forget how to enjoy the place of indistinction. After Elena Kostyleva's presentation on Voina at the 'No Radical Art Actions' conference, the artist Dmitrii Vilenskii asked about Vorotnikov's support for the annexation of Crimea, raising doubts about the group's earlier oppositional position. Kostyleva responded that Voina came up against an invisible wall in their practice with the 'Piss on the Pigs' (*Musor-obossysh*) and 'Cop Auto-Da-Fé' (*Mento-Auto-Da-Fé*) actions of 2011, after which the next step could only be violence without artistic pretentions. Unwilling to take this step, they fled and eventually abandoned their antagonistic stance towards the regime, instead targeting the self-righteous liberalism of their new European hosts. But this is no longer actionism; it is simple posturing.

Again, I do not think this means we can say that the hysteric found her master. Tolokonnikova is wrong to paint late Putinism as a new form of actionism, just as Vorotnikov is wrong to praise the Donbass insurgency from the safety of his Italian exile. Both should know that the Russian regime is not involved in the dramas of subjectivization, whether promoting a new militancy or undermining the law of castration. 'Corporation Russia' is only interested in protecting and, if possible, increasing its market share in the global economy. And, indeed, this is the level at which the Russian actionist tradition might again become useful, occupying spaces within the necrotic body of global capitalism.[19]

Author's note

This chapter reflects the state of Russian actionism in 2014 without consideration of subsequent events or developments.

Notes

1 On the Viennese Actionists, see Brus et al. 1999; on Collective Actions, see Bishop 2012; on the Necrorealists, see Yurchak 2008; on the actionism of the 1990s, see Kovalev 2007.

2 A notable example is the Petr Alekseev Resistance Movement (*Dvizhenie soprotivleniia imeni Petra Alekseeva*). See http://dspa.livejournal.com.

3 The artist has asked that his anonymity be preserved. The action's documentation can be found at www.youtube.com/watch?v=5jzas98dPV8. For the RFE/RL press report of the action; see www.svoboda.org/content/article/26555226.html (both accessed 18 September 2015).

4 Tolokonnikova is referring to Groys 1992.

5 See their conceptually muddled, over-produced response to the murder of Eric Garner by police officers in New York in 2014: www.youtube.com/watch?v=dXctA2BqF9A (accessed 18 September 2015).

6 See documentation of the discussion after the 'Art and Activism' panel: www.youtube.com/watch?v=pj7D024Wl2A (accessed 18 September 2015). Among the participants in the discussion were the poet and philosopher Keti Chukhrov, philosopher Artemii Magun, artist Dmitrii Vilenskii, political theorist Jodi Dean, Croatian curator Antonia Majaca, and political scientist and activist Maksim Aliukov.

7 For more on the theory of hysteria and castration, see Lacan 2006.

8 See Monastyrskii 2011. For a discussion of the Necrorealists and the Mit'ki, see Yurchak 2006.

9 Alexander Etkind has called for caution in using the term 'bare life' in discussions (like those of Yurchak and Santner) of works of art and literature, arguing against the possibility of aestheticizing the incommunicable experience of this condition. Instead, he sees practices like those of the Necrorealists as mnemonic performances or 'victims' balls', in this case commemorating the reduction of Soviet citizens to bare life in the Gulag. While this logic is in principle sound, one should note that the condition of bare life is always linked to representation and its blind spots. One can viciously reduce human beings to bare life – and one can commemorate this trauma – but one can also find it in the place of contradiction between life and power or between real and symbolic bodies, and this is certainly within art's area of competence. See Etkind 2013b, 97–98.

10 For example, as recently as February 2014, Tolokonnikova and Alekhina were met in Moscow's Vnukovo airport by a group of pro-Putin activists waving American flags and wearing chicken masks. The group also brought raw chickens as gifts for the artists. See www.ridus.ru/news/155135. After the 2009 split Tolokonnikova and Verzilov remained in Moscow, while Vorotnikov and his wife Natal'ia Sokol moved to St Petersburg.

11 www.imagebam.com/gallery/j2uu100acnkwnpr4g3xlsx4blbm3ot18/ (accessed 18 September 2015).

12 The verb *pizdit'* (perfective: *spizdit'*) is the most common Russian slang term for stealing. It can also mean to hit someone (similar to the English usage 'to twat someone'), but in this case the various perfective forms take different prefixes. *Pizdit'* should not be confused with *pizdet'*, which derives from the same root but means to talk nonsense or to complain.

13 Aleksei Plutser-Sarno cites this slogan in his *LiveJournal* documentation of the action (Plutser-Sarno 2010).

14 In her presentation on Voina at the 'No Radical Art Actions' conference, the poet and journalist Elena Kostyleva argued that the core question of Voina's practice is 'Kto kogo ebet?' (Who fucks whom?). Kostyleva has never officially claimed participation in any of Voina's actions.

15 This mediating role appears in many of Voina's actions, especially ones involving food. Consider, for example, the cats thrown across the McDonald's counter in 'Mordovan Hour' (*Mordovskii chas*) and the hanged homosexuals and migrant workers in 'We Don't Need Pestel', He Didn't Fall on My Cock!' (*Pestel' na khui ne upal*).

16 Plutser-Sarno – a linguist known for his multi-volume dictionary of Russian swear-words – refers to himself as the 'ideologue' of Voina, although this is largely a misdirection.
17 According to recent reports, the investigator, Pavel Iasman, has since been studying law and even attempted to represent Pavlenskii in his court case over the *Liberty* action. See Nechepurenko 2015.
18 Documentation of the action can be found at www.youtube.com/watch?v=3dS88c9-KSM (accessed 18 September 2015).
19 For an idea how such practices might be on the rise (albeit far less radically so) in the West, see Boyer and Yurchak 2010.

References

Agamben, Giorgio. 1998. *Homo Sacer: Sovereign Power and Bare Life*. Stanford, CA: Stanford University Press.
Bakhtin, Mikhail. 1984. *Rabelais and His World*. Bloomington: Indiana University Press.
Bishop, Claire. 2012. *Artificial Hells: Participatory Art and the Politics of Spectatorship*. New York: Verso.
Boyer, Dominic and Alexei Yurchak. 2010. "American Stiob: Or, What Late-Socialist Aesthetics of Parody Reveal about Contemporary Political Culture in the West." *Cultural Anthropology* 25 (2): 179–221.
Brus, Günter, Otto Muehl, Hermann Nitsch, and Rudolf Schwarzkogler. 1999. *Writings of the Viennese Actionists*. London: Atlas Press.
Etkind, Aleksandr. 2013a. "Petromacho: ili Mekhanizmy demodernizatsii v resursnom gosudarstve." *Neprikosnovennyi zapas* 88. www.nlobooks.ru/node/3432. (accessed 18 September 2015).
Etkind, Alexander. 2013b. *Warped Mourning: Stories of the Undead in the Land of the Unburied*. Stanford, CA: Stanford University Press.
Fanon, Frantz. 1963. *The Wretched of the Earth*. New York: Grove Press.
Groys, Boris. 1992. *The Total Art of Stalinism: Avant-Garde, Aesthetic Dictatorship, and beyond*. Princeton, NJ: Princeton University Press.
Kovalev, Andrei. 2007. *Rossiiskii aktsionizm, 1990–2000*. Moscow: WAM.
Lacan, Jacques. 2006. "Direction of the Treatment and the Principles of Its Power." In *Écrits: The First Complete Edition in English*, 489–542. New York: Norton.
Lacan, Jacques. 2007. *The Other Side of Psychoanalysis: The Seminar of Jacques Lacan: Book XVII*. New York: Norton.
Lan'ko, Mariia and Lizaveta German. 2013 "Petr Pavlenskii: Maidan dolzhen prisutstvovat' v povsednevnosti kazhdogo, kto ego podderzhivaet." *Ukrains'ka pravda* 23 December. http://life.pravda.com.ua/person/2013/12/23/146798/ (accessed 18 September 2015).
Magun, Artemii. 2014. "Istericheskii makiavellizm, ili Pochemu deiatel'nost' Rossii v Ukraine sostoit v tsinichnom kopirovanii Zapada." *Slon* 12 September. http://slon.ru/russia/istericheskiy_makiavellizm_ili_pochemu_deyatelnost_rossii_v_ukraine_sostoit_v_tsinichnom_kopirovanii-1156109.xhtml (accessed 18 September 2015).
Monastyrskii, Andrei. 2011. "Predislovie." In *Kollektivnye desitviia: Poezdkam za gorod*, Vol. 1, edited by N. Alekseev, G. Kizeval'ter, A. Monastyrskii, and N. Panitkov, 9–16. Vologda: Biblioteka Moskovskogo Kontseptualizma Germana Titova. www.conceptualism-moscow.org/files/KD-tom1-small.pdf (accessed 2 April 2017).

Nechepurenko, Ivan. 2015. "How Russia's Most Notorious Artist Convinced His Interrogator to Switch Sides." *The Moscow Times* 26 July.

Nikulin, Pavel. 2014. "'Ni nozh, ni mochku ne vernuli': Petr Pavlenskii – o svoem zaderzhanii posle aktsii 'Otdelenie'," *Bumaga* 21 October. http://paperpaper.ru/zachem/ (accessed 18 September 2015).

Pavlenskii, Petr. 2014. "Dopros Petra Pavlenskogo: P'esa v trekh deistviiakh". *Snob* 29 July. http://snob.ru/selected/entry/77648 (accessed 18 September 2015).

Plutser-Sarno, Aleksei. 2009. "Novaia aktsiia Voiny 'Khui v Ochko'. Pank-kontsert v zale Taganskogo suda: pesnia 'Vse menty ubliudki!'" http://plucer.livejournal.com/157798.html (accessed 18 September 2015).

Plutser-Sarno, Aleksei. 2010. "Novaia aktsia gruppy Voina 'Poshto pizdili Kuru?' ili 'Skaz o tom, kak Pizda Voinu kormila'." *LiveJournal.* http://plucer.livejournal.com/281211.html (accessed 18 September 2015).

Santner, Eric. 1999. *The Royal Remains: The People's Two Bodies and the Endgames of Sovereignty.* Chicago: University of Chicago Press.

Sorel, Georges. 1999. *Reflections on Violence.* Cambridge: Cambridge University Press.

Stefani, Sara. 2013. "Make War, Not Love: Art Collective Voina and the Post-Soviet Bodyscape." Paper presented at the ASEEES Convention, Boston, 21–24 November.

Volchek, Dmitrii. 2014a. "Ekonomika karatel'noi vlasti." *Radio Svoboda* 7 August. www.svoboda.org/content/article/26518544.html (accessed 18 September 2015).

Volchek, Dmitrii. 2014b. "Nozh dlia pokornykh ovets." *Radio Svoboda* 25 October. www.svoboda.org/content/article/26654842.html (accessed 18 September 2015).

Yurchak, Alexei. 2006. *Everything Was Forever, Until It Was No More: The Last Soviet Generation.* Princeton, NJ: Princeton University Press.

Yurchak, Alexei. 2008. "Necro-Utopia: The Politics of Indistinction and the Aesthetics of the Non-Soviet." *Current Anthropology* 49 (2): 199–224.

Zaitseva, Anna. 2010. "Spektakuliarnye formy protesta v sovremennoi Rossii: Mezhdu iskusstvom i sotsial'noi terapiei." *Neprikosnovennyi zapas* 4. http://magazines.russ.ru/nz/2010/4/za4-pr.html (accessed 18 September 2015).

Zupančič, Alenka. 2008. *The Odd One In: On Comedy.* Cambridge, MA: MIT Press.

9   Bleep and ***

Speechless protest

Birgit Beumers

On 8 April 2013 the Russian president signed a law to effectuate a change to the Federal Law Part I, Article 4, 'About Mass Media',[1] banning the use of obscene language (*netsenzurnaia bran'*) in the media.[2] A year later, on 23 April 2014, the Duma passed another law on the prohibition of obscene language in the mass media, cinema, and theatre, which reflects the state's increasing control over culture and especially its language. The new legislation stipulate changes to the existing law on 'The State Language of the Russian Federation' ('O gosudarstvennom iazyke RF'), by adding the outlets of cinema and stage performances to the mass media; by changing the licensing conditions for films; and by levelling fines for administrative offences, i.e. the organization of public performances, the distribution of audio-visual production, and the screening of films without a licence. Law No. 101-F3 was signed by President Putin on 5 May 2014 and came into force on 1 July 2014. The law effectively makes changes to a set of other laws – 'About State Language'; 'About State Support for Cinema of the Russian Federation'; and 'Codex of Administrative Breaches' – while making no distinction between fictional and non-fictional works.

The new law instantly gave rise to a heated debate in the art world over the fate of several films, including Andrei Zviagintsev's *Leviathan* (*Leviafan*, 2014), which had at the time just premiered in Cannes and garnered an award for Best Script, and which was due for release in Russia, awaiting a licence for distribution.[3] Zviagintsev's film was a test case that attracted much attention because of its international status, and because the film exposes the degeneration of moral values in Russian society, targeting primarily figures of (regional) political and religious authority. However, the producer had applied for a license before 1 July and received the classification 18+.[4]

Meanwhile, the new legislation is supported by the majority of Russians: 84 per cent support the introduction of fines for the use of obscene language in the media – even if 57 per cent admit to using vulgar words to express strong emotions (Dobrynina 2014). Eager to expose any attempt of the Putin administration to enforce the legislation and link it to state censorship, the Western media interpreted the new law as a 'move harking back to the cultural conservatism of Russia's Communist years' and 'Soviet-era style legislation'

(Marszal 2014). However, as we shall see below, neither the restriction on vulgar language nor that on on age classification alone represent a fundamental departure from Western practice.

The legal prohibition of obscene language is confined to four words and their derivatives, which are not listed in the actual legislation, but which were subsequently specified by the Federal Service for Supervision in the Sphere of Telecom, Information Technologies and Mass Communications (Roskomnadzor):

> The obscene designation for the male sexual organ, the obscene designation for the female sexual organ, the obscene designation for the act of copulation and the obscene designation for a woman of dissolute conduct, and any lingual units derived from these words.
>
> (Zykov and Kondrat'ev 2013)

There are no restrictions on abusive vocabulary describing homosexual and incestuous acts or defecation, as is the case in UK and US legislation, where such obscene words are normally bleeped out in public broadcasts.[5]

Contrary to the impression created by Western media reports, Russia is not the only country to have legislation prohibiting the use of indecent language in the media; and other countries, too, have reinforced, or attempted to reinforce, the definition of what is permissible and what not. Instead of pointing the finger at the Russian legislation, it might be worth looking at its application and noting two other aspects: first, the fact that Russian legislation differs from that of Western countries in specifically including the performing arts and cinema; and second, the role of obscene language in Soviet and Russian culture in a historical perspective, where it served as a language of dissent from a sanitized, official Soviet jargon, partly determined by the fact that dissident intellectuals had served prison sentences along with criminals and adopted prison jargon, continuing to use it after their release as a sign of dissent (Beumers and Lipovetsky 2009, 49–67).

This chapter explores the use of obscene language in public performances on stage and screen, less in confrontation with the new legislation than as an attempt to forge a language of dissent at a time when the state shows an increased concern with propriety and conduct and with suppressing such a discourse. In contrast to the dissidents of the 1960s and 1970s, the use of vulgar language to express dissent and protest against a status quo today happens largely in the virtual and performative world, thus marking a shift of protest from the real, political arena into a form of spectacle that suggests *a priori* a disempowerment of the actors/agents in the real world. Indeed, Vladimir Gel'man has noted elsewhere in this volume the shift between generations, which has brought with it a shift from word to deed; similarly, Alexandra Yatsyk analyses the use of the body to make statements; in line with this deemphasis of the word, I suggest that words are merely provocative sounds in a recital. (Indeed, consider the emphasis on movement and appearance in the

Pussy Riot case, where fairly little attention was paid to the lyrics). The language of protest resorts to vulgarisms as a replacement for the word as a (now inefficient) political weapon, and the prohibition of this jargon of dissent is effectively a prohibition of the dissenting voice *per se*.

As the Swiss theatre director and journalist Milo Rau, founder of the International Institute of Political Murder (IIPM), has astutely pointed out, there is a fundamental difference between the dissidence of the Cold War era and today's dissent, and it is dangerous to confuse the two. The Western idea of dissidence is rooted in cases such as those of Andrei Sakharov and Aleksandr Solzhenitsyn, which is a romanticized image; today's protest is much more complex, involving issues of state support for anti-state artists and events (Rau 2014, 10–11). The difference lies precisely in the relationship between protest and the state/power/authority: in the Soviet era, protest was articulated in real spaces rather than artificially created and marked performance spaces. Curiously, one of the actor-witnesses in Milo Rau's *Moscow Trials* (2013; see below)[6] made a comment about the 'trials' of Sakharov and Solzhenitsyn, confusing myth and reality: there never were trials against these two figures, who were sent into internal and external exile respectively without any judicial proceedings.[7] Indeed, the form of the trial as a judiciary format belongs more to the Soviet history of the 1930s, when 'show trials' served to constitute examples and display the state's power for terror (see Schuler 2013); yet this strategy would be revised in the 1970s, when exile and house arrest were more common, hushing up rather than exposing. Moreover, the difference between dissidence as protest against an official policy, and dissent – as the articulation of opinions that differ from those commonly or officially held – is important: it lies precisely in the voicing, i.e. the public performance, of such differing opinions. I intend to investigate here the element of (public) performance and display: the game played through abusive, vulgar, and obscene language used to express dissent; the play with images recorded for the camera; and acts of stage performance. I wish to explore whether the ban on obscene language is a question of codes of conduct and propriety, or of the suppression of a discourse of dissent – an act of silencing.

Mat: the language of protest, or language as protest

Effectively, the law against the use of obscene and vulgar language in public (on stage, screen, and television) is part of a general conservative turn in Russia as discussed in Part I of this volume, and has two targets: first, to satisfy public opinion by targeting public order; and second, to legislate against a discourse of dissent. The use of obscene language is a thorn in the flesh of Putin's government as it attempts to introduce public order in a society that was governed by thugs and criminals in the 1990s. Indeed, the language used by figures of authority is often if not obscene and vulgar, then far from impeccable: there is the much-quoted phrase used by Putin himself at a press conference in Astana on 24 September 1999 about terrorists: that they 'will waste in the shithouse' ('my i v sortire ikh zamo-chim'); or the puritan Dmitrii Medvedev's reference to the investigators who searched cameraman Pavel Kostomarov's apartment in December 2012 as 'jerks' ('kozly', literally 'goats'); or a statement from the head of the Ural Regional Centre of the Ministry for Extraordinary Situations (MChS), Iurii Naryshkin, commenting on the impact of a meteorite near Cheliabinsk (Naryshkin, in Pushkarev 2013), which ultimately led to his dismissal.

In the world of literature, one of the most prominent cultural phenomena to promote vulgar language is the so-called New Drama movement, which emerged in the late 1990s following attempts (including of foreign masters) to revive Russia's theatre scene and inject fresh blood into playwriting. The Royal Court Theatre London conducted several seminars in Moscow, promoting the verbatim technique in an attempt to rejuvenate the language spoken on stage and make it more authentic, with the effect that the use of un-edited and un-smoothed vulgar language, or *mat*, became a widespread stage practice. In Soviet times, *mat* was traditionally perceived as the antithesis to the language of culture, permitted only in small doses or for emphasis, or as expression of protest against official culture – and certainly not on stage (Beumers and Lipovetsky 2009).

The use of the verbatim technique, which gave rise to a wave of documentary theatre, accentuated the performative aspects of *mat*. In documentary theatre *mat* is largely a tribute to the hyper-naturalistic discourse of a fidelity to life (which can be aligned with *chernukha* in cinema of the 1990s), rather than a sign of a debilitation of society caused by the landslide of the entire culture. The legalization of obscene language in print in the 1990s had led to much intellectual debate about the socio-cultural functions of this sphere of language, and its prohibition in the new law consequently has repercussions for the discourses of contemporary culture.

Abusive language from a theatrical stage is doubly performative: as prospective verbal action, it is directed both at another character and at the spectator, consciously or unconsciously recording the infringement of a cultural taboo. Moreover, the performativity of *mat* in documentary theatre also gives the plays a distinctly corporeal quality: thanks to obscene metaphors, any social and psychological reaction is instantly unconsciously translated onto the level of corporeal relations. This dominating semantic of *mat* in documentary theatre colours other functions of this linguistic sphere, too: the function of a marker of linguistic freedom from dominating discourse; the function of language of power and submission; the function of linguistic embodiment of frustration and aggression; and as 'direct', nominative language in the sexual sphere (Beumers and Lipovetsky 2009).

Obscene, abusive, non-normative language, then, has long been a form of protest, rejecting official discourses. Such protest is a manifestation, a performance that does not amount to political action. The protest movement today functions, I suggest, in the same way: protests are staged acts of dissent, often – but not always – in artistic form; therefore they require above all a spectator, an audience, a camera more than they do an ally or a supporter.

The silence of protest

The recording of protest on camera is often more important than the act of protest itself. The wider distribution of such recordings effectively happens through social networks, which offer a platform for dissent with officialdom. Moreover, reports on LiveJournal, Facebook, VKontakte, and other social networks are more trusted among citizens, including the intelligentsia, than reports in the mass media, whoever owns them. Social networks seem to empower people, allowing them to document reality from their own perspective; they mobilize and break traditional boundaries of ownership of the 'truth'. Yet telling the story from an individual point of view may be authentic, but it does not necessarily provide an unbiased or full picture of an event. While social media present an alternative to state-controlled media, I suggest that they cannot offer an independent, disengaged, or objective version.

The fixation of protest through various visual media and the diffusion through social networks is a key feature of the protest movement. While the system (police, state) fights protest itself, the distribution of the footage through social media can turn even small-scale events, which might attract no more than a few hundred people, into major protest actions through 'likes' and virtual support. Similarly, a performance staged for a few members of the

Figure 9.1 Still from the Pussy Riot performance from the footage used in *Winter, Go Away*, showing the intervention by church guardians
Source: Courtesy of Marina Razbezhkina.

public can be turned into a mass event through social media. The importance of the mobile (phone) camera that captures events as they unfold offers seemingly un-edited, therefore authentic and truthful, footage, which is also uncensored. However, many events gain significance only through their presence and multiple views on social media and YouTube. Moreover, they are often edited: for example, the actual performance of Pussy Riot in the Cathedral of Christ the Saviour (Fig. 9.1) lasted only 40 seconds, and the amplification system was not connected; the posted footage extends the duration of the performance and provides the proper sound track; furthermore, the footage has been edited and intercut with images from the group's earlier performance at the Yelokhov Cathedral.

> Pussy Riot gained popularity thanks to video clips posted on YouTube in winter–spring 2012, especially after the release on 21 February 2012 of their 'punk prayer' entitled 'Mother of God, Please Chase Putin Away!' [Pank molitva 'Bogoroditsa, Putina progoni']. According to the website of the art group, the clip was viewed 600,000 times in a matter of days. A year later the number of views of the clip on YouTube has exceeded a few hundred million, suggesting Pussy Riot has turned into a global media phenomenon.
>
> (Strukov 2013, 91)

There are two reasons for the importance of social media in the protest movement: the first is that, as the sociologist Lev Gudkov has argued, the protest movement (2011–13, see below) was actually losing authority already in 2012 (see Lonkila 2012). Its leaders, such as Aleksei Navalnyi and Il'ia Iashin, had no agenda for change: 'the leaders of the protest movement have no clear programme of action and cannot offer any perspective for the development of the protest mood' (Gudkov 2012b). Indeed, the protest movement lost impetus: the sense of resignation to the status quo was widespread throughout the period, and only a few people were prepared to actually take to the streets and protest; even fewer believed in having any control over political life (Gudkov 2012a). The lack of initiative is something that Gudkov has traced back to the Soviet past, to a system that stripped man of any responsibility (Gudkov 2004). Although numbers alone do not matter, for comparison, the maximum number of protesters during the Snow Revolution reached 150,000, while the peace rallies in June 1982 attracted 500,000 people (Bonn), and New York's No Nukes Rally one million people. In this instance, the actuality of the protest movement does not hold up to historical comparison at international level.[8]

The arrests during the protest meetings served the purpose of asserting authority, establishing order, displaying state control. However, the media documentation makes many of these events (which could presumably otherwise be hushed up) a true slap in the face of the authority that has little or no grip on – and no understanding of – social networks. Therefore, the images of protest meetings in films – documentary and fiction alike – tell interesting stories of the role of the camera as a tool of protest. The camera documents both protest and its restriction; but the camera image can also be used as evidence in court, as Cristina Vatulescu has demonstrated (2010). The investigative method of filming raises ethical issues: to what extent can documentary footage incriminate protesters, and to what extent can it defend them; to what extent does it record history and to what extent does it make a myth?

The search of the flat of cinematographer and filmmaker Pavel Kostomarov – winner of a Silver Lion in Berlin for his camerawork on Aleksei Popogrebskii's film *How I Ended this Summer* (*Kak ia provel etim letom*, 2010) – on 7 December 2012 is another sign of the potential threat that the state perceives in images of protest. Kostomarov had been shooting with Aleksandr Rastorguev and the journalist Aleksei Pivovarov for the online film project titled *The Term* (*Srok*), posted on LiveJournal since 21 May 2012; the project folded on 21 December after the search and was subsequently taken on by the platform lenta.ru under the title *Lenta.doc* (from 21 January 2013), where the final cut of the film was also published in the summer 2014, after the film's official premiere at Karlovy Vary Film Festival. The film tells of the leaders of the protest movement, fixating their view and actions. The story of the film's release on an alternative platform as well as at an international film festival speaks of the attention that the producers sought beyond the Russian social media, and contradicts Andrew Chapman's suggestion that the use of mobile phone footage and digital cameras empowers people and raises them to the status of a producer:

> *The Term* is not simply a form of political activism by way of its content. Its activism stems from how it encourages digital consumers to become digital producers. The filmmakers are mobilizing new cameramen to travel across the Russian landscape and beyond, to capture the emotion, life and conflict found in everyday life.
>
> (Chapman 2014, 101)

Although footage, and later the film, was available on various platforms, the support of the international festival circuit was clearly an important factor in getting the project international media attention; moreover, the film had a team of professional producers working on the final cut.

This apparent mobilization of the consumer, or the people, connects to an older documentary tradition and is reminiscent of Mikhail Slutskii and Roman Karmen's *A Day of the New World* (*Den' novogo mira*, 1940),[9] covering the day from morning to evening in different locations in the Soviet Union. Accompanied by Iurii Levitan's narrative voiceover, the film was shot by 97 cameramen on Saturday 24 August 1940. The multiple views offered simultaneously from different points in space suggest the omnipresence of the camera, and thereby maximum coverage rather than a selection of positions. Chapman's interpretation that empowerment lies in elevating the daily routine to a national picture in fact echoes dangerously closely the ambition of Slutskii and Karmen's project, namely of presenting a visually and narratively unified nation through the collage of individual portraits:

> *The Term* gently prods at the sore spots of Russian daily life, and overturns dominant hierarchies on the smallest levels, showing minute battles being won on a daily level. It places these moments within a larger historical and national picture, linking viewer-producers who collect stories on the micro level to form a chronicle told on a national macro level. At the heart of these small battles is mobilization and activity of people.
>
> (Chapman 2014, 103)

The empowerment suggested by the fact that history is made by individuals, who are given a camera and who place their footage onto a platform where a mosaic of (hi)stories is built, is somewhat misleading. While it may seem an empowerment to control the footage that later composes history, the official historical narrative is made on another level, and these histories have little or no impact on that story written in the (real) world of politics. In that real world, protesters are arrested, sentenced, and silenced; in the real world, a few people stand in the street to protest, not millions; in the real world, these protests (or demonstrations) – whether by a minority or a majority – are ignored by governments (and this applies not only to Russia). Democracy appears to consist of the demonstration of views, the performance of protest or support for a set of policies, with no bearing on real politics. People demonstrate their views: they have been filmed, they have voiced their dissent – and then the performance is over, politicians get back to business, and 'the people are silent' ('narod bezmolvstvuet'), to use the final phrase of Pushkin's *Boris Godunov*. In his production of the play at the Lenkom Theatre in 2014 director Konstantin Bogomolov provokes the audience early on by projecting these words onto multiple screens for several minutes, leaving the audience to wait for the action to resume, until an actor rises from amid the audience to challenge the tsar. With similar poignancy, the charge of inactivity had been levelled at the public some 25 years earlier in Iurii Liubimov's production of *Boris Godunov* (1982, released 1988) at the Taganka Theatre, where the stage lights were redirected at the audience as the final line – 'Why are you silent?' – was spoken by Godunov (Beumers 1997, 254). The voicelessness of the people was criticized in the late-Soviet era as much as today, with one crucial difference: the audience of the 1980s listened, and got the point: the intelligentsia audience of the Taganka theatre was able to take change into their hands when invited by Gorbachev to help reform the country (see Gel'man in this volume); the audience of 2015 does not even hear the provocation: they are consumers who have paid to be entertained, and they can only whistle and shout at the inactivity on stage. Bogomolov highlights the people's voicelessness (where protest is a staged performance), while the stage action draws obvious parallels between the illegitimate tsar Godunov and President Putin, between the tsar's advisors and the military, religious, and political advisors to the Russian president.

Protest on screen, documentary style

When talking of documentary forms, we should be aware that documentation does not contradict myth-making, whether ideological or individual. The involvement of artists in the protest movement confirms a conflation between fact and fiction, between art and politics. The art groups Voina (War) and Pussy Riot engage specifically in actions designed to challenge the system. Their work, as indeed that of many artist-activists, would be limited in its reach had it not been for the recorded visual and acoustic evidence, be it published on YouTube or in documentaries.

The work with documentary footage thus requires a great degree of responsibility during the shooting and editing process. The strictest form of documentarism today is practised by the students of Marina Razbezhkina's independent school of documentary cinema. The degree project *Winter, Go Away* (*Zima ukhodi!*, 2012) was directed by Elena Khoreva, Denis Klebleev, Askol'd Kurov, Dmitrii Kubasov, Nadezhda Leont'eva, Anna Moiseenko, Madina Mustafina, Zosia Rodkevich, Anton Seregin, and Aleksei Zhiriakov. This film about the protest movement consists of a series of scenes showing protests, footage from the presidential elections, and interviews with leaders of the protest movement (Fig. 9.2). The difference between this and *The Term* lies in the awareness of the object of being filmed. The performative aspect in showing off for the camera may not be an honest form of expression, but it is an authentic form of recording and documenting, as opposed to the 'life caught unawares' approach of *The Term*. Both projects, however, remain dissociated from genuine political engagement or responsibility, and stand instead as a form of escape into another virtuality where problems can be solved, like in reality television.

Where *The Term* and *Winter, Go Away* serve to document the protest movement, films such as *Pussy Riot: A Punk Prayer* (2013) by Mike Lerner and Maxim Pozdorovkin and *Pussy vs. Putin* (2013) by Gogol's Wives, or Andrei Griazev's *Tomorrow* (*Zavtra*, 2012), about the art group Voina, have an agenda: they aim to expose. In the case of Griazev, his film documents the everyday life of the art group Voina, showing not only a number of their political actions but also their private life: leaving the toddler Caspar to discover the world for himself and taking him to protests; arguments within the group; their habits of stealing food from shops and picking clothing from skips. The portrayal of their anarchic lifestyle elicited a sense of misrepresentation and the group twice took the filmmaker to court, once in Berlin and once in Moscow, both times unsuccessfully. Legal action is paradoxically used by protesters to forge their public image.

More interesting here, however, are the two documentaries about Pussy Riot. *Pussy Riot: A Punk Prayer* explores the lives of Mariia Alekhina,

Figure 9.2 Still from *Winter, Go Away*
Source: Courtesy of Marina Razbezhkina.

Ekaterina Samutsevich, and Nadezhda Tolokonnikova – the three women arrested after their performance of the 'Punk Prayer' in the Cathedral of Christ the Saviour on 21 February 2012. The performance on the soleas created outrage, largely among the Russian Orthodox Church and its supporters, because it represented a breach of the code of conduct in an Orthodox Church, where women are not admitted to the area around the Holy Gates. Curiously, Samutsevich holds the view that the Cathedral of Christ the Saviour is no sacral place, but a symbol of power; therefore, she asserts, there are formally no codes of conduct and no restrictions on movement in a cathedral (Rau 2014, 117). The film highlights that CCTV footage helped identify the women. Thus, the documentary explores the use of surveillance cameras against the group, while mobile camera footage serves to promote the group and their actions. The film contextualizes the performance with several preceding actions staged by Pussy Riot and Voina. Largely, though, the film shows the trial and the appeal, drawing on evidence supplied by one of the lawyers of the team (who then wanted to retain the rights to the film and subsequently initiated a court case). The film exposes a certain degree of incompetence on the part of the defence lawyers, both in their visual portrayal (texting during the trial, disinterested in their clients) and in their speeches. The acquittal of Samutsevich after she changed her lawyer adds to this perception, although the film suggests that visual evidence proved that she did not perform on the soleas. The film is remarkable particularly for the interviews with the girls' parents. It also includes footage from the Bearers of the Cross, on the other hand, which largely serves to discredit the opposition (the church, believers) as fanatics. A comparison to the show trials of the 1930s and to the dissidents of the 1960s and 1970s is suggested, but not elaborated further.

It is also interesting to note a fact that is rarely brought into the discussion of the Pussy Riot case: the performance for which they were arrested took place in a public location; their faces were recorded on CCTV, which served to identify the women; the footage was posted on social media soon after the event. However, a few days earlier, on 18 February, another performance took place in the Yelokhov Cathedral, the oldest church and seat of the Patriarch during Soviet years. There, the performance was filmed by Tolokonnikova's four-year-old daughter Gera. The footage was also posted on the internet (and, as mentioned earlier, edited in to the clip of the performance at Christ the Saviour). Yet nothing happened: an old woman told the group that their behaviour was inappropriate, but no further action was taken. For that reason, it appears, they took to the Cathedral of Christ the Saviour. In any charge brought against Pussy Riot one would have expected the prosecution to cite the previous incident to confirm the accusation of premeditated action.

Pussy vs. Putin takes a somewhat different approach, even if drawing on similar footage. It includes footage from various actions staged by Pussy Riot, beautifully shot and edited by the group to suit the way they wish to represent themselves. As such, the film is a cinematic pamphlet.

Both Voina and Pussy Riot have gained attention thanks to social networks and the Internet. Both groups deliberately commercialize their actions while adhering in everyday life to an anarchic form of protest against any social convention. There is a difference between destruction and disruption of public order and provocative artistic engagement, as should become clear from Kristina Norman's reflective chapter in this volume. Documentary footage here serves to create an image, a myth; the diffusion through social media rather than a thoughtful form of artistic reflection by the artists-activists themselves creates a significant contrast with such projects as Norman's *Bronze Soldier*.

Protest on display: fictional images

Fictional film images are, in that respect, more honest about their status: they lay no claim to authenticity, instead emphasizing the qualities of re-enactment, display, and show. While the role of documentary footage has been surrounded by cinematic debate – concerning the use of home videos (Vitalii Manskii in *Private Chronicles. Monologue* [*Chastnye khroniki. Monolog*], 1999); the intrusiveness of the camera (Gai Germanika in *Girls* [*Devochki*], 2005); intervention through editing (Andrei Zaitsev, *My House* [*Moi dom*], 2000) – feature films had seemingly dealt with their relationship to reality in the heated debates around *chernukha* in the early 1990s, and especially the focus on the criminal world.

One of the central charges that protesters levelled at the Putin administration was the multiplication of ministries and administrative offices, and consequently the number of people who work to fill their own pockets. And this is not a new topic: corruption and lawlessness had reigned during the Yeltsin era, and the police force has not since been invested with any degree of trust, competence, or authority. The number of crime serials showing poor policemen heroically fighting crime and often being outwitted by the Mafia rose steeply in the late 1990s and early 2000s.[10] This sense of lawlessness created a situation where people took justice into their own hands: *samosud*, or the appearance of the avenger, has been prominent in fiction films (Oushakine 2013; Goscilo 2010).

The protest movement, by contrast, has made only rare appearances in fiction films. The documentation of the movement and self-publication on social media and YouTube apparently forms a wide enough platform. Sergei Mokritskii's *Protest Day* (*Den' uchitelia*, 2012) is one of the few examples where the protest movement features prominently. The film follows the life of a schoolteacher, who comes from an old intelligentsia family. He teaches Russian literature but is completely incapable of managing his life, having recently divorced his wife. The film records the intelligentsia's inability to sort out their lives, to survive in contemporary Russia. But Mokritskii goes further than that: the intelligentsia has lost not only the ability to master reality, but also its influence on society, not to mention its role as ideological and political think-tank. It stands helplessly in the face of protest – which is carried out in a different form and by a different class and a different generation. Tellingly, the teacher goes against the current – against the flow of the people; he has no idea what is going on; and he ends up, willy-nilly, on a park bank with a hot-dog, sitting next to a policeman – one is a bemused onlooker, the other has a job he could not care less about (Fig. 9.3). Mokritskii's film is maybe the most interesting manifestation of protest because he places his actor into the crowd of an actual march. Moreover, he makes a poignant statement about the different class that composes the protest movement: the intelligentsia, once influential even on the (Soviet) government and ideologists, has been disempowered; the protesters have no illusions about their role in politics: therefore they lack an agenda. 'The women of Pussy Riot are representatives of a new dissidence, which is more decided but, in regard to their relationship to the government, also more disillusioned than most people in the 1980s and 1990s' (Rau 2014, 10).

Of course, protest in artistic form started much earlier than the Snow Revolution of 2011–13, in particular through art exhibitions. Proceedings against artist-activists had taken place already in April 2000, when Oleg Mavromatti staged a self-crucifixion near the Cathedral of Christ the Saviour; a legal complaint from the local Orthodox community followed, and Mavromatti was charged under Article 282 for inciting religious animosity. He subsequently left the country for Bulgaria. Another scandal surrounded Aleksandr Kosolapov's 'Caviar Icon' (*Ikona-ikra*, 1989), on display in the Tretyakov Gallery: an Orthodox group requested the work to be removed in 2005; the request was granted. Even earlier, the exhibition 'Beware, Religion!'

Figure 9.3 Still from the film *Protest Day*
Source: Courtesy of Novye Liudi.

(*Ostorozhno, religiia*) at the Andrei Sakharov Centre Moscow had been van-
dalized four days after its opening in January 2003. Subsequently, it was
not the hooligans but the museum's directors who were convicted and fined
under Article 282.[11] Under the same article, the museum's director and the
exhibition's curator Andrei Erofeev were fined in June 2010 for the exhibition 'Forbidden Art 2006' (*Zapretnoe iskusstvo 2006*) which ran 7–31 March
2007 and showed shelved artworks (see Jonson 2015). Thus, there had been a
series of incidents where the authorities applied the law rigidly; they all concerned religious issues and were based on complaints from Orthodox groups
or representatives of the Russian Orthodox Church rather than political institutions. This may help explain why language (visual, corporeal, and verbal)
stands at the core of the complaints. The artist-activists speak a language
that offends representatives of the Orthodox Church, which seeks to play the
moral judge and influence the state in a way that (communist) ideology had
done in the Soviet era. In other words: not censorship but the law is applied
specifically to root out any action that may be perceived as an attack on the
church and the conduct it promotes. Along these lines, we may also explain
the harsh proceedings against *Tannhäuser*.

The 'sacral' status of the classical text has been at the heart of debates that
developed in the aftermath of the scandal surrounding Timofei Kuliabin's production of Richard Wagner's *Tannhäuser*, which premiered at Novosibirsk's
Opera House on 20 December 2014. After huge critical acclaim, the production was deemed to represent an insult to religious feelings; the local
Metropolitan Tikhon took the matter to court. Kuliabin had interpreted the

opera in a contemporary vein, in which Tannhäuser is a filmmaker who has just completed a film version of the early years of Christ, which he had spent in the grotto of Venus – as a way of linking the mythical setting of the opera's first act to the remainder of the action on the Wartburg. Here, it is not a singers' contest that takes place but a film festival, where Tannhäuser's film is announced with a poster of the crucified Christ on Venus' private parts (Borodianskii 2015). 'Moreover, the slippery relationship between religion and art, i.e. the theme of vulnerability of the "feelings of believers" really does not worry the director. He is concerned with the fate of the artist and the issue of artistic freedom' (Dolzhanskii and Renanskii 2014). On 13 March 2015, the Ministry of Culture[12] summoned the theatre's manager Boris Mezdrich and ordered changes to the show, announcing that it would not finance 'such productions'; following an audit at the theatre, Mezdrich was relieved of his post; the production has been removed from the repertoire.

Once again, there is a parallel to the provocative work of Iurii Liubimov in the 1960s and 1970s, which ultimately also drew the censors' criticism for its exposure of the state's suppression of the artist; in other words: the debate is focused on the limits of the permissible in a cultural system that is largely state-funded. If the stage version of the opera protests against the conflation of art and religion, voicing on stage a fictional protest of the community of film critics against Tannhäuser's film, then this apparently does not lead to a recognition of restrictive policies and their application in the very same case. This is indicative of the blurred line between fiction and reality, between the myth being made and the events as they unfold.

Conclusion: performing protest

Protest, then, is only a performance that expresses the desire for change and the dissatisfaction with the status quo. It is a manifestation in the context of despair, where no real change is possible. It is 'in' to be arrested and to be seen in opposition to the government, society, the establishment, and those who are rich; this is evident in the anarchic lifestyle of Voina. Protest is an act of display without a purpose or an agenda oriented towards the future.

The performative aspect of protest turns the real into a representation, where participants and audience are seemingly in control of the crisis, because of the ritual form. Thus, performing protest becomes part of normalcy. As Guy Debord (1983, thesis 1) suggests, 'Everything that was directly lived has moved away into a representation'. By moving things into a performative world they become controllable, even if this is only within the space of the performance, which is itself an illusion of the real world. Gudkov rightly argues that we are glued to television as an excuse for any action, and suffer from an 'information sterility' (Sokolov 2013): the fault is less with the regime than with society itself.

The question remains to what extent the performance of protest is a uniquely Russian phenomenon. Do we really think that the protest in 2013 of students in Hungary against a contract system or the protests against the dismissal of the artistic director of the National Theatre for homosexuality had any effect? Do we really believe that the protests of students in the UK against the rise of tuition fees have changed anything? Did the Greek referendum in July 2015 change the government's European politics? The list could continue endlessly. Ultimately, the question is whether politics today is not merely a performance of power, in which people should acknowledge that their voice counts for nothing and will not be heard. Protest is the physical and visual articulation of the people's speechlessness or voicelessness. These acts of protests, strikes, and other outcries are a way of compensating for the people's complete and utter helplessness in the face of a world that is run by others, who do not even live in our cities, our streets, our houses.

Protest is staged, using the texts (verbatim) of court trials, of personal memoirs, of witness statements; it has no words of its own. This is the method employed by Teatr.doc in their show *The Bolotnaya Square Case* (*Bolotnoe delo*, 2015), in which they use monologues of the relatives of arrested and imprisoned protesters ('bolotniki') (Fig. 9.4). They present themselves as victims, and therefore as morally strong: in the resignation and suffering lies their

Figure 9.4 The Bolotnaya Square Case at Teatr.doc
Source: Courtesy of Teatr.doc.

strength, following the 'victim complex' described by sociologist Lev Gudkov (2004, 83–120). Molly Flynn has explored documentary theatre in contemporary Russia and drawn a parallel to the show trials of the 1930s as enactment of state terror (Flynn 2014, 314). She has argued that:

> The repetition of verbatim texts in the performance of documentary theatre provides an alternative mode of interpreting and indexing history. By recording and performing their testimonial evidence, the artists at Teatr. doc give voice to otherwise marginalized members of society. They prioritize the subjectivity of the spoken word in contrast to the industry of state media sources.
>
> (Flynn 2014, 316)

Her argument is similar to Chapman's about the use of personal camera footage creating a history through a series of small histories. However, I would extend my comment on Chapman's argument to Flynn also: the empowerment (making history) remains restricted to the virtual media. Similarly, the performances of documentary theatre remain confined to a performance space and restricted to a certain set of replies. One pretends that the actors are participants in the creation of history; the other knows that the actors speak with real words in a fictional space. Thus the enactment of protest, too, is a form of resignation, of stating powerlessness.

Enactment as a form of empowerment is apparently a concept that is alien to Russian culture, as is evident in the re-enactment of the trials against artists in Milo Rau's *Moscow Trials* (*Die Moskauer Prozesse*, staged 1–3 March 2013 at the Sakharov Centre; film version 2014). The performance does not use verbatim texts, but instead some of the main witnesses and participants in the actual trials (against the two exhibitions 'Beware, Religion!' and 'Forbidden Art 2006', and against Pussy Riot) participate in a trial with journalists and activists in the role of prosecution, defence, and chair, while the jury representing a cross-section of society is invited to formulate a verdict: it is liberal, independent, and open; the verdict comes as a surprise (Fig. 9.5). If the actual trials were scripted and rehearsed, genuine "show" trials, then the *Moscow Trials*, a theatricalized show, actually gives the jurors the power to make an independent judgment. The performance is a playing space for freedom, while it is also a withdrawal into a world of art to formulate protest and voice the opinion of the people.

The verdict in Rau's *Moscow Trials* is unexpected: on the charges of offending believers, the jury of seven was quite divided (3/3, with one abstention); on the charge of instigation of religious hatred, the vote was much clearer: one juror pleaded for such a charge and five against, with one abstention (Rau 2014, 151). The trial thus reflects that the people might have decided differently, and that the charges were dictated, arguments rehearsed, and trials are a farce. Only Milo Rau's format returns the power of decision-making and a voice to the people. None of the Russian projects linked to protest recognize

Figure 9.5 The Jury in Milo Rau's *Moscow Trials*
Source: Courtesy of International Institute of Political Murder IIPM/Maxim Lee.

such an empowerment, even if it is in a space defined for play rather than activism.

Indeed, Russian activism confuses the media world with reality when creating protest art that is promoted primarily through social networks. Activism lies precisely in the performative nature of such acts, and in a reflected and thoughtful artistic representation of this protest, as we can see in the works of Kristina Norman, Milo Rau, and other artist-activists. Russian artist-activists want to have a voice, but they have no language and no discourse of protest.

Notes

1 The law had been passed by the Duma on 19 March and ratified by the Federation Council on 27 March.
2 The legislation discussed here covers specifically the media, including online publications of newspapers but excluding blogs and social networks, where different laws apply (Anon. 2014).
3 Similar debates were fuelled by Valeriia Gai Germanika's *Yes and Yes* (*Da i Da*, 2014), which screened at the Moscow International Film Festival in June 2014 and was in distribution from 28–30 June before the new law came into force. See Volkova 2014.
4 See the Ministry's release bulletin, http://mkrf.ru/press-tsentr/novosti/minister-stvo/leviafan-rezhissera-andreya-zvyagintseva-poluchil-prokatnoe-udostoverenie (accessed 24 July 2015). Age classification for all public information was introduced

on 1 September 2012 ('O zashchite detei ot informatsii, prichiniaiushchei vred zdorov'iu i razvitiiu') and comprises five categories: 0+, 6+, 12+, 16+, and 18+.

5 For comparison: in the United Kingdom, Sections 4A and 5 of the Public Order Act of 1986 make it an offence for a person to use threatening, abusive, or insulting words or behaviour that causes, or is likely to cause, another person harassment, alarm, or distress. The Racial and Religious Hatred Act amended the Public Order Act in 2006 to make it an offence (punishable by up to seven years' imprisonment) to use threatening words or behaviour intended to stir up religious hatred. The BBC has sacked staff over prank calls (Jonathan Ross and Russell Brand in 2008) and abusive behaviour (Jeremy Clarkson in 2015). In the United States, the stand-up comedian George Carlin listed the words inappropriate for use on public television in a monologue performed in 1972 ('Seven Words You Can Never Say on Television'), which includes terms for defecation ('shit', 'piss'). US Code title 18, section 1464 stipulates: 'Whoever utters any obscene, indecent, or profane language by means of radio communication shall be fined under this title or imprisoned not more than two years, or both'. Attempts to define 'profane language' have failed in US Congress: in December 2003, a bill to specify a number of profane words based on Carlin's list was rejected: 'As used in this section, the term "profane", used with respect to language, includes the words "shit", "piss", "fuck", "cunt", "asshole"', and the phrases "cock sucker", "mother fucker", and "ass hole", compound use (including hyphenated compounds) of such words and phrases with each other or with other words or phrases, and other grammatical forms of such words and phrases (including verb, adjective, gerund, participle, and infinitive forms)'.

6 Dmitrii Gutov, an artist-participant in 'Forbidden Art 2006', in Rau 2014, 39–40.

7 The most prominent trials were against Joseph Brodsky (for parasitism, 1964); Vladimir Bukovskii (for anti-Soviet agitation and propaganda, 1963); and Andrei Siniavskii and Iulii Daniel' (for anti-Soviet agitation and propaganda, 1965–66).

8 The 'Snow Revolution' started before the Duma Elections on 4 December 2011, where Putin's United Russia gained 49.5 per cent of the votes. On the same day, the nationalistic organisation 'Russkie' held a non-sanctioned demonstration, 'Putin Go!', which led to 258 arrests. On 5 December the Solidarity movement (Aleksei Navalnyi, Boris Nemtsov) demonstrated under the slogan 'Elections are a Farce', leading to 300 arrests. On 6 December a non-sanctioned meeting took place on Triumphal Square, led by Eduard Limonov; the internal military forces arrested 600 people. On 10 December a major protest march followed on Bolotnaya Square (150,000 people), which was not covered on the central television channels. On 24 December 150,000 people demonstrated on Sakharov Avenue. The second phase of the protest movement coincided with the Presidential Elections on 4 March 2012. A month before, on 4 February 2012, people marched on Bolotnaya Square 'For Honest Elections'; on 5 and 10 March 2012 meetings took place in Moscow and other cities. On 6 May 2012 protesters marched on Bolshaya Yakimanka and Bolotnaya Square (ca. 70,000 people), calling 'For an Honest Power. For a Russia without Putin': the event (also known as the 'March of Millions') led to 500 arrests and clashes with the police; several internet sites were blocked, including those of radio station Ekho Moskvy and the newspaper *Kommersant*. On 12 June 2012 (Unity Day) meetings were held on Sakharov Avenue and Pushkin Square (100,000 people).

9 The film's title refers to a literary experiment from 1935, when Maxim Gorky and Mikhail Kol'tsov had published a collected volume under the title *A Day of the World* (*Den' mira*). The project offered a compilation of news from all over the world of events that took place on 27 September 1935. In 1938 Kol'tsov was arrested and in February 1940 he was sentenced to death, thus posing a risk to the film project.

10 Some titles of television serials prove this point: *Streets of Broken Lights* (*Ulitsy raz-bitykh fonarei*, 1997–99); *Cops* (*Menty*); *The Directory of Death* (*Direktoriia smerti*, 1999); *The Crushing Force* (*Uboinaia sila*, 2000–03); *The Agent of National Security* (*Agent natsional'noi bezopasnosti*, 1998–2001); *Detective Dubrovsky's Dossier* (*Dos'e detektiva Dubrovskogo*, 1999); *Hunting Cinderella* (*Okhota na Zolushku*, 1999–2000); *Criminal Petersburg* (*Banditskii Peterburg*, 2000–03); *Bourgeois's Birthday* (*Den' rozhdeniia burzhuia*, 1999–2001); *Rostov-Papa* (2000); *The Brigade* (*Brigada* 2002); *Moscow – Central District* (*Moskva, tsentral'nyi okrug*, 2003).

11 Criminal Law 213: Hooliganism, that is a breach of public order expressing a clear disrespect of society; 'motivated by political, ideological, racial, nationalistic or religious hatred or animosity'. The maximum sentence is seven years, and this article was applied to Pussy Riot. Criminal Law 282: Participation in activities of a social or religious group or another organisation forbidden by court order. This article carries a maximum sentence of four years. Criminal Law 148.1: 'Public acts, expressing a clear disrespect to society and carried out with the purpose of offending religious feelings of believers', carries a maximum of one year imprisonment.

12 See the bulletin of the Ministry of Culture at http://mkrf.ru/press-tsentr/novosti/ministerstvo/pozitsiya-minkultury-po-itogam-obshchestvennykh-slushaniy-po-povodu-konflikta-vo (accessed 24 July 2015).

References

Anon. 2014. Federal'nyi zakon Rossiiskoi Federatsii ot 5 maia 2014g. No. 101-F3. *Rossiiskaia gazeta* 7 May. www.rg.ru/2014/05/07/rus-yazyk-dok.html (accessed 24 July 2015).

Beumers, Birgit. 1997. *Yury Lyubimov at the Taganka Theatre 1964–1994*. Amsterdam: Harwood Academic Publishers/OPA.

Beumers, Birgit and Mark Lipovetsky. 2009. *Performing Violence*. Bristol and Chicago: intellect books.

Borodianskii, Georgii. 2015. "Pravoslavie, nagnetanie, 'Tanngeizer'." *Novaia gazeta* 9 March. www.novayagazeta.ru/arts/67562.html (accessed 24 July 2015).

Chapman, Andrew. 2014. "Changing The Term of Engagement: Casting and Mobilizing Amateur Filmmakers in Recent Projects by Kostomarov, Rastorguev and Pivovarov." *Digital Icons* 11: 95–112. www.digitalicons.org/issue11/andrew-chapman/ (accessed 24 July 2015).

Debord, Guy. 1983. *Society of the Spectacle*. Detroit: Black and Red.

Dobrynina, Ekaterina. 2014. "Ot zloi toski – ne materis'! Rossiiane rugaiut tekh, kto netsenzurno rugaetsia v SMI i blogakh." *Rossiiskaia gazeta* 29 August. www.rg.ru/2014/08/29/mat-v-smi.html (accessed 24 July 2015).

Dolzhanskii, Roman and Dmitrii Renanskii. 2014. "Vagner po-chelovecheski." *Kommersant* 24 December. www.kommersant.ru/doc/2639543 (accessed 24 July 2015).

Flynn, Molly. 2014. "The Trial That Never Was: Russian Documentary Theatre and the Pursuit of Justice." *New Theatre Quarterly* 30 (4): 307–317.

Goscilo, Helena. 2010. "Between the Sword and the Scales, or Celluloid Justice." *Studies in Russian and Soviet Cinema* 4 (2): 137–145.

Gudkov, Lev. 2004. *Negativnaia identichnost'*. Moscow: Novoe literaturnoe obozrenie.

Gudkov, Lev. 2012a. "Chto volnuet rossiian nakanune Novogo goda." *Argumenty nedeli* 17 December. http://argumenti.ru/presscenter/id/110 (accessed 24 July 2015).

Gudkov, Lev. 2012b. "Sotsiolog Lev Gudkov ob ugasanii protestnogo dvizheniia v Rossii i perspektivakh ego rosta." Levada Centre 5 May. www.levada.ru/05-05-2012/sotsiolog-lev-gudkov-ob-ugasanii-protestnogo-dvizheniya-v-rossii-i-perspektivakh-ego-rost (accessed 24 July 2015).

Jonson, Lena. 2015. *Protest and Art in Putin's Russia*. London and New York: Routledge.

Lonkila, Markku. 2012. 'Russian Protest On- and Offline.' FIIA (Finnish Institute of International Affairs) Briefing Paper 98 (February). www.fiia.fi/assets/publications/bp98.pdf (accessed 1 July 2016).

Marszal, Andrew. 2014. "Vladimir Putin Signs Ban on 'Foul Language' in Films, Books and Performances." *The Telegraph* 6 May. www.telegraph.co.uk/news/worldnews/europe/russia/10810862/Vladimir-Putin-signs-ban-on-foul-language-in-films-books-and-performances.html (accessed 24 July 2015).

Oushakine, Serguei A. 2013. "'Address Your Questions to Dostoevsky': Privatizing Punishment in Russian Cinema." In *Russia's New Fin de Siècle*, edited by Birgit Beumers, 175–194. Bristol and Chicago: intellect books.

Pushkarev, Igor'. 2013. "Pochemu my ne opovestili? Potomu chto ego nikto ne zhdal." *Znak* 15 February. www.znak.com/urfo/articles/15-02-20-39/100331.html (accessed 24 July 2015).

Rau, Milo. 2014. *Die Moskauer Prozesse/Die Zürcher Prozesse*. Berlin: Verbrecher Verlag.

Schuler, Catherine. 2013. "Reinventing the Show Trial: Putin and Pussy Riot." *The Drama Review* 57 (1): 7–17.

Sokolov, Mikhail. 2013. "Sotsiolog Lev Gudkov ob obshchestvennykh tendentsiiakh 2013 goda v Rossii." *Rfi* 31 January. http://inosmi.ru/russia/20130131/205267109.html (accessed 24 July 2015).

Strukov, Vlad. 2013. "From Local Appropriation to Global Documentation, or Contestingthe Media System." *Digital Icons* 9: 87–97. www.digitalicons.org/issue09/vlad-strukov/ (accessed 24 July 2015).

Vatulescu, Cristina. 2010. *Police Aesthetics. Literature, Film and the Secret Police in Soviet Times*. Stanford, CA: Stanford University Press.

Volkova, Dar'ia. 2014. "Valeriia Gai Germanika otkazhetsia ot prokata 'Da i Da' iz-za zakona o mate." *RBK* 18 August. http://top.rbc.ru/society/18/08/2014/943485.shtml (accessed 24 July 2015).

Zykov, Vladimir and Aleksandr Kondrat'ev. 2013. "Roskomndzor nakazhet SMI tol'ko za chetyre maternykh slova." *Izvestiia* 25 December. http://izvestia.ru/news/563178 (accessed 24 July 2015).

10 On the (im)possibility of a third opinion

Kristina Norman

After-War is my artistic research project, which took the form of a large-scale mixed-media installation in the Estonian pavilion at the 53rd Venice Biennale in 2009. The study is concerned with the conflict surrounding the so-called 'Bronze Soldier' ('Pronkssõdur') monument in Tallinn, the capital of Estonia. The statue was erected in the city centre in September 1947 as part of a memorial to Soviet soldiers.[1] In the newly independent Estonia the monument became a *lieu de mémoire*: a place of memory, where members of the local Russian-speaking community continued the tradition of celebrating the victory in the Great Patriotic War on 9 May, although officially this is Europe Day. At the end of April 2007 the Estonian government had the statue moved to a less prominent location in a cemetery, a decision that led to riots which lasted for two nights (referred to as the 'Bronze Nights', or 'April Unrest').

After-War is a heterogeneous entity that extends beyond an art exposition. Along with a full-size gilded replica of the Bronze Soldier monument, a kinetic sculpture titled 'Kinetics of Power' and four video pieces premiered in the five rooms of the Estonian pavilion in Venice; the project features an art action in a public space carried out in Tallinn in the former location of the Bronze Soldier, as well as the stormy public reaction to this intervention. On 9 May 2009 I brought the above-mentioned gilded replica, a golden effigy of the Bronze Soldier, to the monument's former location in Tõnismäe Square in the centre of Tallinn, where it was cheered by the local Russian-speaking community who had gathered in order to hold their traditional commemoration rituals in what was now an empty park; it was also met by policemen who resolved the unexpected situation by forcibly removing the uncomfortable object and the artist – that is, me. The intervention attracted extensive public attention, mostly negative, and dominated the headlines of both Estonian and local Russian-language media for a remarkable length of time. The intention of this intervention was to chart the actual state of affairs, amid a seemingly normalized life, two years after the statue had been relocated, in order to address a situation where one part of society insisted that the conflict had been favourably resolved by means of the 'successful police operation' that swept the monument from Tõnismäe and ended the riots, and that there was no need to discuss the causes of the controversy any further, whereas the other part insisted that the conflict remained unresolved.

The fact that *After-War* would represent Estonia at the Venice Biennale was considered unpalatable by the Estonian and Russian public alike. The intervention was proclaimed to be a political provocation. The majority of critics refused altogether to accept the intervention as art. The Estonian-language media demanded that I should be held responsible for the potential consequences that the intervention could allegedly provoke, such as a new wave of street violence, or even murder (Viirand 2009). Among the ethical issues that were brought to the fore was the use of bystanders in the performance. While the Estonian side saw the police as victims of exploitation, the Russian side reckoned that members of the community were instrumentalized. While many Estonians found the work offensive to their patriotic feelings (Elken 2009), Russians objected that their holy symbol was being utilized as an instrument with which to ridicule the community and as a tool to gain personal profit in the art world (Morenko 2009). Largely, my actions were considered unethical because they were individualistic, thoughtless of other people's feelings, and politically irresponsible.

By describing individual parts of the artwork, this chapter tries to map the social and political conditions of the context for the central unit of the project: the public intervention. The intervention proved to have a deterritorializing effect, as it highlighted collective fears that govern society. The reception was impelled by the assumption that, even if addressing some social or political issues, art should preserve a distance from the subject matter, thus staying within a framework of what is traditionally understood as 'aesthetic'. If art action has, or is likely to have, some political consequences, then the artist should be prosecuted on political and legal grounds. As opposed to this commonplace standpoint, my understanding of the role of art resonates with Jacques Rancière's idea of politics, aesthetics, and art being intrinsically linked. For Rancière, politics is a process that is always concerned with aesthetics, i.e. a perceived and sensible reality. He subsumes the link between the process of politics and aesthetics in the notion of the 'distribution of the sensible', i.e. what can be seen and sensed, what can or cannot be said, what is thinkable or unthinkable (Rancière 2004, 12–13). Politics is a rationally motivated action of a subject, and it interrupts the aesthetic regime established by police order, 'which produces, reproduces, and operates the hegemonic distribution of the forms of social participation that are available to individuals and institutions within a particular society' (Yepes 2014, 42). For Rancière, both politics and art have the capacity to create a 'dissensus', a disagreement, the articulation of which is central to the democratic process of emancipation, in the course of which the sensible can be re-distributed and those who were formerly invisible and inaudible are seen and heard (Kangro 2012). Unlike politics, which articulates disagreement in order to achieve definite goals, art offers a dissensus insofar as it claims autonomy and declares its own norm.[2] In the aesthetic regime, art is swayed by heterogeneous forces and is governed by thought that is estranged from itself (Kangro 2012).

The title *After-War* refers to a 'post-' condition, like the term 'after-party' refers to something that follows an official event; here the official event can refer to both the Second World War and the drama of the monument's relocation in 2007. The point of departure for my work was the social cleavage that divides society along the lines of the way in which the results of the Second World War are interpreted by two distinct memory collectives. According to these interpretations, the Bronze Soldier is seen either as a symbol of Soviet occupation, political repression, and mass deportations; or as a symbol of victory over fascism and Nazism, and of liberation of Estonia from German occupation by the Soviet Army.

In fact, what can be called a 'war of monuments' started as soon as Estonia was conquered by and incorporated into the Soviet Union in 1944. All the Estonian monuments that survived the first Soviet occupation of 1940–41 and those that were restored during the German occupation between 1941 and 1944 were listed by the Soviet authorities and systematically blown up. These were mainly memorials of the Estonian War of Independence of 1918–20. In May 1946, to avenge the destruction of the Estonian monuments, two teenage schoolgirls blew up a temporary wooden monument marking the burial site of Soviet soldiers in Tõnismäe, which preceded the Bronze Soldier monument (Kaasik 2006, 1914–15). For this, the 14-year-old Aili Jürgenson (Jõgi) and the 15-year-old Ageeda Paavel were arrested and sentenced to eight years in the Gulag (Faure and Mensing 2012, 293–295).

The case of the Bronze Soldier outlined the power relations established in the society of the newly independent Estonia. The culture of commemoration associated with the monument was clearly a practice of resistance, addressing what Rancière calls 'police order'. Officially, the conflict was presented as a binary opposition between two ethnic communities, but it can also be argued that it was based on inequality between those granted and those denied political participation and visibility within the established order;[3] that is to say, it was about the relationship between an excluded group and governing power, where the monument was used as an instrument of policy. The controversy escalated during the period of the electoral campaign before parliamentary elections in March 2007.

Against the backdrop of rising tensions over the Bronze Soldier, the whole of society gradually became politicized. As in a war, everyone was expected to take sides. At the peak of the conflict, in 2006–07, all intermediate positions were purposefully disregarded and people were made to feel precluded from expressing views that challenge the normalized narratives. The situation worsened particularly after the monument was relocated. Before, it was an officially constructed ethnic conflict, but after the relocation, perceivable internal cleavages appeared within communities. Although in my case an in-between political position can be explained by a mixed Russian-Estonian family background, there are a great number of people with an ethnically univocal background who find it difficult to identify with Estonians or Russians based on the generally established and promoted criteria, and who would like to distance themselves from such forced choices.[4] As an artist, I wanted to react to this polarized situation from a third perspective, positioning myself *between* the communities, memory collectives, and implacable historical narratives.

At the core of *After-War* lies the notion of subjectivization. Rancière conceptualizes the process of subjectivization as 'the formation of a one that is not a self but is the relation of the self to an other' (Rancière 1992, 60). In Rancière's thought, subjectivization is a profoundly democratic process; it is 'the discursive and practical construction of a polemical verification' of equality (Rancière 1992, 60). My project, on the one hand, attempts to make visible the power relations between the community and the state, highlighting a range of practices of resistance that are important in the community's endeavour of establishing itself as a political subject. On the other hand, by means of public intervention I construct my own subjectivity, demanding the right not to take sides. In so doing, I offer an imaginary public sphere where different discourses can be introduced and other subject positions adopted. The notion of a third position that implies being *in between*, standing on the edge, underpins the whole project and defines the way the audience is expected to 'read' its individual parts.

The Central Golden Object

The installation was originally conceived according to the floor plan of the apartment-like exhibition space of the pavilion, which had one central room and four smaller rooms encircling it. In the central room, the golden life-size replica of the Bronze Soldier was hung down from the ceiling by four thin cords, giving the impression of the object actually levitating and being almost weightless, and casting no shadow, as the floor surface under the almost horizontally positioned sculpture was evenly illuminated by spotlights (Fig. 10.1). Conceptually, each room of the pavilion provided the same symbol (the Bronze Soldier) in a different context, offering new ways for it to be interpreted. The golden figure of a soldier wearing a Red Army uniform may visually connect to the tradition of Soviet monumental art, but in its golden lure it may also be related to religious iconography. Depending on the viewer's gaze, it can take on all sorts of connotations, alluding to the symbolic imagery of Christian Catholic or Orthodox iconography, or reminding the observer of a 'golden calf'. By presenting the object in such a manner, I intended to communicate my will to depoliticize the Bronze Soldier and liberate it from the two polarized meanings mainly attributed to it. The 'Central Golden Object', as I titled it, functioned like a floating signifier, the meaning of which had not yet been agreed upon; therefore, the process of its interpretation could potentially take any direction. Stripped from its heavy bronze corporeality, the Bronze Soldier's gilded fibreglass counterpart was proposed as an empty shell, waiting to be filled with meanings by the audience.

Figure 10.1 The Bronze Soldier. *After-War*
Source: Personal Archive of Kristina Norman.

Room One: Tõnismäe culture

In the first room the monument was contextualized as a cultural object, as opposed to its image solely as a symbol of political dissent. A diachronic perspective was offered on the rituality performed in front of the Bronze Soldier monument in Tõnismäe in connection with the 9 May Victory Day celebrations. Two separate sets of archival footage rendered visible the difference between the regimented and estranged nature of official military rituals of commemoration in the Soviet era, and that of grassroots, intuitive, and improvised rituality in post-Soviet time (Figs. 10.2 and 10.3). Footage, in colour and with sound, from newly independent Estonia, starting with records from 1992 and ending with documents from 2007, was projected on to a screen. Soviet-era black-and-white, silent archival footage was played from a small LCD monitor planted inside a narrow tunnel in the middle of the projection screen. In order to look inside the tunnel, the visitors had to walk up to the very surface of the screen and lean a little forward, thus being provoked to make a symbolic bow to the monument portrayed in the video.

The first episode in the black-and-white video featured the unveiling of the monument on 22 September 1947, which coincided with the third anniversary of the liberation of Tallinn in 1944.[5] The Soviet-era footage showed samples of regimented rituality performed at the site of the Bronze Soldier,

Figure 10.2 Ritual gathering at the war memorial in Soviet times
Source: Personal archive of Kristina Norman.

including ceremonial speeches by Communist Party leaders and Red Army veterans; young conscript servicemen in military uniforms lined up; folk dancers in national dress, performing around the eternal flame; and pupils from Estonian schools saluting at the monument's pedestal. Official ritual-ity connected to the memorial site evolved no earlier than during Brezhnev's rule, when the myth of the victory in the Great Patriotic War (WWII) was strongest. In 1964 the 'eternal flame' was added to the memorial's com-position, and formal commemoration rites started to be performed in Tõnismäe on a regular basis: the celebration of the liberation of Tallinn (22 September), Victory Day (9 May), and Red Army Day (23 February). Over the years, the Bronze Soldier became Tallinn's central monument and its meaning expanded to that of a symbol of Soviet power (Tamm and Halla 2008, 33).

The colour footage charted the eclectic grassroots rituality of the post-Soviet era. It showed people laying flowers on the helmet under the Bronze Soldier's arm, putting candles on the pedestal, posing for photos with the statue, or reading poetry. Some people bring an old gramophone with them to

Figure 10.3 Ritual gathering at the war memorial in post-Soviet times
Source: Personal archive of Kristina Norman.

play wartime records; some dance to the music, others sing along. The most peculiar ritual is the creating of a 'carpet of flowers' by sticking cut flowers into the soil. This spontaneous practice was born in 1996, after the reconstruction of the site according to the results of an architectural competition organized by city officials in an attempt to find a way to redefine this Soviet memorial originally named 'To the Liberators of Tallinn' as a more inclusive 'Monument to those Fallen in the Second World War'.[6] Among other rearrangements, the eternal flame was removed and the central pathway leading up to the monument was replaced with a diagonal path that symbolically marginalized the monument in relation to the direction of pedestrian movement on the square, 'forcing the pedestrians to approach the monument as if always in passing' (Kurg 2009, 55). The tradition of making a 'carpet of flowers' was born as a way to win back the area that had changed after the official reconstruction: 'The flowers temporarily re-created the commemorative space for the occasion of Victory Day celebrations, and the territory that had been neutralized was now as if empowered again' (Kurg 2009, 55). The Estonian cultural semiotician Mikhail Lotman has pointed out that some rituality held on the site was connected to the fact that Tõnismäe was a burial ground, where the Bronze Soldier served to mark the graves. According to

Lotman (2007), the tradition of eating and drinking vodka in cemeteries, which was quite popular among Russian people in the Soviet era, is rooted in the pre-Christian Slavonic tradition of *dziady*, ancient commemoration festivals on ancestors' graves. In the video sequence, documents of communal remembrance rituals were interspersed with episodes attesting to the monument's controversial status. Some of these interludes showed incidents of vandalism against the statue. On 9 May 2005, the figure was splashed with red paint; in May 2006 it was painted in the colours of the Estonian flag. Demonstrating how the monument became a potential site of public confrontations between Estonian nationalists and local Russian-speakers was footage from a meeting at the monument organized in May 2006 by a group of far-right activists, holding hate speeches, waving Estonian flags and banners with slogans such as 'Down with occupiers!'. The final episode of the video showed the moment on 26 April 2007 when the site was closed by the police and the monument blocked from the public view by a large tent that covered the entire territory (Figs. 10.4–10.6).[7]

This video installation, focusing on rituals, emphasized the connectedness of the phenomenon of the Bronze Soldier to collective remembering and the process of collective identity formation in the newly independent Estonia, presenting the tradition of celebrating Victory Day in Tõnismäe as a unique culture that was born in this particular location and could be defined as 'Tõnismäe culture'. My aim with this video installation was to counter the representation of such rituals in the Estonian media as a manifestation of barbarity, or as an expression of 'mockery of the Estonian state'.[8] For the Russian-speaking population, the Bronze Soldier is a classic *lieu de mémoire*, a place in which, according to Pierre Nora, memory is crystallized and where it finds refuge. As Nora explains, such memory places are usually associated with turning points in history, when:

> a sense of rupture with the past is inextricably bound up with a sense that a rift has occurred in memory. But that rift has stirred memory sufficiently to raise the question of its embodiment: there are sites, *lieux de mémoire*, in which a residual sense of continuity remains. *Lieux de mémoire* exist because there are no longer any *milieux de mémoire*, settings in which memory is a real part of everyday experience.
>
> (Nora 1996, 1)

In his much-quoted speech from 2005, Vladimir Putin defined what such a 'turning point in history' is for Russian people, and his words had a deep-felt resonance among the politically excluded group in Estonia:

> Above all, we should acknowledge that the collapse of the Soviet Union was a major geopolitical disaster of the 20th century. As for the Russian nation, it became a genuine drama. Tens of millions of our co-citizens and co-patriots found themselves outside Russian territory.[9]

Ever since Estonia restored its independence, the Bronze Soldier has become a tool for the Russophone community in making sense of its collective existence in a situation where the social framework of memory has been replaced, and the new framework does not offer any positive means of identification to the majority of Russian-speakers in Estonia.[10] Inasmuch as no memory work has been done in Russia, Estonia's Russian community has not been offered any new collective frameworks of memory from Russia's side either. The framework remains notably Soviet for the Russophone memory-collective.

Room Two: kinetics of power

In the second room, the Bronze Soldier was presented as a physical object that could be moved in space. The kinetic sculpture titled 'Kinetics of Power' was a gadget similar to advertising hoardings that change their picture with each rotation. In its full circle, the viewer could see photographic records of three main spatial views of the monument: the Bronze Soldier in its original location in Tõnismäe; the memorial site after the statue's relocation; and the monument in its new location in the Defence Forces' Cemetery. The three images replaced each other in mechanical rotation, as if endlessly repeating a magic trick of a 'disappearing monument', or – depending on the mindset and the desires of the audience – of a 'reappearing monument'. Apparently people love magic because they like to be tricked and feel they are seeing something impossible. Even if the method of the conjuring trick is apparent, people appreciate the skills of the performer. In the case of the Bronze Soldier, the main performer was Prime Minister Andrus Ansip, since it was up to his sovereign decision to define the fate of the monument and, ultimately, that of the whole of society. The politician proved to be a skilled administrator, having begun to climb the career ladder as a functionary in the Communist Party and then converting to neoliberalism, making it into leadership positions in the Reform Party. He took up the post of prime minister in 2005 and, after having found the best approach to the issue of the monument – promising to remove the statue from Tõnismäe – he scored an unprecedented victory at the parliamentary elections in March 2007.[11]

The government decided that the monument should be removed from its original site because it was listed as a grave-marker, which made it subject to the Geneva Conventions of 1949 relating to the protection of graves of victims of international armed conflicts. In April 2007, during Open Doors Day in parliament, Ansip publicly alleged that the remains that were about to be exhumed and relocated to the military cemetery along with the monument belonged not to victims of the war, but to a bunch of Soviet criminals and marauders who had been accidentally run over by a tank driven by their drunken comrade. The legal grounds for what the Russian-speaking community interpreted as desecration of the graves was prepared by the Estonian parliament adopting the Military Graves Act in January 2007. The act allowed the relocation of the memorial because of the 'unsuitable site of the grave and

Figure 10.4 The monument to the Bronze Soldier on Tõnismäe Square, erected in 1947
Source: Personal archive of Kristina Norman.

Figure 10.5 Tõnismäe Square after the removal of the Bronze Soldier
Source: Personal archive of Kristina Norman.

the divisive public interest that did not ensure peace for the grave'.[12] Thus the Prime Minister found a way to transcend political, ideological, and ethnic divisions through appeals to the higher value of order (Astrov 2009, 72).

My mechanized rotating sculpture echoed the Estonian political elite's ways of problem-solving, driven by a belief that through a magic vanishing trick it is possible to resolve serious social issues that have to do with collective memory.

Figure 10.6 The monument to the Bronze Soldier at its new site
Source: Personal archive of Kristina Norman.

Room Three: violence

The third room of the installation created a context in which the invisibility of the Bronze Soldier triggers violence on Tallinn's streets. Essentially, it was a video comprising documentary footage of the events of 26 and 27 April 2007, the so-called 'Bronze Nights'. It was a compilation of episodes of violence directed at the police, at private and municipal property, and protesters. Against the background of the media war that accompanied the conflict, and especially the riots, the footage was presented in an unusual manner (Fig. 10.7). The Estonian media presented documents to incriminate the rioters, portraying them as 'Russian vandals', whereas the Russian media (of both the Russian Federation and local Russian outlets) presented the Estonian police as aggressors and the rioters as peaceful protesters defending their rights. My video was rather a commensurate and, at the same time, ambiguous mixture of documents presenting the entire event as a wild carnival, a total acting-out of suppressed tensions.

After the riots had ended, the main daily newspaper in Estonia, *Postimees*, published an editorial entitled 'The Face of the Week: Unknown Russian Hoodlum', claiming that protecting the monument to the Unknown Soldier was only a pretext used by Russians for their delinquent activities: the Russians had finally shown their real face, that of mere criminals. In such a manner the entire Russophone population was stigmatized (Anon. 2007). Elsewhere in the Estonian media the ending of the riots was presented as the result of a 'successful police operation'.

It was a moment of rupture on the level of language for the 'Tõnismäe people', as the take-over of Tõnismäe by the ruling power deprived the community of its vocabulary for what Rancière calls 'verification of equality'.[13] In Tõnismäe, it was the language of rituals that used to be spoken to address the excluding and silencing order. Now that the community was dislodged from the site, which in its specific way had functioned as a physiological apparatus for articulation of the language, 'the demonstrators reached for the easiest means available or the most easily understood vocabulary' (Kurg 2009, 64). Among the slogans chanted by the protesters on the night of the monument's removal were 'Ansip – gravedigger!', 'Shame on you!', 'Fascism won't stand!', 'Bronze Soldier! Bronze Soldier!', and, ultimately, 'Russia! Russia!' The cry for Russia 'demonstrates a change in the means of expression for the counterpublic once its discourse framework had changed, it shows a retreat from dialogue and a move towards separatism' (Kurg 2009, 64). The philosopher Tõnu Viik described the reaction of the Estonian community; he sensed the change in the atmosphere, noticing that protesters were vandalizing not just from a non-existent power-position, but from that of a threat: 'The proximity of Russia and its position in the past century has forced Estonians to look at the threatening Russian protesters with a greater sense of fear' (Viik 2007). In conclusion, one might suggest that the government's monument endeavour resulted in an even deeper division in society, leaving space for only 'either/or' stances and eliminating any possibility for ambivalent positions.[14]

Room Four: action

The last room of the installation framed the Bronze Soldier not as a medium of remembrance, but as an object of commemoration. Seen from this perspective, the golden effigy of the Bronze Soldier can be interpreted as a monument to a monument. For the Russian-speaking community, the symbol died in 2007 in its former role as the Tõnismäe monument. Tõnismäe was declared an ordinary park by the government.[15] In the face of the established order, Russian-speaking people continued their tradition of gathering on 9 May, only now this took the form of a massive pilgrimage. Against several hundreds that used to congregate in the square, now there were thousands of people who went to the military cemetery to lay flowers at the monument and at the graves of the reburied soldiers; then, part of the crowd proceeded to Tõnismäe to make the 'carpet of flowers' and light candles. In an interview recorded on 9 May 2008 in Tõnismäe, I asked people why they continued to come to an empty park; the answer was: 'We have come here to honour the memory of the Bronze Soldier'.[16] A few hours earlier, at the cemetery, I had carried out an intervention in the course of which I handed out for free and sold a number of hand-made souvenir-size Bronze Soldier statuettes. I was fairly surprised to see one of my little sculptures installed by somebody in Tõnismäe, with flowers arranged around it and a candle lit in front of it. My creation was thus used by the community as a tool to symbolically designate their territory. The emergence of the statuette was aired on national television later that evening. It was a clear sign that the phantom of the monument

Figure 10.7 Riots in Tallinn, 2009
Source: Personal archive of Kristina Norman.

lives in Tõnismäe in the imagination of both the Russian-speaking and the
Estonian public alike. I decided to propose a project addressing the issue of
the 'haunted place' to the project competition for the Estonian pavilion in
Venice 2009. *After-War* was chosen by an international jury, convened by the
Estonian Centre of Contemporary Art, which was responsible for the organ-
ization of the pavilion following the delegation of this task to the institu-
tion by the Ministry of Culture. Yet the fact that a project about the Bronze
Soldier would represent the country in Venice received little media attention
in the beginning. It was the appearance of the life-size gilded effigy of the
Bronze Soldier in Tõnismäe on 9 May 2009 that caused the media to explode.

The event itself, as it unrolled *in situ*, had some rather amusing moments for
the audience: a random group of people had gathered in Tõnismäe, unaware
that at certain point they would be transformed into participants in an action
initiated by an artist. The first emotion was that of surprise: people started to
applaud the golden epiphany that they could hardly believe was real. Some
were a little suspicious: 'This must be a provocation. They [the guys who carried the statue from the truck to the site] spoke in Estonian.' But the suspicion

Figure 10.8 The replica of the Bronze Soldier on Tõnismäe Square, 9 May 2009
Source: Personal archive of Kristina Norman.

was immediately brushed aside with an optimistic: 'But the soldier is still ours!' People started hastily posing for photographs with the statue and decorated it with flowers. 'Neat. Nicely done, isn't it? Like a copy! – Yes, same size. Only the pedestal is missing.' It was drizzling, and at a certain point the lightweight sculpture was tipped over by a sudden gust of wind. The community heaved the statue up and moved it carefully to a group of thuja trees to prevent it from falling over again. Within minutes, the police showed up and brutally knocked the venerated statue down to remove it from the site to the street-side. Someone in the group shouted 'Fascists!' at the police, while other voices momentarily tried to discipline the yeller. After an emotional discussion with some of the 'Tõnismäe people' holding flowers in their hands, and with myself, protesting against the removal of my sculpture from the park and accusing the police of robbery, both the statue and I were arrested and deported from Tõnismäe. The whole event, from the moment I appeared with the Golden Soldier effigy, until the police heaved the sculpture on to a truck and drove it away, lasted 23 minutes. The argument that the police used to justify the deportation was: 'There already is such a statue in the cemetery!', while I reasoned: 'But this is not Bronze Soldier, this is a Golden Soldier! Why can't it be here?' (Figs. 10.8 and 10.9).[17]

During a two-week long investigation process, the police came under pressure from public opinion which demanded that the intervention be criminalized and the artist prosecuted. But since the legislation did not offer a basis for

Figure 10.9 The replica of the Bronze Soldier being removed from Tõnismäe Square, 9 May 2009

Source: Personal archive of Kristina Norman.

punishment, I was symbolically penalized with a warning.[18] The confiscated sculpture was returned to me soon afterwards.

When preparing for the intervention, I anticipated that the police could play some role in my artwork, although I could not predict the exact development of the event. I was guided by the presupposition that Tõnismäe park is not a park like any other. I knew I was about to intervene in a place where the established 'order of the police' (Rancière) is most vulnerable. A brittle victory achieved by the government in the war against the monument and its people certainly needed to be safeguarded by the authorities in 'the park'. The victory was fragile because it was not attained politically, and it only could persist in the realm of physical objects and spaces. Such an incident, where an artist gets arrested for walking in a park with her crafted sculpture and for standing around with it to rest a little and converse with random people expressing their admiration for the artwork, can only happen if the whole of society lives in a state of fear and uncertainty. This condition is what I think my intervention revealed, essentially. Moreover, the event showed that the technocratic model of problem-solving has endured over the years. The 'sculpture problem' was resolved by the police following the model used by the government in 2007: uncomfortable objects and subjects should be physically removed from the public eye.

The intervention proved to be highly antagonizing, overwhelming the whole of society.[19] The Minister of Internal Affairs Jüri Pihl made an official statement that this was not art, but a political provocation (Anon. 2009c). To my surprise, the minister's opinion was shared not only by senior artists, who were asked for their expertise (Anon. 2009a), but also by some artists of the younger generation who were active in the field of contemporary art (Anon. 2009b). In the Estonian-language media, I was recurrently accused of ethical irresponsibility on the grounds of a range of imagined scenarios of violence that my intervention could potentially have provoked. The enounced scenarios were symptomatic of a continued discourse of danger associated with the Russophone community, and highlighted that cultural aspects of the Victory Day commemoration are continuously neglected by the majority of Estonians. The articulation of such 'what if?' scenarios also demonstrated that, two years after the relocation, no steps had been taken either by the government or by the media to deal with the collective trauma that the whole of society had experienced during and after the drama of relocation and rioting.[20] The ruling political power rested on its laurels after its victory over the monument. My intervention had cast a die in a board game, adding a dimension of indeterminacy and suspense, which threatened to make the state of the game look somewhat different. The roles of winners and losers, of players and drop-outs, were suddenly called into question, or, in Rancière's terminology, symbolically 'redistributed'.

The Golden Soldier intervention addressed the audience from an ambiguous, 'third' position, which played a crucial role in its reception. Critics used my mixed Russian-Estonian background and my declared in-between political position to discredit my artistic endeavour. The Russian side stated that, as somebody who did not fully belong to the community, I had no right to address the problems of the Bronze Soldier, because I could not possibly understand the sacral nature of the entire issue. The Estonian side labelled me a henchman of the Kremlin, declaring that as a half-Russian, I could not be expected to be loyal to the Estonian state. While claiming my right to transgress the Estonian/Russian dichotomy, I found myself in a minority, representing a collective that had yet to be imagined: a political subjectivity that is yet to come.

Besides other aspects that have been addressed in the current chapter, I think the Golden Soldier intervention and the project *After-War* have been meaningful from a memory-political viewpoint. The installation and intervention continue to participate in the process of history-writing concerning the events of April 2007: *After-War* has been acquired by Kiasma Art Museum in Helsinki, Finland,[21] and the installation has been shown at a number of art exhibitions all over the world. Moreover, the project has become an object of theoretical debate which has been addressed by academics from a number of viewpoints (Weeks 2014; Dixon 2013; Zijlmans 2014). All in all, the story of the Bronze Soldier is incomplete without the Golden Soldier.

Notes

1 The monument was originally named 'Monument to the Liberators of Tallinn'. It features a bronze figure of a Soviet soldier against a stone background. The monument was created by Estonian sculptor Enn Roos and architect Arnold Alas.

2 As Ruben Yepes explains Rancière, 'the autonomy of art hinges on a relative and relational production of a singularity, not on a structural and defining separation of art from the world of habitual aesthetic experience' (Yepes 2014, 40).

3 Out of a total of 1.3 million inhabitants, approximately 30 per cent identify with ethnicities other than Estonian. The majority of these non-Estonians speak Russian as their first language. In the early years of independence, the presence of these people was officially interpreted as a legacy of the Soviet occupation, and the majority of them were legally defined as stateless. Over the decades the percentage of non-citizens diminished: some passed the language exam and were granted Estonian citizenship, while others opted for Russian citizenship. Today there are still around 100,000 people with the status of non-citizen.

4 Professor Eneken Laanes drew my attention to this fact in her review of my MA thesis 'After-War. Projekti lähtepositsioonid ja vahekokkuvõte,' for the Estonian Academy of Arts, 2009.

5 According to contemporary Estonian historiography, Tallinn was not liberated but conquered. Historians have proven that the bodies buried on the site were collected from different locations in and around Tallinn in 1944; these people had died under different circumstances, and only some perished during the military operation of conquering Tallinn (see Kaasik 2006, 1914–1915).

6 The organizers of the architectural competition envisaged that, ideally, the monument should become a site of commemoration also for those Estonians who fought in the Second World War in Nazi uniforms. But due to a lack of financial resources, no major rearrangements of the site to bring about a considerable shift in the monument's iconography were affordable.

7 The police-guarded site was encircled by a fence with signboards carrying the message in Estonian, Russian, and English: 'Please, stay calm. Archaeological excavations in progress'. The tent built to cover the site was indicative of the government actually proceeding to exhume the remains of the Soviet soldiers buried there.

8 Among the Tõnismäe rituals, which were particularly difficult to interpret and created a 'short-circuit' among the Estonian audience, were 'the drinking of vodka in public' and the 'dancing on the graves'. These traditional rites were exploited in the Estonian media as examples of barbarity. The waving of Soviet and Russian flags, the singing of Soviet songs, and other such things were defined by some 'as the demonstration of power position and disdain at the "altar of occupation"' (Arujärv 2007).

9 Vladimir Putin's Annual Address to the Federal Assembly of the Russian Federation held on 25 April 2005. http://archive.kremlin.ru/eng/speeches/2005/04/25/2031_type70029type82912_87086.shtml (accessed 6 April 2015).

10 According to Maurice Halbwachs, collective frameworks of memory are 'instruments used by the collective memory to reconstruct an image of the past which is in accord, in each epoch, with the predominant thoughts of the society' (Halbwachs 1992, 40).

11 Ansip gained the biggest share of votes won by the Reform Party, which won the elections and secured him the position of prime minister for almost two terms, until 2014 when he was elected a member of the European Parliament.

12 Press Release of the Estonian Ministry of Foreign Affairs about the relocation of the monument, 27 April 2007.

13 According to Rancière, verification of equality is an emancipatory practice of the handling of a wrong. In contrast, policy – the process of governing, in which social hierarchies are formed – tries to wrong equality (Rancière 1992, 61–62).

14 Immediately after the riots, the prominent Estonian sociologist Juhan Kivirähk stated that in his opinion the midwife of criminal activity in the streets of Tallinn was the Estonian government, and especially Prime Minister Andrus Ansip. Kivirähk suggested that Ansip should resign because he had destroyed society's internal balance and damaged the state's international reputation. 'The government won its ridiculous battle against a monument, but in the meantime it lost something much more valuable – the trust of its people and society's feeling of security' (Kivirähk 2007). Kivirähk was immediately stigmatized in the media as 'one of those "Red" social scientists', being labelled 'pro-Soviet' or 'communist'.
15 In the first year, in 2007, low shrubs and violas in the colours of the European flag were planted all over the site, as if to leave no space for the 'carpet of flowers'. In subsequent years, as Tõnismäe park was handed over by the state to the jurisdiction of Tallinn's municipal government, the 'municipal flowers' were planted in the second half of May.
16 *Dossier # 109*, a documentary film by Meelis Muhu, about the making of *After-War*; In-Ruum Productions, 2010.
17 Quoted from the video documentation of the intervention.
18 Sten Luiga, the head of the Ethics and Methodology Commission of the Estonian Bar Association, voiced his surprise in the media: 'One could assume that the authorities would substantiate their forceful intervention with a threat to national security, or at least with an attempt to prevent an anti-state misdemeanour. To my great surprise, the police issued a press-release stating that the artist is accused of the infringement of a regulation concerning public amenities which regulates the installation of objects like vases, benches, ash-bins, barriers, and such removable objects in public space. Is this some joke? With reference to the regulation, one could only speak of the authorities' need to chasten the installer if the installed object needed some maintenance or repair' (Luiga 2009).
19 A list of internet links to a fraction of the critical feedback is available on the 'Ethics in Estonia' portal: www.eetika.ee/et/569835 (accessed 30 April 2015).
20 Instead, prejudices and distance towards the cultural Other are continually reproduced by the annual 'celebration' of the 'relocation day' in the Estonian media, using the same stigmatizing imagery of the Russian community as mentioned earlier in this chapter.
21 To a large extent, this circumstance legitimated the Golden Soldier as 'art' for the local audience in Estonia.

References

Anon. 2007. "Nädala nägu: Tundmatu vene pätt." *Postimees* 28 April. http://arvamus.postimees.ee/1655163/nadala-nagu-tundmatu-vene-patt (accessed 25 May 2015).
Anon. 2009a. "Katrin Pere: Kuldsõduri 'sotsiaalsus' varjab sisutühjust." *Postimees* 15 May. http://arvamus.postimees.ee/119487/katrin-pere-kuldsoduri-sotsiaalsus-varjab-sisutuhjust (accessed 25 May 2015).
Anon. 2009b. "Kultuuriinimesed taunivad kuldsõduri autori käitumist." *Postimees* 12 May. www.postimees.ee/117970/kultuuriinimesed-taunivad-kuldsoduri-autori-kaitumist (accessed 25 May 2015).
Anon. 2009c. "Siseminister: pronkssõduri koopia väljatoomine oli provokatsioon." *Postimees* 11 May. www.postimees.ee/117899/siseminister-pronkssoduri-koopia-valjatoomine-oli-provokatsioon (accessed 25 May 2015).
Arujärv, Evi. 2007. "Okupatsioon meis enestes." *Eesti Päevaleht* 27 April. http://epl.delfi.ee/news/arvamus/evi-arujarv-okupatsioon-meis-enestes?id=51084862 (accessed 25 May 2015).

Astrov, Alexander. 2009. "The Work of Politics in the Age of Technological Reproducibility." In *Kristina Norman – After War*, edited by Andreas Trossek, 66–87. Tallinn: Centre for Contemporary Arts (Catalogue of the Estonian Pavilion at the Venice Biennale 2009).

Dixon, James R. 2013. "Two Riots: The Importance of Civil Unrest in Contemporary Archaeology." In *The Oxford Handbook of the Archaeology of the Contemporary World*, edited by Paul Graves-Brown, Rodney Harrison, and Angela Piccini, 561–573. Oxford: Oxford University Press.

Elken, Jaan. 2009. "Kuldsõdur solvab eestlast" [The Golden Soldier Offends Estonians]. *Delfi* 12 May. www.delfi.ee/news/paevauudised/arvamus/jaan-elken-kuldsodur-solvab-eestlast?id=23315371 (accessed 25 May 2015).

Faure, Gunter and Teresa Mensing. 2012. *The Estonians. The Long Road to Independence*. Lulu.com Publications.

Halbwachs, Maurice. 1992. *On Collective Memory*. Chicago: University of Chicago Press.

Kaasik, P. 2006. "Tallinnas Tõnismäel asuv punaarmeelaste ühishaud ja mälestusmärk." *Akadeemia* 9: 1914–1915.

Kangro, Maarja. 2012. "Jacques Rancière'i poliitiline esteetika." *Vikerkaar* 4–5. www.vikerkaar.ee/index1.php?page=Arhiiv&a_act=article&a_number=5441 (accessed 25 May 2015).

Kivirähk, Juhan. 2007. "Uue kolmikliidu verine algus." *Eesti Päevaleht* 30 April. http://epl.delfi.ee/news/arvamus/juhan-kivirahk-uue-kolmikliidu-verine-algus?id=51085132 (accessed 25 May 2015).

Kurg, Andres. 2009. "The Bronze Soldier Monument and Its Publics." In *Kristina Norman – After War*, edited by Andreas Trossek, 49–65. Tallinn: Centre for Contemporary Arts (Catalogue of the Estonian Pavilion at the Venice Biennale 2009).

Lotman, Mihhail. 2007. "Märulisemiootika Eesti pealinnas." *Postimees* 2 May. http://arvamus.postimees.ee/1656091/mihhail-lotman-marulisemiootika-eesti-pealinnas (accessed 25 May 2015).

Luiga, Sten. 2009. "Kuldne puuslik ja õigusriik." *Eesti Päevaleht* 14 May. http://epl.delfi.ee/news/arvamus/sten-luiga-kuldne-puuslik-ja-oigusriik?id=51168519 (accessed 25 May 2015).

Morenko, Konstantin. 2009. "Prazdnichnye provokatsii." *Den' za dnem* (Tallinn) 21 May.

Nora, Pierre. 1996. "General Introduction: Between Memory and History." In *Realms of Memory. The Construction of the French Past. Vol 1: Conflicts and Divisions*, edited by Pierre Nora, 1–20. New York: Columbia University Press.

Rancière, Jacques. 1992. "Politics, Identification, and Subjectivization." *October* 61: 58–64.

Rancière, Jacques. 2004. *The Politics of Aesthetics: The Distribution of the Sensible*. London: Continuum.

Tamm, Marek and Saale Halla. 2008. "Ajalugu, poliitika ja identiteet: Esti monumentaalsest mälumaastikust." In *Monumentaalne konflikt: mälu, poliitika ja indentiteet tänapäeva Eestis*, edited by P. Petersoo and M. Tamm, 18–50. Tallinn: Varrak.

Viik, Tõnu. 2007. "Pronkssõduri konflikti loogika: lähedus jõledus hüsteeria deemon." *Postimees* 26 May. http://arvamus.postimees.ee/1665053/tonu-viik-pronkssoduri-konflikti-loogika-lahedus-joledus-husteeria-deemon (accessed 25 May 2015).

Viirand, Laud. 2009. "Kunsti rahastamine rangemaks" [The Financing of Art Should be Taken Under Control]. *Delfi* 12 May. www.delfi.ee/news/paevauudised/ arvamus/laur-viirand-kunsti-rahastamine-rangemaks?id=23305623   (accessed 25 May 2015).

Weeks, Harry. 2014. "Ethics in Public: The Return of Antagonistic Performance." In *Interactive Contemporary Art: Participation in Practice*, edited by Kathryn Brown, 177–196, London: I. B.Tauris.

Yepes, Ruben. 2014. "Aesthetics, Politics, and Art's Autonomy: A Critical Reading of Jacques Rancière." *Evental Aesthetics* 3 (1): 40–64. http://eventalaesthetics.net/ evental-aesthetics-vol-3-no-1-2014/ (accessed 25 May 2015).

Zijlmans, Kitty. 2014. "Recalcitrant Geographies. National Claims, Transnationalism, and the Institutionalization of Contemporary Art." *Stedelijk Studies* 1 (25 November). www.stedelijkstudies.com/journal/recalcitrant-geographies/ (accessed 30 April 2015).

11 Performing poetry and protest in the age of digital reproduction

Marijeta Bozovic

Avant-garde post–

The constellation of poets, theorists, activists, performers, and intellectuals linked by way of the St Petersburg journal *Translit*, the Kraft independent press, and a number of poetry festivals in Russia includes two, or more precisely, one-and-a-half generations of Moscow- and St Petersburg-based poets: Aleksandr Skidan (b. 1965), Dmitrii Golynko (b. 1969), Keti Chukhrov (b. 1970), Kirill Medvedev (b. 1975), Roman Osminkin (b. 1979), and Pavel Arseniev [Arsen'ev] (b. 1986). The poets in this loosely defined group are markedly leftist in political orientation, occupying a fraught position in post-socialist space and time – and all the more provocative and internationally relevant. Medvedev has had a poetry anthology published in English translation, has been reviewed in the likes of *The Paris Review* and *The New Yorker*, and has published essays in *The New Left Review* and *The London Review of Books*. Golynko has been acknowledged internationally as both poet and critic: most recently, he was a visiting fellow at the prestigious Iowa Writer's Workshop. Skidan has published a bilingual anthology with Brooklyn-based Ugly Duckling Presse; Chukhrov and likely others are soon to follow.

The field of Slavic studies, in many ways still struggling to adapt to the cultural productions of post-Soviet Russia, must reflect the profound changes and politicized aesthetics corresponding to the rise of Putin's Russia – and to the protest cultures emerging in response. This chapter draws from a larger study aiming to bring a new generation of Russian poets to critical attention and exploring what I conceptualize as a contemporary avant-garde; hence the paradoxical use of prefixes in the working title of my larger project: *Avant-Garde Post–*. I hope to contribute a group portrait of poets central to this formation, whose poetic, critical, and activist practices seem paradigmatic, informative, or especially innovative. I study practices ranging from what I term 'poetics of refusal', when the critique of literary institutions makes further publication impossible and transubstantiates poetry into activism, to exquisitely difficult and philosophical poetry in the tradition of Arkadii Dragomoshchenko and his exchanges with the American L=A=N=G=U=A=G=E school.

I am interested in the sites of publication and performance, and in the re-emergence of the avant-garde journal as a venue, art object, collective cause, and social network: today's avant-garde journal has an active presence both off- and online. While poets test the limits of digital dissemination, they also 'embody' their poetics in performances that insist on the physical presence of the poet, at times in potentially dangerous or illegal circumstances. Nearly all of my subjects recognize a precursor in the Conceptualist Dmitrii Prigov, who played the Russian poet as an extended provocative art performance: after Prigov, avant-garde poets today borrow freely from the theories and practices of contemporary art, as well as from new forms of collective theatre. This chapter focuses on the younger poets of Kraft and *Translit*: Medvedev, Arseniev, and Osminkin, and especially on the last as the most pointedly 'performative'. For Medvedev and Osminkin, practices of performing poetry – of performing the Russian poet in a new cultural-historical moment – merge into musical performance with collaborations and collectives like Tekhnopoeziia and Arkadii Kots (among other and more recent incarnations).

Figure 11.1 is an image of Osminkin performing 'Why are you poets...' (*Chto zhe vy poety...*)[1] in a video clip recorded by Sergei Iugov, and edited and published by Osminkin on YouTube along with the accompanying text in 2013. The clip sets a poetry recital against the unlikely backdrop of a train station: unimpressed workers go about their business as Osminkin searches for an appropriate location for what is, in essence, a comically self-conscious avant-garde manifesto, initially available only online, but since released in a

Figure 11.1 Roman Osminkin. 'Why are you poets...'
Source: Still from YouTube. www.youtube.com/watch?v=xnaWug9luQg (accessed 24 September 2015).

collected volume by the publishing house Novoe literaturnoe obozrenie (New Literary Review), with the title *Texts with External Objectives (Teksty s vnepolozhnymy zadachami*), in 2015.

After the subheading, 'About the reasons for the early departure of some and unwillingness to go of other poets' (O prichinakh rannego ukhoda odnikh i nezhelaniia ukhodit' drugikh poetov'), the piece opens with a demand for 'you poets' (presumably the current reigning literary mainstream) to make way, following the brilliant example of the Romantic duellists Pushkin and Lermontov:

why are you poets	chto zhe vy poety
going away so late in life	pozdno tak ukhodite
you're not exactly coal miners	znamo ne shakhtery
you don't go to the factory	na zaboi ne khodite
look instead at Pushkin	posmotrite pushkin
and Lermontov: by bullets	lermontov ot puli
felled at duels	pali na dueli
why aren't you dying, scum?	vy ne mrete khuli?

The comparison with 'miners' (*shakhtery*), workers labouring for a living, may motivate the choice of setting and highlights the contrasting comfort that 'you poets' have been enjoying for too long. (The mission statement printed on the back of all Kraft series books reads: 'The paper on which this text is printed is called "Craft" by the printing industry. The same kind is used by post office workers and in many other technical enterprises. What you are holding in your hands doesn't resemble a "normally made" book of poetry, which corresponds to the vision of the authors whose texts are printed on this pager and in this series [...]').

The stanzas that follow run through the Russian poetic tradition of the twentieth century, focusing exclusively on the deaths of poets such as Nikolai Gumilev, Aleksandr Blok, Sergei Esenin, Velimir Khlebnikov, Vladimir Maiakovskii, Osip Mandel'shtam, Boris Pasternak, Daniil Kharms, Aleksandr Vvedenskii, and so forth. The list is delivered in folksy accentual verse, with comically unexpected rhymes ('bullet/scum'; *ot puli/huli*), wild register-mixing ('mandelshtam, too, fuck'; *mandel'shtam i tot blia*), and sly repetitions. For example, 'the whirlwind of the revolution' *(vikhr' revoliutsii)* is anti-rhymed with the same phrase, inviting laughter at the cliché and implying that the improvising, arm-waving declaimer could think of nothing else. The repetition is all the more striking in a stanza so short that the only new information it allows are the poets' names and the word 'too' (*tozhe*):

look at Gumilyov	glian'te gumileva
the whirlwind of the revolution	vikhr' revoliutsii
look at Blok too	glian'te bloka tozhe
the whirlwind of the revolution	vikhr' revoliutsii

The unceasing feminine endings – common enough in Russian modernist poetry, but striking for a poet who keeps company mostly with free verse-ifiers – add to the impression of pleasurable, self-aware comic verse.

Yet the humour is quite black, especially when paired with the imperative for today's poets to follow in the footsteps of their betters. When Maiakovskii became 'incomprehensible to the masses / your word was heard / comrade Mauzer' (*neponiaten massam / molvil vashe slovo / tovarishch mauzer*). The rhythm breaks on the last line; in the video, Osminkin delivers the line with a militant fist-raise and the footage breaks off, with the recital to resume in a slightly different location after the cut. From here the tone grows only darker:

living in the absurd	zhizn' v absurde kharmsu
unraveled Kharms's nerves	rasshatala nervy
and Vvedenskii from the start	a vvedenskii srazy
had death in his sights	na smert derzhal ravnen'e

What began as generational conflict, a demand that the old make way for the new, and as a list of permutations running through the early deaths of Russian poetry, turns into an Old Testament lineage and an unexpected grave-yard: the folksong version of Roman Jakobson's 1930 essay 'On a Generation that Squandered Its Poets' (Jakobson 1987, 273–300). Is this what a new mili-tancy looks like – a neo-avant-garde eager to throw the literary establishment off the high-speed train of (post)modernity?[2] Osminkin probes post-Soviet fears of a new Left throughout his oeuvre, here quite explicitly:

I'm kidding of course	ia shuchu konechno
live a little longer	vy zhivite dol'she
only not forever	nu ne to chtob vechno
that's not even decent	vse zhe ne prilichno
[...]	
and all the same our books	vse ravno tumany
are opaque to them	nashi dlia nikh knigi
enough with these swine	khvatit s etikh khamov
flip them the bird in our pockets	i v karmane figi

In his video performance of the poem, Osminkin laughs with theatrical omin-ousness after the final lines and storms off – presumably, into the future; per-haps into the past.

Performing the Russian poet: after Prigov

How might we imagine a genealogy of the Russian avant-garde(s)? In 'Socialist Realism: a Post-Scriptum', Evgenii Dobrenko considers Dmitrii Prigov's poetics against the backdrop of the historical avant-gardes of the early twentieth century. Dobrenko offers Prigov's own words in a condensed, insightful summary:

> Discussing the genealogy of 'avant-garde art-producing', Prigov distin-
> guished its three 'ages': 'futurist-constructivist', which was replaced by
> 'reaction against the mechanicalness and planned euphoria of the first',
> by an attempt to prove 'the absurdity of all levels of languages', but
> nevertheless these figures (the OBERIUty) were, according to Prigov, the
> 'cloudy unreflecting bearers of the avant-garde ideology of the first age'.
> And only in the third age ('pop art/conceptualist') did the 'completion
> of the triad' take place, 'the removal of the opposing mutually-directed
> linguistic positions of the first two ages...the affirmation of the truth of
> each language within the limits of its axiomatics...and the declaration of
> the untruthfulness of totalitarian ambitions'.[3]

We can trace the waves of Russian poetic avant-gardes even by looking exclusively at texts about Pushkin.[4] The 1912 manifesto *Slap in the Face of Public
Taste* declared it time to jettison Pushkin from the ship of modernity; but,
like a guilty memory in Andrei Tarkovsky's 1972 film *Solaris*, Pushkin returns
eternally, prompting subsequent generations of would-be avant-gardists and
experimenters to keep throwing him off the ship. When Osminkin cheekily
calls for contemporary poets to be like Pushkin and a host of other Romantic
or neo-Romantic poets, he invites them to die early (and thus on time), not to
write like Pushkin. Thus Osminkin too participates in what we might call an
absurdist tradition of *imitatio Pushkini*.

Building from Prigov's own brief history of Sots-Art, we can add a fourth
dialectical turn with the current generation of avant-garde poets and art-
producers: the paradoxical post-Soviet avant-garde. Adding an extra turn of
the screw, this new generation works from and against Prigov as the Father, as
poets with such divergent writing styles as Skidan and Medvedev have both
suggestively called Prigov in their essays.[5]

Why is Prigov so important to this overtly politicized group of contemporary poets and activists? Prigov brought Russian poetry into the space
of contemporary art: specifically, into the space of conceptualism and
performance. More a poet in quotation marks than a poet, Prigov was a
performance artist playing 'great Russian poet', undermining the logocen-
tric tendencies of Russian culture by taking it to an extreme (see Yurchak
2005). Slavoj Žižek has argued that '*overidentifying* with the explicit power
discourse [...] simply taking the power discourse at its (public) word, acting as if it really means what it explicitly says (and promises) – can be the
most effective way of disturbing its smooth functioning' (Žižek 2000, 220;
emphasis in the original). Alexei Yurchak very similarly defines late-Soviet
parody, *stiob* (Yurchak 2005). Thus, through such actions as his infamous performance of Tatiana's letter to Onegin as a faux Buddhist mantra,

Prigov disturbs the mystified function of the text in Russian culture precisely by exposing it as sacred.

The graphomania of Prigov's enormous poetic output (estimated at around 36,000 poems) in turn disrupts a privileged mode of reading: of exegesis, the close reading of the text for its hidden worth and difficulty, the privileged Romantic mode since at least John Keats, united with the Soviet/dissident preoccupation with Aesopian language that could slip subversive meanings past censors. Through its very bulk, Prigov's oeuvre forces us into a kind of distant reading *avant la lettre*, a reading that moves rapidly across many poems in search of meta-narratives (see Moretti 2013).

The change in strategy opens up new and unexpected possibilities for subsequent generations of poets. We might compare Dmitrii Golynko's rejection of the Romantic and neo-Romantic mode as described in his manifesto essay, 'Applied Social Poetry'. He writes:

> In order to give the poetic utterance an applied character, the poet with a radical gesture renounces the principle of aesthetic autonomy, and also the use of the stereotypical (Romantic and modernist) character of the poet-prophet, demon or eccentric. At the same time he is compelled to free himself from the illusion of artistic independence and to admit his absolute dependence on antagonistic social codes, and on a number of contradictory social voices.
>
> (Golynko 2012)

Golynko's essay is inspired in part by the Polish artist Artur Żmijewski's manifesto, 'Applied Social Art' (*Stosowane Sztuki Społeczne*). Żmijewski argues that art can be used 'for the most diverse goals: as an instrument of receiving and disseminating knowledge, as a factory of cognitive procedures, based on intuition and imagination, as an occasion for learning and for political action' (quoted in Golynko 2012). Following Prigov's innovations, Golynko extends these possible uses of art to poetry, or at least to certain kinds of poetic practice. The translation, however – from Polish to Russian, from visual arts to poetry – leaves remainders and plenty of room for anxiety, not least over the space of reception. A visual work of art, an installation, or a performance has the advantage of physically gathering together an audience, and hence maintains a potential for interactivity and fluid relationships between the performer and audience very different from the ways in which we typically consume poetry – or at least, the way that we did in the twentieth century.

The younger generation of performing poets, including Osminkin, Medvedev, and Arseniev, takes strategic advantage of the space opened up by Prigov. (Osminkin for a period of time even worked with Golynko as his supervisor on a dissertation exploring Prigov's performances.) In an interview in July 2013, Medvedev suggested the following line of descent:

What was Prigov's accomplishment, in large part? In that he learned each time, with a mass of the most diverse methods, to confront the reader with that serious, that modernist approach to art, to the poetic subject, to language in general. That is, you begin reading [Prigov's work] as verse, and then you understand that it is impossible to read it that way, as verse; but as that frame of mind persists inside of you, it creates a conflict. And on that, it seems to me, it all rests. Each time, some kind of neat creation of the unified, logo-centric subject falls apart. And it falls apart namely through an impulse from below, as it were, from the point of view of some kind of new sincerity [...] a kind of direct and immediate and unpoetic discourse. And in that, it seems to me, Roma [Osminkin] has glimpsed some kind of potential for a new democratic approach in Prigov's poetics. And he decided to develop it in a more engaged direction.[6]

Osminkin uses a line from Prigov as the epigraph to 'On Method' (*O metode*), an essay describing his own poetic practice: 'I think that the most democratic literature is not one that is comprehensible to everyone, but one that pays attention to all conventional linguistic gestures' (quoted in Osminkin 2012, 58). In the context of Osminkin's prose, however, the emphasis on democratic literature reads completely differently, and implies concrete political goals.

The poets of *Translit* combine post-Prigov Russian poetics with a transnational left-leaning canon, including not only kindred international performance artists and political artists such as Żmijewski, but also more unexpected English-language and American poets, such as Charles Bukowski (in the case of Medvedev, who in some sense found his poetic voice through translating Bukowski into Russian) and the L=A=N=G=U=A=G=E poets.[7] The latter were in part introduced into Russian verse through Arkadii Dragomoshchenko.[8] As if literalizing a metaphor, Osminkin and Arseniev, the founding editors of *Translit*, met in Dragomoshchenko's special seminar. We accordingly see elements of discourse poetry, found fragments of language, the 'voices of the voiceless', reflected in their work: the pre-formed is performed and revitalized.

Such practices re-politicize and even tentatively re-Romanticize (albeit with accompanying irony) the figure of the poet. Medvedev speaks of a 'weak heroism' necessary in a political moment when cultural figures feel called to social responsibility and even to heroic action, while remaining deeply ambivalent about, and profoundly suspicious of, the heroic posture of the Russian poet. Figure 11.2, for example, depicts Medvedev with other members of his group Arkadii Kots, singing 'The Walls' ('Steny', Lluis Llach's famous 1968 Catalan protest song 'L'Estaca', remade into 'Mury', the anthem of Polish Solidarność in the 1980s, now in Medvedev's Russian translation) inside an *avtozak* police van, when they were arrested while protesting outside of the courtroom during the Pussy Riot trial.

Figure 11.2 Kirill Medvedev and other Arkadii Kots members singing 'Walls' in a
    police van

Source: Still from YouTube. www.youtube.com/watch?v=I3X36Xqd9cw (accessed 24
September 2015).

Recording and disseminating this powerful impromptu music video, one
of several versions available on YouTube, suggests conscious political utilization of the (recently dismantled) cultural capital of the poet in Russian
society.

For Osminkin as for Medvedev, there is an interesting and productive tension between poetry and the musical performances. While the latter
reach a broader audience and are often held in support of political causes,
the former is more likely to maintain a relative autonomy. Yet the two bleed
into one another. As Brian Massumi writes in *Semblance and Event: Activist
Philosophy and the Occurrent Arts*, 'art claims the right to have no manifest
utility, no use-value, and in many cases even no exchange value. At its best,
it has event value' (Massumi 2011, 53). Aesthetic experiment models what
un-alienated labour might look like even as it opens a space for critique, for
emerging subjectivities and collectivities. If we consider aesthetic productions primarily as relational events, the borders between poetry and protest
rock break down, reflecting the poets' actual practice. Medvedev performs
both poems and songs at readings, including the art-historically aware ballad
'Boisia Groysa' and 'Tovarishch Kots'. The latter describes how the police
began calling Medvedev himself 'Kots', after the name of his group (and that
of the Russian translator of 'The Internationale'), effectively illustrating the
fluid continuity between poet and activist, original and translation, and even
between individual and collective identity.

Figure 11.3 Roman Osminkin. 'Jesus Saves Pussy Riot'
Source: Still from YouTube. www.youtube.com/watch?v=nmAb2GBKWkg (accessed 24 September 2015).

Medvedev and Osminkin's texts make free use of poetic biography as well as of current politics, referring to events familiar to their audiences and communities, their witnesses and co-conspirators. Osminkin's best-known song, often paired with Medvedev's 'The Walls', is his original composition in response to the jailing of Pussy Riot: 'Jesus Saves Pussy Riot' ('Iisus spasaet Pussy Riot', 2012). Several versions can be found on YouTube: in the one from which Fig. 11.3 is taken, the cameraman angles down from Osminkin on stage to show a young mother dancing with her child to his words. Osminkin includes the lyrics to his song in his Kraft book of poems and manifestos *Comrade Word* (*Tovarishch slovo*, 2012). On the page he introduces the text as 'a song written in support of the feminist group Pussy Riot on 8 March 2012, which they spent in jail' (Osminkin 2012, 32).

The song manages to be entirely of the moment, an occasional work of protest culture, and to cast the actions of Pussy Riot as a timeless fairy-tale feat – an entirely Romantic *podvig*, or feat.

between the whip of the Cossacks	mezh kazatskoi nagaikoi
and the Chekhists' revolver	i chekistskim naganom
flock maidens armed	v'iutsia devich'i staiki
with militant avant-gardism	boevym avangardom
and on the place of skulls	i na lobnoe mesto
and in the sacred cathedral	i v sakral'nyi sobor
rings the song of the maidens	l'etsia devich'ia pesnia
and a punk-prayer choir	i pank-molebna khor

Osminkin's identification and alliance are overt: the actions of the young women or 'maidens' (inverting the smear campaign run against the young women by Russian media) are recognized as militant avant-gardism: they navigate between the Cossack far right and the Chekhist false left; and they too fight by means of song. The opening stanzas launch into the more jagged rhythms of the chorus:

Jesus saves	iisus spasaet
the patriarch punishes	patriarkh karaet
he's enlightened and well knows	on osvedomlen i prekrasno znaet
the three innocents must be	nado trekh nevinnykh
thrown in the fire	brosit' na koster
and that will trip up every other	i togda zatknetsia vsiakii na iazyk
sharp tongue	oster
[...]	
the three innocents must be	nado trekh nevinnykh
impaled on the stake	posadit' na kol
and that will shut up all this	i togda zatknetsia vsiakii pizdabol
cuntery	

Again we see the mixing of registers in shocking rhymes: the brutal, archaic, and sexual 'impaled on the stake' (*posadit' na kol*) leads to the untranslatable expletive 'pizdabol'. The maidens are now three 'innocents', Christian martyrs whom Christ must surely save. The most famous lines juxtapose Christian salvation with the patriarch's violence, ironically referring to the patriarch as 'enlightened', slipping into the discourse of the other side (the side that believes it knows how to shut up fools, as colourfully put in the stanza's final line). The over-the-top imagery moves from casting the maidens into the fire as witches to impaling them as martyrs, mocking throughout the paranoiac heteronormativity of the Putin regime.

Osminkin's attack only grows more personal from there: the patriarch, initially called by his title, is named and thereby exposed as a mere man; and moreover, one who serves two masters:

it's so nice to decide	kak udobno reshat'
in the name of the lord	ot imeni boga
who gets fattened up	komu zhirovat'
and who's en route to jail	a komu v tiur'mu doroga
Kirill Gundiaev	Kirill Gundiaev
it doesn't do	negozhe kak by
to serve both the lord	sluzhit' i gospodu
and the KGB	i KaGeBe

The unexpected invocation of the former name of the secret police serves as the song's climactic indictment – of Putin's regime and its politico-historical hypocrisies, and of the church's complicity. Osminkin in essence repeats Pussy

Riot's *podvig*, blaspheming not against God but against this particular church and its organized hypocrisies.

Embodiment and poetic bodies

In yet another manifesto prefacing his poetry in *Tovarishch slovo*, Osminkin describes the paradoxical need to combine poetry with action:

> To take the poetic word out of an indifferent mode of existence, and to bring the poet back from the pose of an alienated prophet, poetry must be materialized in a concrete moment in time and space, turning the poet to face unfolding history.
>   Precisely in the moment of the public spoken word, the poet takes onto himself responsibility for his own voice, and thereby accomplishes a socially responsible act [...] The main thing happens: the word is pronounced (materialized) and the act is accomplished, and that means that thought does not remain starry-eyed inspiration, but 'performs itself' into the socium.
>
> (Osminkin 2012, 6–7)

The emphasis throughout is on materializing poetic language through voice and presence, and on the poet accepting responsibility and 'facing' history through performance – on the word made flesh, outlandishly, by 'performing itself' into the body politic.

We can only 'read' such poetic practices using terms such as 'event', 'embodiment', and 'relational art' – following the same theoretical flows and their echoes as influence Osminkin and many of the *Translit* poets (*nota bene* the wealth of references to Walter Benjamin, Michel Foucault, Gilles Deleuze, Jacques Rancière, Alain Badiou, and many more throughout his poetry, essays, and performances). Osminkin's deceptively simple poems demand theoretical accompaniment.

In *Interactive Art and Embodiment: The Implicit Body as Performance*, Nathaniel Stern describes the performing body as 'a dynamic form, full of potential. It is not "a body", as thing, but *embodiment* as incipient activity' (Stern 2013, 2; emphasis in the original). I similarly use the term 'relational', rather than 'interactive', to conceptualize the dissolution of the performer/audience dichotomy: a distinction between the two terms highlights 'what digital and interactive artworks *cannot* do, as well as what they have the potential to do, outside of purely technical terms' (Stern 2013, 63; emphasis in the original). The trouble with the term 'interactive' is in what it obfuscates and elides, in commercial use: 'we must critique the idea that interactivity's supposed provision of choice means it is intrinsically more democratic (or freeing) than other media, and show that such language [...] has been coopted by commercial companies trying to sell us products' (Stern 2013, 22).

Nicolas Bourriaud builds on the primacy of relation, as asserted by Jean-Luc Nancy (Nancy 2000). Bourriaud defines relational artworks broadly as 'invitations, casting sessions, meetings, convivial and user-friendly areas, appointments, etc. [...] vehicles through which particular lines of thought and personal relationships with the world are developed' (Bourriaud 1998, 46). Conceived of as 'public encounters, events, and collaborations', relational artworks strive to move beyond aesthetic consumption (Bourriaud 1998, 78). Poetic practices that aspire to similar embodiment and relational affect rely on performance, audience presence and participation, and site-specific experience. We can only imagine the difference between reading the words of Osminkin's 'Poetic Manifesto of the Movement "Occupy Abay"' (Stikhotvoreniie-manifest dvizheniia 'Okkupai Abai') on the page (reprinted in Osminkin 2012, 31) and participating in their performance at the 'Occupy Abay' encampment during the protests of 2012.

I had the opportunity to witness first-hand a reading Osminkin gave of his poem 'New Laws' (Novye zakony) inside a circle of activists gathered to protest the changing internet laws in the summer of 2013.

it happens you meet an underage girl	byvaet povstrechaesh' maloletku
and right away you make a stern face	i srazu prinimaesh' strogii vid
walk faster past me child	bystree prokhodite mimo detka
I smell sexual maturity's reek	ot vas polovozrelost'iu fonit
but I read all the new laws	a ia zakony novye chitaiu
for paedophilia you won't get me	i mne pedofiliiu ne prish'esh'
you could have thrice the charms of Danae	bud' vy pokhozhi trizhdy na danaiu
but your age is insufficient still	no vozrast vash nesovershenen vsezh

This performance transformed the energy of the otherwise listless crowd and made of the minor protest an event with legs – especially through the ongoing digital dissemination of photos and videos of varying quality taken by the spectators. Osminkin prefaced his reading with the apology that his poems were about the wrong laws, noting that he could not write fast enough to keep pace with changes in the Russian legislation. His piece spoke instead to the still-recent (and then-surprising) laws targeting 'sexual deviancy', purportedly intended to protect the nation's youth from corrupting influences. The list of encounters Osminkin's lyric persona 'sternly avoids' includes an underage girl, a skulking foreign agent, and lesbians; in the last section, Osminkin again uses the term 'maidens', before switching in the final stanza to the untranslatable 'baba' a Russian woman is doomed to remain:

it happens you meet some lesbians	byvaet povstrechaesh' lesbiianok
and right away you make a stern face	i srazu prinimaesh' strogii vid
if you were maidens blameless three times over	bud' trizhdy vy vevitsy bez iz'anov
I'd still smell Gomorrah's reek	ot vas gomorroi za verstu fonit

but I read all the new laws	a ia zakony novye chitaiu
for gay propaganda you won't get me	geipropagandoiu menia ne proshibesh'
in Russia you don't pick your gender	v rossii pol sebia ne vybiraiut
if you're born a broad, as a broad you croak	rodilas' baboi – baboi i pomresh'

Of course, poetic performance and performativity predate the early teens of the twenty-first century. However, such practices read differently after the widespread awareness and recognition of performance art, body art, and feminist art – which Osminkin and fellow poets draw on avidly, queering the Russian poet. As Richard Schechner writes, performance art asks the question:

> 'Who is this person doing these actions?' – unlike theater, which asks about the character doing the actions. Insisting that spectators regard not a character but an actual person (even if the artist embellishes that persona, as Spalding Gray did), actualizes the slogan, "the personal is political'.
>
> (Schechner 2013, 158)

That activist slogan is borrowed from the title of feminist Carol Hanisch's 1969 essay, explaining her bra-burning protest at the Atlantic City Miss America pageant, and reminding us of performance art's roots in feminist art and theory (see Butler 1993). Who are these Russian poets identifying with women, sexual minorities, and decadent foreign thinkers? I read the latest (re)turn of the Russian avant-garde as a combination of powerful local poetic counter-traditions, reimagined through, reinvigorated by – and in solidarity with – international theory and art practice (see Foster 1996). As an explicitly post-Soviet cultural formation, this constellation of sympathetic practices dares to move past the traumas of state socialism to reimagine engaged art and alternative social organization for the twenty-first century.

Poets, activists, and digital media

Legitimizing and bond-forming performances require the poet to be bodily present at protests, arrests, or other charged events; meanwhile, the digital remediation and dissemination of these performances serves to document and share work with a wider community. In the new poetics, offline and online worlds interact with and necessitate one another. While the Kraft books and *Translit* journal appear in hard copy, most materials are readily found online: in portable document format (pdf) on the *Translit* blog or on poets' individual websites, as well as on Facebook, VKontakte, and YouTube.

Figure 11.4 *Translit* blog, with image of hard copy publication
Source: http://trans-lit.info/ (accessed 24 September 2015).

Digital dissemination reflects the way we actually read, share, and reference this material, whereas hard copies provide physical support (Fig. 11.4), serving the purposes of collecting, fundraising, archiving, or signing, personalizing, and gift-giving. (In this fluid on- and offline existence, *Translit* resembles the left-leaning Brooklyn journals of the *n+1* and *Jacobin* variety.)

To take a step back, we might situate the *Translit* blog and related digital poetics against earlier online projects. The most important precursor is Vavilon.ru, the poetry anthology that Dmitrii Kuz'min developed into a web-based publication, 'dramatically expanding both its reach, its frequency of publication, and its archival potential' as early as 1997: Kirill Medvedev comments that 'In this, as in so much else, [Kuz'min] was so far ahead of the rest of the literary field as to be playing in some different game entirely' (Medvedev 2012, 184).

In contrast to the curated encyclopaedia-anthology presented by Vavilon. ru or its successor Novaia Literaturnaia Karta Rossii (started in 2007), we have the anarchic world of free web poetry. Again I quote Medvedev: 'the cheerful amateur graphomania at, say, www.poems.ru is on the whole more attractive than the professional tedium produced by the tenured liberals'. Medvedev has expressed an interest in the unpoliced borderlands of Russian poetry online: 'Since web poetry is a kind of concentrated portrait of the Russian unconscious, a collection of its most painful neuroses, it sometimes manifests itself as an inert, conservative, and very aggressive mass' (Medvedev 2012, 198–199). And this is to say nothing of more concerted recent efforts at the presentation of Russian classics in openly nationalist curator-driven online platforms such as the 'Russian alternative to Wikipedia', Traditsia.ru.[9]

What is the Russian Left to do online – or rather, what do some of the poets of the new Left do? In *24/7: Late Capitalism and the Ends of Sleep*, Jonathan Crary argues that the vast majority of digital usage is based entirely on consumption, and that only a small (to him, negligible) minority of savvy producers make use of online possibilities for aesthetic experimentation and activism (see Crary 2013). Even allowing for such a stark divide between consumers and producers, however, those small minorities of the latter continue to be of interest precisely for their imaginaries of alterity and pushback against a predetermined future.

Before looking at examples of emerging leftist digital poetic genres, we might consider the different uses of the most popular online platforms in the context of protest culture. BBC journalist Paul Mason offers one summary of the functionalities of the information tools used by contemporary activists after what he terms the 'revolutions of 2009–2011'. Mason writes:

> Facebook is used to form groups, covert and overt – in order to establish those strong but flexible connections. Twitter is used for real-time *organization* and news dissemination, bypassing the cumbersome 'newsgathering' operations of the mainstream media. YouTube and the Twitter-linked photographic sites – Yfrog, Flickr and Twitpic – are used to provide instant evidence of the claims being made. Link-shorteners like bit.ly are used to disseminate key articles via Twitter.
>
> (Mason 2012, 75; emphasis in the original)[10]

How does poetry make use of these tools, moving beyond dissemination or simpler forms of remediation? I follow Jay David Bolter and Richard Grusin's use of the term in *Remediation: Understanding New Media*. Bolter and Grusin argue that refashioning within a single medium is

> the one kind of refashioning that literary critics, film critics, and art historians have acknowledged and studied with enthusiasm, for it does not violate the presumed sanctity of the medium, a sanctity that was important to critics earlier in this century, although it is less so now. Refashioning within the medium is a special case of remediation, and it proceeds from the same ambiguous motives of homage and rivalry – what Harold Bloom has called 'the anxiety of influence' – as do other remediations.
>
> (Bolter and Grusin 2000, 49)

The digital is not itself a medium: to paraphrase Lev Manovich, we would do better to think in terms of meta-media (Manovich 2005); in Massumi's phrasing, 'Digital technology is an expanding network of connective and fusional potentials [...] You can take any existing genre of artistic practice and fuse it with any other' (Massumi 2011, 81).

Poetic experimentation online grows complicated quickly. To make sense of digital genres, we are called on alternatively to zoom in, to the close-reading methods of more familiar literary analysis, and to zoom out, to more distanced approaches that take into account platform, popular practices, digital and other anthropologies. The exploration of practices rather than textual units leads us to ask the questions 'how?', 'where?', 'when?' – as much as 'what?' – of a text.

I will run through several examples of poetry online that combine images and text across the major social media platforms. Many Russian poets post their new work (along with rediscovered favourites by others) on Facebook, but Osminkin does so with frequency and invites interaction. Alongside with other playful posts in which he calls himself the 'master of the meme', he posts a draft of 'a little class warfare' (nemnogo klassovoi borby) on 2 August 2013.

Later that day, he adds several more lines through the Comment function, before returning to the poem on 5 August to add the chorus – and to post a YouTube clip of himself singing the piece (accompanied by Medvedev on guitar) and walking the streets of Moscow. The clip was shot on 4 August, the previous day, and the words appear at least partly improvised. The next day, Osminkin adds them to the original posting. The final version (if it makes sense at all to think in such terms; rather, the version he later performs and sends on for translation) includes all the lines, with a few minor textual and formatting changes.

a little bit of class war	nemnogo klassovoi bor'by
a little bit of red terror	nemnogo krasnogo terroru
and the features loved to tears	i barkhatnogo termidoru
of a velvet thermidor	do boli milye cherty

A very different example from YouTube is offered by Kirill Medvedev's video poetry, a remediation of '3 Percent' (3 protsenta), written in 2005 and montaged in collaboration with Iakov Kazhdan in 2010 (Fig. 11.5).

Here, a finished and previously published poem is put to images: less illustrated than expanded and recast. The street setting and the car passing in slow motion hardly 'translate' the language of the poem into visual media, but instead invite us to contemplate the incomprehensible 3 per cent even in this unremarkable scene. The text is read in a neutral male tone (not Medvedev's own distinctive voice) and simultaneously presented in super-title fragments, oddly resembling the new speed-reading applications but to opposite effect. In a sense this digitally remediated poem does the inverse work of the previous example from Facebook: Osminkin begins collaboratively and with multiple media and ends with a poem; Medvedev brings in co-authors and moves into an online existence.

Figure 11.5 'What's there, in those 3 per cent?'
Source: Still from YouTube: www.youtube.com/watch?v=Bv5WmL4kWQ4 (accessed 24 September 2015).

Both cases, however, either begin with or end as something resembling a poetic text. The last example I will give here, a work of experimental performed video poetry by Pavel Arseniev, does not. In 'A Translator's Annotations' ('Primechanie perevodchika', 2013), Arseniev selects found language from Ludwig Wittgenstein's notebooks, translated into Russian, and picks out fragments that suit him in real time, 'censoring' the rest with a thick black marker. The text is thus exposed as always the other – as always a receding chain of others. Notably, this work of found and performed poetry (discourse poetry, in the terms of the L=A=N=G=U=A=G=E school) can only be published in video format embedded in the *Translit* blog.

In schematic terms, projects like Vavilon.ru and LitKarta reflect the hope for a liberal public sphere. Through conclusive lists of the acceptable Russian canon, Traditsia.ru tries to tame and render politically useful its eponymous tradition. More radical experimental practices draw attention to the media and online platforms themselves – and to the way that they shape us.

The limits of digital emancipation

Moving from these examples to concluding thoughts, I return to the offline/online dichotomy. Much of contemporary politically engaged poetry insists on physical performance, on the actual presence of the poet's body, and on physical and ethical risk, as well as on breaking down the walls between performer and spectator, maker and consumer. Readings, concerts, festivals, performances, actions, sit-ins, protests, and encampments like 'Occupy Abay' demand and build the 'strong ties' required for collective action, in Malcolm Gladwell's words (Gladwell 2010).

A number of prominent 'techno-pessimists' have argued against the collectivity-building potential of digital technologies. Gladwell claims that social media create weak ties at best: 'the revolution will not be tweeted'. Evgenii Morozov in particular has denounced 'slacktivism', which he defines as 'feel-good activism that has zero political or social impact but creates an illusion of having a meaningful impact on the world without demanding anything more than joining a Facebook group' (Morozov 2009). Instead, he warns, social media 'can create serious risks for activists, given the increased possibilities for monitoring by state security apparatus' (in Gerbaudo 2012, 8). Meanwhile, Zygmunt Bauman's broader diagnosis is that 'contemporary hardships and sufferings are dispersed and scattered; and so is the dissent that they spawn' (Bauman 2000, 54).[11]

These are important critiques and interventions to an unbounded techno-optimism that presumes faster communication inevitably leads to the increased potential for collective action. However, many scholars, artists, and activists attempt to find middle ground, and to exorcise the online/offline dichotomy.[12] In *Tweets and the Streets: Social Media and Contemporary Activism*, Paolo Gerbaudo suggests that 'social media use must be understood as complementing existing forms of face-to-face gatherings (rather than substituting for them), but also as a vehicle for the creation of new forms of proximity and face-to-face interaction' (Gerbaudo 2012, 13). Gerbaudo speaks of 'choreography' and the 'symbolic construction of public space' on- and offline, witnessed during the organization and implementation of varied international protest events.

Adding poetry to the discussion of protest culture off- and online pushes us to re-examine the relationship between rhetoric and aesthetic, relatively autonomous uses of language and visual media. Analysing the visual turn in contemporary Russian culture, Aleksandr Skidan argues:

> The center of creative work has shifted to the visual arts because (1) they immediately reflect, and partly coincide with, the new technogenic environment, (2) which mobilizes the cerebral and sensorimotor resources of human beings along with the earth's natural resources and outer space. (3) The visual arts correspond to the dominant regime of temporality and synthetic perception established by the mass media. (4) They are inscribed in the culture industry and, consequently, (5) in the capitalist machine, which deterritorializes any form of identity based on linguistic competency.
>
> (Skidan 2007)

Faced with this machine, he asks, 'what is poetry's lot? First and foremost (and this is obvious), exclusion from the machine.' Exclusion alone – even when it takes place within what he calls the technogenic environment – may be considered a success. For poetry, Skidan writes, 'must still invent means for dwelling in the heart of this absolute rupture, for delivering and enduring it as an openness to the future. And, perhaps, as an openness to future (absolutely real) collective actions' (Skidan 2007).

What the work of Roman Osminkin and *Translit* fellow travellers throws back into the discussion of protest culture is the presence of self-conscious aesthetic production, re-created for the digital age: their poetry, despite all genre-bending, still insists that it is poetry. Complex practices claiming the relative autonomy of art imagine, and participate in, the processes of potentially emancipatory subjectivization and collectivity-building.

Notes

1   Translations are mine, unless otherwise marked; whenever possible, they have been checked with the authors.
2   See Boris Groys's famous claim that the 'total art of Stalinism' had its roots in the utopian dreams of the historical avant-garde (Groys 1992).
3   From Dmitrii Prigov's *Manifesty*; translated and summarized by Dobrenko and cited here from 'Prigov and the Aesthetic Limits of Sots-Art' (Dobrenko 1999, 96).
4   Yale University Slavic Languages and Literatures PhD candidate Megan Race makes this argument in an article in progress entitled 'Moi Pushkin i moi Pushkin', offering a reading of pre-Soviet, Soviet, and post-Soviet 'avant-garde Pushkins'.
5   'Golem Sovietikus: D. A. Prigov' (Skidan 2013, 264–258). See Medvedev: 'Post-conceptualism comes after the radical word-play and author-assassination of writers like Dmitri Prigov and Vladimir Sorokin (in his early work) – that is, after the Russian representatives of early postmodernism had become canonical'. Post-conceptualism (sometimes called the 'New Sincerity') 'senses acutely the postmodern death of the author and the necessity for his resurrection and rehabilitation' (Medvedev 2012, 206); translation by Keith Gessen.
6   From the author's interview with Medvedev in Moscow, 1 August 2013.
7   I develop the Bukowski and Medvedev comparison in an article dedicated to Medvedev's poetry (Bozovic 2014).
8   See Sandler 2005, and Skidan, 'Poznanie pyli: A. Dragomoshchenko', in Skidan 2013, 119–126.
9   I am indebted to the ongoing research of Yale University Slavic Languages and Literatures PhD candidate Jacob Lassin on Traditsia.ru and nationalist presentations of Russian poetry online.
10 See also Gerbaudo 2012, 3. In the Russian context, Facebook and its Russian-language rival VKontakte tend to cater to 'Western-leaning' and 'nationally-oriented' users (echoing the nineteenth-century Westernizers and Slavophiles) respectively, albeit with overlap.
11 For a succinct overview of the leading voices of techno-pessimism, see Gerbaudo 2012, 5–9.
12 See Massumi 2011, 16: the virtual 'cannot be treated as a realm apart without being entirely denatured as a speculatively-pragmatically useful concept'.

References

Bauman, Zygmunt. 2000. *Liquid Modernity*. Cambridge: Polity Press.

Bolter, Jay David and Richard Grusin. 2000. *Remediation: Understanding New Media*. Cambridge, MA: MIT Press.

Bourriaud, Nicolas. 1998. *Relational Aesthetics*. Dijon: Les Presses du reel Dijon.

Bozovic, Marijeta. 2014. "Poetry on the Front Line: Kirill Medvedev and a New Russian Poetic Avant-Garde." *Zeitschrift für Slavische Philologie* 70 (1): 89–118.

Butler, Judith. 1993. *Bodies that Matter: On the Discursive Limits of Sex*. London and New York: Routledge.

Crary, Jonathan. 2013. *24/7: Late Capitalism and the Ends of Sleep*. London: Verso.

Dobrenko, Evgeny. 1999. "Socialist Realism, a Postscriptum. Dmitrii Prigov and the Aesthetic Limits of Sots-Art." In *Endquote: Sots-Art Literature and Soviet Grand Style*, edited by Marina Balina, Nancy Condee, and Evgeny Dobrenko, 77–106. Evanston, IL: Northwestern University Press.

Foster, Hal. 1996. *The Return of the Real: The Avant-Garde at the Turn of the Century*. Cambridge, MA: MIT Press.

Gerbaudo, Paolo. 2012. *Tweets and the Streets: Social Media and Contemporary Activism*. London: Pluto Press.

Gladwell, Malcolm. 2010. "Small Change: Why the Revolution Will Not Be Tweeted." *The New Yorker* 4 October.

Golynko, Dmitry. 2012. "Applied Social Poetry." First published in Russian in *Translit* 10/11.

Groys, Boris. 1992. *The Total Art of Stalinism: Avant-Garde, Aesthetic Dictatorship, and beyond*. Princeton, NJ: Princeton University Press.

Hanisch, Carol. 1969. "The Personal is Political." www.carolhanisch.org/CHwritings/PIP.html (accessed 22 October 2016).

Jakobson, Roman. 1987. *Language in Literature*. Edited by Krystyna Pomorska and Stephen Rudy. Cambridge, MA, and London: Belknap Press of Harvard University Press.

Manovich, Lev. 2005. "Understanding Meta-Media." *C-Theory.net* 26 October. www.ctheory.net/articles.aspx?id=493 (accessed 24 September 2015).

Mason, Paul. 2012. *Why It's Kicking Off Everywhere: The New Global Revolutions*. London: Verso.

Massumi, Brian. 2011. *Semblance and Event: Activist Philosophy and the Occurrent Arts*. Cambridge, MA: MIT Press.

Medvedev, Kirill. 2012. *It's No Good: Poems/Essays/Actions*. Translated by Keith Gessen, with Mark Krotov, Cory Merrill, and Bela Shayevich. New York: *n+1*/Ugly Duckling Presse.

Moretti, Franco. 2013. *Distant Reading*. London: Verso.

Morozov, Evgenii. 2009. "The Brave New World of Slacktivism." *Foreign Policy* 19 May. http://neteffect.foreignpolicy.com/posts/2009/05/19/the_brave_new_world_of_slacktivism (accessed 24 September 2015).

Nancy, Jean-Luc. 2000. *Being Singular Plural*. Stanford, CA: Stanford University Press.

Osminkin, Roman. 2012. *Tovarishch Slovo*. St Petersburg: Kraft.

Sandler, Stephanie. 2005. "Dragomoshchenko, Hejinian, and the Persistence of Romanticism." *Contemporary Literature* 46 (1): 18–45.

Schechner, Richard. 2013. *Performance Studies. An Introduction.* New York and London: Routledge.

Skidan, Aleksandr. 2007. "Poetry in the Age of Total Communication." Published in Norwegian translation by Susanne Hege Bergan, in *Audiatur – Katalog for ny poesi*, 2007. English translation by Thomas H. Campbell. www.trans-lit.info/trans.htm (accessed 24 September 2015).

Skidan, Aleksandr. 2013. *Summa poetiki.* Moscow: Novoe literaturnoe obozrenie.

Stern, Nathaniel. 2013. *Interactive Art and Embodiment: The Implicit Body as Performance.* Canterbury: Gylphi.

Yurchak, Alexei. 2005. *Everything Was Forever, Until It Was No More: The Last Soviet Generation.* Princeton, NJ: Princeton University Press.

Žižek, Slavoj. 2000. "Class Struggle or Postmodernism? Yes, Please!" In *Contingency, Hegemony, Universality: Contemporary Dialogues on the Left*, edited by Judith Butler, Ernesto Laclau, and Slavoj Žižek, 90–135. London: Verso.

12 When satire does not subvert

Citizen Poet as nostalgia for Soviet dissidence

Sanna Turoma

The autumn of 2011 saw Russia preparing for the legislative elections held on 4 December, and the spring of 2012 was electrified by the presidential election on 4 March. While political analysts would describe the campaigns as a key moment in Russian 'electoral authoritarianism', cultural scholars would see in this period an explosion of artistic creativity, which was highly visible on the satirical pole of the poetic and political spectrum. The campaigns gave the voters an opportunity to express their discontent, caused by the increasing government control over the media and obstacles to entering the political market as well as the power tandem of the president and prime minister and their change of roles. Though the elections opened 'a window of opportunities for the political opposition' to come 'out of its ghetto' and to initiate a 'mass mobilization and collective action' (Gel'man 2013, 4–5), the organized means of political protest were secondary to the improvised forms of cultural self-expression which symbolically attacked and mocked the authoritarian regime, its institutions, and its leaders. In this chapter, I revisit one the most successful satirical shows of the time, *Citizen Poet* (*Grazhdanin poet*).[1]

Many recent examples, such as Jon Stewart in the US and Bassem Youssef in Egypt, demonstrate that satire is an important form of politically engaged culture in political media.[2] Unlike these shows, however, *Citizen Poet* was not a news show. To be sure, the production team used news materials as its source, and called the project a 'newsical', but, more remarkably, the creators of the show deployed a literary medium which many observers would easily dismiss as marginal or irrelevant to political commentary: the show was, in essence, a series of poetry readings.[3]

Citizen Poet was never broadcast on national TV channels, but it gained momentum on the Internet and social media. The production team consisted of three well-known media personalities, the producer Andrei Vasil'ev, the popular film actor Mikhail Efremov (Fig. 12.1), and Dmitrii Bykov, a well-known Moscow-based poet and author. For political satire in verse, Bykov wrote modernized parodies that played with easily recognizable poems of classical Russian and Soviet poets, applying these literary subtexts to contemporary political events.[4] Reading these texts, Efremov imitated the mannerisms, gestures, and cadence of the parodied poet. The show's satirical spear was targeted mostly at Vladimir Putin and/or the 'tandem' of Putin and Dmitrii Medvedev.[5] It rallied the anti-Putin sentiment of the liberal intelligentsia and those who in social media became associated with the rapidly emerging 'creative class'.[6]

The title of the show related to Nikolai Nekrasov's 1856 poem and its famous lines 'you may not be a poet, but to be a citizen is an obligation'. Nekrasov was known for his satirical verse, which addressed and exposed the social ills of his contemporary Russia and promoted the civic cause of poetry in the age of realism. Nekrasov's lines, in turn, referred to Kondratii Ryleev's famous lines 'I am not a poet / I am a citizen' ('Ia ne poet, a grazhdanin'). Ryleev was one of the participants in the Decembrist uprising in 1825 and was hanged after its defeat. By adopting this title, the show proclaimed its identification with the Russian traditions of politically engaged culture, intellectual dissent, and responsible citizenship.

The online success of the show paved the way for live performances. The team took *Citizen Poet* on a tour of sold-out shows at concert halls, sport venues, and theatres across Russia. In October 2011, for instance, the newsical reached live audiences in Tolyatti, Samara, Kazan, Nizhny Novgorod, Saratov, Volgograd, Krasnodar, Stavropol, and Novorossiisk. In addition to Efremov's performance, Bykov showcased his versatile talent by improvising satirical poems *in situ* responding to topics suggested by the audience. The live performances were a source of financial success for the team (Zhokhova 2012).

The show consisted of 53 poems, most of them Russian. Non-Russian poems (by William Shakespeare, Edgar Allan Poe, and Rudyard Kipling) served as subtexts for three of Bykov's texts. Apart from a few lesser-known poets, Bykov used mostly the Russian literary canon: the nineteenth-century classics (Aleksandr Pushkin, Mikhail Lermontov, Nekrasov, Evgenii Baratynskii, Aleksandr Griboedov, Ivan Krylov); early twentieth-century classics (Osip Mandel'shtam, Aleksandr Blok, Boris Pasternak, Vladimir Maiakovskii, Sergei Esenin, Nikolai Gumilev, Aleksandr Vertinskii); and Soviet writers (Maxim Gorky, Kornei Chukovskii, Konstantin Simonov, Evgenii Evtushenko, Andrei Voznesenskii, Aleksandr Tvardovskii, Bulat Okudzhava, Vladimir Vysotskii, Sergei Mikhalkov). In addition, the show used contemporary poems by Joseph Brodsky, Viktor Tsoi, and Agniia Barto. Apart from Tsoi, a rock musician whose poem was the subtext for a performance making fun of Putin's main campaign speech at Luzhniki ('Everyone dies and I alone will remain'), all the others parodied authors belonging to the high poetic canon. The team also used two Soviet leaders who wrote verses: Iurii Andropov and Iosif Dzhugashvili (Stalin). Clearly, Bykov the parodist relied on the ability of his audience to recognize sources that were familiar from the Soviet education system. At the same time, the successful utilization of this canon points to one of the paradoxes of the show: in many cases the poems drew on a satirical analogy between the current political elite and Soviet rule, aiming thus to expose the continuity of a Soviet-era legacy in the Kremlin's rhetoric and practices of power. Meanwhile, the referential framework of the project as a cultural product (i.e. the meanings and significations it rested on) was rooted in the Soviet-era cultural canon handed down to contemporary Russians as Soviet legacy. This fact prompts an enquiry into the actual target of the show's satire: was the satire actually subversive with respect to the Soviet legacy in the established political, social, or cultural order of contemporary Russian society, which partially drew on these legacies? What problems of Russian politics and society did the show strive to expose? What institutionalized practices, hegemonic discourses, or societal norms did the show question, and how did the regular versification and intertextual play help in this task? Finally, to whom did the show lend a voice? Who was the 'citizen poet', the show's political subject?[7]

Putiniana and the pleasure of recognition

Citizen Poet criticized several aspects of Russia's political and societal developments deplored by those who identified with a Western-style liberal agenda. These were the restrictions of media freedom, violence against political journalists, the Russian involvement in the Caucasus, the corruption of the legal system, the rise of nationalism, the increasing power of the Russian Orthodox Church and its close relations with the Kremlin, and patriotism incorporated into the school curriculum.

To critique these issues, the team used current news items and topics such as the Yukos case that led to the incarceration of Mikhail Khodorkovskii and Platon Lebedev; *Russkii marsh*, the annual demonstration organized by nationalists; suspected embezzlement in the office of Moscow's mayor Iurii Luzhkov; the proposal by the leading health authority Gennadii Onishchenko to deny entry to Tajik migrant workers based on alleged HIV cases; the official project to ban EU vegetables for not meeting Russian standards; and the case of Oleg Kashin, the journalist-activist who criticized a provincial official and was attacked in downtown Moscow.

The main topic of *Citizen Poet*, however, was the presidential candidate Vladimir Putin. One of its most popular performances was 'Putin and the Peasant' (Putin i muzhik),[8] a parody of Aleksandr Tvardovskii's poem 'Lenin and the Stove-Maker' (Lenin i pechnik). Published multiple times as a children's book, the story in verse became one of the main sources for the idealization of Lenin as a kind and wise leader among post-Stalin generations of Soviet citizens. Although written at the end of the 1930s, it became standard reading for schools in the 1950s and 1960s.

Tvardovskii's poem, based on an earlier story by Mikhail Zoshchenko, evolves around an anecdote about a stove-maker and his unexpected meeting with Lenin.[9] The stove-maker does not recognize Lenin, but takes him for an ordinary old man, treating him with disrespect and telling him to move out of his way. He asks the man to tell him his name, and 'the bold-headed, small man' utters 'Lenin'. When the stove-maker realizes that he has been addressing the great leader, he is struck by his own misconduct and sits down in despair. The summer passes and winter arrives. The memory of the unexpected encounter and his disrespectful conduct towards Lenin does not leave the stove-maker. When two soldiers arrive at his house in a snowstorm, he thinks they have come to arrest him. The soldiers take him to see Lenin who, instead of ordering his arrest, has in fact sent for the stove-maker to repair his fireplace. While the stove-maker works on the stove, Lenin works on his books; the stove-maker displays craftsmanship useful for practical needs, and Lenin practises intellectual work useful for ideological ends. Eventually the fireplace is fixed, Lenin offers the stove-maker some tea, and the stove-maker has a chance to apologize for his rude behaviour the previous summer. In other words, the renewed encounter gives the stove-maker an opportunity to show his respect to Lenin, and thus the reader, too, is enlightened: Lenin is not only modest and humble but also kind and forgiving, a patriarchal wise old man and a true leader of the *narod*, the people.

Efremov's dramatized reading begins with a long shot of corncobs (*kukuruza*) stuck on a rake. There is a sound of an engine starting. The camera moves away from the rake and reveals the background: a large black-and-white close-up of Tvardovskii's face on crumpled paper. Next to it appears a text related to the current news item, which frames the poem. It is a quotation published in the newspaper *Kommersant* with the chairman of 'Rodina' (Motherland), the collective farm which Vladimir Putin and Dmitrii Medvedev had visited in Stavropol earlier that week (Fig. 12.2), admiring Putin and Medvedev's harvesting achievement: 'Each did 0.8 hectares! That's something! We never had anyone like these two here before.'

After a short transition, Efremov appears with a rake, impersonating Tvardovskii, still shown in a blow-up on the backdrop. Efremov begins to recite the poem, which opens with a description of a *muzhik*, a poorly-dressed peasant on a corn field: 'In worn-out boots and torn shirt / in his crapulent glory / there walked a farmer on a corn field.'

Suffering from a hangover, yet admiring the corn, he suddenly sees a line of combine harvesters approaching from the horizon. On one of them, as the farmer soon realizes, there are two familiar characters: 'On the harvester, there was the one! / And next to him, the other!' This is Putin and Medvedev, both in designer sportswear with badminton rackets and shuttlecocks in their hands (Fig. 12.3). Before the peasant realizes, Putin has got off the harvester: 'Putin got off the harvester! / Putin! The peasant sat down at once.' These lines are almost a word-for-word citation from Tvardovskii's poem and the stove-maker's astonishment at the old man revealing his identity: 'He sighed, shrugged his shoulders, / Bold, not of great height. / "Lenin", he simply answers. / "Lenin!" The old man sat down at once.'

The idyllic pastoral setting in Tvardovskii's original is turned on its head in Bykov's carnivalesque scene, which exposes the gap between the eclogue idyll typical of socialist realist art and post-Soviet rural reality. Instead of a skilful

Figure 12.1 Mikhail Efremov in *Citizen Poet*

Source: Still from the show on F5. www.youtube.com/watch?v=6e0HcvFt_Ng (accessed 10 September 2016).

countryside stove-maker, Bykov introduces an idle peasant, who is suffering from a hangover. The *muzhik*, which rhymes with *pechnik* (stove-maker), is awakened from his slumber by the sudden sound of combine harvesters, a token of modernized agriculture and technological advancement, which he sees approaching as an enormous army of vehicles on the horizon, violating the pastoral idyll.

Putin gets off the harvester and addresses the peasant, who sits on the ground: 'Why're you shaking, Russian man (*rossiianin*)? That's right, go on, shake.' In his dialogue with the muzhik, Putin describes his and Medvedev's campaign and then explains how the one thing they never thought of ('not in Russia, not in the Union') was to play badminton on a combine harvester. The absurdity of this idea refers to a video blog with Putin and Medvedev's badminton match posted on Medvedev's official Kremlin website, which supported Medvedev's initiative to make badminton more popular in Russia.[10] At the same time, it also refers to Medvedev and Putin's media stunt in Stavropol in October 2011, with the two leaders shown widely on Russian TV channels harvesting corn (six tons each!), extolling the Russian-made combine harvesters, and talking with local farmers (Anon. 2011b).

The more cynical side of the satire is delivered in Putin's reply to the *muzhik*'s question about the two leaders' future plans: 'go either scuba diving on skis / or on a tank to the department of journalism'. The *muzhik*, whose viewpoint the poem assumes, is left in awe, wondering how the leader,

Figure 12.2 Dmitrii Medvedev and Vladimir Putin in Stavropol Krai, 25 October 2011
Source: Kremlin.ru (CC-BY 3.0 Unported).

Figure 12.3 Putin and Medvedev playing badminton in a corn field, in a photomontage
inspired by *Citizen Poet*
Source: www.youtube.com/watch?v=6e0HcvFt_Ng (accessed 10 September 2016).
Author of the image unknown.

ready to take a tank to a school of journalism, can manage without a drink (vodka):

> What can you say, what can you propose,
> lying in horror in the stack? –
> How can you do that without a drink? –
> Well, I just can, uttered he [Putin].

Tvardovskii's poem adapts a folklore-like plot, in which a simple man encounters a political leader and is reformed, revitalized, and enlightened by this encounter. In Bykov's parody of this convention, however, the *muzhik* comes out of the meeting more perplexed than enlightened. Meanwhile, the subtext evokes a parallel between Putin and the Soviet leader. Medvedev plays second fiddle, as in many of the popular representations of the two, and fades away when the dialogue between Putin and the *muzhik* begins.[11]

One of the central images in the poem, in both the textual and the visual representations, is corn (*kukuruza*) (Fig. 12.4). In the political imagery of the Thaw period, which Tvardovskii belongs to, corn is associated with Khrushchev. The massive planting of cornfields was one of Khrushchev's failed attempts to modernize Soviet agriculture. In addition to Lenin, Khrushchev is the other Soviet leader referenced in the poem's satirical reappropriation of the Soviet cult of political leadership.

'Putin and the Peasant' makes fun of Putin and Medvedev, and aims to expose Putin's affinity with Soviet politics.[12] The show repeatedly pointed to the resemblance between his public image and Soviet-style leadership. However, even when mocking this affinity, *Citizen Poet* nevertheless contributed to the overwhelming fascination with Putin's persona in Russian print and online media. The show mentioned Putin in 24 of 53 poems, and in 14 he was the main subject matter.

Rather than undermining the Soviet-style personality cult, the poem and the performance, in fact, contributed to the cult of personality surrounding Putin and supported by official image-building as well as unofficial cultural production. This 'Putiniana', as Helena Goscilo (2013) points out, endorses the importance of Putin's leadership in the popular imagination whether it is produced with or without satire and parody (see Cassiday and Johnson 2010).

The show invited the audience to laugh at Putin's persona and his authoritarian leadership, but it did not challenge the audience to look for an alternative. Instead, the crux of 'Putin and the Peasant' and other performances of the show was the process of exposing the affinity of Putin's official image with the Soviet-style personality cult. With the enjoyment of recognition came the sense of belonging. The show did not stimulate a need for change but, on the contrary, created a sense of contentment, the nostalgic pleasure and reassurance of generational and/or educational identities. Being able to understand what Putin's leadership signified, what its political roots were, and how its significations were reconstructed through literary and cultural references created

Figure 12.4 Illustration to a critical piece titled 'The Children of Corn', on Putin and Medvedev's visit to a farm in Stavropol

Source: Website of *Russkoe natsional'noe edinstvo*. www.rusnation.org/sfk/1110/1110-32.shtml (accessed 10 September 2016).

a sense of collective and mutual understanding even for those who were too young to have experienced Soviet schooling first-hand. It created a bond of belonging not only to the generation of those born in the Soviet Union and schooled on Tvardovskii's story, but to a cultural competence that was a standard in the imaginative normalcy of Soviet society among the educated classes. While exposing the hyperbolic media stunt of Putin and Medvedev's cornfield extravaganza, which in the Russian context cannot escape associations of the Soviet-era display of achievements of agricultural and technological modernization, it also articulated a nostalgic relation with the Soviet past through a pastiche of a standard Soviet-era children's story in verse. 'Putin and the Peasant' and the entire project presented a case of 'stylized expression of nostalgia for the Soviet past', which Julia Cassiday and Emily Johnson acknowledge in their analysis of 'Putiniana' as a major mode of cultural production in post-Soviet Russia (Cassiday and Johnson 2013, 49–51).

Political leadership vs. dissenting cultural leadership

Citizen Poet appropriated the Soviet poetic canon as cultural capital and collective memory shared and cherished by its audience. In this respect, it is an example of post-Soviet symbolic practices that thrive on the loss of collective belonging caused by the disintegration of the Soviet Union. The disintegration and the loss of political identity was a recurring theme in *Citizen Poet*, although Bykov's take on it was often ironic and critical. One such ironic instance was the reinterpretation of Lermontov's lyric poem 'Clouds', in which Bykov commented on Gennadii Onishchenko's initiative to deny entry to Tajik migrants for the ostensible reason that they carried tuberculosis and HIV.[13]

> In the past we used to be great,
> We amazed the world with our sweep and vileness,
> Nowadays we do deals with the Tajiks,
> And send all the Tajiks to the farm.
>
> (Bykov 2011)

Analysing the cultural condition caused by a sense of collective loss and the overwhelming culture of post-Soviet nostalgia it spawned in Russia after the mid-1990s, Serguei Oushakine recognizes 'retro-fitting' as one of the major artistic methods of post-Soviet nostalgic production of culture. Rather than 'the process of political restoration', this mode of cultural production borrows past forms: 'It is the familiarity of the old form that becomes crucial' (Oushakine 2007, 453), as he writes, quoting Fredric Jameson's well-known postulations about the importance of an '"image at which [...] the mind can stare itself out"' (cited in Oushakine 2007, 453). This method, and the attitude towards the past it promotes, articulate 'a longing for the positive *structuring* effect that old shapes could produce, even when they are not supported by their primary contexts' (Oushakine 2007, 453–454; emphasis in the original).[14] For example, the first print collection of *Citizen Poet* had a cover that showed Efremov wearing a top-hat and silk scarf, and smoking a pipe with a mischievous grin on his face. Framed by the show's title with a reference to nineteenth-century politically engaged culture, the photo evoked an unidentified poet set in an unidentified earlier period, creating a vague nostalgic aura, induced also by the sepia background which imitated the style of old photographs. In fact, Efremov's attire and the image were originally used in a performance in which Efremov impersonated Daniil Kharms, the early twentieth-century satirist and author of absurd anecdotal stories about, among other things, Russian literary classics. The news item was the announcement of Russian actor, performer, and former priest Ivan Okhlobystin that he would step up as a candidate for the presidential election and seek the support of the Russian Orthodox Church. The *Citizen Poet* team used the occasion to expose the absurdity of the electoral campaign as a whole. Bykov's pastiche of Kharms's playful poem, itself an allusion to Samuil Marshak's children's poem 'The Poodle' (Pudel', 1925), was retitled 'Father Ours', and incorporated both Efremov and Bykov as fictional characters in the absurd plot.

Although Bykov used Lenin to create the satirical analogy of the Soviet-style cult of personality, the poem evoked not the historical period of Lenin's

Figure 12.5 Book cover for *Citizen Poet*

life but the historical period during which the poem was integrated into the mainstream of Soviet culture, namely the period dominated by Khrushchev's leadership in the 1950s and 1960s. Tvardovskii's poem was written in 1938–40, but the reprints started to appear in 1955, continuing until 1990. The subtext of 'Putin and the Peasant' was not only Tvardovskii's text, but also his persona and the entire Thaw period, during which the so-called thick journals became an important channel of cultural and social debate. Tvardovskii was the legendary editor-in-chief of one of the leading journals, *Novyi mir*. His career covered several Soviet decades, starting in the 1930s. During the Second

World War he became a popular wartime poet, winning the Stalin Prize for Literature three times. But it is the post-Stalin 1950s and 1960s that he is mostly associated with in Russian cultural mythologies. Tvardovskii made the decision to publish such milestone works as Il'ia Erenburg's *People, Years, Life* (*Liudi, gody, zhizn'*, 1961) and Aleksandr Solzhenitsyn's *A Day in the Life of Ivan Denisovich* (*Odin den' Ivana Denisovicha*, 1962). These works initiated a public polemic about the political violence of Stalin's regime.[15]

'Putin and the Peasant' retro-fits Putin into the Soviet narrative of political leadership, but, more than that, it also retro-fits its author and actor, Bykov and Efremov, into the narrative of *dissenting cultural leadership*. It creates an analogy between Bykov and Tvardovskii on the one hand, and between Efremov and the actors of the 1960s, who were instrumental to Khrushchev-era liberalism, on the other. Not everyone in the contemporary Russian audience would necessarily recognize Tvardovskii – he is not an iconic figure like Maiakovskii, for instance – but the method of having a blown-up image of the poet behind Efremov, used in all the performances, reinforced the idolization of poets and writers. It also re-evoked Soviet iconography and its role in the cult of personality. The black-and-white image on wrinkled paper, as if it had been tossed away and then recovered, induced a nostalgic ambience for the performance in visual terms.

In Efremov's case there was a more personal connection to the 1960s, which many Russians were aware of, and which re-evoked the same narratives of the cultural liberalism of the 1960s that Tvardovskii did. Mikhail Efremov is the son of the famous Soviet theatre director Oleg Efremov, who, not unlike Tvardovskii, was at the forefront of liberal cultural politics during the Thaw. He was one of the *shestidesiatniki*, the generation of the Soviet 1960s, who formed the core of the post-Stalin artistic and cultural elites in the period of late socialism (see also Smeliansky 1999). This real-life affiliation, apparent also in the physical resemblance between father and son, reinforces the ironic yet utterly nostalgic evocation of the Soviet 1960s.

The representation of the *muzhik* also refers to past Soviet narratives. The *muzhik*, a target of Stalinist collectivization and often a passive onlooker in the technological advancement imposed on him by the enthusiastic Soviet modernizers, represents the immutable, unchangeable essence of the Russian provincial subject (see Siegelbaum and Sokolov 2004). His bewildered sincerity lays bare the leaders' ruthlessness. Yet, at the same time, the *muzhik* remains outside the political agency granted to both Putin and the poet framed in the narratives of official (Putin) and dissenting cultural (Bykov) leadership. The poem also creates a binary opposition between the capital city as the location of both political and cultural power, and the provinces without any such power. The centre–periphery dichotomy, when reimagined in the context of the 1960s, calls forth a gamut of popular representations of educated metropolitan views of the provinces in Soviet life and popular culture, film, and literature, be it a field trip by university students (going on *ekspeditsii* or *na kartoshku*, the obligatory trips schoolchildren and students would take to help on a kolkhoz), or a journey to a native village by an educated but alienated Soviet man living in the city. The village (*derevnia*), as Petr Vail' and Aleksandr Genis attest in their popular *The 60s: The World of the Soviet Man* (1998), became the destination of the Soviet youth's *Wanderlust* at the end of the 1960s. These narratives represent rural Russia and its inhabitants as the immutable, unchanged essence of Russian identity.

To be sure, Bykov and his team's re-reading of this narrative is ironic, and yet the representation of the *muzhik* in all its irony presents the *muzhik* to the urban educated audiences as an archaic *tableau vivant*, a nostalgic image from the past untouched by change and stripped of political agency. This brings me back to one of my initial questions about the show's political subjectivity.

The nostalgic subjectivity of post-Soviet liberalism

In addition to the role of poetry as a popular form of social and political dissent, another Soviet legacy the show brought forth was the use of the radio as a medium of communication. The fact that *Citizen Poet* attained fame on the radio, i.e. on Ekho Moskvy, which is one of the leading liberal radio stations in Russia, created a point of reference, to the necessity of radio for mass communication in the Soviet era. Radio itself is a nostalgic medium in the age of digital revolution and social media, although in reality it was the latter that provided the channel for the show's accessibility and success as a popular phenomenon.

Affiliating the authors of the show, by way of impersonation and pastiche, with canonical figures of Soviet literature and theatre did not aim to restore the context of Soviet politics understood as the politics of the Communist Party and the Central Committee. Nevertheless, the aesthetic devices of the show were not entirely free of restorative effects. The method of visual and textual retro-fitting led to a *dissenting politics of nostalgia*, which retrieved not only past forms but also past contents of 1960s Soviet liberalism. My reading of *Citizen Poet* recalls Mark Lipovetsky's argument about the resilience of the liberalism of the 1960s in post-Soviet cultural and intellectual production. Lipovetsky argues that this discourse, which he ascribes to the technical intelligentsia of the 1960s and their strong cultural impact on Soviet society, was 'the foundation and core of the specific late-Soviet and post-Soviet strands of liberalism', shaping its cultural mainstream (Lipovetsky 2013, 110 & 116).

The subject position of this liberalism was rooted in an understanding of the priority of the cultural field as the field where political processes take place. Not affected by the profound critique of the Enlightenment's legacies, informing, at that time, the emergence of post-structuralist theories and intellectual formations in the West, which, in turn, questioned the epistemological fundaments of knowledge production and subjectivity, Soviet intellectual or non-conformist academia produced a brand of liberal thought which was fundamentally an essentialist construct, manifest in its predilection for binarisms and cultural hierarchies. In this understanding, culture comes across 'as a set of "eternal" values rather than as a dynamic and contradictory process [and] reverent protection of established hierarchies rather than subversion' (Lipovetsky 2013, 118).

According to Lipovetsky, the Soviet liberalism of the 1960s presupposed a separation between Soviet political power (*sovetskaia vlast'*) and the field of intellectual and cultural production, where dissenting cultural politics would take place. This was the precondition for the intelligentsia's self-understanding, which, as Lipovetsky argues, resulted in the 'double-consciousness' characteristic of late-Soviet and post-Soviet Russian intellectuals. The fact that Soviet history has not been 'worked through', by which Lipovetsky points to the avoidance of responsibility for some of the grimmest moments and traumatizing experiences of that history, has enabled the overwhelming post-Soviet nostalgia industry as well as 'the replication of many cultural and social practices of late socialism' (Lipovetsky 2013, 123).[16]

The subject position of this discourse was predominantly a masculine position. Women, even if sometimes authors of major literary works, were usually represented as passive bystanders, denied independent agency. The national canon of literary luminaries *Citizen Poet* evoked and promoted was entirely masculine. The team used only one female poet as a subtext, although twice. This was Agniia Barto, a popular Soviet children's writer. The gendering of national identity in Russian literary and cultural production is a well-researched topic (see Goscilo and Lanoux 2006). In *Citizen Poet* women remained outside this identity-building and, perhaps more importantly, female voices were excluded not only as agents of *vlast'*, political power and decision-making, but also as a vehicle for its critique.

Meanwhile, as Lipovetsky's argument about 1960s liberalism continues, irony became the main strategy with which to face disappointment with the socialist utopia and other Soviet meta-narratives (Lipovetsky 2013, 117). This position was also shaped by an understanding that the subject was in a 'double opposition: to the state and the "people," to the absurdity of the regime, on the one hand, and to the idiocy of the "uneducated masses," on the other' (Lipovetsky 2013, 119). The position was, then, simultaneously anti-totalitarian and anti-democratic, and this, again, was tied in with the intelligentsia's self-understanding of its role as the main agent of societal and political modernization (Lipovetsky 2013, 121).

Citizen Poet recycled and re-established Soviet legacies passed on through cultural memory and practices.[17] These legacies informed the understanding of Russian national identity, gender order, social hierarchies and binarisms, and the very concept of culture. In this sense, the show exhibited what Lipovetsky calls the 'neotraditionalist turn' that, in his view, took place in Russia in the 2000s (Lipovetsky 2013, 118).

The show's anti-Putinism was constructed on the Russian traditions of creative and intellectual dissent and, more specifically, on the legacy of 1960s liberalism and its opposition to Soviet power with the complex of intellectual positions vis-à-vis the people. 'Putin and the Peasant' illustrates this poignantly. The poem's critique of Putin is rendered by re-evoking the narrative of the Soviet-style cult of personality, while the authors' political stance is articulated by affiliating them with the narrative of 1960s dissenting cultural and intellectual leadership. Meanwhile, the peasant – as a token of the authentic essence of Russia – is retro-fitted into the narrative of the backwardness and uneducatedness of the Russian people in rural areas.

The word *muzhik*, in its contemporary and traditional meanings, is instrumental to an understanding of how the nostalgia towards Soviet liberal legacies works in the poem. The word's primary meaning is a male peasant or farmer (*krest'ianin*), or a male of the lower classes (*muzhchina-prostoliudin*).[18] In the early Soviet period, it also had counter-revolutionary connotations, as opposed to a worker (cf. Sperling 2015, 36). In contemporary Russian usage, however, it can refer to a man in general, associated often with emphasized masculinity: a *muzhik* is a 'real guy' rather than an effeminate male or homosexual. It is also a word that has become associated with Vladimir Putin, as Valerie Sperling shows, drawing on Oleg Riabov and Tatiana Riabova's sociological study. The image of a *muzhik* as a personification of Russian masculinity became part of Putin's legitimation strategy: 'Putin's image was brought into line with the muzhik mold, as his presidency coincided with the rise of the muzhik as a masculine type' (Sperling 2015, 37).

By referring the *muzhik* back to his original haystack, Bykov does not expose the new significations the word has acquired. Instead, he strips the word of its contemporary significations to communicate a nostalgic attitude to past eras, to the nineteenth-century classics, and, moreover, to the Soviet era.[19] Efremov's comic characterization of the *muzhik* in his reading of the poem re-evokes stereotypical representations of the *muzhik*, with the original meanings of rural backwardness, uneducatedness, and ignorance. In short, this *muzhik* represents the masses, the simple but authentic 'people' (*narod*), bewildered by the leader's plans with their absurdity and brutality.

The political subject of *Citizen Poet* was not the peasant, the political and social underdog of the narratives of Soviet history, but the imagined audience – a cultural, or rather *cultured* reader, listener, and consumer of intellectual entertainment wealthy enough to purchase a ticket to the show, and competent enough to enjoy its intertextual play. The political subjects of *Citizen Poet* were those who identified with the lyric subject of Bykov's poetry and his nostalgic subject position. They shared cultural and political fundamentals, such as the understanding of literary education and high culture as a priority, a self-sufficient entity articulated in opposition to political power (*vlast'*). To some extent, the major political theme of *Citizen Poet* was a nostalgic re-evocation of the liberal intelligentsia of the 1960s.

Citizen Poet and *kul'tura*

Engaging in an ironic yet nostalgic interplay of identity constructions, Bykov forced the audience to demonstrate literary erudition and cultural competence.

His use of canonical materials invited his fans to take part in the processes of textual and visual retro-fitting, recognizing and debating vaguely familiar narratives, and re-evoking them through allusions and references. The show reinforced the status of Russian high-cultural and canonical literature and educated Russians' understanding of culture's role in society, its educational and civilizational role.

This aspect of *Citizen Poet* was pointed out in a televised debate, which galvanized Russians involved in cultural and intellectual production during the 2012 presidential campaign. The debate took place on the channel Rossiia 24 on 13 February 2012 between Nikita Mikhalkov and Irina Prokhorova.[20] Prokhorova, who until the debate was known mostly among Russian academics and the Moscow elite – the international Slavic community knows her as the founder and director of the leading academic journal in humanities and social sciences, *Novoe Literaturnoe Obozrenie* (*New Literary Review*) and the publishing house of the same name – stepped out of her obscurity and became a nationwide luminary by fiercely but eloquently arguing over cultural politics with Mikhalkov.

The host Anna Shnaider started the debate by bringing up the topic of political satire and its recent popularity in Russia. She asked the guests what they thought of the phenomenon and its significance in Russian society. She did not mention *Citizen Poet* by name, but it was obvious she had in mind the satirical show, which was at the height of its popularity at the time. Furthermore, her comments on the fact that satire linked Prokhorov to Mikhalkov made it clear which satirical project she had in mind, since the *Citizen Poet* team had used both as its topics.

Mikhalkov needed no introduction: since the 1960s he has been one of the most popular actors and filmmakers and, with that, a powerful player in Russian cultural politics, especially in the Moscow-based film industry. In 2007 he signed an open letter addressed to Vladimir Putin, in which four influential cultural players appealed to the then Prime Minister to become a presidential candidate for re-election 'on behalf of all Russians working in creative fields' (Tsereteli et al. 2007).

In the debate, Mikhalkov represented Putin's supporters, while Prokhorova was campaigning for her brother, Mikhail Prokhorov. In other words, the debate was between a male conservative and self-proclaimed nationalist known for his Kremlin connections, and a female representative of Western-oriented liberal opposition close to the oligarch circles. Mikhalkov dismissed *Citizen Poet* outright by referring to it as *stiob*: 'everyone practices it [*stiob*] as best as they can', he said, using the term in an evaluative sense as a sign of banal and flat humour.[21] Just a couple of days earlier, Bykov had produced a parody of Mikhalkov's father Sergei during Mikhail Prokhorov's campaign event in St Petersburg.[22] Efremov impersonated Sergei Mikhalkov and delivered Bykov's parody of Mikhalkov's well-known children's poem 'A song of friendship' (Pesnia druzei). The title of the parody 'Whoa, What a Campaign!' was a reference to the poem's repetitive chorus line 'whoa, what a company', which in the poem evokes a group of 'good neighbours and happy friends'. In Bykov's re-reading the company was that of those Russians who, in the freezing cold, rallied *en masse* to protest against Putin's campaign and re-election.

For Nikita Mikhalkov, this parody was a mere *shutka*, a joke. Irina Prokhorova responded to this parody in a different tone. In her view, the rise of political satire bespoke of general discontent and people's disappointment with leading politicians. She compared the popularity of political satire to the popularity of the political anecdote in the late socialist period of Stagnation. She evoked an analogy that many of the *Citizen Poet* satires drew on – that is, the analogy between the onset of Putin's third re-election and late-Soviet rule.

Throughout the debate, Prokhorova spoke eloquently for the importance and maintenance of cultural and educational infrastructure, the institutional foundation of Russia's cultural production. She criticized the current leadership's rhetoric of modernization efforts, and drew the viewers' attention to the regional inequality of current cultural politics. In the spirit of her campaign work, she emphasized that Mikhail Prokhorov was the only presidential candidate with a set of goals to improve the funding and work of Russia's cultural institutions.

For most of the debate, Mikhalkov contented himself with the role of a listener. His unwillingness to argue with Prokhorova may have had to do with her rhetorical skills, but it also reflected the fact that they both shared a concern about Russian cultural heritage and the resources available for its maintenance. The concern about the state of Russian culture united Prokhorova and Mikhalkov, whose political stances seemed worlds apart. The Soviet 1960s, during which Mikhalkov began his acting career by personifying a Moscow youth in Georgii Daneliia's epoch-making film *Walking the Streets of Moscow* (*Ia shagaiu po Moskve*, 1963), gave rise to both Soviet liberalism and Soviet Russian nationalism. An essentialist understanding of Russian culture was crucial for both intellectual formations.

In post-Soviet Russia the word culture, *kul'tura*, has retained some of its high-canonical meanings that were institutionalized in Soviet times. Anna Akhmatova is *kul'tura*, but Pussy Riot not necessarily so. High culture enjoys great social prestige. *Kul'tura* is still associated with *kul'turnost'*, which was canonized in the Stalinist period as the result of extensive campaigns to teach to Soviet citizens basic cultural values, good manners, and standards of personal hygiene. An educated person (*obrazovannyi chelovek*) is expected to also be a well-cultured person (*kul'turnyi chelovek*) with polite manners and appreciation of high arts. S/he knows the cornerstones of Russian national culture, paintings and music, and can recite Pushkin by heart. This kind of perception of culture is closely associated with an understanding of national culture as a fundamental basis of national identity. In Russia, this is a traditional realm of the intelligentsia and its self-proclaimed mission of maintaining and spreading cultural texts and values.

This understanding of culture entails a nationalist concern for Russia's cultural condition. This concern, again, brings together Western-oriented liberals and patriotic conservatives, who all share a belief in the value of Russian culture as national heritage and resource. The success and popularity of *Citizen Poet* seemed to rest, at least partially, on this unchallenged position of culture.

This conservative approach to canonical culture also explains, together with anti-Putinism, the success of the intertextual play based on literary classics that *Citizen Poet* enjoyed. Satire is a classical literary genre, which, as Amber Day reminds us, 'has always been an aristocratic art – disdainful and imperious, conscious of style, and suspicious of the mob' (Day 2011, 9). *Citizen Poet* attests that satire's associations with classical literature are still strong, at least in post-Soviet Russia.

Conclusion

Citizen Poet ended as a radio show and touring newsical after the presidential election in March 2012. The ending was widely publicized on social media and the last live concert advertised as 'the last concert in freedom'. The concert took place outside Russia, in London, which used to be the refuge of nineteenth-century political radicals and famous exiles such as Alexander Herzen. The final shows in London were sponsored by contemporary political exiles, now linked to the post-Soviet oligarchy. The sponsor was Evgenii Chichvarkin, known to the Russian audience as a wealthy eccentric, who – after making a fortune in the 1990s in mobile phone retail – was implicated in several court cases and, as a result, settled in London. Then, *Citizen Poet* was again performed in London the day after the election, and the event was advertised as *grazhdanskaia panikhida*, a 'civil memorial service' for the show. The final poem, 'On the Death of a Project', was dated 5 March, the day after the presidential election, which also happens to be the day of Stalin's death. This irony was foregrounded by the choice of the subtext: 'Utro' (Morning), a lyric poem by Iosif V. Dzhugashvili, also known as Joseph Stalin. By publicizing the ending before the re-election, and thus anticipating the inevitable result, the creative team sought to expose the absurdity of Russia's elections and the fact that there were no real political alternatives in Russia.

The irreverence and wit of Bykov's parodic pastiche hit a nerve with Russian liberal audiences, disillusioned after the euphoria of the 1990s and educated on the nostalgic ironies of post-Soviet reality. At the same time, the show was anchored in a gamut of Soviet legacies to which it related nostalgically. The materials that the team used strengthened the position of Russian canonical high culture, as it was institutionalized by Soviet education, and reinforced the sense of collectivity, which the common enemy, the political power identified with the Kremlin and the traditional enemy of Soviet liberal intelligentsia, further supported. The show made fun of political power and also of Russian national culture, but it did so within the paradigm of that very culture, without challenging its role as the cornerstone of national identity. Challenged by commercialized and globalized cultural practices, Russian national culture was revitalized and refashioned for the purposes of political satire. The satire, however, did not mock the fundamental structures of society; it did not challenge or question Russian cultural, gender, or ethnic hierarchies or other social binaries.

Lipovetsky has argued that the technocratic discourse of the 1960s had an enduring influence on the cultural mainstream of late-Soviet and post-Soviet liberalism. I argue that *Citizen Poet* was anchored in the legacies of this liberalism, and the show's success had to do with the nostalgia it communicated towards the subject positions and cultural foundations characteristic of the liberal stance of the late-Soviet period and its dissident culture. The political subject of the show was a nostalgic subjectivity, which identified with the longing for the collective sense of identity based on an understanding of culture's primacy over political power, yet cherishing culture as a primary field for anti-power critique. Ironic yet nostalgic, this show continued late-Soviet intellectual legacies, which in turn drew on dissenting intellectual traditions of the nineteenth century. Each pastiche and impersonation of a Russian or Soviet poet's voice retro-fitted Bykov and Efremov into the literary canon, a product of institutionalized Soviet cultural practices.

The show was critical of political power and exposed its unruliness and corruption through satirical laughter and parody. However, the show lacked subversive vigour, which would have questioned and exposed the hierarchal fundaments of Russian institutionalized practices, hegemonic discourses, or societal norms. Critical of the political elite, it was not, however, critical of the essentialist cultural hierarchies which support this elite. The nostalgia for Soviet legacies undermined the subversive power of its satire, preventing it from becoming a cultural force in transforming Russia's civil society. Its satire did not subvert as much its nostalgia healed. The satire was rooted in the conviction of satire's potential as entertainment rather than in its potential as a socially and politically transformative force. As early as 2000, Serguei Oushakine asserted that the ubiquitous reuse of Soviet symbolic vocabulary had made the Soviet era 'the object of a permanent attachment' (Oushakine 2000, 1009–1010). This, he claimed, had halted the development of Russia's civil society. The nostalgic use of the legacies of Soviet dissidence in *Citizen Poet* points to the permanence of this attachment.

Notes

1 *Citizen Poet*, or *Poet and Citizen*, as it was first called, ran first on the TV station Dozhd' (Rain), then on the radio station Ekho Moskvy (Echo of Moscow), and on the internet portal F5 from February 2011 to March 2012. It became news in Russia after Natal'ia Sindeeva, the executive director and main stakeholder of Dozhd', decided to withdraw the show from the internet TV station after learning about a poem about Vladimir Putin and Dmitrii Medvedev, which she found too 'personal' and, possibly, offensive to Medvedev. In an interview on Dozhd' she repeatedly referred to her responsibility as the owner and executive manager to keep the business going, implying that it is necessary for a successful media

business to maintain good relations with the country's president: www.youtube. com/watch?v=uBsg797k6qI (accessed 6 June 2016). The show's YouTube site can be found at www.youtube.com/user/GrazhdaninPoet (accessed 6 June 2016). The presidential candidate and party leader of Pravoe Delo (Right Cause) Mikhail Prokhorov, who is also a celebrity and one of Russia's wealthiest men, sponsored the production and appeared as a guest in live concerts. F5 was owned by Prokhorov's media company Zhivi! (see Zhokhova 2012).

2 Amber Day has asserted that there has been a 'renaissance' of political satire taking place in the world media. She has identified three genres: 'the satiric documentary, the parodic news show, and ironic, media-savvy activism' (Day 2011, 2). 'Whether or not satire has become verifiably more popular, satiric media texts have become a part of (and a preoccupation of) mainstream political coverage, thereby making satirists legitimate players in serious political dialogue' (Day 2011, 1).

3 Satirical verse and socially engaged, political poetry have boomed in Russia in recent years. Roman Leibov places *Citizen Poet* in the literary history of the genre he calls 'occasional political poetry', using it as an example of the Internet's role in the genre's recent reverberation. Leibov recognizes in Bykov's occasional verse a successor to 'Russian lofty civic-minded poetry' (Leibov 2014, 199). Leibov's article offers a useful overview of Russian political poetry in the 1990s and 2010s. On recent social and political poetry in Russia, see also Marijeta Bozovic's and Jonathan Brooks Platt's contributions to this volume, and Butov 2014a and 2014b.

4 I consider Bykov's renderings of Russian classics to be pastiche with parodic features and satiric aspirations. In the Russian formalists' definition the object of parody is art, while the object of satire is reality. For Mikhail Bakhtin, however, satire and parody were inseparable. According to Bakhtin's renowned theory, the novel originated in folklore narratives and the carnivalesque worldview imbued in them. Satire is characterized by critique and laughter. It exposes human and social weaknesses and vice. There are two distinct types of satire: one with timeless human vice as its target and the other that targets contemporary, often political or societal problems. More recent theoretical configurations have emphasized satire not as a genre but a mode of writing; what makes writing satirical is its tone and aspiration. In this chapter, I subscribe to Day's precept of letting irony, satire, and parody overlap conceptually with each other to highlight them as a discursive strategy rather than an aesthetic and poetic device (Day 2011, 2). For satire, see also Griffin 1994. Pastiche, a widely used term in cultural criticism, has recently triggered a large amount of theoretical writing. As a genre it is usually associated with such concepts as homage, travesty, burlesque, and especially parody. One of the common ways of distinguishing between parody and pastiche is to see parody as a work that makes fun of or mocks something, in opposition to pastiche, which does not (see Dyer 2007, 40–41). Rather than denying pastiche its comical elements as Fredric Jameson (1983) and Gérard Genette (1982) famously do, I draw on definitions which highlight parody as polemical, critical, and akin to satire but which grant pastiche the option of a comic effect. As Margaret Rose puts it, pastiche is, unlike parody, 'neither necessarily critical of its sources, nor necessarily comic' (Rose 1993, 72). Another distinction between pastiche and parody as imitative practices, which I find useful to keep in mind, is Mirelli Billi's formulation that pastiche focuses on the similarities of two texts, whereas parody stresses their differences: 'parody is transformative, pastiche is imitative' (in Dyer 2007, 47). For the history and conceptualizations of pastiche, see also Nyqvist 2010.

5 On Putin and Medvedev's appearances in national news broadcast, see Cassiday and Johnson 2010, 683. For an analysis of Medvedev as Putin's satellite in popular imagery before Putin's third re-election, see Cassiday and Johnson 2013, 56–57.

6 Richard Florida's (2004) discussion of 'creative class' has become a point of reference and identification in and around the protest movement. See, for instance, the contributions to the journal *Neprikosnovennyi zapas* 92 (2013), www.nlobooks.ru/node/4219 (accessed 6 June 2016).

7 I will explore these questions by analysing the project as recorded on the show's YouTube site and in the two printed volumes *Grazhdanin poet. 31 nomer khudozhestvennoi samodeiatel'nosti* (Citizen Poet. 31 Issues of Artistic Amateur Performances) and *Grazhdanin poet. Na smert' proekta. Grazhdanskaia panikhida* (Citizen Poet. On the Death of a Project. Civil Funeral). These hard-cover editions with ample illustrations, documenting the making of the show, and with DVDs attached, include the poems Bykov wrote and Efremov performed during the period of 14 February 2011 to 5 March 2012 (Fig. 12.5).

8 In September 2015, a search for 'Putin i' (Putin and) on Yandex, a popular Russian search engine, resulted in the suggestion 'Putin i muzhik' as the second hit after 'Putin i Kabaeva' (Putin's alleged long-term mistress).

9 Mikhail Zoshchenko's story was based on an anecdote about Lenin in oral tradition (Hellman 2013, 403–404). See also Roman Leibov's account of the apocryphal origins of the story (Leibov 2013).

10 http://blog.kremlin.ru/post/191 (accessed 9 May 2016).

11 For Medvedev as Putin's satellite in popular responses, see Cassiday and Johnson 2013, 56.

12 Bykov has also used Putin as a character in his fiction (Rogatchevski 2013, 138–139).

13 In reality, the initiative stemmed from a diplomatic conflict between Tajikistan and Russia, caused by the arrest of two pilots (one Russian, the other Estonian), who were sentenced in October 2011 to eight and a half years in prison by a Tajik court for illegal border crossing and smuggling (Anon. 2011a). The pilots were eventually released (Anon. 2011c). Onishchenko's initiative did not result in a decision to ban Tajik migrants, a cheap source of labour in Russian urban areas, although there were round-ups of Tajik migrant workers in Moscow and some were deported (Schwirtz 2011). The subtext is Mikhail Lermontov's 'Clouds', which he wrote in St Petersburg at the height of his literary fame and before his departure for his final exile in the Caucasus (see Nikolaev 1994, 334).

14 The projects were Ekaterina Rozhdestvenskaia's cover art, Farid Bogdalov and Sergei Kalinin's remake of a Repin painting, and photomontages of political leaders inserted into classical paintings by various artists.

15 The journal had become the target of harsh criticism before these controversial publications. In 1954 *Novyi mir* and Tvardovskii were criticized for publishing writers who had adopted a 'subjectivist' approach to literature and its ability to depict reality which, in turn, questioned the foundations of Socialist Realism. Tvardovskii was the target of a smear campaign in *Pravda* and was summoned to a meeting with the Secretariat of the Central Committee of the Communist Party. Khrushchev himself chaired the meeting, which Tvardovskii did not attend. He is known to have had periodic drinking bouts, which, together with his role as the champion of liberal literary politics, secured him a place in the Russian narratives of dissenting writers and civic actors. See Kozlov 2013, 72–78, 171–208.

16 For post-Soviet 'nostalgia industry', see also Nadkarni and Shevchenko 2004, and Kalinina 2014.

17 Mark Lipovetsky finds a 'substitute' in 'all cultural authorities of the liberal mainstream – for late Soviet cult figures'. Bykov is, in his view, a substitute for Evtushenko (Lipovetsky 2013, 119).

18 See, for these contemporary meanings, the Russian Wikipedia: https://ru.wikipedia.org/wiki/Мужик (accessed 9 May 2016).

19 See, for instance, the standard dictionary examples from Turgenev, Gogol, and Chekhov's works used in the Ozhegov Dictionary: http://dic.academic.ru/dic.nsf/ ogegova/111130 (accessed 9 May 2016).
20 The debate is available on YouTube: www.youtube.com/watch?v=f0Xzc8hGpM0 (accessed 9 May 2016).
21 For a scholarly discussion of *stiob*, especially in late socialism, see Alexei Yurchak's often quoted definition of *stiob* as 'an ironic aesthetic' that 'thrived in late socialism'. It was a parodic genre that 'differed from sarcasm, cynicism, derision or any of the more familiar genres of absurd humor'. *Stiob*, as Yurchak defines it further, 'required such a degree of *overidentification* with the object, person, or idea at which [it] was directed that it was often impossible to tell whether it was a form of sincere support, subtle ridicule, or a peculiar mixture of the two' (Yurchak 2006, 250; Boyer and Yurchak 2010, 181).
22 Sergei Mikhalkov (1913–2009) was a Soviet children's poet known, among other things, for writing the lyrics for the Soviet anthem during Stalinism and readjusting them twice: for a 1970s Soviet version and, again, for the version used as the national anthem of the Russian Federation since 2001.

References

Anon 2011a. "Onishchenko: Tadzhiki raznosita VICh i tuberkulez." *Grani.ru* 14 November. http://graniru.org/Politics/Russia/m.193085.html (accessed 9 April 2016).

Anon. 2011b. "Prezident i prem'er obsudili s agrariiami mery podderzhki sel'skogo khoziaistva." *Vesti.ru* 25 October. www.vesti.ru/only_video.html?vid=372825 (accessed 9 May 2016).

Anon. 2011c. "Tajikistan Releases Russian and Estonian Pilots." *BBC* 22 November. www.bbc.com/news/world-europe-15835483 (accessed 9 April 2016).

Boyer, Dominic and Alexei Yurchak. 2010. "American Stiob: Or, What Late-Socialist Aesthetics of Parody Reveal about Contemporary Political Culture in the West.". *Cultural Anthropology* 25 (2): 179–221. www.culanth.org/articles/94-american-stiob-or-what-late-socialist-aesthetics (accessed 5 May 2016).

Butov, Mikhail. 2014a. "Political Poetry in Russia: 1990s–2000s." *Russia beyond the Headlines* 1 October. http://rbth.com/literature/2014/10/01/political_poetry_in_russia_1990s_2000s_40279.html (accessed 6 June 2016).

Butov, Mikhail. 2014b. "Political Poetry in Russia: 2011–present." *Russia beyond the Headlines* 3 October. http://rbth.com/literature/2014/10/03/political_poetry_in_russia_2011_present_40335.html (accessed 6 June 2016).

Bykov Dmitrii. 2011. "Sbitye letchikom, F5, 21 November 2011." *LiveJournal* 21 November. http://ru-bykov.livejournal.com/1214192.html (accessed 27 October 2016).

Cassiday, Julia A. and Emily D. Johnson. 2010. "Putin, Putiniana, and the Question of a Post-Soviet Cult of Personality." *Slavonic and East European Review* 88 (4): 681–707.

Cassiday, Julia A. and Emily D. Johnson. 2013. "A Personality Cult for the Postmodern Age: Reading Vladimir Putin's Public Persona." In *Putin as Celebrity and Cultural Icon*, edited by Helena Goscilo, 35–64. London: Routledge.

Day, Amber. 2011. *Satire and Dissent: Interventions in Contemporary Political Debate.* Bloomington: Indiana University Press.

Dyer, Richard. 2007. *Pastiche.* London: Routledge.

Florida, Richard. 2004. *The Rise of the Creative Class.* New York: Basic Books.

Gel'man, Vladimir. 2013. "Cracks in the Wall: Challenges to Electoral Authoritarianism in Russia." *Problems of Post-Communism* 60 (2): 3–10.

Genette, Gérard. 1982. *Palimpsestes. La littérature au second degrée.* Paris: Éditions du Seuil.

Goscilo, Helena. 2013. "Russia's Ultimate Celebrity: VVP as VIP *objet d'art.*" In *Putin as Celebrity and Cultural Icon*, edited by Helena Goscilo, 6–36. London: Routledge.

Goscilo, Helena and Andrea Lanoux. 2006. *Gender and National Identity in Twentieth-Century Russia.* DeKalb: Northern Illinois University Press.

Griffin, Dustin. 1994. *Satire: A Critical Reintroduction.* Lexington: University Press of Kentucky.

Hellman, Ben. 2013. *Fairy Tales and True Stories: The History of Russian Literature for Children and Young People.* Leiden: Brill.

Jameson, Fredric. 1983. "Postmodernism and Consumer Society." In *The Anti-Aesthetic: Essays on Postmodern Culture*, edited by Hal Foster, 111–125. Port Townsend, WA: Bay Press.

Kalinina, Ekaterina. 2014. *Mediated Post-Soviet Nostalgia.* Huddinge: Södertörn University.

Kozlov, Denis. 2013. *The Readers of Novyi Mir: Coming to Terms with the Stalinist Past.* Cambridge, MA: Harvard University Press.

Leibov, Roman. 2013. "'Kto on?': Epizod iz istorii transformatsii russkogo shkol'nogo kanona". *Acta Slavica Estonica* IV: 203–232. www.ruthenia.ru/canon/Лейбов_Майков.pdf (accessed 9 May 2016).

Leibov, Roman. 2014. "Occasional Political Poetry and the Culture of the Russian Internet." In *Digital Russia: The Language, Politics, and Culture of New Media Communication*, edited by Michael Gorham, Ingunn Lunde, and Martin Paulsen, 194–214. London: Routledge.

Lipovetsky, Mark. 2013. "The Poetics of ITR Discourse: In the 1960s and Today." *Ab imperio* 1: 109–131.

Nadkarni, Maya and Olga Shevchenko. 2004. "The Politics of Nostalgia: A Case for Comparative Analysis of Post-Socialist Practices." *Ab imperio* 2: 487–519.

Nikolaev, P.A. ed. 1994. *Russkie pisateli 1800–1917. Bibliograficheskii slova'r.* Vol. 3. Moscow: Bol'shaia rossiiskaia entsyklopediia.

Nyqvist, Sanna. 2010. *Double-Edged Imitation: Theories and Practices of Pastiche in Literature.* Helsinki: University of Helsinki.

Oushakine, Serguei. 2000. "In the State of Post-Soviet Aphasia: Symbolic Development in Contemporary Russia." *Europe-Asia Studies* 52 (6): 991–1016.

Oushakine, Serguei. 2007. "'We're Nostalgic but We're Not Crazy': Retrofitting the Past in Russia." *The Russian Review* 66: 451–482.

Rogatchevski, Andrei. 2013. "Putin in Russian Fiction." In *Putin as Celebrity and Cultural Icon*, edited by Helena Goscilo, 131–159. London: Routledge.

Rose, Margaret. 1993. *Parody: Ancient, Modern, and Postmodern.* Cambridge: Cambridge University Press.

Schwirtz, Michael. 2011. "With a Russian in a Tajik Jail, Moscow Aims Its Reprisal at Migrant Workers." *The New York Times* 16 November. www.nytimes.com/2011/11/17/world/europe/russia-rounding-up-tajik-workers.html?_r=0 (accessed 9 May 2016).

Siegelbaum, Lewis and Andrei Sokolov, eds. 2004. *Stalinism as a Way of Life.* New Haven, CT: Yale University Press.

Smeliansky, Anatoly. 1999. *The Russian Theatre after Stalin*. Cambridge: Cambridge University Press.

Sperling, Valerie. 2015. *Sex, Politics, and Putin: Political Legitimacy in Russia*. London: Routledge.

Tsereteli, Z., T. Salakov, A. Charkin, and N. Mikhalkov. 2007. "Pis'mo prezidentu Rossiiskoi Federatsii V.V. Putinu." *Rossiiskaia gazeta* 16 October. https://rg.ru/2007/10/16/pismo.html (accessed 9 May 2016).

Vail', Petr and Aleksandr Genis. 1998. *60-e: Mir sovetskogo cheloveka*. Moscow: Novoe literaturnoe obozrenie.

Yurchak, Alexei. 2006. *Everything Was Forever Until It Was No More*. Princeton, NJ: Princeton University Press.

Zhokhova, Anastasiia. 2012. "'Grazhdanin poet': istoriia sluchainogo biznesa na $3 mln." *Forbes* 6 August. www.forbes.ru/sobytiya/lyudi/84882-grazhdanin-poet-istoriya-sluchainogo-biznesa-na-3-mln (accessed 25 May 2016).

Index